# *sound advice*
# ENCYCLOPEDIA
# OF VOICE-OVER

## & The Business of Being a Working Talent

By Kate McClanaghan

Dedicated

to

**Dr. David Karsten**

My friend. My former professor.

My first professional cold shower.

You never held my naiveté against me.


And Jeff Finney for his unflappable commitment

to excellence, honesty and true friendship.

# Contents

- Coaching
- When You Record Your Demos
- Direction of Your Demos
- In Preparation for Recording Your Demos
- At the Demo Recording Session
- On the Job

## III. Postproduction: Promotion and Getting Work

- Soliciting Feedback
- How to Determine Whether Your Demo Is Competitive
- The Purpose of a Demo Postcard
- Postcard Printing and Bulk Mailing
- What to Include on the Demo Postcard
- Reproducing Your Demos
- C-Shell CD Cases and Labels

- Establishing Your Brand Identity
- What You'll Need Designed
- Friends Don't Let Friends Design Their Graphics
- What You Can Expect From a Graphic Artist
- How to Art Direct Your Graphics
- What Makes a Graphic Great
- What to Avoid
- What If You Hate Everything Your Graphic Designer Presents
- *Before* Signing off on Your Graphics

- Your Domain Name Is *Not* Your Web Site
- What Happens if You Inadvertently Let Your Domain Name Expire
- What's in a Domain Name
- How to Create the Most Effective Site
- New Web Technology
- QR Codes and Your Web Site
- The Importance of a Voice-over *Only* Web Page

- Do I Need a Headshot to Land Voice-over?
- Before and During the Shoot
- Reproducing Your Headshots
- Résumés

- *Why* You Need an Agent
- *Your* Job
- Your Target Audience
- The **Sound Advice** 8-week Promotional Process

- How to Promote Yourself to the Producers
- The **Sound Advice** Regional Mailing Lists
- The **Sound Advice** Overall Direct-Mailing Process
- Where the Work Is Online
- Promotions to Casting Directors
- The Social Networks

# Foreword

The purpose of this book is to enlighten anyone who may *have*—or may *desire* to have—a career as a working talent. This text should be of great use to those wishing to learn more about this business in depth, especially with regard to directing, as well as acting for commercial, voice-over, stage, film, and television.

The approach of this book is derived in large part from my personal experience; you could say I have a rather unique vantage point. By profession, I'm a casting director. I've been a freelance commercial copywriter and producer for many, many years. Additionally, I've been a professional voice-over and actress since I was a child.

**Sound Advice** is what I had been looking for since the beginning of my career: the most thorough, most current, custom-tailored approach to the entertainment industry. I founded **Sound Advice** to be the single, most helpful source for budding talent to get the best possible jump-start on their careers, as well as a place for established talent to sharpen their tools. This book is a direct product of producing and coaching literally *thousands* of individual talent and from producing and voicing literally scores of commercial, industrial, promo, and animated productions.

We began by concentrating solely on commercial voice-over in our Chicago studio and, over the years, discovered how effective our approach really is in every medium, regardless of experience level, location, or even the specific aims of the individual talent.

Beyond my personal experience, we have *extensively* surveyed numerous casting directors, talent agents, film directors, commercial producers, and copywriters. What you have in these pages is the benefit of their collective input and experience, as well as my own observations and experience. As a result, the information in this book is as objective an approach as you will find. It's based firmly on very good authority.

Let's assume you're after what we're after: to work steadily as a professional talent, earning a decent living while scratching your aesthetic itch. It can be done. People do it every day. However, as with any small business, it helps to be as systematic and as efficient as possible. That's where **Sound Advice** comes in.

After all, this is your small start-up business you're embarking upon here. This business requires attention to detail on many fronts: in your performance, in the production and marketing of your demo, in your pursuit of representation, and so on.

The problem, however, is that far too many people will focus on details that are of no consequence to the overall goal of establishing and maintaining a career in this business. The purpose of this book is to help you maneuver through the industry minefield with greater ease than ever before—even if it may be contrary to popular belief.

If you are, or once were, established in this business, the most recent changes in technology may have left you in the dust. Technology is fully incorporated into our lives, our work, and certainly into the talent industry like no other time in history. These advances continue to occur as they have over the course of a few short years, and they're not expected to slow down anytime soon.

Even if you have embraced technology fully, you need to know how it applies to this field. It's a whole other skill set. If you resist change, your career will ultimately fail.

So many of us were taught as actors to rely solely on our wits and physical prowess on stage that we forfeit any real advancement of our careers by omitting the most *basic* computer and self-promotional skills.

Trust me, this is the voice of experience speaking. Certainly technology had always been my personal Achilles heel. Granted,

I'm a producer, but I have an engineer who knows the technology necessary to bring my project to fruition.

Okay, so what do you need to know to adapt? There's no short answer, but you will find answers in these pages.

With any luck, and with some dutiful application, this reference book will help you discover what you have to offer as a talent *right now*, help familiarize you with simple, accessible technology to make yourself known and stay on top of the game. How well you integrate and master the advice we have defined for you here will only aid in your success.

As H. G. Wells once said, "Adapt or perish."

Since the latter really doesn't appeal, we'll focus on the former.

I hope it serves you well!

If you apply what you learn here, I'm very confident, it will.

KATE

# I. Preproduction

**Preparing to Deliver Your Best**

# Chapter 1: Going the Distance

"Great works are performed not by strength,
but by perseverance."
—Samuel Johnson

At **Sound Advice** we're often asked, "What's it take to go the distance in this business?"

There's no single answer. There are four: pursue, persist, prepare, and promote. These four components are absolutely vital to succeed at ANYTHING, let alone an acting or voice-over career. It's your responsibility to ensure these elements are continually in play as they are required of you no matter how far along you may be— regardless of whether you are just beginning, or if you have been established and are aiming to raise your game to the next level. They are a constant.

Whatever you accomplish in this business, you'll succeed only if you *pursue* it. Nothing will come to you, no matter how much talent you may have. Even with the benefit of nepotism, it's ultimately up to you to run your career. This is _your_ business and no one else's. Own it. Opportunities are what you make of them.

You have to set your sights on your immediate goals, and then **persist** at them, and often beyond what you might first consider a comfortable margin. Additionally, developing and then maintaining your skills requires persistent dedication. This element only *increases* with success, not the other way around—contrary to what many novices may think.

So, if you find you're easily frustrated or simply give up after a few months of training or even after only a year or two of promotion, then you may never honestly know for yourself what you could have created without real, long-term **persistence**.

**Preparation** means continually developing your abilities, and along with *ongoing* promotion, this requires *patience*. Allow yourself to continue to develop your skills. Agility is not naturally intuitive and talent can atrophy with lack of use. It takes attention. Otherwise your skills won't be sharp when called upon at a moment's notice, and they *will* be tested. Without persistence you will serve only to undermine your own confidence. Your confidence is directly related to your integrity as an artist. Regardless of your position, no matter how affluent you may be, no one can afford to lose his or her integrity. Even "natural talent" will degrade and weaken if not continually honed.

To add to this, your success is contingent on continual and repeated **promotion** far more than anyone in this business has previously ever lead you to believe. Consider it your staple from this point forward. It's up to you to drive attention to yourself through your very best promotional efforts. And with that thought in mind, as a rule: never set your sights on securing "just one audition," or "one big break," or "wait until the time is *just right.*" If so, you will secure only ONE audition, ONE break, and the time will never arrive because you never took the time to properly promote yourself. The time is right when you decide it is, so make that NOW. Make a decision as to what you want in your life and work toward those goals. In doing so you'll accomplish far more than you ever imagined possible.

Every audition is a form of promotion, yet so many artists repel the idea of promotion that this could easily account for the scores of talented souls who have fallen into oblivion. If you leave your career alone I promise *nothing will happen.* It will slip through your fingers.

No one who has ever scored an Oscar accepted it saying, "This was so easy. I don't know why you guys don't all have one. It was a piece of cake!"

Nope. Anything worthwhile is accomplished from hard work and lots of it. And a good deal of that work comes from consistent and constant promotion. Consider it as much of your job as the performance itself. This is how we make ourselves known and familiar. Promotion comes with the territory and can't be ignored if you intend to succeed as a working talent.

The fact remains that talent who persist at promotion, while honing their performance skills, will make themselves known and valuable. What they may lack performance-wise at the onset of their careers will strengthen and develop from experience, but not from a single coaching once every eight to ten months, or a half-hearted promotional blitz once or twice a year.

Those who become consummate professionals make it their business to run their own careers rather than leave it to chance.

However, keep in mind from the moment you decide to commit completely to establish (or further) your career it will seem as if all the forces in the universe will set out to thwart you. Not because you shouldn't be pursuing this field, but rather the complete and utter opposite. It's an occupational hazard that will test your mettle at every turn. And while you may be a strong sprinter at the onset of your career, aim to go the distance. It's far more rewarding if you do.

And even with a thorough road map to follow, as we've laid out for you here at **Sound Advice**, you're the one who has to dedicate yourself to the task of getting it done. Certainly your odds are far greater with us than without us, but it's still work and you're the one who has to do it. No one will give it to you, or create it for you. You can't purchase it, but you can invest in yourself effectively and prepare to deliver what's needed and wanted of you so you're ready at a moment's notice. And that is extremely rewarding on many, many levels.

So, when you find yourself losing patience, and no doubt everyone does in every small business from time to time, rather than dwell on being frustrated, put your attention into your *pursuits*, in your *preparation*, and in your *promotion*. There's always something you could be doing RIGHT NOW to forward your goals.

In other words, just do it!  And procrastinate tomorrow.

# Chapter 2: FAQs and Myths

"Truth is stranger than fiction."
—Mark Twain

### 1. What exactly is a voice-over?

A voice-over is when you hear only the voice on any form of production but you don't see the actor who's speaking. A radio commercial is a voice-over. The narration on any film, stage, TV show, commercial, animation, Web site, phone prompt, promo, movie trailer (you name it) is a voice-over. A voice-over is anytime you hear only the voice of the actor.

### 2. What is a voice-over demo?

A voice-over demo is a professional representation of the work you do best and what you want MORE of. This is how it will read to every professional source that listens to your tracks, so it better be up to the task. They will assume that *you* feel your demo is the very best you can do. So if it's not, that's a problem.

A demo is a handful of *well-produced* pieces that define your contribution to that specific genre or style of the voice-over industry: commercial, narration, animation, promo, or Spanish.

There are essentially five separate and distinct demos geared specifically to service five very different areas of voice-over work, which we cover in detail during our one-on-one Orientation.

*We can deliver this service via video conferencing (Skype), or in person. Check out www.voiceoverinfo.com for more information.*

There are specific standards required of each demo genre designed to accommodate the needs of the producers for these styles. The object of the demo is to take the guesswork out of the equation in order to make hiring you an easier task.

No matter the genre, most producers are looking to cast talent who sound conversational, professional, and honest. In other words, they want you to *sound like yourself.*

To hear examples of our demos, visit our **Sound Advice** Web site at: www.voiceoverinfo.com.

### 3. Why do I need a voice-over demo?
Well, frankly, you can't get voice-over work without one. Much like if you don't have a headshot and résumé, you can't secure on-camera work.

You need a demo to get a talent agent and to promote yourself to copywriters and producers at advertising agencies (known as ad creatives) and to anyone else who produces work that requires a voice-over.

It could be you have a friend or family member who offers you the occasional opportunity to do a job or two prior to having a demo. That's fortunate, but if you hope to continue in this business you'll certainly need one.

The whole idea of having a demo is to take the guesswork out of the casting equation. Once we've listened to your demo we should have a very clear idea of what sort of work you're best suited to deliver and most likely to land, what you actually sound like, and how you animate the text.

In short, the best definition of a demo is: a professional "demonstration" of what it is you do best and what you want MORE of.

## 4. Can't I just get a "makeshift" demo to start me off?

This is probably the greatest misconception novice talent have with regard to this industry.

"I'll get a good demo later."

Problem is: Your demo is your professional calling card.

The fact is, you *cannot* secure a proper talent agent (and therefore regular auditions or steady voice-over work) without a professional demo. Pure and simple.

If you promote a half-baked demo, that is precisely how any professional contact will view the best you can do.

The *cheap imitation demo* you submitted will speak to your level of commitment, putting your professionalism at risk. The recipient can only deduce that you feel this is the best representation of your very best abilities.

Talent agents, casting directors, and producers must use your demo to submit you for projects. It's a direct reflection on them if they submit less than reputable options; it lowers their professional status with people who are counting on them.

You have to consider who is receiving your demo. For instance, the audience for your commercial demo (the standard demo track required of *every* voice talent), is made up chiefly of advertising creatives. Creatives don't understand why you would create a representation of your work that was anything less than professional. It wastes everyone's time. And yet the industry is flooded with them.

Keep in mind your demos are auditioning for you in your absence better than 98 percent of the time. It speaks volumes to your aesthetic level, your skill, and your understanding of what's expected of you as a professional.

Granted, you may be just starting out in this field, *nevertheless* you are still held to the very same professional standards as everyone else. There is no beginner, intermediate, and advanced job out there. Each job is considered to be as professional as the last. Every client you voice a project for expects the top of your game, the top of your profession, regardless of whether the job is union. You're expected to consistently offer the very best of your abilities— always. And this standard begins with your demo tracks.

So, if you create a cheap, thrown-together, single-recording-session demo, mixed inside an hour or two, you will have just thrown away $850; $1,750; $3,000 or whatever you happened to spend on it. If the spots on your demo don't sound like actual, well-produced national television spots, you will not be considered for any work, and thereby miss the opportunity to "land work first" in advance of investing in a proper demo as you had originally intended.

The fact is you can't land voice-over work with a poor example of what it is you do best.

## 5. How much does a demo cost?
This is the single hardest question to answer regarding the subject of voice-over. It depends on so many factors and variables, such as:
- Are you a complete novice?
- Are you a relatively seasoned actor, but voice-over is a new medium to you?
- How much training or career guidance will you need to focus your efforts most effectively?
- Do you have an agent? Does he specialize in voice-over?
- Are you planning on promoting your demo?
- How current is your knowledge of the business and what's required of you?
- Are you technically inclined and able to record auditions from home?
- If you're a well-established talent, do you have an effective game plan to secure work?
- How many demos are you planning to tweak or have produced?

These and numerous other specific elements all factor in to what it will take to produce your demos. At **Sound Advice** we prefer to approach each talent individually and custom tailor their demos according to an overall promotional plan.

If you shop around, you're likely to hear demos range in cost anywhere from $850 to upwards of $10,000 per track, which can only add to your confusion. Rates can vary widely so you have to consider what you're getting for your investment.

The fact is you need to approach this business as a start-up.

According to business consultant and author, Steve Blank, *"A start-up is an organization formed to search for a repeatable and scalable business model."*

And, *"A business model describes how your company creates, delivers, and captures value."*

In other words, you need a game plan to run your voice-over/acting business as a small business based on what you're trying to achieve. Namely, a realistic timeline in relation to the amount of effort you invest with relation to: your product, your performance, your promotion, your demos, auditions, your demo Web page, and postcards.

The cost of your demo must reflect what you're getting for your money and what you're trying to accomplish. So when determining rates among demo producers, do your best to avoid back-tracking by enlisting the most-cutting edge, up-to-date, full-service, and supportive options, otherwise you'll only frustrate yourself and push your career goals further from your reach.

**6. I'm a pro. I want to stay on top of this business and its continual changes. What do you suggest I do first?**

Even if you have been working and training as a professional for a number of years, you may be harboring outdated or flat-out incorrect information with regard to your career and how to navigate it.

If you were once doing well and you're not anymore, there may be a few simple adjustments you need to employ to turn your career around, provided you're willing to confront them.

If you're doing well and want to increase your efforts, even better! Successful people never sit back and let it rest if they intend to maintain their success.

This is an extremely kinetic, ever-changing industry and what held true two years ago has already changed dramatically and may not be the case in today's market. All the more reason why so many seasoned voice-over vets benefit from our **Sound Advice** one-on-one Orientation. The information we impart to you is ahead of the curve, given our unique vantage point as industry professionals, producers, and casting directors.

### 7. Will you tell me if I can't do this?
There are plenty of people of varying degrees of expertise who are more than happy to quickly tell you "you can't"—sight unseen, without ever testing your mettle.

At **Sound Advice**, we'll tell you if you're not applying yourself. We'll let you know what you *should* be doing and *how to* apply yourself in nearly any situation in this field.

We'll even back you up and be there for you many years after we've trained you and produced your tracks. We're in this for the long haul and expect you are too. In fact, if we invite you to do a demo it's because we believe in you and that you will take what you've learned from us and run with it. If we produce your demo tracks, in many respects we are *endorsing* you, so we want you to represent us well. That's vitally important to us, because this is precisely how it reads to the industry and to our professional colleagues.

But, if you're asking, "Will we tell you whether or not you can join this 'very exclusive club called voice-over'?" No, we will not.

NO ONE has the right to tell you whether you can or cannot have a career in this business—or any other for that matter! It's elitist. And, to be perfectly honest, you don't have to take that form of browbeating from anyone. Ever. Nor should you.

Granted, a great many people are not all that forthcoming with information in this industry, they hold their cards very tight to their chest. It could be they're afraid you may discover how little they actually know about the subject. Or maybe they view you as a threat to their livelihood. Perhaps they are under the misconception that there is not enough work to go around and you might cut in on their business. To add to this, these individuals may not know as much as you know after simply reading this book or taking our **Sound Advice** one-on-one Orientation.

Frankly, there's plenty of room in this industry for everyone— provided you're trained and prepared to deliver your best. There's been more than a 900 percent increase in the amount of voice-over being produced annually than there has been in years past. This can easily be attributed to the rapid expansion and melding of media through Netflix, Hulu+, the relatively recent addition of more than 2,000 standard channels available on cable, on the Internet, games, animation, commercial and corporate demands, and assorted new media is now considered commonplace in the entertainment industry—all of which require voice-over of some form or another.

Besides the fact, no one does what you do quite the way you do it!

### 8. What do I need to get started in voice-over?
Besides objective training to continually develop your skills and confidence, you'll need a professional support system to back you up, some sense of what your job as a professional entails, and, of course, well-produced demos that best represents you.

You need at least one talent agent who specializes in voice-over, who has a good idea of what it is you bring to the table, and, most importantly, who is willing to include you regularly on auditions.

You'll need a flexible work schedule that allows you the freedom to audition and book jobs during standard business hours. (We suggest you maintain your day job until you're making at least three times more than what you're making now to support yourself.)

You'll need professional, well-designed graphics that are smart enough to draw the interest of industry professionals to listen to you and your demos.

You'll need a *single-page* Web site devoted *solely* to your voice-over work where your demos can be heard. You'll need postcards to broadly promote your site, thereby broadly promoting your demos.

But, most of all, you'll need tenacity and a real commitment to continue to develop your skills and promote yourself and your demos. Just like developing your performance skills, promotion *never* goes away. These are a constant if you intend to work. You get out of your career whatever you put into it.

At **Sound Advice**, we custom-tailor coaching packages, which we deliver either in person in either one of our studios, or via video conferencing (Skype).

### 9. Can I do voice-over part-time?

Sure, if you happen to know a producer who has enough work to keep you so busy they want your voice on absolutely everything and they do nothing but national spots for a variety of major market products or services.

The fact is, part-time for any other business is 20 hours a week. If you were to dedicate ten hours a week to working your skills and another ten hours to promoting your demos, you stand a far greater chance to becoming a *full-time* working talent. But that means you absolutely must put in the hours!

So, dedicate yourself to working on your career for no less than 20 hours a week. Or *part time*, if you will.

If you're only just starting out, positioning and prepping yourself for what the job takes to be a working talent requires at the very least 10 to 20 hours a week. This is how you become a professional. It takes commitment.

Becoming a steady, working talent takes a great deal of persistence, just like any other small start-up business. That's realistic, and from our experience, incredibly effective.

### 10. Is it realistic to consider my acting career as a start-up or small business?

Not only is it realistic—at **Sound Advice** we absolutely insist on it. While you're expected to be skilled enough to simply "play" during the session, every other aspect of this business demands you approach it as a proper profession.

Our intention is to give you the greatest opportunity to study this field by giving you step-by-step training and specific advice when it comes to establishing yourself as freelance working talent.

### 11. Do I have to have acting experience to pursue voice-over?

No, you don't. Stage work or improvisation is not the high watermark for whether you will book work in film, TV, or voice-over. There are scores of successful stars who can back that up.

Would it help? *Absolutely*, because it allows you to tell a story, use your imagination, develop a character, and establish a viewpoint other than your own. All of these attributes are vital to performing in any medium.

### 12. To do voice-over I need to be able to do character voices and dialects, right?

Not really. Most of the work available honestly doesn't typically call for you to sound like anyone *other than yourself.*

In fact, having random character voices and phony accents featured on your demo is considered unprofessional as a whole for the simple reason it sounds amateurish. Maybe one in 30,000 spots are specifically for a French guy or a German guy. Even then they are more likely to hire someone who actually is French or German or what have you. So, do not waste the time on your demo.

Now, this doesn't mean you should stop playing or creating original characters. It's just that what's the most marketable is you being YOU!

If you happen to speak French, German, or another language fluently, then sure, a little of that further in on the demo is totally appropriate depending on the demo you're producing. But never lead with it in the first 30 to 40 seconds unless it's your native tongue for a standard commercial track in English.

*C'est si bon!*

For examples of what extremely marketable demos sound like, visit our demos page at www.voiceoverinfo.com and hear for yourself.

**13. But, I have all these character voices I do. Everyone says I should be making millions. Right?**
If you truly have something you can do repeatedly (without hurting yourself and others), that is *original*, then an animation demo is in order.
A commercial demo, however, is what's required of every talent first and foremost and that means more affects than accents.

Commercially you'll be hired for more mainstream work first, due to the fact that it's the bulk of what's out there. That doesn't mean the straighter stuff lacks wit or is without imagination in any way. It's just that most commercial work doesn't tend to call for out-and-out cartoon-y characters, which is precisely why you shouldn't feature these characters unless the demo is geared specifically for animation.

None of this should squelch your character work—these things are not without merit. Just don't limit yourself to continually "being someone other than yourself."

The objective of your demo is to define who you are and how you are perceived in a major market.

An animation demo is a specialized thing. It's honestly not for everybody and usually reliant on where you live to glean the greatest return.

Generally, for commercial work and games, if they want a character, they will listen to your tracks and then call you in to audition for it.

As far as impersonations go, as remarkable as they can be—they are not the first things you want to open with either, I'm afraid. In fact, if that's all you do the field is rather limited.

If you're predominantly a character actor it's perfectly appropriate to blend humor and personality-driven material with the straighter, more mainstream commercial deliveries that dominate this work. Pepper gingerly with character affects. Easy does it. It's a balancing act.

## 14. What does a talent agent do? Do I really need one?

The talent agent submits you and is the primary liaison between you and the work. They know what a job is worth and are there to negotiate or broker a deal between you, the talent, and the client who needs your services.

This is the most thankless job in the business, yet vital to your bottom line as a working talent.

Question is: Does your agent get called for auditions and work that match your career goals and your type? Is the work appropriate to what you'd successfully land?

(Refer to Chapter 18, How to Get an Agent, for more detail on what an agent does, what you can expect from him, and what he expects from you.)

## 15. How do I get a talent agent?

At **Sound Advice** we have an extensive game plan that has met with a great deal of success for every talent who has utilized it fully.

(See details in Chapter 18, How to Get an Agent.)

## 16. Why do I have to promote my demo? Isn't that my agent's job?

Maybe you're one of those people who repeats this mantra everyday: "I hate promoting myself. I hate it, I hate it, I hate it. Besides, I have no idea how to go about it." (Hmm. Maybe that's why you hate it.)

Maybe you think someone else is supposed to handle all your promotion. If you do you will be abandoning your career to those with less heart and drive than you do!

Or maybe you consider promoting yourself to be "boastful" and therefore embarrassing. Or you "don't want to be a pest." Get over it! It's an excuse! You're avoiding what needs to be done if you're going to work at all in this business.

This is a business basic: If you consistently promote yourself and persist at it—you're going to work. You may not start out as the most talented guy in the room but your ability will increase with continually exposing yourself to the auditions and the work until finally you're cornering the market on whatever it is you do best!

However, there is a right and a wrong way to do it. If you already have a demo and you're not promoting it, check out Chapter 19, How to Get Work, for more details about our incredibly effective, continually updated mailing lists and detailed marketing plan designed to maximize your efforts.

**17. How do you know when you need a new demo?**
If you have a professionally produced demo but you haven't landed a proper agent or are working steadily, then consider the following before completely throwing the baby out with the bath water:

- Does your old demo run almost two minutes (or more)?

- Do your agents handle much voice-over?

- Have you sent out repeated promotional mailings to producers and potential clients for at least two years? If not, then you really have no idea whether the demo works for you.

- Has it been four years or more since you last updated your demos? Depending on your age range and the changes in the market, you may need to tweak an otherwise effective demo.

- Do some of the spots on your demo sound like fake commercials rather than actual national spots?

- Have you landed a few good national television spots that you could add to your current demos?

- Does your demo sound great to you, but your graphics aren't professional? (See Chapter 15, Graphics.)

Take a listen to some of the demos featured on our **demos** page. Does your demo compare to the level of professional production heard there? If not, you're not even in the ballpark, and it's time to professionally upgrade your demo.

*If any of these questions apply to you, contact **Sound Advice** to make the world right again. Give us a call in either location for more help: 773.772.9539 or 323.464.0990.*

### 18. Can and should I get talent agents in various regions?

While there are numerous online options today that offer small, random jobs to those just getting started, if you intend to make a career out of voice-over you'll need a talent agent who can offer you work that best suits you as a professional.

Fortunately today it's possible to secure representation from a variety of talent agencies in numerous regions throughout the country, if:

- Your demos are competitive
- You can audition from home
- You continually promote yourself
- You keep yourself open to auditions, and
- You keep your skills sharp!

(See Chapter 18, How to Get an Agent, for the process to secure representation.)

### 19. Do I need a headshot to land voice-over?

No, you need a headshot to land stage and on-camera work, such as commercials, film, and television.

In fact, we've found it far more effective in voice-over to *avoid promoting your demos with a headshot entirely*! Those likely to hire you would much rather imagine what you look like than actually *see* what you look like.

Further, if your headshot is not up to date, or is a poor or inaccurate representation of you (which sadly is too often the case for far too many talent), you'll being doing yourself this added disservice.

Celebrities, young adults under 15, and mature adults over 70 are *possibly* the exception here, but even in these cases—it's not necessary to ever have a headshot for voice-over.

Again, the objective of the voice-over demo is to let us imagine *who you are* and *what you are talking about* more anything else.

Overshadowing that objective undermines the effectiveness of the demo tracks.

At **Sound Advice**, we strongly suggest you keep your on-camera promotion separate from your voice-over. You have distinctly different missions with each of these career aims.

That said, our statistics have found that talent agents and managers who would represent you for *both* on-camera as well as voice-over will have a greater understanding of your commercial aesthetic, professionalism, and skill if they listen to your demo tracks when considering you for representation. Our **Sound Advice** clients are more likely to increase their on-camera work with the presentation of demos produced with **Sound Advice** by a significant margin (greater than 40 percent).

But the opposite, having headshots to promote the demo, unfortunately, has the counter effect.

We equate to seeing what the actor really looked like who voiced Fred Flintstone. Unless you actually knew the fellow, it's something of a buzz kill. You want to be left imagining the cartoon character, not the man himself.

(See Chapter 17, Headshots and Résumés.)

### 20. Will a casting agency represent me?
No, casting directors are hired by ad agencies, production companies, independent directors, and producers to cast work. They don't represent talent. Talent agents and managers do.

Casting directors hold auditions for animation, games, film, TV, commercials, etc., but generally they are paid to bring in the talent that most effectively meets the demands of the production or project.

(See Chapter 18, How to Get an Agent, for more details.)

### 21. How do you get paid if you're nonunion and you did the job from your home recording studio?

As a nonunion talent, you will be hired, on occasion, by your smaller-market agent or local vendor to voice random work such as in-house tutorials, training films, brief Web promotions, etc.

At **Sound Advice**, we urge you always to work through an agent in order to keep the work you do above board and, whenever possible, to ensure a proper pay rate.

However, today, due to the advent and rampant use of the Internet as a resource for "chop-shop" voice-over work, many talent have become one-stop shops. That is to say, talent have put themselves in the position of negotiating their own rate (often when they have little if any idea what the project is truly worth), and acting as recording engineer (utilizing their home recording setup and skills), and bookkeeper as well as voice-over.

While we don't encourage this, the fact it exists in the marketplace today can't be denied. Has quality and professionalism suffered for it? Yes, without question.

Nevertheless, should you find yourself in this position early on in your career, keep in mind you are setting a precedent with any client when you establish a rate with them at the start, and there's no real turning back. But if you want to ensure payment, it's always best to have the client pay half up front, through a PayPal account you've set up for yourself, and then the balance upon delivery.

Even if the client is a friend, we urge you to keep this policy. Otherwise you may find you did the work of five people at bargain-basement prices, and your efforts will remain uncompensated.

Treat this business as a business, and concentrate your efforts on becoming a *voice-over*, rather than a jack-of-all-trades, master of none, which sadly has become the state of our industry to great extent.

### 22. How much time should I expect it to dedicate to this before my career to gets off the ground?

At **Sound Advice**, we encourage you to treat your work as professional talent as a start-up business. It's a well-known fact that starting any small business requires you dedicate a minimum of three full years to establishing yourself. It's no different with this profession.

We suggest you start out by committing yourself to this work like it's a part-time job. If you dedicate a minimum of 20 hours a week into your career, what's considered part time by any other business, you will stand a greater chance of working FULL time as a working talent. So, by all means—make it your aim to work *part time* as a voice-over.

Refer to Chapter 13, What's Expected of You as a Talent, to follow the series of actions to take whether you are beginning or experienced. They are listed in groups of weekly targets in order to help you accomplish your professional goals and include vocal warm-ups, promotion, coaching, and much more.

### 23. I'm not all that computer savvy. Will that hurt me as a voice-over?

To land work as a professional talent today, whether you're in voice-over, or *any other industry* for that matter—you do have to have some command of technology in order to keep in step with current professional standards and demands, otherwise you run the risk of your talents dying with you, left completely unattainable, unacknowledged or severely under utilized. Therefore, if technology is not your forte, you MUST then ally yourself with trusted, reliable options familiar with the specific demands of the acting profession, especially voice-over.

While we are not Web or IT consultants at **Sound Advice**, we confidently recommend **Web site marketing partner, Ron Martin**. http://ronmartinwebdesign.com/sound-advice-clients

He can assist you regardless of your location (or his), provided you have a computer and high-speed Internet access.

Then again, you could enlist the tech skills of your very talented 15-year-old son or your tech-savvy 32-year-old niece. However, they (and therefore YOU) are missing some critical info that will save you a great deal of time, money, and effort when it comes to this industry.

Therefore, we suggest you leave it to the professionals, especially Ron.

(See Chapter 7, Advancing Technology, for more info.)

### 24. Do I have to have a home recording studio to successfully land steady voice-over work?

It doesn't hurt!  In fact, you open yourself up to a great deal more opportunities nationwide, if not internationally, as a voice-over.

That said, if you're not all that tech-savvy to begin with—we suggest you concentrate efforts on being a talent, first and foremost!  Get at least eight months to a year under your belt and then branch out into recording your auditions from home.

Regardless of your background with recording auditions or even actual sessions from home, at **Sound Advice** we can't recommend Erik Martin of **HomeRecordingStudioDesign.com** enough!

Erik is the "PRO's Pro," yet approachable, affordable, and experienced enough to understand what you need as you need it.  He makes life EASY for every strata of voice-over.  And that makes it far easier for you to land a greater volume of work from a greater variety of sources!  GENIUS!!

Regardless of your location, HomeRecordingStudioDesign.com offers personalized service for every strata of home-recording assistance, through online video tutorials, as well as support as technology changes and your skills improve.

(To be sure to you know what to ask Erik, check out Chapter 7, Advancing Technology, ahead of time.)

### 25. How much do you get paid?

There's really no short answer for this question, but we'll do our best to narrow the field for you, because your rate of pay varies *widely* from job to job, and whether the project is a union job or not.

There are a variety of factors that play into the equation, such as whether the job is a commercial voice-over or for on-camera. Whether the job is for television or film, union or nonunion, broadcast or nonbroadcast, aired in a major metropolis or more rural location. The amount of reuse or repetition of airplay (which incurs residual pay if it is a union job) further plays a vital role as to what the project is worth.

If the job is a nonunion, regional radio spot, it's likely to be a buyout. This means there is one set fee paid for the job, and the talent will not see residual payment for repeat airings (like you would for union work). Internet jobs are *always* buyouts, regardless of whether they are union or not. They run anywhere from $1,500 on the low end to the multiple thousands of dollars depending on the length of their agreed usage.

For a nonunion, regional buyout you're likely to be paid anywhere between $150 and $550, whether the voice-over is for broadcast or not. However, since the job is nonunion, you're likely to get paid whatever fee you may have agreed upon in advance.

(See Chapter 20, How Union Work Works.)

### 26. How many auditions can I expect it to take before I start landing work?

It varies dramatically from one talent to the next and depends on whether you are doing whatever you can to make yourself available to the work that suits you best.  Even if you are doing everything "right," it may take, *and often does*, as many as 200 to 300 auditions before you ever land a job.

Then again, you may take off like a rocket and begin to work steady after only one or two auditions. It's not common or very likely, but it can happen.

We've discovered most talent generally harbor the misconception that it should take no more than five or six auditions to book your first job, then they expect to book *every other* audition from there on out for the rest of their career.  Wonderful thought, but mathematically, this is a gross improbability.

The fact is, auditioning regularly is half the job of being a working talent. The more you audition, the more likely you will secure steady work for yourself.

Auditions are your greatest promotion, provided they are not your sole form of promotion. If so, you'll ultimately find you have fewer and fewer auditions and therefore fewer and fewer opportunities to work.

Here's the thing: If you're easily frustrated or far too impatient and rely *solely* on one to two auditions a month, then it could *and probably will* take from now until doomsday for you to begin to work steady.

Auditioning alone requires skills that must be mastered and continually developed. The more you drill them, the better off you'll be.

Go into every audition like you're already booked on the job— deliver a finished performance. Then once you've delivered the best audition you're capable of—MOVE ON! Put it behind you. Stop counting the jobs you *didn't* get and start figuring out your next promotional blitz and to whom.

At **Sound Advice**, we offer a service called **Practice Auditions** to allow you the opportunity to keep your audition skills sharp, while developing your home-editing ability! Check our site for more details: www.voiceoverinfo.com

### 27. Is there such a thing as an overnight success?

I have to say I've seen a number of people happen into the honey pot relatively overnight. Of course, a number of elements clearly played a part in such rocket rides including: timing, skill, a terrific willingness to take a risk, a very astute talent agent, and personally knowing the individuals who hired them.

However, the talent who succeeds right out of the gate, with very little experience or preparation, is not likely to know what to do next. How they managed to succeed thus far may completely elude them, so maintaining a career beyond their initial achievement quickly becomes the challenge that follows. Success is likely to fade away as fast as it occurred. The term one-hit wonder was created for just such occasions.

## 28. How soon after the audition do you hear whether you got the job?

Usually you'll hear within a day or two, although it may take up to a week or more. So keep your cell phone on hand and charged up, and be sure to check your e-mail often. If you auditioned for the job, they will need to hear you're confirmed if they do cast you. If you don't confirm as soon as possible, they may go with someone else for fear you can't be relied upon, or because they're on a tight time line.

It's important to note that you hear only if you *got the job*. They don't call everyone who auditioned and tell them, "Sorry, you didn't get the spot." That would be incredibly time-consuming, not to mention a really lousy job, you know? So you're not likely to hear how close you came to nailing it. If they were pleased with what you did they will call you again on future projects.

Also, it's not likely you'll learn who they actually cast unless your agent booked the talent, or if you happen to know the talent personally.

## 29. How do I determine what I do best in commercial voice-over?

Do what you know and concentrate on your own demographic.

For a more extensive study of television as a medium and the commercials you'll find there, refer to Chapter 8, Determining Your Commercial Strengths. This exercise will help you build your frame of reference. Further, it will broaden your observation of the current commercial styles you'll be expected to play, and you'll increase your ability to deliver the goods when you are directed to do so.
What you're likely to discover in this commercial study is precisely what's required from you, and that's to *be who you are*. That's far more interesting than nearly anything else you can play.

## 30. What if no talent agent agrees to represent me?

Pursuing the talent agents is a gradual process.

You have to continue to faithfully follow the process laid out in detail in Chapter 18, How to Get an Agent.

You must consistently apply this process until you are happy with the agents representing you and the amount of work you're landing. With the technology to which we have access today, you now have a greater opportunity to secure representation from talent agents all over the country, not just in your local vicinity.

You must pursue representation until you find agents who know you well and work you steady. Persistence and preparation is key to success in landing proper representation—so stay with it until you do.

### 31. If you're technically "with" a talent agency, but you haven't been called in for an audition in a while, what should you do?

If the agent knows you well, and it's been three or four months, give her a call—but be brief and to the point! Certainly, "out of sight, out of mind" applies here. You need to make your presence known and valuable. Not just for a single call or e-mail, either—it's time to make a steady diet of checking in and making yourself available to the work. This requires repetition.

If it's been six months or more since you've been called for *anything*—you're officially starting over, my friend. A phone call is not appropriate. Instead, you're going to need to resubmit from the ground up because these folks probably don't know you from Adam.

In fact, all the players at that agency could very well have changed in the last six months to a year. Stranger things have happened. This is a very kinetic business. The receptionist is now booking print work, the voice-over agent is on maternity leave, and the on-camera person is now someone you caught cheating at poker when you lived in the dorm. (Remember the dorm? Yeah, me either.)

Anyway, be sure your promotional materials are up to date regardless of your situation. No one can submit you for anything if they're not.

If you know the agent well enough to call and touch base, then give her a ring and let her know you'd "like to drop off some recent headshots. Would this afternoon (or tomorrow) be a good time?"

If she doesn't want to see you—she is likely to tell you at this point and you can peddle your papers elsewhere. Otherwise, she'll tell you when is actually most convenient for her. Don't be surprised if it isn't until the beginning of next week. That's a good sign because it means she's busy and can't be bothered with idle chitchat. (Of course, I don't know any busy person who can be bothered with idle *anything*. You?)

Ask her what the agency's policy is on "checking in." If the agency does have a checking-in policy, it usually entails you calling in every other week for a brief "Hey, hi, how are you" thing. Every talent agency is different, and if you hope they treat you as an individual, you need to treat them in kind. Your agent may prefer e-mails to phone calls or the other way around. The agent may prefer you let her contact you. My primary agent will call and we'll have a *10-second conversation*. Literally. And we're on great terms.

As you're getting to know your agent, snail mail a single demo with a note or a photo-postcard or something small and industry-related every other week until you've established a steady working relationship. This will also keep you in her forethoughts and readily available should an appropriate job arise.

### 32. Can I get work without a headshot or a demo?
In a word: No.

If you expect to work in front of a camera or onstage—you MUST have a proper headshot. By the same token, if you intend to do voice-over, you MUST have a proper demo. No one can hire you without it.

Far too many would-be talent have a cheap attack when it comes to their most vital tools: their headshots and voice-over demo. They spend as little as possible thinking they can get by with makeshift headshots and demos. Ultimately, all they manage to accomplish is racking up lost time and money. The fact is, even if a friend is in the position of helping you by offering you an opportunity—he can't submit you to those casting the role without either of these all-important assets.

You could be the most talented thing this side of Timbuktu. But the fact remains: It'll die with you if you aren't professional enough to invest even that much into PROPER headshots and demos that will represent you when you're not there.

But in order to produce the best possible demo, it's imperative you have training *before* producing your demo.

Training is a constant and should be a ball continually in play for every talent, regardless of experience level.

### 33. How do you put an on-camera reel together?

An on-camera reel is similar to a voice-over demo as it features your on-camera work for commercials, television, film, or corporate industrials.

These categories are mutually exclusive of each other because they are used for different purposes. If you intend to land more film, for instance, your reel should feature film.

Just like the voice-over demo, naturally, your on-camera reel should reflect *what you do best, and what you want more of*!

However, unlike the voice-over demo, none of the segments used on your reel should be created solely *for* the reel. Unless, of course, your last name is Coppola, or the Coen brothers offered to write and shoot something that features what you do best. Heck, who'd need anything else if that were the case?

Instead, the rest of us mortals collect copies of each spot from the producers who hired us. This is known as collecting your elements. Then we hire a *professional* editor to edit them together. Each scene should reflect the top of the action, the top of the emotion.

An on-camera reel is a montage (about three minutes long at the most) consisting of visually appealing material that best defines you as an on-camera actor and the type of work you intend to land more of.

It's important to note, you do *not* need to have an on-camera reel to land on-camera work. Reels are used more widely in Los Angeles and New York City and are now found almost solely online (as opposed to reproduced on DVD).

If you've managed to isolate a single scene featuring you in a recent *CSI* episode, for example, it's perfectly appropriate to include just that scene or two on your **castingnetworks.com**, **castingfrontier.com**, and **actorsaccess.com** page, in lieu of a full on-camera reel.

Other than that, a great source for material for your on-camera reel (and to develop your on-camera experience) would be to pursue student film work with up-and-coming directors in film schools such as the Art Center College of Design in Pasadena, California, NYU Film School, and Columbia College Chicago, to name a few.

# Chapter 3:
## The Purpose of a Voice-over Demo

"My passions were all gathered together like fingers that
made a fist. Drive is considered aggression today;
I knew it then as purpose."
—Bette Davis

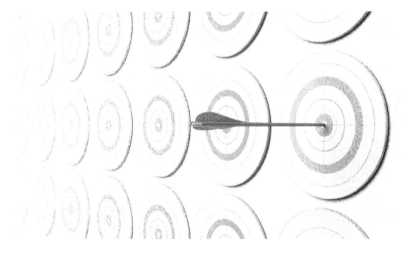

Your demos are expected to be a professional *demonstration* of what it is you do best, and what sort of work you're aiming to *secure more of*. Voice-over demos, like on-camera reels, are meant to define who you are professionally and what work you do best.

While there are no absolutes when it comes to what should and shouldn't be included on your demos, probably the most important factor to consider is: what effect (or work) are you attempting to attract? And are you servicing the talent needs of the producers most likely to hire you?

Which leads to the next inevitable element to consider: What does the *producer* need and want to achieve from your demos? As a novice (or even "intermediate") talent it's highly unlikely you might even venture an accurate guess.

> # The best definition of a demo is: what it is you do *best* and what you want *more* of.

At **Sound Advice**, we have extensively surveyed those most likely to hire you to take as much of the guesswork out of the demo production equation as possible. Producers are generally attempting to "sell" you, as a talent, to their clients, directors, and to various creatives.

Each demo track targets the specific area of the industry you're aiming to work in and areas that can best define your greatest assets.

Producers who utilize your demos do so to discern whether to audition or simply hire you, therefore your tracks must fulfill the producer's professional needs and standards.

The following are a few good standard guidelines to follow as to what is expected of your tracks for strong, competitive, professional voice-over demos.

# Types of Demos

There are essentially five types of demos to service producers who hire voice talent in five separate areas of the industry, although there are no real absolutes. Demos are, by design, created to fulfill the very specific needs and demands of their target audience: the producers most likely to hire us as voice-overs.

The most successful voice talent have no less than two and as many as four demo tracks to open themselves up to as many employment opportunities as possible. By doing so, these talent service the needs of their talent agents as well, because it's impossible to land steady work as a voice-over without having a proper demo.

## 1) **Commercial demo**

(Also known as a *commercial announce* demo)
Length: 1:00 to 1:10
Target audience: Commercial producers, copywriters, and casting directors

The commercial demo is the single most important demo any voice talent can have. This track alone is what talent agents require from their clients most, as it can potentially offer you the greatest return on your initial investment as a working talent, and thereby subsidize the next level of your acting career. This is provided your commercial track represents you well and you continually promote it! Again, you cannot effectively pursue voice-over without a proper demo, most especially a commercial track. Those casting will listen to it and either hire you or call you in to audition you and ensure you can deliver what's on the demo.

The commercial track consists of approximately five to nine segments of national TV spots or extremely well written, well-produced radio spots. If they are not the real thing, they must in no uncertain terms sound like they are. Each segment must reflect the style of commercial work you are best suited to land. The demo should take the guessing game out of what you do best and define your professional aesthetic level.

Each spot should flow effortlessly and quickly from one to the next without breaks. Each spot should cross fade smoothly, one into another, rather than those old demos where one piece would fade out entirely, and then we'd suddenly hear another spot fade up mid-sentence or mid-action, as if you were turning the radio dial. It's confusing and unprofessional.

Instead, each spot on your demo should sound like different producers produced each piece at different times, in different studios. The track should show a variety of commercial styles, a variety of attitudes and vocal expressions, all of which you can re-create again and again anywhere else at a moment's notice. Each segment should spark the imagination, allowing us to quickly and effectively imagine what each commercial might look like in earnest. The listener must be convinced each segment actually aired as a well-produced national TV commercial.

Utilizing commercial copy ripped out of magazines should be avoided completely. It's extremely obvious to any professional producer these scripts were written for print, because it sounds like it especially when read aloud. Print copy is meant to be read in your head while you're at the dentist or getting a pedicure. Besides you were likely drawn to the ad in the first place because of all the pretty pictures.

At **Sound Advice** we write, modify, or pull copy (scripts) for our clients specifically to ensure the material used on each demo is fresh and, most importantly, *best suits and defines the talent themselves* in commercial voice-over. Our aim is to make each spot sound familiar, both production- and performance-wise, and to give the listener the impression they may have heard these spots from your demo somewhere before. That can be accomplished only if the spots truly define the talent's greatest commercial assets. This is how we ensure the talent is well suited for that style.

The best way to discover and study the commercial styles you're most likely to book is by recording and observing them as illustrated in Chapter 8, Determining Your Commercial Strengths.

Your commercial demo should not contain impersonations, extreme character voices, dialects, or dialogues. (If the first thing anyone asks after listening to your demo is "Who's the other voice?" this demo failed you. This is YOUR demo. You have a minute. We either get that you can act from the expression and imagination you exhibit in what you have here, *or we don't.*)

Your job is to *convey the concept* that's playing out in this commercial. Such as security, intelligence, understanding, warmth, wit, experience, problem-solving, ease, effortlessness, real interest, or point of view, to name a few. Put simply: What are you talking about? Does it sound like you know what you're talking about without being sell-y?

A commercial demo should define who you are, *naturally*. If you're used to playing a character, other than "being yourself" then this can be a rather confusing proposition. You may feel vulnerable at the very prospect of "just being yourself." This is where the training comes in, especially improvisation. Studying voice-over, and especially commercial work can actually *heighten* ALL your acting skills in any medium, especially if you master (or at least make peace with) this one precept of "being yourself."

(See Chapter 6, Identity, Branding, and Type, and Chapter 13, What's Expected of You As a Talent, for more information.)

Keep in mind, just because you were actually hired and paid to voice a commercial does NOT mean that spot belongs on your demo. Many spots you book may never grace your demo, simply because the production may be less than adequate, the spot is poorly written, the subject is not all that savory, or it just doesn't represent the *very best* you can do. Again, a demo is what you do best and what you want *more* of, and unless that's the case it should not be included on your demo. A lot of work we find ourselves doing, especially at the onset of our careers, can and often is slightly less than wonderful.

## 2) **Narrative demo**
(Also known as corporate announce, industrial, narration, or nonbroadcast)
Length: 1:15 to 1:45
Target audience: Corporate clients

The corporate announce demo consists of four to seven narrative segments, each ranging from about 15 to 20 seconds in length, that are geared toward corporate training, sales, medical, point of purchase, and the like. They generally contain nomenclature indigenous to the field they are communicating to and are used in convention presentations, staff instructional videos, Internet tutorials, etc.

These tracks often feature reads that have been inspired or even mirror Discovery Channel, History Channel, Animal Planet, HGTV, Food Network, and the like. This track is used to promote your skills to narrate cable programming, not just industrial text.

If you have a corporate background, you have a great leg up in industrial work. You already have some notion of the corporate mindset.

Strong cold-reading skills come in very handy in this area as well, especially on the session, as it's extremely rare that you would be auditioned for narrative voice-over. Generally, you are booked directly off the demo itself. Considering nearly 45 percent of all voice-over work is narration, it's nearly impossible to secure this form of work without a narrative demo.

As with the commercial demo, a variety of narrative styles should be featured on this demo track, and, once more, each segment should appear to have been produced at a different place, by a different producer.

## 3) **Promo demo**
Length: 1:00 to 1:10
Target audience: Promo producers at networks and affiliates (such as ABC, NBC, and CBS) and cable stations (such as Bravo, HBO, HGTV, A&E, IFC, and TLC)

To give you an example of the type of work promo entails: "All this month on Lifetime Television…," "*Next* week on Lifetime Television…," "This week on Lifetime Television…," "Tonight on Lifetime Television…."

The promo voice-over may define the channel, the program, the station, the series, and may be one of many (which is most often the case), or the only one. As you might imagine, most promo work offers a great deal of repeat business for the voice-over, as most promos seldom air for more than a week or two at a time, although some can run for a month.

The work often leans toward the melodramatic, the animated, the extreme, or the hyper-real. For instance, when it comes to evening news and suspense programs, this work can sound very sensational. The talent often assumes an extreme persona.

Example: "He was wicked. She was wild. Together they went on a rampage the country continues to talk about. The legend of.... Tonight on *Project Runway*."

The ultimate objective of this demo is to secure repeat promo work, by becoming the voice for the ABC News in St. Louis, for example, or maybe for the Independent Film Channel (IFC). Your voice in part becomes the station's identity, even in smaller markets.

Penn Gillette (of Penn & Teller) was the primary promo guy on Comedy Central for a number of years when the station first came to be, giving the channel an irreverent, playful identity. The rest is history. With promo work, as in narrative voice-over, you're most likely to be cast directly from your demo.

It's not likely you'll have many auditions for these jobs, so the demo is a must if you intend to land this sort of work!
It's important to note promo is neither union nor nonunion work, it's completely deregulated. In other words, you would not be subject to residuals as you would with commercial work, but again there's far more repeat business.

Additionally, you are expected to have a home recording setup for this sort of work, or at the very least, access to proper recording capabilities (including a digital patch), which would allow you to book promos for networks, network affiliates, and cable stations anywhere in the country.

While a bulk of promo work is cast out of New York and Los Angeles, the average promo voice talent can live anywhere from Maine to Miami, Seattle to San Antonio. Most promo voice-over talent have initially established themselves in commercial voice-over.

## 4) **Animation demo**

> Length: :45 to 1:00
> Target audience: Animators, animation producers, animation casting directors, and game producers

We may be experiencing the Golden Age of animation right now, yet easily 70 percent of all voices utilized in animation work today are known celebrities, which would explain why a bulk of all animation is done in Los Angeles.

According to Wes Stevens, president of the VOX talent agency in L.A., "Unfortunately, the one market that just does not work well long-distance, at all, is animation. I hate to make it that black and white, but that is not a market that phone patches easily, unless you are a celeb or established. Introducing and developing a client would not be productive long-distance."

Food for thought.

That said, an animation demo should consist of nothing but *original* characters. However, this is NOT a character demo. A character demo consists mainly of commercial work with character voices or affectations, not that we recommend anyone create a character demo—regardless of how much of a character you may be. (More on this below.)

Also, if you have dead-on impressions of existing, known, animated characters—while these abilities are exceptional, the fact remains there are working professionals you are imitating and it's not likely you'll replace them, especially, for instance, if the voices you do best originate from the creator of the animated series, such as Seth McFarlane. Take heart, these are extremely valuable skills, they simply aren't correct for use on an animated voice-over demo.

The fact is many rank-and-file animation talent (many you may never know by name) are likely to voice far more mainstream, realistic, characters. Granted many of these roles may sound somewhat overly dramatic, like something you might find on *Johnny Quest* or *Ben 10*. These are more affectations than full-blown characters.

Straighter, more realistic characters have their place on this track as well so don't neglect them. There are moms, dads, real kids, and such; these are roles that need to be cast as well. The animation field is often overwhelmed with wacky characters, when all that's needed is an honest, natural delivery. The more natural you sound in any given situation, the better—even as an animated character.

Regardless, each animated segment on an animated track should depict the height of the action of the scene, and the height of the emotion. There are likely to be eight to ten selections total in a single minute-long animation demo. That's it. NO LONGER than a minute, according to the most seasoned talent agents that represent the most successful animation actors.

Typically, producers and directors of animation and animated series will listen to your track and then audition you based on the fact that you have qualities they are interested in. They will put that to the test and challenge your ability to create on the fly.

And just like there are film genres and commercial styles exhibiting the popular animated styles that best suit you vocally, your animated demo track should define the type of work you're best suited to land. For example, consider which animated styles influence and inspire you, or that you happen to be the most familiar with:

- **Hanna-Barbera** (*Huckleberry Hound*, *Yogi Bear*, *Top Cat*, *The Flintstones*, *The Jetsons*, *Magilla Gorilla*, *Josie & the Pussycats*, *Cow and Chicken*, *Dexter's Laboratory*, *Johnny Quest*, *Johnny Bravo*, *Scooby Doo*, and the *Smurfs*, to name a few.)

- **Warner Brothers** (Bugs Bunny, Sylvester, Tweety Bird, Granny, Porky Pig, Pepe Le Pew, the Tazmanian Devil, Daffy Duck, Marvin the Martian, Foghorn Leghorn, as well as, more recent options such as *Power Puff Girls*, and feature films such as *The Iron Giant*, also director Tim Burton's projects such as *Corpse Bride* and *The Nightmare Before Christmas*.)

- **Disney** (Classic Mickey Mouse, Donald Duck, Goofy, *Snow White*, *Bambi*, *Beauty & the Beast*, *Little Mermaid*, *Aladdin*, *Pocahontas*, *Princess and the Frog*, *The Lion King*, *Tangled*.)

- **Pixar**  (*Toy Story, Monsters Inc., Up, The Incredibles, Finding Nemo, Wall-E.*)

- **The Simpsons** This show is in a class unto itself.  It not only the longest-running animated series to date, but this ensemble of exceptionally talented actors and creator, Matt Groening could be credited for being the very catalyst for propelling the Golden Age of animation into the mainstream and commercially viable.  (Which is always good for future business.)

- **Seth McFarlane**  (*Family Guy, American Dad, The Cleveland Show.*)

- **Other options to consider:** Anime, *Speed Racer, King of the Hill, Johnny Phantom, Beavis & Butt-head, The Rugrats, South Park, GI Joe, My Little Pony*, and also study Cartoon Network, Nickelodeon, and ABC Family.

It's worth noting that contrary to popular belief, not everyone in voice-over is expected to have a great variety or capacity for character voices, as you may discover while studying many of the examples listed above.  Of course, if you are able to pull off some terrifically kooky voices that will blow away everyone who hears it, by all means feature them on your animation track.  (Your spontaneous, improvisational skills can be put to good use here.)

It's important to note, most animation work requires you are actually in the studio with the director, where the animation will be rendered, rather than having the ability to voice your animation from a remote location.  Therefore if you are in the Los Angeles area, you stand a far greater opportunity to book animation than in other areas.

For more inspiration and options to reference a great variety of animated work, check out the Big Cartoon Database at www.bcdb.com.

5) **Spanish demo**
    Length: 1:15 to 1:45
    Target audience: Spanish-market commercial producers
    and copywriters

The amount of work in Spanish voice-over due to "equal time" offered by larger market channels and various global translations has absolutely exploded in recent years, offering no less than an 800 percent increase in employment—provided the talent

a) Has a competitive voice-over demo, and
b) Can achieve the performance demands of a neutral dialect and acting ability.

The dialectal accent featured primarily in Spanish voice-over heard in America can be considered a "neutralized" Spanish dialect. It's a somewhat Americanized sound that is void of any specific Spanish accent, so it's neither predominantly Mexican, Puerto Rican, Cuban, nor Castilian (from Spain), for instance. It's a *neutral* Spanish dialect that is the most sought after on the Spanish demo.

To clarify, *The Global Advisor Newsletter* recently offered greater insight into Spanish translation and narration as it is used in today's markets and on the Internet:

*According to Telemundo, this "neutralized" Spanish is the middle ground between Colombian Spanish, that they consider too fast and terse, and some Caribbean accents that are, in their opinion, too slow and imprecise. For Telemundo executives, Mexican Spanish is "the broadest-appeal, easiest-to-understand Spanish." Needless to say, not everyone agrees, particularly Colombian television and cultural critics. Many Colombians believe that their version of Spanish is the purest spoken. But the article also mentions that about eighty percent of Telemundo's potential audience— households whose viewing habits are monitored by Nielsen—is Mexican. Could it be that Telemundo is merely providing good customer service and localizing their message to the requirements of their largest audience? The bottom line is that Telemundo is doing better against their major competitor, so they must be doing something right.*

*The "neutralization" process should also include paying attention to variations in grammatical constructs, such as pronoun to verb correspondences. An example, is the "voseo" that consists in the use of the pronoun "vos" instead of "tú," followed by the corresponding form of the verb—"vos sabés" instead of "tú sabes" (you know). The "voseo" is common in Argentina, but used also in other Latin American countries. It should not be confused with*

*"Vosotros sabéis," the form used in Spain, but not in Latin America. Other examples are "tú sabés" (instead of "tú sabes") used in Uruguay, for instance; and forms like "tú tenís" (you have)—a variation on "vosotros tenéis" and "tú tienes"—used in Chile. "Neutral Spanish" uses "ustedes" instead of "vosotros" for the second person plural and "usted" for the second person singular. Therefore "you know" (where "you" is singular) is "usted sabe" and the plural form is "ustedes saben."*

This neutral quality can be readily identified as it is employed in commercials, training films, industrials, and so forth when the voice-over states the product or service with an accent that is clearly American English amid a primarily Spanish voice-over.

A Spanish demo should include both commercial selections and corporate industrial blended seamless with full professional production. Like the English counterpart, the Spanish track, when done well, will most often allow the talent to secure employment directly from track, rather than require further auditions.

The voice talent for this track are <u>always</u> expected to be fluent Spanish speakers, with <u>no</u> exceptions.

If the natural dialect of the voice-over is from Mexico City, for instance, then offering one segment that features this dialect is perfectly appropriate. However, Castilian is far too proper for American (and even South American) acceptance. It generally doesn't read as conversational, as the other Latin dialects do here in the States.

The greatest problem Latin talent contend with is poorly translated copy. This is referred to as "Spanglish," which is English that is often translated literally into Spanish rendering the narration useless as it makes absolutely no sense. Any fluent Spanish-speaking individual can offer how routine this problem really is. For instance, a Spanglish translation would be a direct English translation such as "the blue sky," which, correctly translated in Spanish, would read "the sky blue."

Other obstacles include copy that lacks any real imagination, spots that are so hard-sell and over the top it's impossible to take them seriously, and, of course, production budgets that are a far cry from the mad money generally thrown at English-speaking consumers, at least by comparison.

Yet the demand is there for ongoing, steady work in Spanish, and it continues to be on the rise as it has over the last decade.

If you speak Spanish, French, Italian, Russian or any other language *fluently*, combining commercial and narrative work on a single demo track offers you the very best opportunity for voice-over work.

## Demos We *Don't* Endorse and Why

### Dialogue demos:

These are demos, or even segments included on commercial demos, that supposedly "show the talent can act." This is an outdated notion, and there is absolutely no use for them. They can confuse the listener as to who the demo track is ultimately promoting. If the first thing asked after listening to a dialogue demo (or a demo with dialogue included on demo track) is "Who's the other guy?" then that demo has failed you. The objective is to promote you in a minute.

### Character demos:

If you have some really amazing, *original* characters (and I don't mean impersonations), or *affectations of your own voice*, it's perfectly appropriate to include one or two *further in* on your commercial demo track, rather than dedicate an entire demo devoted strictly to character voices. According to our extensive surveying, those looking to hire you are far more interested in hearing you *sound like yourself*. And that a bulk of the work available is commercial announce, so concentrating your efforts on this work above and beyond any other form of voice-over is more beneficial to you. Also, we discovered more genuine, natural voice-overs are a far tougher bill to fill. For character work you will be auditioned, as those holding the casting are clearly looking for something specific and they will know what they are after once they hear it!

Also, if characters are a big part of what you do, then reserve *a precious few* segments on your *commercial announce demo* to demonstrate your sense of humor and affectations, rather than

47

dedicating an entire demo track to characters and dialects you will rarely, if ever, be called upon to do.

A character track will only serve to read as self-indulgent if it doesn't serve the needs of the producers you're attempting to promote your skills to.

What's ruined the character demo for folks who probably really *should* have one is the simple fact that, just as so many people consider themselves exceptional drivers, everyone thinks they have a sense of humor. (How do you account for all the accidents?)

In the meantime, make sure your agent knows you are more than capable at presenting unique, original characters if this is your forte, and be sure to offer an animation demo, which will further open you up to even more opportunities.

## Jingle demos:

If you're a singer and you have a couple of fully produced professional albums out that are current and represent your musical style, editing a few excerpts from fully produced existing tracks would suffice very nicely as a jingle demo. But, frankly, unless you're already connected with or have connections with a busy jingle studio, you will not have access to a steady amount of jingle work to justify creating a demo dedicated to securing this sort of work.

A bulk of this work is done in New York and Los Angeles. Frankly, even in these locations the industry has taken to securing music, for a good deal of commercial and film, from artists who are already produced. Securing music from small, unknown bands found on iTunes or cdbaby.com, for example, is generally cheaper, faster, and easier than starting from scratch these days. Such is the ad and film business today.

Certainly, if you do hook up with a recording studio that is interested in having you among their roster of vocalists for projects that may pop up, you should know you are expected to sight-read with great fluency. You must be able to adapt to a variety of musical styles on a whim such as reggae, rap, hip-hop, salsa, jazz, country and western—whatever the project may require. You must equally have a great proficiency to blend into harmonies and to effectively take the lead on a moment's notice if that's needed of you. The expectations are steep, which is why very few succeed with any consistency. Most jingle singers are often one-hit wonders, so to speak. The pay for national commercial work (on a SAG-AFTRA job) is quite good and affords the jingle singer residuals just like national voice-over work.    But for the most part steady work is few and far between for jingles.

## Audiobook demos:

In years past, formidable publishing houses would secure having their more beloved titles read for audiobooks (books on tape) by the author or by celebrities, which could account for so few audiobook voice-overs ever becoming all that well known. Certainly Tony Award-winning actor Jim Dale, who read the Harry Potter series here in the States, has become a star among these ranks, but there are precious few he can call his contemporaries. Audiobooks are generally an obligation to the publisher, but most talent do it as a labor of love rather than this work being something that can sustain a living.

Since online publishing giant AMAZON acquired Audible.com (and transforming it further into acx.com), many novice voice talent find themselves entertaining the thought they can "practice" voice over while getting paid for it by accepting audiobook jobs offered through various pay-to-play sites (such as voice123.com and voices.com) and freelance job sites like eLance.com.

Aside from the occasional children's book, they typically find themselves in way over their heads when it comes to the actual demands of agreeing to such a project. The reason being: these projects consistently require you record, edit, produce, perform, re-record, fix, change, and deliver what would (under any other circumstances) be handled by a professional recording studio, a seasoned recording engineer, a producer, a casting director, a talent agent, _and_ perform (up to as many as 25 characters or more, which on it's own is a remarkable feat)—all for sub-par rates based on "finished" hour.  _Finished_ being the operative word here, meaning the length of the final production, not the number of hours it took you to create this beast.  Which, by the way, usually works out to be any where between 45 and 75 hours of work on your part over, regardless of your how adept your editing prowess might be.  (Keep in mind, we want you to be a *voice talent*—not a professional recording engineer.) Therefore, voicing the audiobook itself is only a small fraction of the job, all for a bargain basement rate that generally works out to be about $3 to $6 an hour considering the average audiobook is a novel is 250 to 350 printed pages in length.

Do the math. Would you consider this work worthy enough to warrant a demo? I wouldn't.

Additionally, as if that weren't enough, if you listen to many audiobooks, you'll find there's a vast inconsistency in production values from one to the next.

Stamina is required for this work, something no demo can honestly convey. It's grueling work—often peppered with tough text, unusual nomenclature, and occasionally odd language. You sit in an isolation chamber, for six to nine hours a day for about a week or two and are paid a pittance for the honor.

## Station-imaging and Radio Air-check demos:

Unlike commercial, narrative, promo, Spanish, or animation voice-over demos, where we go out of our way to make each spot sound like it was produced by a different producer at a different studio, the production on both station-imaging (e.g., "96 FM! The Home of Rock & Roll!") and air-check demos for radio announcers are meant to sound very even and almost uninterrupted, as though they were created by taping the radio live. (This may be what you originally thought demos should sound like if you didn't know what we're striving for. There's different criteria needed for a proper voice-over demo that deviates dramatically from air-check and station-imaging tracks.)

Disc jockeys and radio announcers are expected to have both station-imaging and air-check tracks. These are to show what the radio personality would do on-air during his show and to exhibit how he does big announce-style promos for a variety of radio stations. These demos are generally presented to program directors and general managers at various radio stations by talent seeking work in radio. These demos are entirely self-produced and created by editing excerpts from past shows the DJ has done, focusing on the most dynamic personality-driven shows. Station-imaging tracks sound as if they are on the threshold of being over-produced;

peppered with booms and swishes and sparkle effects for emphasis on reads that are extreme and over the top.

We don't produce air-check or station-imaging demos at **Sound Advice**. The fact is, most people in radio dream of doing voice-over as freelancers, and certainly that's our aim for these very steadfast, committed individuals as well. However, the sad thing about radio is, no matter how much we love it—it simply doesn't love us back. The problem is it's the devil they know, which is very hard on those who have committed so much of their lives to this work. But, far too many radio talent have developed such deep habits in terms of performance and self-production, the prospect of doing anything else is almost too much to bear. There are typically far greater rewards from being a freelance voice talent, but old habits, as the saying goes, die hard.

(See Chapter 4, Radio, Radio, for more details.)

## Political demos:

Before every election we are subject to so many political ads, we can't hear ourselves think.

At **Sound Advice**, we purposefully avoid creating these demos for three primary reasons:

- The work is far too infrequent to warrant
- You must be an unshakable advocate for
  a single party or candidate (and few honestly are)
- We'd rather not add to the mudslinging

Plenty of demo producers or freelance recording engineers would happily take your money to create a political track for you during an election year, but we'd rather opt out. It's extremely doubtful it would pay for itself, unless you've already secured an inordinate amount of this work, or are slated to be the official voice of a specific candidate. (In which case we wish you both the best of luck!)

## Trailer demos:

Since the legendary Don LaFontaine passed away, many would have thought this aspect of the voice-over industry would have miraculously opened up for scores of others to work. However, once again, the numbers simply don't support it. Studios typically produce only <u>one</u> feature film a month each, beyond that they buy up indie films to support the demand. There's not enough call for trailer work to support having a demo produced to service this aspect of the industry if the return is less than likely. Once again, unless you have already established yourself in this area, we don't recommend investing yourself in this demo track.

## How Many Demos You Need

Upon survey, and according to most marketing experts, when offering clients an excessive number of options they tend not to choose anything. They become overwhelmed and completely shut down. This occurs when presenting too many demo tracks on a demo Web site as well. We've discovered ad creatives prefer *no more than five demo tracks* per site.

> For example:
> Track 1: Commercial demo
> Track 2: Corporate narration demo
> Track 3: Promo demo
> Track 4: Animation demo
> Track 5: A single *full commercial read**

*A full read is not necessary, but a nice option if the performance helps define the talent.*

On every demo track, the flow of one selection to the next is essential to exhibit the most professional and therefore the very best results. Each demo should exhibit point of view, attitude, imagery, convey thought, and a variety of expressions.

As noted above, no track should extend much longer than 1:10, except the narrative and Spanish tracks (1:45, tops). Anything more than this can overwhelm the listener and make them feel anxious, much like waiting too long at a poorly timed stoplight. We don't want to repel the listener—we want to leave him wanting more.

As long as your demo tracks are well produced, they represent you well while exhibiting what you do best in each genre (commercial, narrative, promo, Spanish and/or animation), and as long as you promote yourself thoroughly, you should be in fine shape.

## The "Demo" of a Demo

It's _never_ appropriate or effective to present MAKESHIFT, HALF-BAKED DEMOS to a talent agent or producer, especially when you know it's not up to professional standards! If you do, you will be wasting their time _and yours_. Just try getting a talent agent to listen to your demo the _next_ time, even after it's been completely redone. Agents are people trained to _recall_ talent. They're likely to think, "I remember this guy. He doesn't know anything about this business."

No one wants to be put in a position to reject you. Chances are they will simply avoid you upon your next attempt.

One of the common excuses we often hear for turning in a bad demo: "I'll do a better demo later, after I've landed some work and made some money." Unfortunately, that day is likely never to come due to the fact you've offered such a poor example of your professional work from the start. Your standards will be too low to be considered professional or viable.

Another excuse is: "The agents and casting people won't remember me from my crummy demo." To that I have to say, would you like to test me? I remember a three-minute phone call I had 12 years ago with a talent I've never met. I remember what was said, what breed of dog he has, and what his day job was. As a casting director I'm practiced in remembering people, especially talent!

Additionally, if you record all your demo tracks in one day, it will _sound_ like it was done all in one day, by the same producer, at the same studio—which completely defeats the purpose of the demo.

Furthermore, any demo producer that will record you all in one day is not giving you the opportunity to develop your ability on mic and transfer your skills to this medium.

Keep in mind; the goal here is to _establish_ yourself professionally. You want to become memorable _in a good way_! Produce your demo properly the *first* time and you won't have to make excuses for yourself at a later date or desperately try to play catch-up with your career by doubling back. You'll alleviate your overall frustration considerably if you do.

Ironically, many novice talent often pose the question, "Why doesn't someone give me a chance?" The answer is, if you present an unprofessional, substandard demo to an agent, they can only assume you don't know what you're doing, which would be the truth.

Do it right the first time. If you're going to produce a demo, *invest in yourself*. That's the only way to afford yourself the opportunity to see a return. It will be far more cost and time effective if you do.

*For strong examples of what truly professional, entertaining demos should sound like, check out our* **Sound Advice** *Web site,* **www.voiceoverinfo.com.**

# Chapter 4: Radio, Radio

"They say you better listen to the voice of reason.
But they don't give you any choice 'cause they think
that it's treason. So you better do as you are told
… you better listen to the radio."
—Elvis Costello

It's a common misconception that if you're in radio then you must be in voice overs, when in fact, they are two separate and very different worlds. The truth is if you *are* in radio—it's very likely you *wish* you were in voice overs. Precious few successfully discover how to move from radio to voice overs because, much like theater, people in radio will starve for their art.

Most of the yearly graduates from various universities and trade schools for broadcasting and production often find themselves becoming one of the great nomadic populace that dedicate themselves to radio: in part because they love the medium and also due to their initial aspirations to becoming a voice actor. Radio seems a logical enough route at the onset should you want to get into voice overs.

However, after dedicating years to small and medium market radio, requiring these committed individuals do five to eight shows a week (typically six to eight hours long a piece), as well as write, voice, and produce no less than 150 station promos a week (to keep the station afloat with endorsement and advertising money), and all for a meager paycheck that is typically $5,000 to $8,500 *below* poverty level. The main thing driving these people is their love for the medium and the fact that radio has become the devil they know. There's comfort in what's familiar.

To add to this, people in radio find themselves out of work every six to eighteen months and not for any fault of their own. These are extremely dedicated people by and large, but due to the fact that the small- or medium-market station they found employment with in Baton Rouge, for instance, changed formats from adult contemporary to all talk, or the station was bought by Cirrus, or perhaps they simply hit the pay limit at that station and they are now being replaced with people who are $2 less an hour. (Can I get a *Grapes of Wrath* reference here, please?)

As pitiful a picture as I may be painting here, the plot thickens when you discover many bad performance habits are generated with all those years in the radio trenches. Hard-sell deliveries don't translate well to commercial or narrative voice-over. Unfortunately, radio talent tend to develop a very sell-y sounding delivery that becomes ingrained in every read and is very hard to break. Even though you might think all that experience in front of a mic would add to their value as a voice-over, these talent typically address the mic the same way for *everything* they do, regardless of what the script requires of them. So their deliveries aren't exactly natural or versatile, which can be a real deal killer in voice-over.

To make matters worse (yes, there's more) these talent are used to delivering one take and one take ONLY. Now, as a novice, you might think being One-Take-Jake to be some sort of selling point. Instead, it's the polar opposite: To be a successful voice-over you're expected to offer *options* with each take, rather than offering the same inflection again and again with little or no variation from one take to the next. The reason being: you're trying to satisfy the production demands of a number of people, and to take direction (if

56

and when it's given) and apply it immediately. This isn't done in a single take and serves only to make a radio talent feel as if they failed in some way, simply because they aren't used to this standard commercial process in which most voice overs are professionally produced.

There are literally masses of radio talent roaming the country, attempting to suss out a living in the industry they know and love: radio. So, it stands to reason, these are the folks who populate and drive pay-to-play (P2P) sites such as voice123.com and voices.com, both popular voice-over job sites among radio talent that offers nonunion talent paying voice-over opportunities from all over the country and Canada.

## What's Your Rate?

Professional voiceovers have only recently had to ponder the question, "What's your rate?" Historically that's a question a producers, casting directors, and talent agents answer, not talent. Yet in radio circles, where they are used to writing, voicing, and producing hundreds of spots a week for local station vendors, professional recording engineers are replaced with hurried edits off a radio talent's laptop; seasoned producers, casting directors, and talent agents are replaced with anxiety-driven, bargain-basement rates to vendors that would probably rise to the occasion if they were given a realistic estimate.

Instead, radio talent, so worried they will not get the job unless they dramatically low-ball the rate, act on this dreadful misconception: "I'll give them the first one for $5, and charge a higher rate later on." To that I say, "Good luck!"

The problem is you set a precedent with the first job you do with a new production client. And if you tell a new client your rate is $5, for instance, they will expect that *same* rate again on the next job. In fact they'll base their next budget on the original quote you offered. So, why would they use you again if your rate suddenly inflates to $250 on the next booking? *($250 is the average rate for a voice-over on a basic nonunion small-market radio spot.)* You can't very well charge 50 times what you initially charged and expect to hang on to that client for continued business, even if you did forewarn them. They probably won't remember and will only have canceled checks in their past accounts to go by with the original devalued rate. The point is, this won't make your client happy, and rightfully so. Would you be okay with that if you were in their shoes? Charging below-basement rates to new clients serves only to devalue your work and the work of others in the profession, as well as devaluing the worth of talent agents and recording engineers alike, whose skills and expertise are completely overlooked in this scenario.

Low-balling your rate in this manner will not serve to land you steady work or even further your mission to move from radio to voice overs.

Our best advice to you when it comes to offering a rate for your services: Stay out of it! Instead leave it to the professionals whenever possible, namely a seasoned talent agent. NEVER hang a shingle out saying you cost $X amount as a flat fee. There is NO flat fee for performance. Why? Because there are far too many variables in the equation! *Every* production is unique and so are the demands of the project, therefore the value of the job (your rate) should be based on the project demands, the intended usage and length of usage according to the standards established by the union (SAG-AFTRA). Besides you're only undermining your own true authority as a professional by offering a rate that most clients would certainly oblige if offered. Blindly offering a rate out of fear and anxiety will only further distance you from discovering how to move from radio to voice overs.

A rate for your skills, personality, and performance is determined by the *intended* and ultimate use of the final audio—not how long the final audio will be, and it never has. Regardless of the suggested rates offered on various pay-to-play online casting sites that only serve to benefit the client and not the voice talent.

The primary purpose behind a client employing professionals (casting directors, producers, and talent agents) is the simple fact that these industry veterans have experience in determining what the value of a particular job might be. For instance, whether the project will be created for commercial use, Internet, new media (iPad, Twitter, smartphones, Facebook, or games), cable, network, trade show, interactive, animation, and/or corporate narration.

How long the vendor intends to use your final performance in any combination of the list of above options or repurpose any portion of your performance, all factor into the ultimate value of the voice-over (or acting) job. I'd say that's well worth their meager rates, wouldn't you?

Ironically, in recent years, with all the added forms of media your work could ultimately end up in, the value of these key professionals has diminished. Without an experienced producer, casting director, and/or talent agent, to safeguard the true value of your work, talent have been left to their own imagined value. With little or no experience, talent have readily been giving away their services through the continued use and abuse of many of these online voice-over job sites, which is unfortunate. Radio talent, especially, have even less experience determining their value and often exhibit greater desperation by attempting to low-ball their rate beyond any normal standard in order to win the job on these sites. As the saying goes, desperate people do desperate things. Coming from a radio background they will do-it-themselves rather than employ an agent or leave it to the professionals.

## For the Love of the Game

It's understandable how so many people can completely devalue themselves for the love of the work. Actors have been doing just that since time immemorial. They're simply trying to earn a living.

But when we're referring to voice-over, we're generally referring to a mass medium, rather than an intimate theater setting, and we're speaking of a recorded performance that can be repurposed again and again, adding to the value of that performance. This makes the following cautionary tale all the more pertinent.

Would-be voice talent Elwood Edwards voiced "You've got mail," among the other notable AOL prompts back in 1989, prior to the Internet becoming such an established utility. He wasn't paid a dime for his time. A few short years later his iconic statement became the title and central theme of a major motion picture starring Tom Hanks and Meg Ryan. So, not only did Elwood's voice greet millions of individuals prior to opening their e-mails, it was used in trailers, had broad theatrical release, played on network television, and had been broadcast on cable and commercials. Had he been paid what the job was worth, he would have incurred residual pay in the hundreds of thousands, by today's standards.

In a PR move to reduce the possible backlash that might follow, AOL compensated Elwood in 1998 with a buyout (flat fee) of approximately $80,000 and had him sign a release putting any possible future compensation to rest. He was happy, AOL was happy. Of course, if he had continued to receive renewals and residuals for "you've got mail" he would possibly have incurred as much as $3,500,000 to date.

Certainly this is an unusual case, but you could say every case is unique.

The bottom line is it doesn't matter what the length of the final audio is, what matters is the intended and ultimate use of the final audio that determines the true value of the job. It's well worth mentioning, since so many radio talent base their ridiculously low rate on the "fact" that final audio will only be "five seconds or less." This has *nothing* to do with what you should be paid for your voice-over, and it never has.

This is where voice over training, discovering how to be a voice actor, and learning how to do voice overs will improve any seasoned radio talent's game tremendously—no matter how much experience and what you may know already about radio, *every professional* stands to elevate their career to a dramatic extent by seeking voice coaching. Every potential client likely to hire you believes you are a voice actor, and therefore you need to consider yourself as such.

Not all voice over classes offer this viewpoint, but then, unlike **SOUND ADVICE,** they haven't extensively and repeatedly surveyed more than 12,000 of your potential employers nationwide as we have.

### Air Checks

The on-air demo for a radio talent is known as an *air check*. They consist of numerous clips from radio shows the radio talent (DJ) has actually done without the commercials and music. They are used to secure jobs at radio stations and are submitted to program directors (PDs) for this very purpose. The production on these demos is expected to be very even and consistent, the complete *opposite* of what we are attempting to do when producing demos to secure voice-over in commercials, corporate narration and industrials (Co-Ed), promos, animation, and Spanish language. The simple reason is that we are attempting to make each spot sound as if it were produced in a different studio by a different producer for a different product service, or show. This is yet another great disconnect between these two worlds: radio and voice-over.

## A Hat for Every Head

The benefit of voice-over job sites such as voices.com, voice123.com, and voplanet.com is that they offer small-business owners and many nonunion talent opportunities to assist one another.  For example, if a small-business owner in Charlotte, North Carolina, has a very limited budget of say $500 to $750 a month to produce a couple of radio commercials, and you have a simple home recording setup with which you can record (not *produce*, but simply *record*) those spots, then both parties can get a good deal, proving there actually is a hat for every head.

What's a good deal? Getting paid a rate you're comfortable with as a talent, and conversely, as a vendor, paying a rate you can live with comfortably as well.  It's not a good deal unless it's a good deal for both parties.

If your gut tells you you're giving away the candy store, then don't! Good judgment goes a long way.  If you honestly don't have any idea what the true value of a job is, turn it over to a dependable talent agent.  It's well worth the 10 or 20 percent commission you'll pay him and will probably secure even more opportunities with the same vendor due to the fact your agent can *confidently* offer the true value of the job.  Commerce is confidence.

## The Most Lucrative Voice Work Going

Of all the sites that offer voice talent opportunities for work, Voicebank.net is head and shoulders the ultimate—and not just nationwide but internationally as well. Voicebank not only offers the most voice-over auditions (both union and nonunion), but also the most lucrative voice work in the business.

The talent listed on Voicebank aren't subjected to random, often inappropriate evaluations either, as they are on voice123.com. Additionally, the projects offered on Voicebank are generally sent through various talent agents, rather than scores of individual talent and are primarily for national campaigns. They also don't suggest you establish a flat rate for yourself either, they stay out of that. They simply let professionals conduct business as professionals.

Voicebank predates any of the established casting sites by a number of years, including the premier on-camera casting sites such as ActorsAccess.com and CastingNetworks.com. This is where the seasoned voice-over professionals do business and where you should be included as well, if you aren't already. This is not to say every talent agent on Voicebank is flawless or every job offered will break the bank in your favor. But it's the saner, more stable route that offers radio talent (and all other professional voice talent) a source with which to find proper representation and access to bigger, more consistent, higher paying voice-over jobs. And isn't that what we're all ultimately aiming for? (Yes. It is.)

## Technique & Training

If you've spent a better part of your career in radio, it's very likely you lack training, especially when it comes to technique and taking direction.

Technique training can be rather tricky. Especially when it's commonly thought in our field "there's no single approach considered more effective than another." We hope to challenge that. As we see it: Acting is acting is acting. And voice-over... IS acting.

At **Sound Advice** we propose a rather unique approach: there are only a handful of technical demands you must master with each medium, however the same basic principles apply to every performance regardless of whether it's for voice over, film, television, commercial, or some other recorded media.

The concepts we impart to you in this chapter are just a few of our own signature training, which we consider *the **Sound Advice** Approach*. We offer one-on-one coaching in either of our two studio locations in Chicago or Los Angeles, or through the use of Skype provided you have stable Internet service.

Having coached more than 10,000 people to date, varying in ages from 4 to 89, I've managed to determine what I consider the common denominators of what the actor experiences and needs to know and do on any given job, and further, what those who have hired him expect and need. **Sound Advice** has offered me a fascinating opportunity to observe and define a few steadfast tools here that can only assist the entire production, regardless of the medium, if employed with consistency.

That said, there are a few **common misconceptions** in the way, right out of the gate, such as:

- The folks who have hired you are after a single, perfect take
- You'll be required to do only a take or two and then you're done
- Those who hired you *know what they want*
- You'll receive direction that will determine your delivery

Most of us have the idea that those folks on the other side of the glass on a voice-over session will be feeding us every nuance and notion. Now, this may be something of a lightning bolt striking from the blue, but you are not likely to get *any* direction at all! The direction you do get will be limited, if not flat-out confusing. So you must be sure to define your terms if you are ever offered anything you don't fully understand.

Technique is the process you apply to achieve results in a performance or promotion. This term literally applies to *every* single aspect of this business—performance, promotion, marketing—it's a vital component to achieve any form of success.

Ironically, no one is interested in seeing or being made aware of your technique any more than any one wants to be made aware of your DNA. Yet, like DNA, it's the stuff that holds the whole delivery together. The difference is technique requires development in order for it to blend fully into the scenery and become a natural part of your professional fabric.

Generally, it's most commonly associated with performance. Method acting, Meisner, Linklater, and Lessac are some of the better-known modern techniques that make up so much of the American acting training palette. Well-schooled talent should be familiar, at least in theory, with these over the course of their career if for no other reason than to have a reference of them should the need arise. They all have their merits, to a greater or lesser degree.

As you might have guessed, when it comes to creating a process for running the business of your career, a bit more structure is required. Even the notion of incorporating order and routine into the mix is usually met with resistance by most artists. Yet without it, it's not likely their art or therefore their performance will endure.

And if it's true that great art endures because it continues to communicate, then I'd like to take that one step further. I tend to think art continues to communicate because it remains accessible— much like pop culture.

For art, like anything worthwhile, you must persist. In fact, in order to accomplish ANYTHING you must persist, but certainly that's especially true when it comes to your career.

(See Chapter 11 *The SOUND ADVICE Approach* for more details on improving your performance and creating a more natural delivery.)

# Chapter 5: Kids and Young Adults

"When child actors act well they're just reacting to situations, and they're acting very real because their life experience is so short; there's no history to fall back on."
—Mariel Hemingway

I was stage struck as child. To me, acting wasn't just a fun way to play (which it was) it was a flat-out quest that continues to drive me today. It's a driven passion that keeps me going, even when met with great opposition.

To a parent this has to be one of the biggest concerns: coming to terms with the fact that your child will face continued opposition as an actor, whether from snarky competitors who don't appreciate being bested, or after delivering a strong, confident audition only to discover someone else booked the job. This is tough pill to swallow for an adult let alone a young performer. Yet, in spite of everything, young talent dedicatedly continue and their desire to press on remains. That determination has to be encouraged on occasion, and on occasion, you may find your young actor encouraging you! An inherent positive outlook is required of both of you.

Maybe it can go without saying, but your young actor needs your encouragement, support, and that you act as a proper manager, often without any experience or notion of exactly what that might entail, which is precisely why we've included this chapter.

Here at **Sound Advice** we've trained and produced demos for well over a thousand young performers over the years ranging from age 4 through 17 to great effect. In fact, the results have been so extraordinary, many of our young talent return years later as adults with the intention to repeat the success they enjoyed when they were small. Which is why we contend, a child with a voice-over demo is like a kid with a loaded gun—they're bound to hit something.

It's imperative you embrace the technological advances this industry requires in order to run your child's career and keep you in good, quick communication with agents and managers. Even if you're completely up-to-speed and have embraced technology fully, you need to know how it applies to this field. If you resist change, the future of your child's career will ultimately fail.

Actors are typically taught to rely solely on their wits and physical prowess, which should be true for kids, provided the parents aren't skirting their obligations of running their children's careers and forfeiting any real career advancement by omitting the most basic computer and self-promotional skills.

Part of the beauty of being a young adult or child actor is this truly is the _only_ time the actor can actually walk into the audition or job and simply act. As an adult actor you must handle all the administrative, financial, technical, communication, and scheduling logistics involved with establishing and maintaining a career in this field. Instead, all of those duties fall to YOU! All your child or young adult actor should ever worry about is stepping into an audition, onto a set or booth… and just "play". (They don't call a "play" a play for nothing.) Allowing your child the freedom to do just that means you're doing your job well.  And it *is* a job!   This certainly explains why so few child actors continue in the business into adulthood. They must have had powerhouse parents who flawlessly maintained the administrative aspects of running their small business that gave the child ample opportunity to concentrate solely on performing. When they move on to adulthood, they suddenly discover that 90% of success is administrative.  The rest is showing up and delivering goods.

With any luck, and with some dutiful application, this trusty reference book will help you discover what you have to do to help your young actor realize their dreams, and ultimately yours as well.

Our best advice: Give your young talent room to create and play, while you (the parent) maintain a sane, stable, reliable, organized support system for both your child as well as the professional who relies on them. Producers, casting directors, and talent agents need to know they can count on you to arrive on time with your young performer prepared, well fed, and rested. This means it's up to YOU to safeguard your child from undue stress and worry. Making sure your young talent is prepared for every audition and supplying them with the professional tools and continued training necessary to work professionally in this business is the other half of this very challenging role you'll play in your child's career.

## Training, Demos, and Headshots

Your young actor needs more than a new pair of shoes every few months.  As an actor, his training is *ongoing*, his headshots will need to be updated continually and, if he has a voice-over demo (not all kids do), he will need to update his materials with some frequency, especially if his promo doesn't look or sound like the young performer actually walking through the casting agent's door. It will be a tough sell to secure a talent agent, talent manger, and book work for voice overs, land commercial acting jobs, or establish their acting career without the proper tools expected regardless of whether they are just starting out or not.

Headshots of babies with sunglasses and cake on their faces are adorable on Facebook, but less than professional, regardless of whether a "professional" photographer shot it or not.  Costumes are not appropriate either. Neither are "selfies" taken from smartphones.

Just honest expressions, with a variety of emotions are all that's required. A proper talent agent will help choose a few good "looks."

Kids with voice-over demos work—provided they have access to a talent agent that handles both kids and commercial voice-over, and provided the voice-over demo sounds like real, *national* commercials. If your child can't easily re-create what's on his demo, that demo will be misrepresenting his abilities. However, a well-produced voice-over demo can act as a remarkably effective tool to better define your child's public personae and what sort of commercial work he's best suited to book. Without the benefit of having a proper commercial on-camera reel, an effective voice-over demo can offer producers and directors a better idea of how vivid your child's imagination really is and how it applies to a mass medium like commercial work.

## Honest Representation

It's important to mention you will NEVER pay a talent agent to find work for your child or buy access to casting opportunities. Not in any professional setting anyway.

Talent agents are paid a percentage (usually 10 to 20 percent) of whatever productions or print jobs your child books. But no funds should ever be required of you in advance of securing work.

There's honestly no real litmus test to determine whether the information you're getting from a purported talent manager, acting coach or talent agent is true. Even the Better Business Bureau isn't what it used to be.

The best advice is seeing and speaking with other parents and children who are getting quality auditions and bookings through this same source. Determine in advance of signing anything whether these other families are happy with the results they've been getting and why. Have they gotten paid? If so, how recently? What was it for? How long did it take to get paid?

Ultimately, trust your gut. If it walks like a duck and quacks like a duck, it's probably not a fish. Poke around. This is your child. And always consider where you are. If you're in a rural area, is it likely your child will be exposed to steady opportunities—probably not.

You may have to go out of your way, but ask LOTS of questions. It's really YOUR job to be your child's advocate and learn whatever you can to best manage your child's acting and voice over career.

## The Coogan Law and the Coogan Account

Knowing the legal ins and outs of having a child in this business can be daunting. It has a long history, which is probably best illustrated in the life story of Jackie Coogan, a child star discovered by Charlie Chaplin, who initially found fame in the classic 1919 film *The Kid*. He became the youngest star in the business and earned a lucrative salary during the 1920's and 1930's. Under California law at the time, his earnings belonged solely to his parents, who ultimately pilfered away all of his savings by his 21$^{st}$ birthday. Jackie sued his mother and former manager and as a result the Coogan Law was in effect by 1939 with the intent to protect the earnings of young actors in a similar situation.

Today the Coogan Law, modified to further protect child actors in January 2000, affirms that earnings by minors in the entertainment industry are the property of the minor, not their parents. According to the SAG-AFTRA Web site: "Since a minor cannot legally control their own money, California law governs their earnings and creates a fiduciary relationship between the parent and child." This change in California law also requires that 15 percent of all minors' gross wages must be set aside and deposited within 15 days of employment into a blocked trust account commonly known as a Coogan Account. Employers will require a Coogan account number from the parent upon securing a role.

Not all banks offer Coogan Accounts, and even many that do may not have employees who are familiar with the term. Explaining you are interested in opening a blocked trust account for your child should clarify what you're attempting to accomplish.

Check the SAG-AFTRA Web site for a list of the banks that offer blocked trust accounts. Coogan Accounts are required if your child or minor will be working in the states of California, New York, Louisiana, or New Mexico.

## Work Permits

Most states require a general work permit prior to hiring a minor in any form of employment. These vary widely from state to state, and most states require a letter from your child's school indicating your child is in good academic standing prior to issuing a work permit.

You'll need a copy of your child's birth certificate among your child's legal documents and to acquire proper work permits. Considering minors must have their Coogan Account Trustee Statement attached to their work permits at all times, it would be a good idea to open your Coogan Account before securing the work permit. It's best to check with your state's Department of Labor for questions and applications.

Generally, the I-9 is the Employment Eligibility Verification form used to confirm an individual's right to work in the United States and to establish identity. According to SAG-AFTRA, a valid passport is the most useful form of identification for minors. It confirms both identity and right to work. School identification cards (with picture), Social Security cards, and birth certificates are all used to prove the right to work and identity for minors.

To learn more about I-9 documentation requirements go to www.formi9.com.

Parents or legal guardians are required to provide a W-4 in order to indicate the rate of federal payroll tax withholding and use the personal allowance worksheet on the top of the form to calculate the number of exemptions. If the minor is incorporated, a different form is used. Always consult a tax professional familiar with child performers' work regarding tax payments and exemptions.

## Education

Parents with young children who have a good run in commercials or on a series, for example, often anticipate that the income generated from these high-earning periods can be put to good use later for the child's education. However, it's important not to put off until tomorrow what is genuinely required today: A good education is often an actor's greatest resource. The ability to hone expert study skills, strong reading, and writing skills are always required of an actor and are tested constantly in this business.

The definition of a minor, according to SAG-AFTRA, on commercials is 15 years and under, and for motion picture and television, and non-broadcast industrials is under 18 years of age.

## School-aged Minors

On a school day, school-age minors may work as follows:
- Ages 6 to 8—four hours (maximum of eight-and-one-half hours on the set)
- Ages 9 to 15—five hours (maximum of nine-and-one-half hours on the set)
- Ages 16 and 17—six hours (maximum of ten-and-one-half hours on the set)
- On days when school is not in session, school-age minors

may work an additional two hours a day
- On all days, the minor must have at least one hour of rest and recreation and one half-hour meal break
- By prior arrangement with the studio teacher, up to two hours of school may be banked (stored) to offset additional work hours on other days; there must be at least one hour of school on each day the minor's regular school is in session

## Preschool-age Minors

Minors who are 6 months through 5 years do not attend school on the set, even though they may attend preschool or kindergarten on a regular basis.

Work hours are as follows:
- Ages 6 months to 2 years—two hours (maximum of four hours on the set)
- Ages 2 years through 5 years—three hours (maximum of four-and-one-half hours on the set)
- Minors 6 months through 5 years must have at least one hour of rest and recreation
- Minors 2 to 5 years must also have one half-hour meal break

Compulsory education requirements vary from state to state. In California, for instance, excused school absences for children in the entertainment industry are limited and, it might surprise you to learn, independent home schooling is not legal. Each school must follow the local school district's jurisdiction requirements in which the minor resides. Again, according to SAG-AFTRA, "out-of-state home school arrangements are not automatically recognized. Parents should establish a solid working relationship with the minor's school as soon as possible."

Every school is unique, especially since your school may not receive their average daily allotment (ADA) of funding for a minor absent for work reasons. All the more reason to develop a good working relationship and communications with school administrators and teachers. Some schools are very accommodating to children working in the industry, while others discourage it.

On a set, SAG-AFTRA contracts require the producer supply a teacher if your child is working three or more consecutive days. This doesn't apply to voice-over, generally, but it's good to know.

## Sheepskin

The California High School Proficiency Examination (CHSPE) is a state-sponsored examination offered periodically throughout the year. This is the legal equivalent of high school graduation recognized by the Labor Commission. If a minor obtains a CHSPE certificate, he may work as an adult, with no requirement for observing child labor law or attending school on set. Most CHSPE certificate holders still attend their regular schools. Not all states have tests similar to the CHSPE, and the State of California does not necessarily honor similar exam results from other states. Whether a university would honor CHSPE as valid high school diploma is a variable as well.

## Auditions

If your child comes to life for you and you alone, and clams up in front of others, or responds only in one- or two-word responses—just like adults, this is a deal killer. It's doubtful your child should continue. It may seem like a no-brainer to mention it, but exposing children to opportunities against their will or under pressure will _not_ result in a positive outcome in the short or long haul.

EVERYONE experiences nerves. Surviving them is the key. Redirecting nervous energy into performance energy is done by simply allowing yourself to BE nervous, rather than fighting it. (This is true for you as the parent, as well!)

The more comfortable your young performer becomes with the process, the more realistic the expectations, the more he can be himself and the more honestly conversational and communicative he can be during the audition/interview process—the greater his likelihood for booking the job.

Even with exceptional headshots, which will need to be reshot every 4 months until they are almost 30 (no kidding), with a remarkable on-camera reel, and an incredibly well-produced commercial voice-over demo—all auditioning for them in lieu of their presence—your vivacious youngster needs to "bring it" consistently to every audition. The only way this comes about is from exposure. And that translates into scores of auditions—and you clocking in loads of miles on your car, as chief transport and all-around organizer.

For what it's worth, SAG-AFTRA contracts allow commercial auditions for minors after school provided they conclude prior to 8 p.m. Motion picture and television and non-broadcast industrial auditions for minors are allowed after school and must conclude before 9 p.m. Considering most casting is done online, with very little interaction with the casting office, you may find you need to remind your agent or those casting that your minor is not permitted to leave school early. Ask for the time frame in which the casting office is holding interviews or auditions to accommodate both school and the agency.

Auditions are an art unto themselves. The more of them you do, ideally, the better you get.

The fact is, no one is all that keen on auditions, producers and talent alike. It's nerve-racking for both sides of the production process; those casting are worried you're better on your demo or in the audition process than you will be on the job, and talent are just plain worried about what it is they don't know.

On one hand, some talent become expert auditioners, but can't deliver when ultimately put to the test. They often harbor the erroneous notion that once booked they are expected to deliver a flawless performance in one single take after which the entire studio will explode into spontaneous applause and then they can go home. The only real difference between the audition and the session is the number of takes. A booking may require 5 takes, or it may require 55 takes. (It varies dramatically from job to job, and from director to director.) Whereas on the audition, we usually get only one or two takes regardless of the project, regardless of the medium.

Still others are only good once they land the job, but bridging the gap from unemployment to employment remains the eternal dilemma and demands they master the art of the audition.

I know, I know. I can hear all those young hopefuls, pining, "Can't someone just take a chance (on you) so (you) don't have to go through this ridiculous process." In a word: no. Creatives and talent agents alike look good only *if you do*—and if you don't pan out, they feel the brunt of your professional missteps even more directly than you ever will as a talent. (This explains the cold, harsh reception you're often met with when you first embark on securing representation, doesn't it?)

## A Numbers Game

Auditions are promo. And, especially for voice-over, they aren't and should never be the sole form of promotion, due to the simple fact that relying on a *single* talent agent from a *single* region to supply you with enough auditions is not a viable option. Statistics dictate that it generally takes between 150 and 200 auditions to book a job. If you're getting two to three auditions a week from the *one* talent agent, you have then it'll take you *a year to land a single job*! You have to increase the odds in your favor. One of the great benefits of voice-over is the fact that you can (and should) secure numerous talent agents in a variety of regions across the country. With consistent, targeted promotions driving traffic to your voice-over demo Web site, you can effectively be cast directly off your demo. You'll increase your odds by a significant margin if you do.

In order to land a job, for both voice-over and on-camera work, *auditioning* is generally required of nearly every rank and file talent. And to make the best use of valuable production time, headshots, voice-over demos, and on-camera reels (promo) are generally used in advance of your audition to determine whether you're the correct type, look, style, and personality required for the specific casting project.

Voice-over demos and on-camera reels can act as an effective substitute for an audition on occasion, in large part because they are thought to be the best example of what you have to offer as a professional, and what sort of work you are seeking *more* of. So if your professional tools are not up to date or are low grade and makeshift, you may be keeping yourself from landing jobs you might be perfect for.

After submitting your promo, you may be called in for an audition. The more auditions you do, the more you make yourself known, and the more familiar you'll become to those most likely to hire you.

## What Do They Want Your Child To Do

Consistently your young actor will be told to "just be yourself." Those casting will want your child's interpretation of the script; in other words, the most dynamic, spontaneous, natural, honest person they can be.

Most casting sources *know what they don't want* rather than what they do. (You may even hear, "We'll know it when we see it.") And as a result, many novice talent set out to determine what a client might want from them using deductive reasoning; they attempt to rule out all the don'ts rather than concentrating on the do's. Problem is: Your young actor can't tell themselves how NOT to do something. Instead, they need to concentrate on what they want in the equation.

For instance, if you tell yourself "DON'T think of a banana". Or "DON'T think of a cat". It's an impossible proposition. Yet, a good deal of direction you may be given will be, "The first paragraph was great, but don't do what you did on the end. Do something else. And…rolling…"

This is where effective coaching comes in. You have to tell yourself what you *want* in the equation, not the other way around. At **Sound Advice**, we've been imparting how to self-direct and avoid this trap for nearly 20 years to scores of talent, young adults and kids alike.

## How Auditions Are Held

How auditions are held refers to the manner in which casting is being done. This varies widely from project to project, commercial to film, on-camera to voice-over, let alone from one production company or casting agency to another.

Some initial on-camera casting calls will have you scheduled to be seen at a specific time and location. You'll sign in, read the rather vague direction ("Know-It-All" or "Bully"), and you'll wait to be called with a burgeoning room full of kids who either a) look exactly like you, or b) couldn't be more different from you. (Take your pick. Expect both scenarios.)

Scripts and/or descriptions are typically available where you sign in.

When you do go in to deliver your audition, you may or may not be told where to stand. Look for a mark on the floor. It's usually shaped like a T. You'll slate your name and then be expected to go directly into your performance. Most casting agents and assistants guide you through this, as it behooves them to get the best possible read from each submitted talent, but it helps to know how it works for the exceptions.

On union auditions they *must* have the lines displayed in front of you on an easel, usually next to the camera or placed where they will ask you to look slightly off-camera. Often in initial commercial auditions you are not expected to have your lines perfectly memorized (sometimes the lines have changed overnight from the sides posted on the casting site) and it's acceptable to refer to the posted lines on the easel. Be familiar with the lines but able to change the lines you have rehearsed.

It is best to be better acquainted or memorize any lines for the callback. (Again, copy can change in an hour as the ad creatives' work becomes more intense as the actual shoot is probably in a few days.) On-camera callbacks will be in a room with the head casting director, and often the director, the producer, any number of ad creatives, and possibly even the client.

Often in castings where there are few or no lines, your young actor will be asked questions and expected to answer directly to camera, often about their own life experiences. "Have you taken a family road trip before?" or "Do you play soccer? Are you any good?" "When you're not acting, what's your favorite thing to do?" "Do you have a crush on anyone? Do they like you back?" Those casting are looking to see how your child expresses themselves, how they interact with others, including strangers, and to discover their most precious, most valuable possession—their own unique personality.

This is where spontaneity and improvisational skills are essential. It doesn't matter if they are a great basketball player or not for the Kool-Aid commercial they are auditioning for—but it does matter whether they engage, connect, and animate in front of the camera and with those they are on-camera with as well as those they are not. I always tell even adult actors, *you're paid to have a pulse.* It's more important to animate the *concept* than the words on the page. This is true for on-camera and voice-over alike.

(See Chapter 12, Auditions, for more information.)

## Work-a-Day World

The SAG-AFTRA contract governs minor's work hours everywhere in the United States unless stricter work hours are mandated by the state. Workday rules are as follows:

Starting with babies, in California, infants 15 days to 6 months of age may only be on the set between the hours of 9:30 a.m. to 11:30 a.m. or 1:30 p.m. to 3:30 p.m. No infant born prematurely may work until he/she would be at least 15 days old if born at full-term. SAG-AFTRA producers have agreed to observe these restrictions in other jurisdictions.

- Ages 15 days to 6 months—twenty minutes to two hours maximum on the set
- Minors may not work before 5:30 a.m. or after 10:00 p.m. on evenings preceding a school day (work days must end by 12:30 a.m. on nonschool days). The minor's final workday must be concluded at least twelve hours before the beginning of the minor's next regular school day
- On a school day (determined by the calendar of the district where the child resides), school-age minors must receive at least three hours of instruction. Maximum allowable hours and times of instruction vary by grade level
- Minors through age 15 must be accompanied at all times by a parent or guardian. Minors age 16 or 17 may work without a parent or guardian, but are entitled to have a parent or guardian present. The parent or guardian is

entitled to be within sight and sound of the minor at all times

- Minors who are high school graduates are exempt from the child labor laws and may work on the same basis as adults

## Emancipation Proclamation

Theatrical production (television programs, motion pictures) tends to go on for long work hours, sometimes 12 hours or more. Obviously, the longer an actor can legally work the more favorable the casting process can be. Enter: emancipation! No, it has nothing to do with Abe Lincoln, the Civil War, or ending slavery in America. Emancipation is a legal process by which a minor (anyone under 18 years of age) can legally be declared by a court of law to be considered an adult. The emancipation process and its effects vary from state to state. However, in California, emancipation does NOT excuse a minor from the compulsory education requirements nor from the child labor laws. Therefore, in California, an emancipated minor will not gain any advantage in the casting process, but it does allow for the production to save some budget costs considering no teacher is required on set, the minor can continue to shoot longer hours, and the parents are free to leave the set to take care of other personal and family functions that are bound to arise.

## Can't Imagine Doing Anything Else

So, in conclusion, clearly there's a lot to know regarding young performers, and we're only scratching the surface. All your child needs to concern himself with is "the play's the thing." It *should* be play for them. That's what will make them valuable to any production and happy in life. The happier the child, the more stable the performer. Besides, most young actors can't imagine themselves doing anything else.

Your child will usually let you know what he needs and wants. You simply need to be open to hearing what he is *actually* saying, rather than what you might be projecting on him due to the fact you've invested so much time, money, and energy into his career. Your child might play along simply because he doesn't want to let YOU down, and that never works out well. It has to be the child's call, or you will *both* be wasting valuable time, energy, and sanity.

Hopefully this book and especially this chapter will conserve on all of these and more.

If your child isn't all that committed and finds himself more interested in piano or baseball or dance, so be it. Most kids want it all. If you can manage it, let 'em have it. They'll only be more well-rounded individuals from the experience. It's not pleasant working with unhappy humans, especially when those humans are small.

You may have thought this chapter was going to make your life easier. At this point, you might just get a glimpse into what most adult actors must do for themselves and wonder how they manage. The answer: not very well. They didn't have a parent like you to offer them lots of room simply to create! Thanks, Mom and Dad!

Speaking of managers, should you feel you need one, and you live in either New York or Los Angeles, we suggest you contact your local SAG-AFTRA office for suggestions for reputable options specializing in kids and young adults. Otherwise, these responsibilities ultimately fall to you. (Insert either "Congratulations" or "With my sympathies." Your call.)

# Chapter 6: Identity, Branding, and Type

"The particular human chain we're part of is
central to our individual identity."
—Elizabeth Stone

"Who am I?" Now there's an age-old philosophical question.

Well, once upon a time, in an alternate universe, I was the perfect Peter Pan type, a sprightly, high-spirited tomboy who was both physically agile and able. And, if it wasn't for a few frighteningly high notes in the "Little Lamb" solo, I was once the ideal Louise in *Gypsy*: a character that does a complete 180, going from a shy, awkward introvert to a sexy, confident sophisticate.

Fast-forward twenty-some odd years later and it would be safe to say that identifying me with either of these two characters is not only a stretch—it's flat-out comical!

Okay, so what does that tell us? Your type can and *will* change. It's bound to eventually. Age range alone will see to that.

Certainly there is a germ of that sassy Peter Pan in me still that now plays out as the fun mom, and that awkwardly bashful girl–turned–sexually confident sophisticate that was Louise now reads as the confident authority, sometimes with a noticeable, vulnerable crack in her armor just to raise the stakes. And, ironically, what was once Louise is now Mama Rose.

Generally, I'm best suited as the trusted best friend or neighbor, comic relief or not. (In life as well as on camera.)

All these things ultimately make up who I am and how I'm perceived in an instant as these all deal with *type*.

Type can be elusive in this business for a number of reasons. Reality is often subjective. Additionally, you may discover yourself growing into a type you've never played or out of one that once seemed the most comfortable to you.

The bottom line is: How you read as a talent and what you innately bring to the role speaks volumes before you even utter a sound. How you look (your face, your build) already have an entire performance built right into it. Your presence, whether you realize it or not, says a great deal.

Hopefully, it's saying what you intend it to say. Now there's the rub.

In advertising, we identify with a product or service by its brand identity. This identity is carefully sculpted and established through well-planned promotion and product placement. It often takes years just to come up with a name like Häagen-Dazs or Lunchables, and even longer to establish a reputation like McDonald's or Macy's. As a rule every brand is intended to evoke familiar concepts designed to appeal to specific demographic audiences. These things don't come about on their own, although they're certainly expected to appear that way.

The term branding comes from advertising. It allows you to differentiate yourself from the competition and, in the process, to bond with your audience and create loyalty. Branding is the process of making something distinctive in the marketplace. In a mass medium, to communicate effectively you must be able to convey your point quickly and distinctly, otherwise you may confuse, or, just as bad, underwhelm the viewer/listener.

The term identity comes from marketing. The idea here is if you can easily identify with the product, you can readily determine its value. (Sounds more like casting at every turn.) If you find the subject is something you can identify with rather quickly, you are more likely to embrace it. It will appear familiar, even if it may be something new. This is primarily why type is as important as it is.

Okay, so identity and branding deal with making a product recognizable and representative of something specific.

That's what we do when producing your demo at **Sound Advice**. Determining your type as a talent, for both on-camera and as a voice-over, utilizes many of the same features when developing a brand identity.

As Americans we've been raised on a steady diet of commercials. You're probably far more familiar with identity, branding, and type than you even realize. As a captive and consistent TV viewing audience, we've been saturated with branding.

What speaks to us most from a mass medium speaks to us *individually* first. As actors we're no different. When we first start out in the talent business, we take comfort in the knowledge that no one does what we do.

"I'm me. I'm the only one of me. I don't want to be compared with anyone else."

To be honest, that's not the issue, unless you make it so.

While it's true no one does what you do quite the way you do it, you are, certainly at first glance, perceived as a very specific type. This is true whether you embrace this concept or not. You may as well like it at least a little bit, because without type no one will be able to identify with you *or* establish your value to their future production—and that, my friend, is a cold, hard fact.

So, your type is in large part *how you read to others*; how you come across; how you appear as your personae is conveyed to the viewer. In short, it's who you *are* in the most basic, broadest sense. Identity and branding speak to your specific color, nuance, and creation.

## You and Mass Media

First of all, to clarify, the term media refers to *multiple* forms of mass communication, such as stage, film, television, commercial work, Internet, cable, print for magazines and billboards, and radio, to name a few. A medium would be a single form of any of these.

That said, today's talent are generally expected to be well versed in all forms of media. This means understanding what is needed and wanted from you should you be cast to perform in any or all of them.

Most talent focus their efforts by specializing in one form over another. However, if we don't venture beyond what we know, we tend to limit our viable options professionally.

All that said, it's unrealistic to expect *every* talent to be appropriate for *every* job that comes down the pike. We're all well suited for a variety of work, and yet many of us may specialize in just one or two aspects of this business. And that's fine, if that suits you.

Consider, for example, an established working actor who began his career in radio. Later this talent became a disc jockey, and from there got into improvisation and stand-up. Later this talent expanded his skills into stage, commercials, and sitcoms. This eventually evolved into film, cable, and back into commercials again, and even animation and spokesperson work. Of course, voice-over plays a prominent role in all of these forms of media.

I use this example due to the fact that this is the course many talent have taken, whether well-known or rank and file. This will continue to be the case as long as the industry exists if you anticipate being a steady working actor. It's simply the nature of the beast. The point is: In today's market, we're expected to master multiple disciplines.

Technology has evolved to the point where a single performance can be transferred to numerous media outlets: your film performance can be played on the Internet, on your smartphone, iPad, on cable, and on network television. Yet the same performance demands were required of you regardless of all these different forms of media.

This is what can be observed as the ongoing *melding of media;* what was once solely on television is now playing at the movie theater and on the Internet and so on. Therefore, what was once considered a great divide from one medium to another is more symbiotic than ever before.

So mastering a variety of media might not be as much of a stretch as you once may have thought. It does require mastering a few technical skills within each art form, but beyond that, the truth is... acting is acting is acting!

We're often told, from some highly professional, well-meaning persons that, "Voice-over is a very different skill set. It's not at all like other forms of acting!"

We hear the same adage applied to the various other media of which we are "expected" to be just as skillful in.

Approaching each new form of media as a dramatic departure from what is familiar is a trap. It's a common misnomer that only serves to throw perfectly capable talent under the bus. So instead of approaching a new medium as if it were alien, do your best to *embrace it*.

## Versatility

As stage actors we're taught we're supposed to be *everything*. And certainly that's the general consensus regarding acting as a profession. You're supposed to be as well versed with Shakespeare as you are with Arthur Miller, as comfortable with comedy as you are with pathos, able to tackle *Medea* and turn around and just as easily play in a sitcom. For what it's worth, *none* of these tasks are all that easy. They all demand a tremendously high skill level from you as an actor, yet we're told *that's* being versatile, *that's* the job, and it's simply what's expected of us.

Well, as much as I love him, Shakespeare is not for everyone. I've come to this conclusion after sitting through hours of poorly performed productions of the Bard (hours of my life I will *never* get back) performed by actors who love the text and are quite good in numerous acting styles, just not this one. ("I wish him the very best—*elsewhere*," as my mother used to say.) Of course in some cases there are those who will never master this particular style, it may never have any bearing on whether these talent continue to work with any regularity. The talent in question might be incredibly successful in some other genre of the industry.

Essentially being versatile has to do with three things:

> 1. Classically, versatility has referred to whether you are as skillful at becoming a persona far different from yourself, or whether each character you play is a dramatic departure from the last.

> 2. The ability to transfer your skills from one medium to another also denotes versatility. With advancing technology, mass media continues to meld into a single, more versatile source. The more you familiarize yourself with the few technical demands required in each medium, the more confident you'll be to deliver the best possible performance.
> *

3. Versatility speaks to making yourself *flexible* enough to be prepared for whatever the production requires of you. For example, in theater, you typically have at least two weeks of rehearsal and then a week of previews before a production opens. Yet it's on the rarest occasion in recorded media you'd be required to deliver only one perfect take. It's certainly preferred you deliver your very best from the first take until the last, but a variety of inflections offered among repeated takes, within the parameters of the production, are most consistently needed and wanted from you.

* *This could account for so many stage actors having such a tough time transitioning to a new medium such as commercial or film. They often give themselves too long a runway to get off the ground, even though they're perfectly cast for the commercial, type-wise.*

## Who Are You?

Acting is a card game: The objective is to lead with *trump*; lead with POWER. In other words, establish yourself with what it is you do best.

Sounds easy. However, you may be too close to it to determine for yourself how you're perceived. This speaks to type. It's not uncommon, even if you've been pursuing a career in this business for a number of years, you may only stumble upon the work you're best suited to land as a type.

If your type changes or falls out of favor with the trends, a complete reevaluation of who you are and how you're perceived needs to be done if you hope to continue in this business.

Nothing stays the same, and type is no exception. If you had been relatively successful at one time and now you're not, something changed. It may be your marketing or the fact that you stopped making yourself available to the work. You may have changed agents. Then again, it may be your type has changed or the market has changed and those who once had a call for your type now require something else. There are a handful of factors that could be at play here, and determining how you're perceived *right now* is a very good place to start. You may find you typically do best with what interests or entertains you most.

We meet talent every day at **Sound Advice** who we'd consider extremely marketable for commercial work, yet far too often the talent don't consider themselves commercially viable. This may occur for a variety of reasons. It may be due to the fact that, in the case of many stage actors, we are generally taught to repel ANYTHING commercial, as this would be considered "selling out." Unfortunately this mindset has managed to impede more talent from establishing themselves professionally and making a stable living in this business. It's quite the stigma to overcome, especially if it's been drilled into you for four years or more in theater school.

Yet, it's a little-known fact that many well-known, respected film directors have managed to keep themselves gainfully employed between film projects for decades now directing commercials. Apparently, this fact has eluded all those "well-meaning" acting coaches who are often responsible for perpetuating this notion of selling out. It's a trap and not designed with your best interest.

## Determining Your Type

If you're just starting out or starting over, you may feel some pressure to fully define your type, establish your brand, your identity. You may have the idea that you can't just go out there *not* knowing who you are. Well, my friend, talent *do* just that, to a greater or lesser degree, every single day. They have as far back as anyone can remember. It's perfectly fine to have a *general* idea of where you'll book and how you're perceived—at least for the time being.

Typing a talent is often rather subjective. On one hand, typing allows a talent agent, casting director, producer, or director to get a handle on who you are in the *broadest* terms. On the other hand, it ultimately *defines* you as a very specific individual and sets you apart from the masses.

Thus, the confusion surrounding "type": It's very easy to become lost in this paradox.

Let's back up a minute. Let's start with the question, "How are you perceived?"

To break it down, you must have some idea of the sort of roles *you would do best*. You would never have pursued acting *in any capacity* if you didn't have at least *some* idea of what it is you bring to the table.

> How you read as a talent and what you bring to the role speaks volumes before you ever utter a sound.

Are you a character actor? Are you a romantic lead? Are you the bad guy? Are you the good guy?

It's very likely you fall into one of these types. *This* is where you begin as this is most likely how you're perceived first and foremost.

Breaking with conventional wisdom, the first professional auditions you go on you'll discover you're continually asked to "just be yourself." "Well, who the heck is that? I got into this business to 'be' someone else!" Most talent feel far more comfortable remaining safely behind the character they've created, rather than exposing their vulnerability as themselves. What a frightening prospect. Besides the whole thing is completely confusing. No wonder determining your type is such a conundrum.

You have to ask yourself, "What roles am I MOST LIKELY to play?"

Do yourself a favor and keep it simple.

## Here are a few types in the broadest of terms, especially for film:

| | |
|---|---|
| Romantic lead | Young female romantic lead (ingénue) |
| Comedic Sidekick | Villain |
| Hero/Heroine | Action Hero |
| Leading Man or Woman | Character Lead |

There may be more, but for now, even with these few it's likely you see yourself in one or more of these categories.

## A Variety of Work

Actors are generally taught to pursue *everything* all at once. We are told we're supposed to be as skillful at performing Shakespeare as naturally as Arthur Miller, *The Sound of Music* as comfortably as *Reservoir Dogs*, or a commercial for *TOYS R US* as easily as an episode of *The Walking Dead*.

While you very well may be well suited for *each* of these examples, this *can't* be said for every actor. And while it's advantageous to be as prepared and agile a talent as to make yourself available to the greatest amount of work you possibly can, being *everything* is not necessarily what you do best, nor should it make you any less valuable as a talent.

Discovering what you do best and concentrating your efforts, while continuing to develop and diversify your skills in a variety of areas, is always the best policy. You may find success in a specific area of the business, such as corporate narration. If that area of the business becomes short lived for whatever reason, the industry shifts suddenly requiring only nonunion talent—then your primary source of work may deplete entirely and this could be out of your control UNLESS you have other options as to where to focus your efforts and support yourself.

Certainly we are taught, from numerous sources as budding talent that *mastering all performance styles* and offering a *wide range of characters* is how to be read as versatile. And while it's true, you would be considered versatile if you were masterful in these areas, the fact remains today, as a working talent, mastering a variety of media genres is just as important—if not more so.

## Being Someone Else vs. *"Just Being Yourself"*

Let's say you have an established public personae such as Larry David (*Curb Your Enthusiasm*). It's doubtful that early on in your career you'd be considered versatile performance-wise. But that doesn't limit Larry David's, or other personality-driven actors like him, ability to be a successful talent in film and television. (And you'll notice stars like Tina Fey and Martin Scorsese are not above applying their skills to commercials, as they have done for American Express and a handful of others.)

So we can deduce from these examples, as well as scores of others, that mastering a variety of performance styles and characters is not necessarily the high watermark of a successful, working talent. Certainly not everyone is correct for everything a casting director may have a call for.

Nevertheless, the very first direction you are most likely to hear, as you walk into an audition, regardless of whether the project is a McDonald's commercial, a small role on *CSI*, a prominent role in the next hit HBO series, or a voice-over for a corporate industrial client is to "just be yourself"!

I don't know about you, but early on in my career, I always found this terribly confusing as a talent. Yet as a producer and casting director, it's honestly what we need for just about every project. Certainly this creates a terrific contradiction in the actor, especially after dutifully studying that he should "become someone else."

Let's face it this is a horrible prospect as a talent. This contradiction stems further when we successfully "lose ourselves" in roles, as we've been encouraged to do from all of our very best training. The prospect of "just being yourself" is often abhorrent to any self-respecting actor.

Yet, consistently this is precisely what we're asked to do at nearly every audition and every session or shoot. Didn't we become talent because, in large part, we enjoy *becoming someone else* and fully assuming another point of view that's often a dramatic departure from our own? Aren't we expected to be versatile?

So what's a talent to do when consistently, audition after audition, job after job, he's met with, "just be yourself"? You simply have to make peace with this notion by developing a realistic, natural, grounded, honest personae that is *a true extension of yourself* that you can comfortably play through. This seems to be the best answer. This especially applies to you if you find this direction confuses you completely and keeps you from nailing the audition or callback, regardless of how correct for the role you may be. Once you have gotten yourself a little more grounded professionally by exposing yourself to numerous auditions and jobs, you'll find this *performance personae* allows you to meet the demands of casting sources, while satisfying your own aesthetic sensibilities.

So, why is there is this great separation between our acting training and probably the most common, most basic direction you're likely to hear? Aren't you supposed to be someone else as a talent? Isn't that what acting is?

*Not necessarily*. If it were, then Spencer Tracy screwed up horribly. If you were looking to cast a film and wanted Spencer Tracy, you got… Spencer Tracy. If you wanted Clark Gable, you got Clark Gable.

Of course, if you were to have asked either one of these classic Hollywood icons, "Do you feel your performances were *dramatically different* film after film?" You can be sure each would feel they offered a terrific departure from one film to the next. Of course! They're actors!

Well, whether either of these film giants were versatile or not, is completely subjective. The fact is we love what they brought to the roles they graced, and we will continue to do so for years to come. Both became known for a style that was their own and ultimately personified something specific. Yet neither one of these two ever gave you the impression they were ever acting.

In fact, when you're auditioned, you're more likely to be asked *not* to act. In fact, the ability to confidently conceive the concept of the role, and of the project as a whole as a talent, will prove to be one of your greatest assets.

As for your type, it's quite possible you have only a rough idea of what that might be, regardless of your experience level. But, if you've been concentrating your efforts in musicals as the romantic female lead (the ingénue), and you find yourself auditioning as a college student trying to manipulate her mom into buying a new computer at a commercial audition, it's quite possible you may feel a bit like a fish out of water. You may even walk away from an audition thinking you weren't at all correct for the role or that you did poorly, when in fact you were simply taken out of your comfort zone as the ingénue. And that can be an odd and uncomfortable experience.

Building your comfort zone as a talent is an ongoing process. We're challenged on this point continually throughout our careers, so be careful not to confuse this experience with what you would and wouldn't be correct for professionally. It's not likely every medium will be immediately intuitive. Better than 90 percent of what we do deals with training and experience.

You'll learn more about who you are and what you bring to the table by exposing yourself to as much work as you possibly can in the field you are attempting to expand into.

## Dualities and Contradictions

It's no secret this industry is riddled with contradictions. And not all performance situations will feel all that natural and comfortable; especially as our role in the production equation continues to require greater technical demands from us.

This is also true when it comes to the direction we are given, of which precious little is typically imparted. For instance:

> Warm authority
> Bigger, more natural
> Faster, more relaxed
> Sensitive indifference

Life is full of dualities and this industry is a lot like life. And life is full of contradictions and complexities. Thus, the adage "the devil's in the details."

The greatest characters you'll play will be a bundle of contradictions. Forrest Gump was wise in many ways, yet he was…Forrest Gump. The name alone has become a euphemism for stupid blunders.

Butch Cassidy and the Sundance Kid and Thelma and Louise were criminals and yet, simultaneously, heroes.

For instance, as voice-over we're often told at auditions they are looking for a "non-announce announce." Sounds confusing at first blush, but honestly, no one wants you to *sound like an announcer*, even though you are assuming the role of the announcer. They want you to sound real, as if every word on the page is what you actually think and you are simply thinking out loud. In other words, they want you to be yourself! (What else is new?)

What adds to the confusion surrounding being yourself is the fact that we are sometimes expected to play the antithesis of who we really are. In other words, we are asked to play against type. Hmm. Do I sound like I'm talking out of both sides of my mouth? I very well may be.

Dualities make up a great deal of the direction we are given, the roles we portray and it even plays into who we are and how we read as individual talent, too.

Julia Roberts established herself as a vulnerable girl-next-door type, she was always (somehow) the "victorious against great odds" ingénue (*Mystic Pizza*, *Steel Magnolias*, *Pretty Woman*). She scored an Oscar with *Erin Brockovich* when she took that ingénue and added to it (by playing against type, mind you) the strong, potty-mouth, provocatively dressed single mom. Talk about dualities and complexities.

## Playing Against Type

Barry Williams, the actor who played Greg Brady on the now infamous 1970's TV show *The Brady Bunch*, once spoke on a talk show about how each role on the show was based on the kid who played it—with *one* exception. Apparently, according to Williams, Susan Olsen, who played the youngest Brady, Cindy, was a devious little imp on the order of a bad seed, yet she played against type as the sweet, innocent girl we all came to know and (gulp) love.

If this is true, then Susan Olsen, even as a small fry, was playing the antithesis of who she really was. Yet even as a kid, she played the role flawlessly.

One of classic Hollywood's most well-known talents, Edward G. Robinson (or Eddie, as he was called by his friends) was actually one of the sweetest, kindest fellows you'd ever want to meet and work with—the polar opposite of his *Little Caesar* tough guy, gangster image that made him famous.

James Cagney, on the other hand, was a true-to-form tough guy and wouldn't hesitate to stick a grapefruit in your face for looking at him sideways. As legend has it, Cagney was known for actually being that hard-edged sort that wouldn't take the slightest flack from anybody. Even in his last role in *Ragtime*, Cagney played the crooked public official—the man was always either the cop or the killer, even to the bitter end. He either played into his type or directly away from it. Regardless, he was someone you'd prefer to have on your side.

Not long ago, Cary Grant was named the number one movie star of all time, and it made me think: Was he playing against type, or was he true to his public persona?

## The Ultimate Movie Star

Actually, Cary Grant didn't become the ultimate, sophisticated hero until he had first played *himself* to a great degree. The sophisticated romantic lead was practically the antithesis of who he was initially: one Archibald Leach of Bristol, England. In fact, when an interviewer once stated, "Everybody would like to be Cary Grant." Grant replied, "So would I."

However, the role that made him a star was a role that played very close to what he knew, up close and personal: a cockney con man in *Sylvia Sydney* opposite Katharine Hepburn. He was the love interest, naturally. But more than that, he was something of a mysterious man of the world who was playful and, true to form, a performer in a traveling vaudeville show. This was just what Archie Leach himself had done as a youth when he left home at 14 to join a troupe of knockabout comedians known as the Penders.

After that role in *Sylvia Sydney*, Grant played opposite Katharine Hepburn again in *Holiday*, where he played even closer to who he really was: a lowbrow amongst the upper crust. Ultimately, as the story went, he was far too good for them, rather than the other way around. This role depicted him as a fellow who, when he found himself in an uncomfortable situation, would make himself at ease by entertaining himself and others with the same sort of acrobatic tumbles and comedic fumbles that he had performed in hundreds of performances with the Penders boys. This made him endearing to us as an audience and made him seem comfortable no matter where he was in the world—something of a wish fulfillment for any die-hard fan.

Grant and Hepburn repeated this winning formula in Howard Hawks' *Bringing Up Baby*. It was a magical combination and one they both knew quite well. You could say, to the benefit of generations of audiences, the pair were growing up together on film.

Ironically enough, the next role of major import in which Grant played opposite Hepburn was in *The Philadelphia Story*, which gave him a higher social status. At the opening action of the film the two had *grown up together* and they were now formerly husband and wife due to his debauchery and drinking. This time Grant's background was elevated to match Hepburn's, as she had been raised in upper-class New England society in real life.

So, you could say Katharine Hepburn played what she knew to begin with as well. After all, *The Philadelphia Story* was even written for her.

Hepburn was a tomboy—just as she had played in *Sylvia Sydney*, a girl dressed as a boy. She was the perfect contemporary Viola from *Twelfth Night* come to life. She was one of the first female public figures to wear pants. Her mother had been a well-known feminist, views she personally shared and touted. It was more than scripted monologue that surfaced in *Adam's Rib* with her other well-known partner both on- and off-screen, Spencer Tracy.

In summary, scanning the early careers of these two beloved actors we take away a body of work that defined these two iconic Hollywood personas. Again, *dualities* play into all of this. It's who you are and *this* will play into how you'll most likely be cast.

## The Ultimate Working Actor

If Cary Grant is forever the ultimate movie star, then the title for ultimate working actor has to go to Mr. Charles Lane.

Who is Charles Lane, you very well may ask? It's more likely you'd know his face (*and demeanor*) than his name. Charles Lane was—and *is* the consummate character actor. You always knew what you were going to get. This is what made him valuable and could easily be attributed to why he worked as long and as much as he did.

**CHARLES LANE**

His type has afforded him decades upon decades of work. In fact, if he weren't such a defined type, it's not likely we'd recognize him or what he brought to every production he graced. He found his niche and it's worked for him for more than 100 years, as he lived to be 102.

Born in 1905, this centurion has managed to appear in nearly 100 television appearances and *more than 250 movies*, not the least of which was *It's a Wonderful Life* in which his character stated, "It's no skin off my nose, but someday, Mr. Potter, this bright, young man is going to be asking George Bailey for a job!"

## The Great Fear of Being "Typecast"

There's a prevalent fear among actors of becoming pigeonholed: confined to playing the same sort of character or genre until they're identified only as Sam Spade from *The Maltese Falcon*, Fonzie from *Happy Days*, or Edward from *Twilight*.

Well, *that* would be a very good problem to have, to be honest. I realize this is a rather novel viewpoint, but I encourage you to focus on defining your true type first and then branch out from there.

Think it through for a moment. Once you're established as a good solid *type*, you can later stretch beyond those parameters to create *anything* you wanted from there. Play *against* type, if you will.

Of course, you may later expect the same successful response you received when you first "hit." But you won't make your mark without first establishing yourself with who and what you are clearly seen as first and foremost.

There are numerous talent who have made a dramatic leap from one public identity to another: Hilary Swank, Jodie Foster, Clint Eastwood, Brad Pitt, Tom Hanks, and Halle Berry, just to name a few. But they all did this only *after* they established themselves in this industry as very specific types.

Tom Hanks was someone both men and women could love! He was easily one of the very first character leads, but more a comedic-romantic lead. Examples: *Bachelor Party, Big, Volunteers, Splash*, and even *Bosom Buddies*.

Brad Pitt was a handsome wild card. He might be dangerous. This guy was never your average romantic lead, but that's what he was up for. He's either played the sexy predator or is after the predator, even as a young guy. He could be considered the romantic rogue. Examples: *Another World* (daytime drama), *Dallas* (nighttime drama), *Thelma & Louise, A River Runs Through It*, and *Se7en*.

Clint Eastwood started out the tough, long-weathered, "real" guy who just happened to be a cowboy. Come to think of it he still is. The tough, long-weathered, "real" guy who just happens to be a... (you can fill in the blank).

Jodie Foster always appeared wise beyond her years; smart, but vulnerable. Examples: *Freaky Friday, Bugsy Malone, Taxi Driver* and even her signature, *Silence of the Lambs*.

Hilary Swank plays the dedicated, physically agile, yet personally vulnerable types—her roles break from traditional female stereotypes. Examples: *Buffy the Vampire Slayer* (the film), *The Next Karate Kid, Boys Don't Cry, Million Dollar Baby, Amelia*. Okay, maybe she hasn't deviated from her initial type after all. But it's certainly worked to her advantage.

So maybe this pigeonhole business isn't such a bad thing after all. Maybe in many cases it helps define us. Halle Berry went from playing a cracked-out, jittery junkie in Spike Lee's *Jungle Fever* to *BAPS* to *This is Dorothy Dandridge* to her Oscar-winning role in *Monster's Ball*. And, she managed to keep her Revlon gig rolling through half of it.

In the end, all these examples tell us quite a bit:

- Play what you know first, then branch out from there once you're established. It's not only okay to be yourself, it's your strong suit—like Cagney.

- Use skills you've cultivated in other areas, like Grant used his comedy, tumbling, and acrobatics, crafts he honed as a teenager.

- You have a type sewn into your face whether you personify that type in real life or not—like Hepburn as an aristocrat, or Robinson as a gangster, or Cagney as the ultimate authority, or Grant as the romantic leading man.

- You can also play against type and find your niche, like Robinson.

- Lastly, versatility has as much to do with mastering a variety of media as it does performance styles. And you don't have to be everything but do need to know what you do best.

Concentrate on *who you are, first and foremost*. This tends to be the antithesis of conventional training, but you are far more likely to be cast for being *yourself*. That can be the hardest thing to play, especially when there's no effort in your performance.

Frankly, no one is interested in seeing you work at a character. After all, if you're *everything*… <u>nothing</u> comes to mind.

When it comes to voice-over, you can break down types basically into three (very broad) categories:

**The Unusual Voice**. This is a voice that is unequaled and difficult to compare. This one may not be correct for everything but, with a generous serving of *tenacity*, it can and will catch on. (Examples: Wallace Shawn, Rosie Perez, Jennifer Tilly, Peter Lorre.)

**The Personality-Driven Voice**. This is a voice that simply has a good, natural tone, because this person sounds like himself. He sounds knowledgeable and comfortable in his skin. What sets this voice apart from the rest is the willingness to convey a point of view (POV), naturally. There may even be a dialect, slight impediment, or affect on this voice. None of that matters provided the talent is committed to the POV, and the delivery sounds like the text is what he actually thinks, what he has experienced personally. (Well-known examples include: Owen Wilson, Holly Hunter, Peter Coyote, Tommy Lee Jones, Wilford Brimley, and Martin Sheen.)

**The Salt and Pepper Voice**, as I call it. This is a voice that's correct for so many things, so many national campaigns, it can be used effectively in nearly everything. (Examples: Two steadfast, rank-and-file talent come to mind: Debbie Kellogg and Pete Stacker; both well-established, hardworking voice talent from Chicago. These folks so effectively provide the "mental wallpaper" required on so many projects they are scarcely acknowledged, but if you stopped and thought about it—you'd think: "That voice sounds familiar.")

## Know Thyself

Best advice: You shouldn't worry so much about whether you're going to become pigeonholed. Instead, concern yourself with the fact that you may be too vague conveying who you are during your next audition and those auditioning you can't quite get a handle on your point of view. Concentrate on mastering what you do best and make yourself available to whoever might have a use for it so you can ultimately do whatever it is you intend to do. Thus is the way of the artist.

The moral to the story: *Do what you know*. Master that. See where that leads you.

Most folks consider themselves reasonably self-aware. That said *most folks* think they are good drivers and that they have a wonderful sense of humor. Of course, insurance rates and YouTube would prove *most folks* wrong.

While you may have glimpses of blinding clarity into who you really are and how you are perceived, there's a pretty good chance most of the time you're too busy getting on with living your life to stop and lock this one down without a fair amount of experience under your belt. There's something to be said for the benefit of distance.

Sometimes it's best to surrender to not knowing—it's often only then you discover what it is you need to know.

## An Exercise in *Defining Your Type*

If you honestly don't have any idea of how you are perceived in the industry or where to focus your efforts, then we have some work to do.

Ask yourself: Which well-known actors are you compared with most often (in life and in the industry)? Why? What qualities do you share? Describe these actors in terms of type. What is it about you that's different? Give yourself four or five descriptive qualities that define the known talent you're most similar to and four or five that set you apart.

Just keep it simple.

In acting, like life, you sometimes feel like you have it all figured out, and then, in the very next moment, you suddenly find you're reinventing the wheel all over again. So, understand this is and it will continue to be an ongoing process.

The industry requires a great variety of types, it always has—regardless of all the cookie-cutter fem-bots and boys in Hollywood. Being yourself as an individual has more merit and ease than anything else.

Today we have more than *two thousand cable stations* that come standard with basic cable. That translates into a great deal of television, film, promo, narration, animation, and commercial work at the end of the day.

# Chapter 7: Advancing Technology

"All art relies on technology—whether it be a proscenium arch or
what have you. We are constantly bumping up against it, evolving
technology in a way to convey our art. [Ultimately, technology]
changes the way we
work in that art form."
—George Lucas


Change is inevitable.

How well we adapt determines how well we survive. HG Wells
said it best, "Adapt or perish."

Artists in particular have *always* had to adapt to continue to
communicate and to remain employed in their field.

Michelangelo took the Sistine Chapel gig even though he was
primarily a sculptor. He adapted to paint as a medium over his
preference to sculpture, not to mention the rather awkward format
(the chapel ceiling) and the rather monumental subject (both
Heaven and Earth) all to great effect. You could say the job raised
his game a bit. So maybe there's something to be said for
diversifying into other media beyond those with which you're most
familiar.

Those who are slow to adapt to the advancing technology our
industry requires from us will quickly find much of their business
evaporate into thin air. You could have the greatest skills and most
remarkable potential, but it will die with you if it's not available and

forwarded in the formats currently being used by the very industry professionals from whom you intend to secure work.

So, whether you happen to be a technophobe or technophile, here are a handful of things you need to know to keep in step with our industry in order to make yourself available to the work and to comply with the demands of this very progressive, aggressive entertainment business. These are technically the most common advances in use at this writing, but keep in mind, in a few short months, years, and decades even these will become obsolete. Nevertheless, adapting to the most current advances will certainly effect how well you communicate with those most likely to hire you. Passing off these responsibilities to someone else may ultimately result in the complete and utter *extinction* of your personae on the casting radar because you'll be at the mercy of others to communicate for you. And that could easily lead to the evaporation of your career. So pay attention. You'll likely find advancing technology actually makes things easier for you, not the other way around.

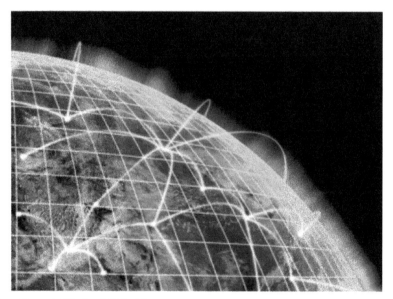

## The Great Digital Divide

If you were born *prior* to 1975, chances are computers elude you to some extent, unless you've worked in a field where technology plays a dominant role. Unless you've made a concerted effort to expose yourself to the current technological advances, it's likely you may have fallen behind on what you need to know to advance your career as a talent.

It wasn't that long ago that MP3s became a standard production element or the Internet became a common utility. When they did, it left scores of very skillful talent out in the cold. Suffice it to say, the industry hasn't been the same since. Prior to that, embracing technology was never really required of talent. Your agent would call your "service" and you'd show up the next day at the studio and that'd be the extent of it.

The upside of this former audition process was it afforded talent face time with casting directors, and fewer talent were called in to audition for each project. However, times change. While technology today may offer far more talent the opportunity to audition for the same project, the benefit is there's at least 10 times more work to audition for than in years past.

And, as always, you'll only manage to survive to the extent you're willing to learn how to make yourself known and available to the work. Whether your work relies on if you can be reached, via text, voice mail, and e-mail. You can make yourself known, via your Web site, online casting services, Facebook, LinkedIn, and electronic submissions. We now have commonplace advances designed to make your life easier. And they will... if you embrace them.

Exhale. You may find you enjoy this. Enter: *The Jetsons*.

## Recent Turn of Events

Once upon a time, voice talent traipsed all over town for auditions all day long and on a daily basis. The upside of this audition process was that talent could actually meet and greet the people who were casting for voice-over; ask them questions; get the real story directly from the horse's mouth. This is now a rarity by today's standards, unless you're in New York where 25-35% of the time talent might audition in front of casting directors for commercial voice over jobs.

Additionally, the talent agents could spend more time serving the producers' needs, negotiating contracts, scheduling talent for auditions or bookings, and personally getting to know YOU—their talent pool, rather than playing casting director (without the benefit of being paid to do so).

The downside of this former auditioning process was far less job opportunities. There's been a *1200 percent* increase in the amount of voice-over work in the past six years alone. That's more than a boom—that's a flat out, off the charts unprecedented expansion. Question is: how do you access this work?

It only stands to reason the role of the talent agent has irrevocably expanded and altered in recent years as well. Today's voice-over market dictates talent agents become amateur recording engineers and expert casting directors whether these are their skills or not—and this in addition to their already weighty workload of understanding the producer's budget demands and the true value of the job in talent terms. Talent agents responsibilities more than doubled, yet their pay remains a mere 10 percent of whatever the talent makes, and 20% if the agent is strictly representing nonunion. (Honestly, who'd want this job?! No wonder there is only a precious few considered extremely valuable.)

This dramatic shift went pretty much unnoticed by the average talent, as many up and coming producers demanded more and more from these dedicated souls. In the meantime, scores of remarkable talent resisted adapting to a few simple digital advancements needed to accommodate their agents and the producers that hoped to cast them. Ultimately, these talent found themselves scratching their heads wondering where all their work had gone.

Well, it had gone digital. More specifically, it could be found on the Internet by way of *Voicebank.net* to anyone who cared to look. Any talent agency that neglected to subscribe to Voicebank found themselves left out of the most lucrative and important auditions.

The fact is there's never been so many projects requiring voice overs as there are today: Cable has expanded to more than 2,000 stations with most basic subscriptions, Netflix and Hulu+ offer online viewing options complete with commercials and tutorials—all requiring unique attention performance-wise and all paying a determined value that varies widely from project to project and producer to producer. These employment opportunities were completely unprecedented a few short years ago simply because access to the basic technology is now available over the Internet or on your mobile device.

For a few bucks a month added to your cable bill, a DVR (digital video recorder) offers you the ability to record literally months of programming, making accessibility to current broadcast Pop Culture and the commercials that play during these programs an unlimited resource for research and study. Driven by consumer demand this massive mutation of media continues to spillover to smart phones and tablets, and provides new sources of revenue for every experience level of talent who are at once preparing and offering themselves further accessibility to work in this ever-expanding industry.

As mass media continue to merge, the lines dividing film, cable, network TV, the Internet and New Media blur, therefore determining what a job is worth requires an even more savvy, more experienced and adaptable agent than ever before; someone who understands the needs of the producer and the value of an effective talent.

But like most small-business owners, freelance talent, much like their dedicated talent agents, often find themselves running their small business the same way they did when business was thriving, way back in the day before their type changed, before demand changed in the industry, and prior to all these mad technical advancements, which can keep a valuable freelance talent's career from moving forward. Inadvertently overlooking what's required of you as a talent in order to even get called in for an audition without honest inspection of your immediate and long-term goals can waste a great deal of time and money, and cause a great deal of unnecessary frustration.

## Your Small Business

Seems *all* small-business owners, regardless of their field, harbor a deep desire to get their business to run on automatic. It's understandable—they've worked hard, and now they'd prefer simply to set it and forget it. But frankly, if we've learned anything in recent years, nothing works left to its own devices.

Considering this is your business _you_ have to run it if you expect to get anywhere and every avenue that offers you a greater opportunity to promote yourself and secure work is an advantage to you. Most successful, seasoned business owners will tell you that it generally takes three to five years to establish any small business. Marketing alone requires no less than eight repeated impressions before the recipient is likely to remember you or act on your promotion.

What does this tell us? Tenacity and consistent promotion is vitally necessary if you expect to expand any business, but especially in the entertainment field. And everything in this world is either expanding or contracting. It's either improving, albeit slightly and steadily, or it's _not_.

Voice-over is no different. This is a remarkably dynamic industry, which is vitally dependent on multiple media, promotions, communications, and the technologies that drive them.

That's never going to change. That much you can always count on.

## The Technical Tools _Every_ Talent Must Have

In order for art to meet commerce, employing a few technical tools is necessary if you intend to establish and further your career as a professional talent. Mastering these tools is essential as they offer opportunities to communicate professionally with the most current elements utilized in the industry today.

In most cases, these items will audition for you when you cannot be physically present. They will define you as a professional to agents, producers and casting professionals. If done properly, they will offer continued access to the work and will make the very best impression to those most likely to hire you. In most cases, the following items will define you as a professional, which is the whole idea.

## Voice-over Demos and Web Pages

Today, the primary format for your demos is MP3, rather than compact disc (CD), and if you're not online—you simply don't exist. MP3 files of your demos should be available on your *single-page* Web site, a site devoted strictly to voice-over.

Of course, you may feel it necessary to establish an on-camera site as well if you're pursuing on-camera work. The truth is an *on-camera site* is optional. At SOUND ADVICE, we feel it's more important and money better spent to include your headshots, demos, resume and on-camera reel (if you have one) on ActorsAccess.com, CastingNetworks.com, for instances, to be considered for various on-camera jobs.

Your voice over only Web site should display your name as a branded logo, your demos in MP3 format, and your contact information. That's it.

(See Chapter 16 Websites for more details on what you should and shouldn't include on your web site to create the best effect.)

MP3s have all but replaced having a CD of your voice-over demos, except to promote your self to a small handful of talent agents, considering fewer and fewer talent agents require a disc.

(Also, see Chapter 14 Producing Your Demos & Various Promo to determine the details necessary to effectively promote yourself.)

## The Standard Audio File Format: MP3

The MP3 file is the standard file format used to distribute audio on the Internet and used by voice talent to e-mail auditions to their agents. While MP3 is not the latest and greatest compressed audio format, it *is* the tried-and-true *standard* for compressed audio files. MP3 is nonproprietary and will play on a variety of players on *any* computer. It is a *compressed* audio file format, popular because it retains most of the quality of a CD at about a tenth of the file size.

*Uncompressed* formats, like AIFF and WAV files, are the same quality as a professionally reproduced CD or even better. (Remember CDs?) However, they are also big honking files that weigh down busy e-mail in-boxes, if they even show up in an e-mail at all. These are a big fat no-no and should be avoided. As for RealAudio, Windows Media, and other brand-name formats, a listener would have to download and install a proprietary player to hear your material, and the audio quality is inconsistent. This is why MP3 remains the standard.

All of the auditions you record at home and e-mail in to your agent will be in MP3 form, as opposed to AIFF or WAV files.

With MP3s, the higher the bit rate, the higher quality the MP3 and the larger the file size.

Bit rate could be considered the sound equivalent to depth of field in a photo, or focus for clarity.  Since the lowest bit rate would sound awful, and the highest bit rate would defeat the purpose of using a compressed format at all, it's best to use a bit rate between 128 kbps and 192 kbps, as these are generally considered the accepted standards.

Sending an MP3 of your demos is perfectly acceptable today. E-mailing a direct link to your Web site where your demos can be easily accessed is also an effective way to promote yourself to a talent agent or a potential employer, just not the ONLY way to promote yourself.

## QR CODES

QR Code stands for Quick Response Code. These are typically black and white, square two-dimensional, matrix bar codes used as mobile tagging devices.  They can be scanned with a simple app from any smartphone or iPad tablet.

QR Codes can (and should) be designed to lead directly to your Web site, for more effective interactive marketing and promotion.  These links to your site are then "bookmarked" on the mobile device of the individual who scanned your QR Code from your promotional postcard or résumé.

The idea is to drive substantially more traffic to your voice-over Web site, where your demos can be heard, from your targeted audience (producers) on the very thing they rely on most: their mobile devices (iPhones, Blackberries, and iPads).

The fact is producers count on their mobile devices more than standard laptops.

QR Codes cost nothing to create (provided you know what you're doing), and the app to scan QR Codes is free as well.

Provided your Web site wasn't designed primarily in Flash, and can easily be seen on mobile devices, utilizing QR Codes on your promo converts a simple postcard into an interactive device.

Considering e-mailing a direct link to your Web site is typically met with a big, fat DELETE, and we've seen better than an 80 percent increase in traffic to sites utilizing QR Codes on their promotions and a 10 times return rate within the first month of scanning the QR Code in the first month. This could be the greatest advance in promo since the invention of the postcard!

(Details about promotional logos and graphics can be found in Chapter 15 Graphics.)

## Headshots

Headshots are needed primarily in **JPEG files** (no more and no less than 72 dpi) to post to online casting sites, on your own on-camera Web page, and to your agents' Web sites (if they have them), for electronic submissions (e-mails) and, on occasion, as a standard color print (hard copy) headshot.

A headshot in a JPEG file at 72 dpi (or dots per inch) means this digital file is small enough to send in an e-mail and can be seen on just about any computer screen with the least amount of effort. A casting director or producer is likely to have quite a few thumbnail headshots in JPEG files on her desktop to consider for the roles she may be casting. She'll click on one and it will blow up to full size. It MUST have your name on the JPEG file itself, so everyone knows who you are.

You can obtain a JPEG of your headshot, even if yours were shot on film, by scanning your clean master shot (from the photographer).

## Résumés

If you are e-mailing your résumé to an agent or casting director, or posting it to a Web site, it should be a PDF (Portable Document Format) file. PDF files are like a picture of a printed page meant to be e-mailed, and posted on the Web, and consistently viewable on any computer.

The Mac OS allows you to create a PDF directly from your document via the print window; unfortunately, Windows (PC) does not, so you will need to buy Adobe Acrobat. Cute PDF is another option.

It's easy enough to do online, if you do a quick search.

## Google Voice (Optional)

Agents and potential clients need to reach you—and fast! However, you may have some hesitation as to whether to put your own cell number out there for the wide world to see and use on your Web site. Or maybe you have a job that would make it difficult or awkward to include your most accessible cell phone number and you'd prefer to keep your immediate business separate from your budding acting business. Fear not, there's an easy answer!

Google has come up with a great solution! They give you a *free* phone number that can be forwarded to any of your existing phones.

For example: a potential professional contact would call your Google Voice number, and you can set it to ring on as many different phone numbers as you like. Offering you access to the call while keeping your existing phone numbers discreet. When the call goes to your voice mail it will go to your Google Voice mailbox, which will have your own specific greeting designed just for those professional calls.

Voice mails will automatically be transcribed into text and sent as an e-mail or a text message to you! So, it's great for getting calls regarding auditions and bookings.

## Mac vs. PC

For many years, there has been a legendary derision between these two platforms, but with advances in technology, the gap between Windows-based PCs and Apple computers has narrowed considerably.

Yet, Mac remains the dominant platform for creative endeavors and can be considered the industry standard for numerous reasons. Certainly Mac OS X is the preferred platform of advertising creatives, in part because some of the programs used to edit and mix commercials, television, and film all run primarily on Mac, or at least run more consistently and effectively on a Mac.

Additionally, for a home recording setup either one will do, provided you know how to use it.

## Hi-Def (HD), the RED, and 3-D

In the past few years, television and film have merged to a great extent and have changed the standard format from video to high definition, Hi-Def, or simply HD. All content produced for broadcast is now consistently HD.

HD is as light and easy to shoot as video. It takes a much smaller crew (by about one-third) than traditional film and can record for up to an hour on a single magazine—whereas a standard 1,000-foot film reel allowed only 10 minutes of shooting. HD offers the average filmmaker versatility and affordability that film never did.

The RED camera was introduced a few years back, which records all footage directly to flash or hard disk storage (the camera's internal hard drive). This camera has essentially reinvented cinematography and shooting film and TV. More and more feature films and TV series are being shot on a RED, but not exclusively.

Shooting in 3-D has increased dramatically in recent years, and not solely for film or games, but for TV as well.

So what does all this mean to an actor? In many cases, directors will let the scene continue when shooting on a RED or in basic HD, so you might need to keep the action going where in the past, on film, you would have been asked to act in shorter increments. Many Hollywood managers often tell their young stars, "Go do an Indie film this summer. It'll keep
up your street cred." In addition to that, Indies allow these talent to become familiar with acting in this medium and performing and often improvising for the camera during longer intervals.

As these new digital mediums evolve, so will the demands and requirements of what is needed from you as a talent adapt and change.

## Home Voice Over Recording 101

The most common question we hear with regard to home studio setup, regardless of the experience level, is: "What mic should I use?" No short answer because just as your voice is unique, so is the mic that you choose to record it with.

And yet every recording engineer (or salesman at Guitar Center or Sam Ash) you run into will happily offer up what his favorite go-to mic is and why everyone should get it. Frankly, this is a rather dangerous proposition because if you run out and purchase that mic it's very likely it will run you about $850 or more.

Well, you can't blame the guy. You asked, "What sort of mic would you get if you were recording at home?" And he told you. (Simple enough question, or so you'd think.) And you might bring it home, all proud at first, and then suddenly you realize, "How do I plug this thing in?" So, you head back to the engineer and he looks up at you from his console, bleary-eyed, "Oh, uh... Do you have Pro Tools?"

Okay, it's official. You just dove in *way* over your head and you're sinking to the bottom of the lake. So, you scramble back to Guitar Center or Sam Ash or some such to return the mic. Only they won't take the mic back, because, by law they can't. It's a hygienic thing. Mics are the single piece of gear that cannot be returned.

Here's the thing: You missed a few steps. (Sorry 'bout that. Leave it to me to point that out to you at this stage. I realize I'm stating the obvious, but bear with me.)

The truth be told, the most important thing you need to be—is THE VOICE TALENT, especially if you're not technically minded to begin with. Don't try to be a professional recording engineer. You'll eventually need a good basic understanding of how to create an audition from home, but only so you can establish yourself as a professional voice-over *first and foremost*. But, baby steps, please. If confronting recording an audition from home is too much for you when just starting out, you'll want to utilize every professional option you have within reach. There are always far more than you might ever suspect and you're gonna need to put them to good use in the beginning. There's a learning curve to all of these elements.

If, on the other hand, you <u>are</u> rather technically minded and you want to create a home-recording setup for yourself, we still advise you to *keep it simple*. Otherwise you'll end up a professional recording engineer more than a professional voice-over. It's important to mention because far too many people geek out completely on purchasing more gear than they'll ever need, especially when your primary goal here is to be a voice-over.

## Choosing Where to Record at Home

For home recording regardless of your skill level (yes, even you meek, worrywarts who can't tell your on-button from your delete key) we *strongly* recommend you first consider WHERE you intend to record. The objective of having the ability to record from home is to record the best possible auditions and the occasional corporate narrative. In this way it will allow you to be the most-accessible, effective voice talent possible. Your home recording set up must be custom-tailored to your specific technical skill level—just like our training at **Sound Advice** for performance and promotion.

## Auditioning from your iPad or iPhone

Probably the easiest, most-workable home recording and editing option EVER can be done using an iPad or iPhone thanks to the TWISTED WAVE APP available (for $9.99) on iTunes. Considering scores of people have either an iPhone or an iPad (the fastest selling device ever sold) missing any audition ever again is practically inexcusable.

There are two versions of this application: one for the iPad or iPhone, the other for use on lap or desktop Mac computer. The lap/desktop version is available from their website for $79.99.

The simplicity and quality of your recording, and editing your remote auditions with TWISTED WAVE is so extraordinary you might just get carried away! It's a lot of fun!

Twisted Wave is the recording software we recommend most if you have a Mac because it is so easy to use and it's the least expensive editing option available. We want to be a voice talent—NOT a professional recording engineer.

And to make the process even easier we recommend the digital book **iVoiceover. Super. Simple. Recording.** ($6.99) by **Erik Martin** of **Sound Answer** available on iTunes for the best insights into using Twisted Wave for voice-over. His book takes you step by step through recording (tracking) and editing your auditions. There's still a learning curve, but Erik's book will help a great deal and for a nominal charge.

## Professional Assistance

Every one needs help in sorting out their home audio set up from time to time, or technical assistance to insure the quality of their recordings meet industry standards. This is where our head of production, producer **Jeff Finney**, lends his expertise. For the equivalent of our hourly coaching, we also offer technical guidance over Skype. This way we can see, as well as hear, the challenges you may be facing to offer the best, most frugal solutions possible. (See our Services on www.voiceoverinfo.com for more details.)

## Tools & Online Casting Options

There are numerous online casting options these days, the most important of these are: **Voicebank.net**, for voice-over auditions of every type; **CastingNetworks.com**, primarily, but not exclusively, for commercial on-camera auditions; **ActorsAccess.com**, primarily for theatrical (film and television) and commercial auditions, and **CastingFrontier.com**, mostly for commercial work and **NowCasting.com**.

Until you are included on these sites, you honestly don't exist to just about anyone worth while casting talent throughout North America and much of the U.K., whether that work is union or not.

Managing your own postings on these sites offers you far more control over your destiny than you ever had in the history of the entertainment industry. We suggest you post at least 4 different "looks", your commercial voice-over demo and an on-camera reel, provided they are all done professionally and they represent you well.

## Pay-to-Play Web Sites

The downside is many small market clients who utilize these Pay-to-Play sites (often for the first time production) will ask whether you are a studio and able to record, *edit and mix* the voice tracks you are being hired for as a voice-over. If you aren't—just say so. There's such a thing as over-promising what you honestly can (and should) deliver for the price. These sites offer *voice-over projects*. If they honestly require full production, refer them to us, or a reliable, local studio you've worked with in the past. Otherwise, you are offering services that may far exceed what you're hired to deliver: voice-over.

With the introduction of various Pay-to-Play (P2P) sites, such as **voicehunter.com**, **voices.com** and **voice123.com**, nonunion talent now have greater opportunities than ever before from these casting sites devoted to posting voice-over auditions from across the country and around the world for a broad range of productions. These sites often offer free introductory opportunities, but are most effective when you register for a yearly subscription (usually for about $395).

While there are various Pros and Cons to utilizing these sites, we do suggest, once you have your voice-over demos, you register with one or more of these sites and complete the profile describing your greatest assets and abilities to increase your rate of return on your demos and auditions.

PROS:
- These sites offer an average of 10 to 20 auditions a week, varying in value between $75 to $2500 per job if booked

- The average booking ratio from auditions is 1 out of 100 from these sites, which is substantially greater than the standard 1 in 200 or more auditions you can expect under any other circumstances

- The likelihood of booking jobs directly off your demo is better than 50% of the time from these sites (provided your demo is professionally produced)

- These sites offer you opportunities from across the country and around the world you normally would not have access to

- Landing even a few low-paying projects, when you're first starting out, helps instill confidence to continue in this field while offering you the opportunity to see a return on your initial investment sooner rather than later

- Allows you the opportunity to build repeat business with various clients as you become their vocal brand

CONS:
- These sites force talent, who typically aren't accustom to determining the value of their performance or the media it may be reused in, to come up with a rate. Talent agents, producers, and casting directors typically determine (and legitimize) what talent are paid

- These sites often offer sub-basement level rates on projects that would pay far more and ultimately degrade the actual value of the work by setting a poor precedence with production clients who could (and should) pay up to 20 times more for the talent

- The occasional unscrupulous payment practices (i.e. not getting paid) which the site cannot (and will not) be held responsible for

- These sites offer rate sheets to "assist talent in determining their rate" with options that often don't apply to voice-over, don't correctly apply to the project or job posed, or are below standard rates you would typically earn had you gone through a reputable nonunion talent agent

- Pay-to-Play sites are basically eHarmony/Match.com-style sites for voice talent, connecting clients with voice talent.

How well you suit a clients needs is dependent on how well you complete the profile that suits the specific logarithm created per each site. Problem is: most talent will complete their initial profile and neglect to update or revisit this key attribute once a month or so. This may effect the talent in a negative manner if it's not properly maintained, considering the P2P site logarithm will continually modify according to industry and Internet trends that may leave your profile in it's dust by doing so

- Talent come to rely solely on these sites rather than using them as a tool to first establish their small business as working voice talent without graduating to union projects or securing effective representation with union-franchised talent                                                                    agents

- Some P2P sites place arbitrary demands and restrictions on talent for "auditioning too much" and randomly rate each talent which implies "servicing" potential talent buyers who use the site for free, while undermining skillful talent who are paying to utilize the benefits of the site

- Some of the information offered from various blogs and promotions on these sites impart inaccurate or outdated industry information

- Talent tend to promise more than they are able to deliver production-wise with various jobs offered on P2P sites, and get in over their heads by ultimately over-promising and under-delivering; in most cases talent are simply required to record and upload the raw recorded files to the client's designated site rather than supply a finished production

- Talent rarely have the experience or expertise to determine appropriate practices and agreements talent agents understand and offer. P2P sites often post projects that ask for more than the talent can honestly deliver. Eager to please and land work, talent often find themselves out of their depth agreement-wise. They end up agreeing to rates that are well below budget-basement for the voice talent's skills, let alone agreeing to all the "extras" many small budgets might require. (These are a few of the chief reasons you WANT a talent agent.)

After all that food for thought, it's important to point out we *do* encourage talent to pursue voice-over projects by making P2P sites part of establishing yourself in this field. They are a fact of life if you intend to work in this field.

Besides, it's imperative your demo is included on as many sites as possible where numerous voice talent are cast, not simply through your talent agent on their sites or through voicebank.net. Knowing some of the various demands and obstacles in advance should only make your ability to manage your own voice-over career far easier.

At **SOUND ADVICE**, we've worked with scores of radio talent in overcoming the various obstacles of transitioning from relying solely on radio to becoming a full-time, professional voice talent.

(See Chapter 4 Radio, Radio for more details and insights.)

## Voicebank.net

The majority of national union (as well as non-union) voice-over auditions are held on **Voicebank** (www.voicebank.net) every day.

Voicebank taps into the national talent pool and invites a good many established talent agencies throughout the U.S., Canada, and the U.K. to more voice-over auditions than any other single source in North America. It is the industry standard, and all nationally recognized ad agencies employ its resources in order to hold auditions and cast voice talent.

Your voice-over agent will post your demos on the agency Voicebank page after agreeing to rep you.

## Social Networking

Promoting your demo Web site at least two to three times a week through your Facebook, LinkedIn pages and over Twitter is an effective way to use social media. Your friends will help promote you, which can only help your overall promotional efforts, provided you make an effort to connect with as many worthwhile sources as you can.

While businesses are required in today's working world to maintain a presence on Facebook (for promotional purposes), LinkedIn is the appropriate social networking site to use to connect with professional contacts and groups as an individual or small-business entity. Twitter offers interested parties links to demos, web pages, your talent agents and the like.

Basic Internet etiquette should ALWAYS be applied in these instances. Remember: When you're online, you're in public! Keep it professional. Keep it clean. Keep it positive and pleasant. You'd be surprised what might come back to haunt you.

### Establishing (and Protecting) Your Professional Reputation Online

It's very likely that anyone considering hiring you—a talent agent, employer, or producer concerned with his own professional image—will very likely to Google you first, prior to working with you, especially for on-camera work. That Facebook page you have for social reasons could very well put the kibosh on future jobs or professional relationships you're attempting to build if mishandled. Your professional reputation could be destroyed in a single Google search unless you keep it professional, use it well, but USE IT.

## Various Sites That Matter

Whether you're at an audition or on a session, it's far better to know what you're talking about than it is to simply guess. Best advice: When in doubt, look it up! If you're not sure about pronunciation or meaning of a certain word, turn to **Merriam-Webster Online** (www.m-w.com) or Dictionary.com. There's a feature that will even allow you to hear a sound bite of how to say the word you're not sure about.

It always helps to know more about the subject if you're doing a narration and have never come across the topic before, so check out **Wikipedia** (en.wikipedia.org). While Wikipedia's information is not infallible—it's written and edited by its own readers—you'll learn enough to sound interested and knowledgeable. And that's precisely the goal.

Next time you're watching TV and you notice an actor that you recognize from *somewhere* but can't seem to place it—or you're wondering where someone on the A-list got her start—that's what **IMDb, the Internet Movie Database** (www.imdb.com) is for. IMDb is a vast repository of information. The site's mission is to catalog every pertinent detail about a movie, from who was in it, to who made it, to trivia about it, to filming locations, and even where you can find reviews and fan sites on the Web. You'll also find information on TV shows and even video games. This can be a wonderful tool for filling in the gaps in your reference base.

**Hulu.com** is a site that offers television programs and scenes of shows, both canceled and current, for free viewing online. This site allows you to study film and TV in detail from the comfort of your computer. (Hulu Plus also offers even more access to programs for small monthly subscription.)

Additionally, it's worthwhile to Google your own name every six to eight months. This way you'll have some idea what a potential talent agent, producer, or client might view about you online. If there is any inaccuracies or inappropriate items you need to address, you can better confront it or correct it rather than be broadsided by it.

## Three Forms of Patch

The beauty of being in voice-over today over any other time in history is the fact that every session is as near as a simple "patch." By that I mean a studio in one region of the country—say Austin, Texas—can easily patch with another studio, say, in Bridgeport, Connecticut. The form of patch generally depends on the budget of the project and the production demands.

There are essentially three forms of patch: phone patch, ISDN, and Source-Connect. (The latter two are both considered digital patch options. Then again, considering phone lines are now digital, you could say they're ALL digital patch options.)

Phone patch is cheap technology that utilizes basic phone lines, and in some instances can be replaced with Skype from many home-recording setups. It's used when the production budgets are extremely tight, usually for recording voice-over for nonunion corporate narration, or on small- and medium-market radio and TV projects. It's cheap because the client doesn't have to patch in from another studio to offer direction. In fact, the client is usually in his corporate office or even driving in his car and he patches in to ensure you (the voice-over) are pronouncing everything correctly.

Phone patch is often used to get approvals at the end of sessions, whether it's a patch session or not. The downside of phone patch is the poor quality offered to the client when listening in. To you, the voice-over, it simply sounds like the client is on the phone. As for the client, a phone patch usually sounds like a phone held up to a phone, which isn't great, but it's better than nothing and serves its purpose on tight-budget sessions.

While ISDN is generally the production industry standard, it's been used consistently in most professional recording studios for more than 18 years. Proof positive why you should never underestimate how slow small business (and most recording studios are small businesses) are to adopt change.

ISDN is extremely expensive to install, maintain, and operate. To add to this, there are probably only two ore three guys left at AT&T in Chicago and maybe four or technicians left in Los Angeles who are equipped to install or even service ISDN because this technology only continues to exist for this very esoteric industry known as *voice-over*. (Okay, radio and video conferencing also utilize ISDN as well, albeit infrequently due to the cost.) The fact is ISDN is an antiquated technology that's expensive and will be phased out entirely before long, especially if the phone company has anything to say about it. It's simply not worth it to them to maintain this service.

ISDN as a digital patch requires both studios (the one the voice-over is recording in and the studio you're patching with in another location) to have two designated digital phone lines. Additionally, where ISDN is concerned, a rather expensive device (known as a codec) is required to send and receive data over these dedicated lines. The data in a voice-over recording session would be each of your recorded takes.

The other form of digital patch, Source-Connect, utilizes broadband Internet and a software codec in place of having the phone company install two very expensive phone lines and codec, yet it offers the same core benefits as ISDN.

Source-Connect works just as well as ISDN, frankly. Sometimes better. And it's certainly improved in recent years. Many of the naysayers likely haven't used it since it first came out, and either they weren't patient enough to stick with it and figure out its finer points, or they simply remained with the devil they knew—ISDN.

Personally, the feature I like best about Source-Connect over ISDN is that a forgetful recording engineer can't leave the ISDN on over a long weekend at the end of a session with Source-Connect and rack up a $7,000 long-distance bill. It's a frightening experience, and I don't know a studio that hasn't had that happen at least once.

Another nice thing about Source-Connect is there's a lowered single-user rate, so it's more affordable than the professional version if the voice-over is a recording engineer and has Pro Tools as well as the chops to navigate the session. But, it should be noted Source-Connect is NOT for the novice techie.

The benefits of digital patch (either ISDN or Source-Connect) are:
> a) You can record, edit, and mix in either the studio

you're tracking in, or the studio you are patching with

b) Allows both the talent (in one studio) and the client (located in an entirely different studio) to conduct the session as if they were in the same studio. It actually sounds as if the client is in the control room while you're in the booth. (Apart from the obligatory two-second digital delay that's apparent between takes when the client is directing you.)

c) You can easily bridge to a studio that has ISDN with Source-Connect as well, so it's not like you can connect only with other studios that have Source-Connect (or vice versa)

ALL forms of patch, as all technology, are subject to the occasional hiccups and issues, especially in the hands of those lacking the true experience and wherewithal to correct or trouble-shoot the problem, therefore we can't recommend enough that you concentrate your efforts on your voice-over skills, first and foremost.

So, as I mentioned earlier—it bears repeating, sometimes it's simply best to *leave it to the professionals*, even if you consider your technical skills to be "above average." Of course, I only mention this because most people consider themselves wonderful drivers and to possess a great sense of humor. Statistics, on the other hand, tell a different story.

At **Sound Advice**, unless you're already a rather seasoned recording engineer, we generally recommend you leave professional recording, mixing, and editing to the professionals. Don't plan on utilizing digital patch sessions from your home recording studio unless your production skills are far and away exceptional, otherwise you will over promise and under deliver, which is never a good idea. And you will undermine the real reason you're even attempting to master all of this—because you're required to be a voice-over first and foremost. If your skills are mainly as a voice-over then concentrate primarily on your performance instead of developing your recording abilities beyond mastering your auditions from home, and refer any bookings you land to a local professional studio that will work with you.

Chances are there are numerous small, professional studio options within just a few miles from where you are right now that will offer you a lowered studio rate should you or your potential production client require you patch with them on a project. In any case, you now have a working knowledge of what is likely to be needed and wanted from you, especially if your would-be client is in another region, which opens up your employment options by a dramatic margin.

## ipDTL

ip stands for Internet Protocol and DTL stands for Down The Line.

This is a very promising Web app created by British-based tech company In:Quality designed to replace the extremely expensive, rather antiquated technology known as ISDN, the industry standard used to connect one studio with another for professional voice sessions and various radio broadcasts.

ipDTL is potentially the simplest, most cost-efficient option to be introduced to date to patch voice talent with producers from nearly anywhere in the world provided both parties have Google Chrome, stable Internet access, and at least one of the two parties has a subscription to ipDTL. At this writing, this App is yet untested, but has the potential to record high quality, possibly "better-than-ISDN" audio, according to their site and various online enthusiasts, using your basic broadband connection.

ipDTL doesn't rely on expensive proprietary hardware and pricey phone lines like ISDN. Yet, like ISDN and SourceConnect (the most popular broadband patching option thus far), ipDTL offers a professional grade option for audio recording, which delivers a similar experience as being in the same studio as the client, even though they may be across the country or half the world away. Like these two previous options, the client sounds as if they are in the Control Room while you are in the booth.

The PROS (seem to be):

a) An inexpensive connection to potential production clients without having to enlist an additional recording studio

b) Simple to install and use for even relatively novice home recording studios

c) Access to clients the world over you may never have had access to with such ease or clarity

d) The ability to edit the session DURING the session, as if you're in the same studio from either side of the recording session

The CONS:

a) Getting tried-and-true ISDN or SourceConnect production clients to bridge with you on ipDTL may prove difficult. (No one likes experimenting with actual gigs. It can cost you more than you initially bargained for.)

b) It's still too early (at this writing) to determine what issues may crop up considering this option is so new. The fact is we have yet to fully assess the overall pros and cons of ipDTL.

Currently this exciting new option could very well allow us, as SOUND ADVICE, to record your demo from your simple home recording set up with minimal added expense, provided your home studio sound quality meets our recording standards, while offering you greater opportunities to patch with potential producers on future bookings.

The key word here is: potential!

For more information, visit:
http://www.youtube.com/watch?v=mH_h-PK5VCs

## Skype

Skype is a wonderful free Internet option you can find easily online to stay connected with friends and family, even if they happen to be in another country, by virtue of video conferencing. It utilizes the Internet and your basic built-in computer video/audio capabilities.

We offer voice-over coaching and consultations at **Sound Advice**, which are simply done using Skype allowing voice talent across the country, as well as the world access to our approach and production.

In fact, Skype is a great, *cost-free*, alternative for the traditional studio phone patch by utilizing the audio-only chat option or the multiple-user option for more than one client to be included on the session. No need to purchase a Skype phone number, just open an account and download the software and you're in business.

We consider the clarity and ease of Skype to be far superior to the standard phone patch option utilized in most professional studios over the last few decades. (You can learn more about this through Erik Martin's HomeRecordingStudioDesign.com.)

Learn more here: http://www.skype.com/en/download-skype/skype-for-computer/

## FTP

FTP is the abbreviation for file transfer protocol. An FTP site is like a virtual filing cabinet, typically part of an existing Web site where files can be stored, but it requires a user name and password to access the stored files. So, if we back into it, FTP simply means "*how to* transfer a file." FTP is faster and more reliable than e-mail for transferring files.

This "virtual filing cabinet" can store scripts (as PDF files, docs, or docx), audio files (such as MP3 or WAVs), fully produced commercials or industrials (in .mov format and several others). It offers access to a server via the Internet where pertinent files can be securely kept. When you have many digital files you need to make available to someone else, such as audio files from a voice-over session, they are most often uploaded (or *posted*) to an FTP site.

In addition to FTP there are file-sharing services that are becoming very popular, like yousendit.com, CyberDuck, DropBox, and various others. They are completely Web based (no additional software needed). They even offer starter plans that are free.

So, at the end of a session, when a producer you just did a voice-over for asks you, "Can I FTP this spot to you?" you will now know what they are referring to and you will reply, "That'd be great!"

Just make sure that producer has your e-mail address so they can send you the FTP site's address, user name, and password. Double check that you have the producer's and the recording engineer's e-mail to remind them to send you the links where you will find the fully produced spots.

## Practice Auditions

There's certainly a learning curve to developing your basic recording and simple editing of your auditions. Therefore, every opportunity that develops your self-directing skills, the better. So, once you have determined WHERE and HOW you will record your voice-over auditions from your mobile device, tablet or home computer, you'll need to develop your editing skills to record and edit your auditions. These skills are NOT immediately intuitive! It takes time and practice to offer an audition you can confidently deliver. You don't want to advertise to talent agents you're available for auditions and then find yourself unprepared. You want you new talent agents to confidently endorse you. THEREFORE… we recommend our exclusive and practical service called **PRACTICE AUDITIONS.**

This is eight full weeks worth of exercises and challenges to help you hone your home-editing skills, while playing with the copy currently used today on many top auditions.

How it works: We randomly e-mail you scripts throughout the week for eight weeks, most with pending deadlines just like you can expect from real auditions. For instance, you might receive two auditions on Monday, nothing on Tuesday, three on Wednesday, one on Thursday and nothing on Friday.

These won't be real auditions for actual jobs, but you should treat them as such. The object is to practice recording, editing, and returning your auditions quickly and well within their deadlines.

Our engineer will let you know whether you are too far off mic or too close, too low or too loud, and whether you sent it in on time. The more you do, the better you get and the sooner you can put your attention back on your performance, where it belongs. They are only meant for you to practice your skills from your home-recording setup. The goal here is to give you the greatest opportunity to deliver your very best—always.

The best way to learn from any and all of this remarkable technology... is to just do it!

## Most Common File Types

| File Type | What is it | Usage |
|---|---|---|
| **Audio Formats** | | |
| .WAV | Full quality, uncompressed audio file | Used on CDs and for broadcast-quality audio, used for commercials, film, TV, etc. |
| .AIFF | Full quality, uncompressed audio file | Used on CDs and for broadcast-quality audio, for commercials, film, TV, etc. |
| .MP3 | Good quality, but compressed audio file | Used to email your auditions and demos; used on your voice over web site |
| **Video Formats** | | |
| .MP4 | Small video file with quality | You might receive a commercial you did in this file format |
| .MPEG | Older format, larger video file; moderate quality | You might receive a commercial you did in this file format |
| .JPEG | QuickTime Movie | You might receive a commercial you did in this file format |
| **Photo Formats** | | |
| .JPEG | Digital file for photos and pictures | Headshots are typically sent and stored in this format. |
| **Document Formats** | | |
| .doc | Microsoft Word Document | A text document; occasionally used for scripts or sides |
| .docx | Newer format Microsoft Word Document | A text document; often used for scripts or sides |
| .PDF | Portable Document Format | A document that can contain text and graphics; used most often for scripts or sides. |

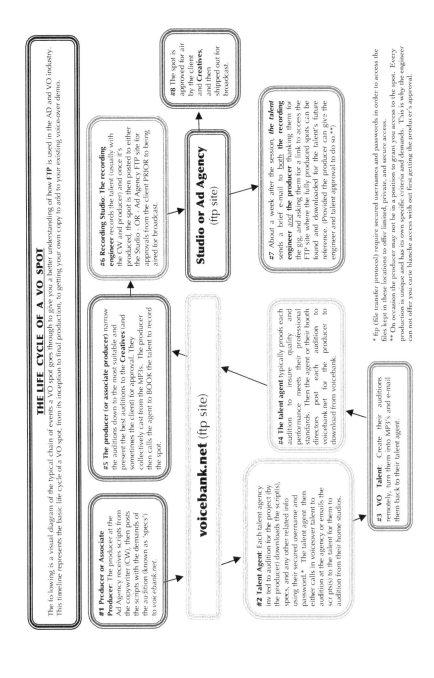

# THE LIFE CYCLE OF A VO SPOT

The following is a visual diagram of the typical chain of events a VO spot goes through to give you a better understanding of how FTP is used in the AD and VO industry. This timeline represents the basic life cycle of a VO spot, from its inception to final production, to getting your own copy to add to your existing voice-over demo.

**#1 Producer or Associate Producer:** The producer at the Ad Agency receives scripts from the copywriter (CW), then posts the scripts with the demands of the audition (known as 'specs') to *voicebank.net*.

**#2 Talent Agent:** Each talent agency invited to audition for the project (by the producer) downloads the script(s), specs, and any other related info using their secured username and password.* The talent agent then either calls in voiceover talent to audition at the agency or emails the scripts to the talent for them to audition from their home studios.

**#3 VO Talent:** Create their auditions remotely, turn them into MP3's and e-mail them back to their talent agent.

**#4 The talent agent** typically proofs each audition to insure quality and performance meets their professional standards. Then the agent or their booth directors post each audition to voicebank.net for the producer to download from voicebank.

**#5 The producer (or associate producer)** narrow the auditions down to the most suitable and present the best auditions to the **Creatives** (and sometimes cast from the MP3s. The producer collectively cast from the MP3s. The producer then calls the agent to BOOK the talent to record the spot.

**#6 Recording Studio: The recording engineer** records the talent (usually with the CW and producer) and once it's produced, the spot is then posted to either the Studio – OR - Ad Agency FTP site for approvals from the client PRIOR to being aired for broadcast.

**#8** The spot is approved for air by the client and **Creatives,** and then shipped out for broadcast.

## voicebank.net (ftp site)

## Studio or Ad Agency (ftp site)

**#7** About a week after the session, *the talent* sends a brief e-mail to both the **recording engineer** *and* **the producer** thanking them for the gig, and asking them for a link to access the FTP site where the fully produced spots can be found and downloaded for the talent's future reference. (Provided the producer can give the engineer and talent approval to do so.**)

\* ftp (file transfer protocol) require secured usernames and passwords in order to access the files kept in these locations to offer limited, private, and secure access.

\*\* On occasion the producer may not be in a position to grant you access to the spot. Every production is unique and has its own specific criteria and demands. This is why the engineer can not offer you carte blanche access with out first getting the producer's approval.

# Chapter 8:

# Determining Your Commercial Strengths

"There will come a time when passion will leave you. Curiosity will sustain you!"
—Heywood Hale-Broun, actor/sportswriter

The single most valuable and unexpected attribute you can develop from doing commercial work, aside from gaining the knowledge that you can feasibly earn a healthy living in this field, is the fact that you can hone your aesthetic skills as a professional actor by transferring your performance skills from one medium (such as stage) to another (television).

From landing commercial work, not only can you earn union status (SAG-AFTRA) but you also learn you must be ready for anything and on very short notice as a talent. With some tenacity you're bound to discover you can subsidize your entire career very nicely with commercial work rather than relying on the food-service industry to pay your bills.

Commercial work can raise your game as a talent in a variety of ways. This means you need to study the commercial styles from the ground up. If commercial work is relatively foreign to you, then employing the following process will help make studying the medium as a whole easier and more affordable.

To begin, you need to concentrate on your own demographic.

Demographic is a term used by marketing guys to establish who buys what, who does what, who likes what and when. Are you a 30-year-old guy who is single, something of a slacker and plays poker every Saturday night with other guys just like yourself? Fine. You're homing in on your demographic. Do you eat fast food five times a week and work out once a month? You're getting warmer. That's also part of your demographic.

As we've covered, chances are you're more likely to book a job based on what you already know first and foremost. So if you've been trying to be something that's a bit of a stretch for you—try for a moment to stop shoving yourself into a mold you might not fit. Too often, we're taught we're supposed to be someone else. We're asking you to abandon that concept for a while.–We're not saying stop trying new things, but perhaps this entire notion we're suggesting might contradict the approach you've been taking.

Why is it that every ingénue wants to be a character actor, every character actor wants to be the lead, and every lead wants to be seen as a comic when he's, in fact, a natural straight man? (Do you have any idea how tough it is to cast a really good straight man?)

The following study has been created to help you narrow the field on what you're best suited to land commercially.

## Your Ongoing Homework: *Building Your Reference Base*

Just as there are stage and film styles, there are commercial styles you need to become familiar with. Studying the medium will define what sort of work you're best suited to book, and whether that be film, animation, commercial voice-over work, commercial on-camera, or television.

You may have heard the familiar business adage: "Do what you know." Well, that certainly applies to performance to a great extent as well.

As your auditions increase you'll discover the people you're auditioning for will consistently refer to specific commercials and TV shows as a point of reference. If you're the right type but have no idea what they are referring to, you will be at a considerable disadvantage. But if you employ this form of study for a minimum of three to five hours a week you will greatly increase your knowledge of popular culture and will have a greater chance to deliver what's needed and wanted at the audition and on the job.

Pop culture is the common language of casting directors, producers, copywriters, and directors. They are most likely to describe what they're looking for by using the most current references they can think of that are closest to the collective artistic vision of the project. This is a grand opportunity for you as a talent—*if* you've done your homework. You'll be thrown these pop-culture bones and you're expected to catch them, rather than let them sail right over your head. If you apply yourself to the following form of study you will have a greater chance to pick them up and run with them.

> Pop culture is the common language of casting directors, producers, copywriters, and directors. They are likely to describe what they're looking for based on current references from television, film and popular commercial campaigns.

Advertising creatives generally have a tough enough time articulating what they need and want from you at a session. And when it comes to voice-over, you're likely to be directed by the copywriter, the creative who wrote the spot. (Occasionally, the copywriter will defer to the producer or recording engineer for input). Regardless, these individuals do not always know how to direct, whether they know what they want or not.

This would explain why the greatest post voice-over session complaint most actors have is, "They didn't give me any direction beyond, 'It's a non-announce announce, warm and friendly—go.'"

The truth is it's *our* responsibility as talent to offer options at every audition and every session and with every take. This is required of us with little or no direction at all. Therefore we must self-direct to a great extent. We're expected to offer plenty of performance options *within the parameters of what's being asked of us*. They expect us to be decisive in our delivery as we are expected to be a vital part of the creative process.

By the same token, if we are given direction we're always expected to apply that direction in the very next take. This requires agility, which is what we must glean from training and why we never cease sharpening our skills. The knife cuts both ways.

Nevertheless, on a voice-over session as in any performance, they're looking to you to bring a pulse to the text, which can appear flat and ordinary upon your first few read-throughs. Initially, the script may seem to lack imagery, emotion, or personal point of view. It's your job as a talent to bring life to the words. Creatives and various clients typically assume you have something to bring to the table without their input and will leave you to your own devices. You do have a great deal to create with, you know, if you've come to play.

You're paid to have a pulse, so start pumping some life into that dead fish. A script can look pretty flat on the page until you start fleshing it out with some real spirit of play! So, play!

So where to begin? If you've done your homework as we've laid it out for you here, you're not as likely to be thrown off guard. In fact, you'll feel quite stable. You need to get your land legs by thoroughly studying the medium, namely popular commercials, television, and film.

Here's your homework and how you do it: Commit yourself to studying popular television and commercial styles by asking the following questions for no less than three to five hours *a week*. The more you do it, the easier this work will become because you realize a great deal about mass media you probably never considered before, and you'll understand it on an entirely different level.

A word of caution: Don't fool yourself into thinking you can simply watch a whole lot of television without the ability to play it back and expect to get the same results. Do yourself a favor and honestly study this stuff as we suggest below. You'll be very surprised how much you will glean from even an hour or so of this study.

Besides, it's FUN!

## How to Study Commercials and Television

We have a great advantage these days. Technology is on our side to study television, film, and commercial work with greater ease than ever before due to the now commonplace DVR (digital video recorder).

If you don't own a DVR we recommend you rent one through your local cable service for a nominal monthly fee to best study the medium in which you intend to work. Or, if you don't have cable and a DVR, check out **iSpot.TV.** You may not readily discover which commercials play during what shows, but you *will* be able to view many current commercials and have the luxury to observe the following details.

Here's what we suggest:

First off, (if you're using your DVR and cable) record the shows you watch religiously, commercials and all. The commercials that play during the shows you never miss are already geared to your demographic. They know you're watching. You need to study them thoroughly. Follow the list of items to observe on the next page.

Second, record popular shows that you've heard of but haven't yet seen in order to stay on top of the popular references. Begin by studying the top ten on the Nielsen ratings. A quick Google search will turn up the weekly listings of the top shows.

Again, if you don't have the luxury of cable TV and a DVR and you're looking to study the top TV shows, we recommend you enlist the assistance of either Netflix or **Hulu+** for a small monthly fee.

The objective here is to *build your reference base*. In other words, you can't play it if you don't know what they're referring to. Therefore, the broader, more extensive your reference base, the more likely you'll be able to apply the direction you're given at auditions and sessions. On a commercial audition, you're likely to receive direction based on current popular television, commercial, Internet, and film. No matter how close you may be to the type they're after, if you don't understand the frame of reference they give you, you won't be able to play it and will miss out on a true opportunity.

If you don't watch much TV, then you certainly have your work cut out for you. (And, of course, Netflix is a great source to catch up on various popular series you may have missed that shape the culture or define a style or character.)

Dedicate yourself to watching a good *eight hours* of programming a week for a month. For instance: the *Today Show, Parks and Recreation, The Big Bang Theory, Ellen, NCIS, The Voice,* the evening news (as depressing as that may be), *The Simpsons* reruns on Fox, something on HGTV, something on the Food Network, TLC, History Channel, Animal Planet, and maybe a little something on IFC (Independent Film Channel), like *Portlandia,* or *Comedy Bang Bang* on Sundance Channel. The idea is to record a good cross section of material. Try to discover examples that cover nearly every demographic.

Other cable channel options worth studying: HBO, AMC, TCM, TBS, and always from the four networks: ABC, NBC, CBS, and FOX.

Beyond becoming familiar with what's current commercially, the following exercise is likely to build your overall observational skills and allow you to discover the commercial styles you're best suited to play.

When you play back what you've recorded, whether you're viewing familiar programs or not, have a pad of paper and a pen handy and make note of the following:

1. What is the spot for?

2. Is the commercial for a product or service you would find nationwide? Or is it a local service or product?

3. Would you do the voice-over? Even if it's only the tag (i.e., "It gets the dirt out." Or "SC Johnson, a family company")?

4. Does the commercial appear to be well-produced?

5. Would you appear on-camera in the commercial, film, or TV show? As what role?

6. Do you use the product/service the commercial is promoting?

7. Do you wish you used/had the product/service (but maybe can't afford it—yet)?

8. Are you personally opposed to the product/service?

9. How many voice-overs are on the spot? (There is often more than one.)

10. Is there an unusual character affectation in one or more of the voices, or is it a more natural delivery?

11. What is the overall emotional tone of the spot? Is it solemn? Hopeful? Sarcastic? Playful? Stoic? Confident? Is it edgy? Is there an attitude? Is it witty?

12. Is the commercial, film, or TV show personality driven? Are these personality traits you have also?

13. Does the commercial tell a story?

14. Who is the voice-over talking to? Is it more than one person? (Even as an announcer?)

15. Does the delivery seem very personable and conversational?

16. Does it seem the voice-over is "thinking out loud"?

17. Listen to the ad without looking at it. Do it again. Do it again. Do it again. Just listen to the delivery without looking at the image. Does it have a great deal of imagery even without looking at the picture?  Or is it the other way around?

18. Does the voice-over start out quiet and become very loud as the spot progresses? Or does the voice-over remain fairly consistent, volume-wise?

19. How close to the mic was the voice talent likely to be when the spot was recorded? Is the voice-over intimate? Is it more boisterous? Somewhere in- between?

20. Does the delivery tell us anything about the person doing the voice-over?  Does it sound like a personal point of view (POV)?

21. Is there a change that occurs in the delivery?

22. Which words are emphasized, if any at all?

23. Is it a well-produced national commercial? Is it a half-baked local commercial?

24. Is it a 15-second-, 30-second-, or 60-second-long spot?

25. Does the voice-over speak from the moment the commercial begins until it ends?

26. Is the commercial mostly images and music with the voice talent coming in only once or twice for emphasis?

27. Observe when the voice comes in with the picture. Does the voice-over start a sentence take a break and then finish the thought in stages?

28. Is the action of the commercial humorous and the voice-over more conservative? Or is it the opposite: the voice-over is more humorous and the action more conservative?

29. Does the music match the emotion of the voice, or does the voice-over counter completely with what's happening on-screen, including the music?

30. Does the voice-over sound effortless?

31. Does it sound like the voice-over is simply thinking out loud?

32. Does the voice-over sound like they know that they're an approachable authority?

33. Do you recognize the voice? Is a celebrity doing the voice-over? Or have you heard this voice or quality on other commercials?

34. If it is a celebrity voice-over, is there a voice-over in addition to the celebrity spokesperson?

35. Is this a commercial voice-over style you feel you could easily play?

36. Does the program you've recorded have a great deal of narration? If so, what is the tempo, emotional tone, and general vocal quality of the voice-over featured?

37. Does the voice-over sound sell-y, stiff, choppy, or forced? Does it sound like the voice-over is reading?

38. Is it a promo spot for a program, special station, or channel?

39. What's the probable age range of the voice(s) and characters on the spot: Under 16 years? 18-25 years? 25-35 years? 35-45 years? 50 plus? Retirement age?

40. Does the voice talent's age seem to coincide with the age the commercial, film, or program is geared to reach? Or is it the opposite?

41. Is the spot aimed for a gender-specific audience? Is the same gender delivering the voice-over? Is the same gender featured on camera?

42. Is this spot airing during a show you watch frequently? Or a program you've never seen and maybe might never watch?

43. Do you recognize this same spot from other media, such as radio or the Internet?

44. Does this commercial appear to be one in an ongoing campaign?

45. Have you noticed other commercials on air that have a similar theme or style to this one for other unrelated products/services?

46. Do you recall seeing this spot on the air (on and off) for a year or more?

47. What is the principal actor(s) in the commercial wearing? What color is it? Style of clothing? (Do you have clothes of this type in your closet to wear for auditions, if you're pursuing on-camera work?)

48. If the voice-over were on-camera, how tight a shot would you say he/she'd be in? Extreme close-up (ECU)? Close-up (CU)? Medium close-up (MCU)? Medium shot (MS)? Long shot (LS)? Wide shot (WS)?

49. Observe the commercials you got lost in more closely. Make note of what it was that drew you in.

50. Have you seen the same commercial play during your favorite shows also play during programs you never watch? Notice what these commercials are for, the time of day they usually play, and who their target audience might be.

Dedicate at least three to five hours a week to this form of study for a solid month. What you'll learn will absolutely astound you.

Ultimately, you'll discover that the object of the game here is to simply be who you are because being yourself is far more interesting than watching you *try* to be something you're not. Watching an actor shoehorn into something artificial or forced is an effort to watch and is counterproductive.

Being yourself is *real*. It's honest. It's simple. And it requires far less effort than you may have ever perceived. There's tremendous power in simplicity. Put it to work to your advantage.

# Chapter 9:
# Developing Your Vocal Skills

"Elocution is oratorical or expressive delivery, including the graces
of intonation, gesture, etc.; style or manner
of speaking or reading in public; as, clear,
impressive elocution. Eloquent diction."
—Oxford English Dictionary

Developing and keeping your vocal skills agile is a constant in this
business. Much like any muscle, if you don't work them out
regularly they will atrophy and cease to work for you when you
need them most. This is why it's vitally important to your
professional credibility and overall confidence that you keep your
skills honed. Considering you MUST be able to re-create what you
have on your demo with very little effort, it's imperative you keep
your vocal skills sharp.

If the only time you are working your chops when you arrive on our doorstep to coach, then your career will begin and end at our front door. You're ultimately responsible for whether you succeed. How well you're able to deliver what's promised on your demo has to be your prime mission. It takes dedication.

So, with that, here are the keys to kingdom. Try not to lose them in the couch.

## Noteworthy

It's worth noting our **Sound Advice** Vocal Warm-Up is compiled in large part from surveys of several certified speech pathologists, completely independent of one another, as well as from a handful of extremely successful voice talent who swear by these techniques.

Speech pathologists (speech paths) in particular know the true value of drilling vocal combinations in order to develop and correct articulation and diction. This is precisely how speech paths can effectively assist a four-year-old with a stutter to speak with fluidity, and someone who's survived a stroke to regain his ability to speak. Imagine what these exercises can do for _you_ assuming you aren't playing through such obstacles or handicaps. These exercises will allow you to master your vocal prowess provided you dedicate yourself to making this warm-up part of your weekly regimen. You have to make it your business to do so.

In recent years, speech pathologists have suggested you AVOID recording yourself while running through your vocal warm-ups, as you will only serve to drill inaccurate intonations, sound placement and improperly articulated sounds you're bound to create in the initial weeks of applying these techniques. Findings show playing back personal recordings of running through vocal warm-ups solidify _improper vocal habits_, rather than the other way around. So we discourage it. Instead, it's best to follow a recording of that supports proper placement and tonal accomplishment, such as with our **Sound Advice** VOCAL WARM-UP. This will allow you to practice articulating the correct sounds you need to drill to develop proper enunciation and the most effective elocution.

(An MP3 version of our SOUND ADVICE Vocal Warm-Up can be purchased from our site: www.voiceoverinfo.com.)

# The Condensed Sound Advice Vocal Warm-up

This process is exclusive to **Sound Advice** and designed to offer you an even greater command over your vocal skills, especially when maintained as a steady regimen. These techniques are designed to assist <u>every</u> talent *regardless of skill level.*

Make it your goal to do this warm-up *at least three to five times a week*, ideally in the morning, to develop a greater mastery over your articulation and diction. You'll find you will develop greater vocal agility, which will make you a far more valuable voice talent and actor.

Be sure you're well hydrated and stand facing a mirror.

We recommend tea-temperature warm water during the session to gently slough off all the "cobwebs" from your vocal chords and keep you well hydrated. Cool or cold water before and after, just like after a workout.

Okay, START!

1. "OOO" siren a musical scale from low to high (never high to low)*

   Purpose: To smooth out vocal cracks in your voice (which are technically breaks in your pitch) using a musical scale from low to high ONLY; to get you to use your body to back up your voice through gesture (and to take a good deal of your attention off giving your mouth full responsibility for creating all your sound); to fine-tune your diction and build your vocal agility.

   a. Keep your head level rather than tilting it upward while going up the scale

   b. Vocalize an "OOO" sound (as in the word 'room') in a steady and deliberate scale, from low to high

   c. Motion upward with your hand to coincide with your voice; your body backs up your voice

d. Do not speed. Slow down, take your time to allow for more control and to build agility

e. Your sound should taper off (or soften at the end) once you reach the top of the scale in order to avoid employing tension in your throat and mouth

f. Repeat 8 to 10 times in a row

NOTE: If you hit a crack (as you are sure to do at any time when running scales low to high during these exercises) then add two to three more "OOO" scales. The next scale that follows will have far less, if any, pitch break quality. Each additional scale will further smooth out any breaks in your pitch and correct your muscle memory.

*According to speech pathologists, randomly running scales high to low only instills cracks (known as pitch breaks) in your voice. To correct this they recommend running scales low to high ONLY. It may come as a surprise, but apparently running scales high to low will actually incorporate breaks in your pitch—something we're trying to avoid and alleviate completely.

2. Buzzing the lips
Purpose: To warm up your front articulators using a musical scale again from low to high ONLY; to get you to use your body to back up your voice through gesture, while smoothing out pitch breaks (cracks) in your voice and keep your voice supported and sounding younger, longer.

a.   Keep your head level rather than tilting upward as you gradually voice the scale, low to high

b.   Make a motorboat sound with your lips (like a child would do) by placing a subtle hum just behind your lips

c. Do a scale low to high while buzzing your lips, while gesturing up the scale with your hand. (Your body backs up your voice)

d. The sound should simply decay (fade away) at the top of the scale rather than end abruptly

e. Repeat at least 8 to 10 times

Note: Don't be discouraged if you don't find the "buzzing your lips" exercise naturally intuitive. Your cell phone wasn't immediately intuitive either, was it? It probably took three to four weeks. So keep at it!

If at first you find your buzzed lips sound encompasses the entire expanse of your lips, your sound will not be specific enough to achieve the effect we're going for and achieve the results we're trying to master. If you're not doing it correctly, you'll be expelling far more air than sound when you buzz your lips. If this occurs, hold up two fingers in front of your mouth, as if you are pretending to smoke. Aim your buzzing lips sound between your two (slightly parted) fingers. Get some sound behind your lips and start motorboating! Then add a scale from low to high behind it.

If you find buzzing your lips is difficult and discover you're not buzzing your lips at all, then you're centering your sound too far back in your mouth or in your throat at present.

It's worth mentioning every child on the planet who learns to speak buzzes his lips. Children do this the world over, for a good three years as their ability to speak clearly develops. So we're going back to basics. You can do this. It's just been a while. (If you are having a tough time buzzing your lips, you're mumbling and you don't even know it!)

Sound follows thought. Place your attention just out in front of your mouth by about two or three inches. With continued application of this exercise, your articulation will become far more agile and your diction more specific. Nothing fine-tunes your diction quite like buzzing your lips, so keep at it.

3. Stick out your tongue in a full, long stretch as if a doctor is looking down your throat, as you say "Aaahhhh."

Purpose: Since your tongue is one of the longest muscles you have, you need to stretch it before working it out; doing so will allow for greater dexterity of articulation, elocution, stamina, and diction and ultimately will decrease the opportunity for mouth noise.

a. Keep your head level rather than leaning forward or move your head down with your sound throughout this exercise

b. Make an elongated "aaahhh" sound (as in apple) sound as you hyperextend your tongue out of your mouth as far as you can

c. Your hand gestures should coincide with the movement of your tongue

d. Be sure to place your sound out in front of you, rather than swallow it or center it in the back of your throat

e. Open up the back of your throat with the elongated "aaahhh" sound, as if a doctor is looking down your throat. The sound should never have a choking quality or be focused/directed through the back of your neck. Instead, this is done without tension

f. Let the sound soften at the end rather than tightening. Creating tension such as this is known as a glottal stop. Avoid it. Keep everything easy, but hyperextended

g. Repeat six to eight times

4. LA-NA-DA-TA-GA-ING-KA
This item is credited to have originated from seasoned pro, vocal coach, and vocalist Raven Kane. I have no idea where she came upon it.
Purpose: This exercise allows you to work each area over the surface of your tongue through specific isolations and articulations to develop cleaner, more agile repetitions.

a. Throughout this exercise keep your head level, leave your mouth slack, and isolate the movement of your jaw (keep your mouth open about half an inch). Focus your sound directly out in front of you on each vocalization. Watch yourself in the mirror to ensure you're keeping your mouth still forcing your tongue to articulate each of the following sounds

b. Vocalize: LA-LA-LA-LA-LA. Using only your tongue to create the sound. Repeat at least 12 to 16 times

c. Next, continue to isolate the movement of your jaw, forcing your tongue to articulate the sound: NA-NA-NA-NA-NA. Repeat at least 12 to 16 times. No nasality. Focus your sound directly out in front of you, rather than up in your face or back in your throat

d. Vocalize: DA, TA, GA, ING, KA concisely as you can and consecutively. Again, keep your jaw still, your mouth slightly agape. This forces your tongue to articulate these sounds. Speak as clearly and carefully as you can. With each repetition the sound will be more articulated. Place your sound directly out in front of your mouth

e. Repeat this exercise in its entirety six to eight times through. Do it with purpose—placing the sound directly out in front of you

Your vocal warm-up is now completed. You should have far greater stamina and cleaner diction even after a single application of these exercises in their entirety. So, you can just imagine what continued application will do for you: You'll be vocally fit in a few short weeks.

## Two Weeks to Create a Habit

A single vocal work out is one thing. Vocal fitness takes time.

Experts say it takes two weeks to create a habit. It's no accident then that it will likely take about two weeks for you to make a habit out of this warm-up to gain some of the greatest benefits from these exercises just like any workout. However, it may take a month or more before you see the difference for yourself.

153

The important thing is consistency. So, stay with it. You have everything to gain with consistency and commitment.

## Follow Up

Follow the **Sound Advice** Vocal Warm-Up with cold reading a book out loud, such as a children's story like any written by Dr. Seuss or *Alice in Wonderland* for an additional 20 to 30 minutes to increase your cold-reading skills.

We strongly encourage you to practice this vocal warm-up standing in front of a mirror, especially for the first month to establish a stable receipt point for your communication (namely YOU). After that, you can then relax that requirement and do your vocal warm-up in the shower, or while you're driving in the car on the way to work, to your agents, or a session.

Dedicate yourself to maintain this regimen no less than three to five times a week to keep your vocal skills sharp and to tone your cold-reading muscle.

## Catch Your Breath

When you first find yourself in front of a mic in a booth, you're likely to find yourself surprised to discover how much you sound like Darth Vader—at least every time you take a breath. Your attention may be directed there by a novice recording engineer, or maybe by some rookie producer, or quite possibly without their help at all—you managed to introvert into every breath all by your lonesome.

To this, I have _one_ thing to say: Breathing is an involuntary action. You have to do it. It's not only expected, it's required.

*Shallow breathing* can and should be avoided by allowing yourself to come back to neutral (a fully relaxed state) with which you exhale completely prior to beginning another take. And as we mentioned from the beginning, you must make a habit (muscle memory) of returning to this grounded position before uttering a sound.

154

As for undue attention on your breathing and whether you need to do anything else beyond focusing your attention on the work at hand and creating, all I can say is: There's a learning curve here. Relax. Get yourself into neutral. Exhale and GO. Your breathing will manage itself for the most part. Beyond that we're talking about phrasing, which is an entirely different subject.

(See Chapter 11, The **Sound Advice** Approach.)

> Vocal agility, much like your performance
> skills, is not immediately intuitive.
> It takes continual practice.

## Diction, diction, diction

For additional fine-tuning of your diction AFTER our vocal warm-up, try this short exercise that helps develop mastery of rhythm, alliteration, and imagery.

This exercise is just for fun; the warm-up above is far more imperative and effective in developing proper mastery of your vocal prowess so you will be able to rely on your skills at a moment's notice.

Try this exercise very slowly and methodically at first for accuracy and precision. Over enunciate every word and syllable. Then gradually pick up the pace each time through, delivering each item directly to yourself in the mirror. Take each item off the page and direct your communication into the mirror.

Do your best to read with accuracy *no less than three times through*. Add this to your regimen two to three times a week, especially during the first six to eight weeks of making a routine out of your vocal warm-up.

Look up any words you don't know *before you begin*, so you know what you're talking about. I realize that's a novel concept, but humor me. It's a very good habit to get into. You'll not only increase your vocabulary, you'll actually expand your entire understanding as a whole. Imagine that.

155

Speaking of which, be sure to *imagine* each item in motion as you speak. If you only imagine a still life, your delivery will suffer. An engaged imagination has the greatest impact on your inflection. (There's a reason they call it animation.) Notice how every time you imagine each item, each time through this exercise, something new comes into the equation. Your imagination continues to create whether you like it or not. You'd be wise to acknowledge this fact and incorporate it into each take and performance. The very same thing occurs with each and every take on a session or an audition as well. This is your greatest tool. Use it! Acting is a time art (an art reliant on time for effect), and you're expected to *play*! So, have fun!

One hen,

Two ducks,

Three squawking geese,

Four limerick oysters,

Five corpulent porpoises,

Six pair of Don Alverzo's tweezers,

Seven thousand Macedonians in full battle array,

Eight brass monkeys from ancient, sacred crypts of Egypt,

Nine sympathetic, apathetic, diabetic, old men on roller skates with a

defined propensity towards procrastination and sloth,

Ten lyrical, spherical, diabolical denizens of the deep

who haul stall around the quo of the quay of the quivery,

all at the same time.

*This diction exercise is known as the "Announcer's Test," as it originated at Radio Central New York in the early 1940's as a cold-reading test given to prospective radio talent to demonstrate their speaking ability. It's quite the litmus test and a terrific enunciation exercise!*

## Taming the Whistling "S" Sound

The following exercise is precisely how to de-"*s*" a sibilant *s* without the benefit of *digital* editing assistance.

According to the speech pathologists I have interviewed, ALL men have some issue with the *s* sound. I honestly don't know if that's true, but I have seen more than my share of guys who seem to have an unprecedented amount of attention on creating this sound.

Regardless, *everyone* has a whistling *s* quality from time to time, some more than others. The following exercise can be a lifesaver on session, even for singers.

**For a solid 30 to 60 seconds** (NO cheating)... **make an *S* sound (SSSSS), then a *T* sound (TUH), followed by a *Z* sound (ZZZZ).** Repeat these sounds consecutively and concisely again and again.

Each sound should come out independently—at no time should the sound you make ever sound like "stuz," "stuz," "stuz." That would defeat the purpose of this exercise and result only in making you feel foolish. (Not that any of these exercises have so far. Shall we revisit the "Lucille Ball"? I rest my case.)

Done correctly, this works EVERY TIME, provided you do it long enough and don't rush it.

So take your time. Spend at least three and half to five seconds to get through one full round: "SSSS," "TUH," "ZZZZ," and then repeat. You're correcting your muscle memory and effectively de-"s"-ing your sibilant *s* sound.
The difference is incredibly effective and immediate.

If you are aware of *s* issues in your speech, add this exercise to your vocal warm-up regimen.

## The Sound Advice Cold Reading Exercise

This workout is intended to help you build your cold-reading skills as well as your vocal range and stamina. We're also attempting to expand the vocal variety in your delivery, offer you more control of your sound, and where you are placing it. PLUS, it will bring you up to date on current events, depending on the text you choose to read.

The objective of the **Sound Advice** Cold Reading Exercise is to *get the words off the page and into that mirror* with as much ease and fluidity as possible. Ideally, this should be done in the morning, at least two to three times a week.

This exercise should FOLLOW our vocal warm-up, as it does in this chapter, but it should *never* replace it.

To begin, go online and find *The New York Times*, *The Chicago Tribune*, or *The Los Angeles Times*, or choose a book or other reading material you've never read before. STAND in front of a mirror and read each story *out loud*.

Look up any word that you don't know or fully understand. Oxford Dictionary online is awesome, thorough, and FAST! Look it up *quickly* before moving on. I mean it, LOOK IT UP! Save yourself, save the session. Otherwise you'll shut down right where you stand if you don't. You'll continue half-heartedly *if you continue at all* if you DON'T KNOW WHAT YOU'RE TALKING ABOUT! So, get into this habit here and now. It will serve you well on sessions and auditions. Just do it. Other than that, make sure you have plenty of water.

## Section I:

To start, get yourself situated standing in front of a mirror with the intention of placing your performance into it.

You have to entertain yourself to find your audience and that includes developing your vocal technique.

### The Over-the-Top Delivery

From the very beginning, read the first story/lengthy paragraph on the page out loud and as animated and in as exaggerated a delivery as you possibly can muster. Go *way* too far. No dialects*, no forced volume or pitch, just an *over-the-top* (don't-worry-that-delivery-is-completely-inappropriate-for-the-text) sort of delivery.

At **Sound Advice**, we call going over the top *stretching the canvas*. This is based on the notion that like the artist Jackson Pollack you should stretch the canvas and slap some paint around. Don't be afraid to make a mess. You should never hold back and always prepare yourself to go further than you originally thought might be appropriate from the very start of *any* performance. There's nothing but discovery in it. ALWAYS challenge yourself to "go too far" from the very beginning of every performance to garner the greatest results, including this exercise.

Now, move on to the next story or lengthy paragraph.

*Dialects and speed are nearly impossible to back out of once established in your muscle memory delivery. They will dominate the performance that follows and should be avoided when attempting to stretch the canvas, or go too far.*

## The Speedy-Slow Delivery

With the second story, try reading the first paragraph very, very slowly and methodically, completely over-articulating every syllable. Then follow this paragraph by reading the next very quickly, still maintaining the very articulated, concise requirement as well as you can. Alternate back and forth with every other paragraph in this way for about six to eight paragraphs. It should become easier as you go.

Keep your attention on: Am I being understood? Am I getting across what I'm talking about?  COMMUNICATE!  Your goal is to be understood. Every delivery inevitably boils down to making sure the listener really gets what it is you're saying.

## The Reporter Read

On this story/paragraph read with the cadence of a cliché news reporter. ("This is Sandra Dolittle, reporting from the Pentagon. Back to you, Chet.") Assume the personae: a somewhat staccato, rather ridged and announce-y read, as if you were Walter Cronkite. Go over the top in that direction.

Again, be sure to take those words off the page and put them into the mirror—start to get more specific with this requirement.  Take the words off the page and into the mirror.

As a reminder: If you see any words that you thought you knew but really don't, look them up. Then move on to the next story.

## The Straight-Ahead Read

Drop all the pretense you have employed in each of the previous stories or pages and simply deliver the read straight out, simple as that.  Take the words off the page and focus them into the mirror to yourself as honestly and articulated and as *real* as you actually are.

There you have it.  Your natural, unadulterated voice; warmed up and honest.

You may move on to Section II, if you are up for the challenge, or if you find it difficult to place your sound.

## Section II:

Section II was created to develop these skills with some precision. This section concentrates on controlling your sound. The goal here is to establish more of a vocal range through placement.

Throughout this section we're concentrating on *imagining where your sound is centered*.

Imagine your sound is coming from a particular place on your body—picture it originating from there. This takes some repeated practical experience to master, but rest assured, it can and *should* be done to best control your sound, so keep trying even if during the first few weeks it doesn't feel like you're getting anywhere. (Remember it takes at least TWO weeks to make a habit out of *anything*.)

If you feel your voice is rather monotone or unvaried, this is the exercise for you.  Besides, you'll continue to develop your cold-reading skills!

### Center Your Sound Between Your Knees

Starting with the first paragraph on the page, imagine the center of your sound is placed down between your knees. No matter how deep your voice may actually be—this subbasement is *below* your natural, normal low.

"Ahhh" yourself down into this lowest of lows. Picture the center of your sound between your knees while vocalizing the "ahhh" sound. Make sure your knees are loose, your feet shoulder-width apart, and your mouth slack and easy.

Now begin reading with a monotone in this register, imagining your sound is centered there. This is a subbasement low that is below your natural lowest point. Rock the read just above and just below

160

this level back and forth.  Continue to read through that first sentence or two.  Exploring this deep, dark, low sound.

Once you've established this sub-low-end vocal quality, read through another sentence, gradually finding the next subtle register above it.

Move up to that quality, as if this low-end sound is centered in your lower belly.

## Center Your Sound in Your Lower Belly

With the next few sentences, we'll pull it up one notch. Imagine that your sound is now centered in your gut, your lower belly.

Create that "ahhhh" sound to bring it up there. Rock the sound back down into your knees and then up to the gut, down to the knees, up to the gut.

Your ability to trust the difference will increase after a few weeks of doing this, so don't be too hard on yourself.  Sound follows thought—just place it there. Eventually you'll know for yourself what *you* consider to be the next step above or below. It's still low; it's just a bit above your lowest, subbasement low.

Go ahead and read the next paragraph or sentence or two, still with a bit of monotone in your voice. That's fine. Then slide back down into that sub-low centered between your knees.  Keep reading.

Be sure you're not straining through any of this. Keep it nice and easy. Move through the read, alternating between the knees and the gut, until you feel fairly stable with where the sound is originating from—in this case, your gut.

Next, try moving the sound from the gut up to the next elevated level: just below your rib cage in your solar plexus.

## Center Your Sound in Your Solar Plexus

We're gradually moving up the center of your body, placing your sound in a new location with each sentence or two or paragraph. Place your hand over your solar plexus as you read. Imagine your sound centered here and resonating from this location.

Let the sound drop down into in your gut again, make note of the difference in that monotone—use the "ahhh" as needed to find it, and then move back up to centering your sound in your solar plexus again. Keep reading.

Next, try moving the sound into your chest, just above this center register, then back into the solar plexus again.

Move that sound back up to the gut, back to your solar plexus. Remain there for a *phrase* or two, and then back up into the chest. Keep reading. Don't slow down. Move back down into your solar plexus.

## Center Your Sound in Your Chest

Place your hand below your rib cage on your solar plexus again. Then move your sound up to the next level, into your chest. Continue reading, using the "ahhh" sound for placement. Go back to your solar plexus, then back up to your chest again. Keep reading.

Now fully center your sound in your chest. Keep reading.

NOTE: *You may have noticed none of this is all that natural sounding yet. I totally understand. Keep going. Again, this is about getting more command on your own placement of sound. With that you will broaden your vocal range.*

Next, move the sound into your throat voice, then back down into your chest where you've centered it. Then back up into your throat—don't strain; nice and easy—just simply center your sound there for a phrase or two, and then back down into your chest.

Move back down to the solar plexus and back up again. Use that "ahhh" sound as needed to find the center of your sound. Move that sound up into your chest and then gradually up into the throat voice again briefly, and then back down into the chest voice with a half a sentence here and whole one there as you read.

## Center Your Sound in Your Throat

Keep reading your way up into your throat voice, then back down to your chest. Then back up into your throat.

Go easy here! No tension, there should be absolutely no straining in any of this.

Move your sound back into your chest voice and further down the line into your solar plexus again. Rock your sound down in there, while you continue to read. Keep it moving, then come up to the chest and center it up in your throat again. Keep everything loose and easy—no straining.

At this point, from your mouth on up, the length of what you're reading will be even shorter spurts—just phrases and jibs and jabs.

## Center the Sound _Under_ Your Tongue

Begin by imagining your mouth is so loose the only articulation you have in it is up and down, and it's left slightly agape. Center your sound under your tongue (as odd as that may sound).

Imagine you are scooping up each phrase off the page and pouring them into your mouth. WITHOUT THE BENEFIT OF DICTION—let those words _sloppily spill out as you say them_. Read one full sentence in this manner. Focus your delivery into the mirror. Direct the intention of what you are saying there, but only a modicum of articulation is employed. (You're going to want to speak with more articulation after this.) The words should stream off the page, into your mouth, and the _intention_ of each phrase should be focused into the mirror.

You may get through only one or two full sentences here, but

make it your total intention to relay what it is you're trying to say off the page into that mirror.

This deprivation of diction is intended to make you long for it. If it takes another sentence or two to get that, then add another. Keep going using this loose and sloppy "blah-blah-blah" sound to maintain your sound being centered just under your tongue.

## Send the Sound Out Through Your Face

From that sloppy-mouthed business, move very quickly through the following: blurt your sound directly out from your face and sinuses, especially alongside your nose.

Send that sound up and out your sinuses. Quickly blurt out a phrase or two—keep moving.

Follow the sinuses by sending your sound up and out through your eyes. Don't think—DO! And do it quickly! Just a quick phrase—maybe two, tops.

Then—eeeeek, next phrase—send the sound out of your forehead! Next phrase out the top of your head! QUICK! (Great-sufferin'-succotash!) No straining—just shoot that delivery out fast and furious!

Then drop it! (Phew!)

Little light-headed? Take a sip of water. Look at yourself in the mirror. Still with us? Fine.

Finish the sentence you may have started directly out in front of you.

## Place Your Sound Directly (and Easily) Out in Front of You

Imagine sending your sound directly out about two feet in front of you, allowing it to bow out to the left and right, just above your shoulders. This sound is authentically YOU.

You have full mastery of your voice, it's comfortably warmed up and easy, fully supported with every handicap dropped and out of your way. (Exhale.) You're now ready for anything!

Nice going, Ace. You're officially ready to roll.

# Chapter 10: The Health Department

"Happiness is nothing more than good health
and a bad memory."
—Albert Schweitzer

The best defense is a strong offense, or so the saying goes, and when it comes to your health that means eating well, taking supplements if necessary, getting plenty of rest, and maintaining a healthy routine.

However, when we're up against it, and maintaining these things has been taxed to the hilt, or they simply aren't a commodity, here's a little help and TLC that will right what's wrong.

Bookings and important auditions often come when you least expect them; therefore, keeping yourself healthy and fit is an integral part of making yourself available to the work. If you're so ill you can barely peel your head off the pillow, you're going to have a tough time delivering the goods in a session or at an audition.

Since Murphy's Law will render your vocal cords dry, strained, and abused on the morning of your first professional recording session—in part because so much attention is placed on your voice—I have compiled here a few tried-and-true home remedies to help restore your stability and confidence, so you can deliver without having to make excuses.

### 'Scuse Me?!

First of all, it's not in your best interest to walk into a session and inform the room—in a painfully hoarse voice—"Sorry, my throat's killing me! (cough, cough) But I figured we'd try a few takes anyway. I took three buses to get here! (a-choo!) 'Scuse me! (sniff) Ugh, my head's killing me. At least I made it here, right? I figure I can fake my way through it—I mean, what the heck. Besides, I'm so broke—I really need this job! (cough, cough, cough)."

One word: gag.

You will earn NO ONE'S sympathy by reporting your physical (or personal) ailments to everyone within earshot at a professional session. You will, however, make those trying to produce a Clio Award-winning commercial nervous about the fact that, thanks to you, they may miss their deadline, possibly go over budget (since they will probably have to replace you), or worst of all, get fired themselves for not delivering the final production when it was promised. And all due to one forlorn little voice talent who didn't have the sense to get her act together and do the job (that'd be *you*).

If you're in such bad shape, YOU SHOULDN'T BE THERE! Inform your agent *a day ahead of time* that you're too ill to attend the session. It's rare that you'd be completely unaware of an oncoming health problem the day before—so rare that it's considered downright childish to wait until the morning of the session to bail on the job due to illness.

As you might have guessed, this is frowned upon in any work environment. If you're coming down with something, the number-one rule is this: COMMUNICATE! Let your agent know as soon as possible if you have the flu or think you may be contagious. You never know. They may be able to move the session!

Otherwise, you're likely to kick such a dent in your professional reputation that you could very well lose any potential work that may have come your way from this client in the future! Simply put, showing up unable to deliver the goods, and not allowing the production team time to replace or reschedule you, is bad form.

That being said, if you are truly blindsided by an illness the morning of a session, you'll have to determine the situation for yourself realistically at that time and contact your agent as soon as you're *certain* you won't be able to attend. If you continually keep in good communication with your agent and avoid pumping up the volume on the personal drama, they will surely field this one for you.

If you're in the emergency room or something of that nature, once again, do your best to keep your agent informed. If you can't call personally, make sure someone near and dear to you gets in touch with your agent. It's a simple matter of communication—it can solve the world's ills faster than anything! If your agent is a seasoned vet, believe me: He's seen it before.

## A Pound of Prevention

There are a number of common minor ailments that often befall a voice talent.

Please note: If you have a chronic condition, please consult a proper physician. The following home remedies are meant only for minor ailments. They are intended to tide you over when you simply need to get through the session. That said, I wouldn't have devoted an entire section of this book to these small gems if I hadn't experienced significant and consistent improvements with literally scores of people.

Keep in mind that it's always best to err on the side of caution by avoiding obvious abuses to your health and well-being. Smoke-filled rooms and staying up all night like a frat boy during rush week are bad ideas, especially the night before a major audition or recording session. Some health abuses can (and should) be avoided. Your reputation won't bounce back as fast as your body if you put yourself in harm's way and can't rise to the occasion when it's expected of you. Preparation involves a bit of prevention, sometimes. Use your better judgment and avoid having to fake it.

No industry professional is so gullible and burden-free as to accept excuses over results. They still need to get the job done. Giving an agent, producer, or director a problem to solve or an obstacle to overcome makes you a burden. Avoid it.

## Losing Your Voice

If you find yourself crippled by laryngitis, a voice-over's greatest nemesis, visit this site designed by six vocal experts and doctors: **www.voiceproblem.org**

> If you're under the weather, or are at the onset of losing your voice and your agent calls you for an audition... *you are expected* to sit this one out. This will no doubt go against every fiber of your being, but if you show up sick and get others sick you will not be making fans. You will only serve to undermine your own professional credibility.

On this site you'll discover that there are two types of laryngitis, differentiated by how long the inflammation lasts. Acute laryngitis is a short-lived inflammation of the larynx, lasting up to a week or slightly more (though it seems an eternity!). Chronic laryngitis is simply an ongoing or prolonged inflammation. Naturally, if you don't take care of the former, the latter will result (that's why I bring it up).

Laryngitis is not necessarily contagious. There are a variety of causes, including viral or bacterial upper respiratory tract infections (some of which may be infectious to those around you) and reactions to fungi or molds. Other, less common causes include: exposure to highly concentrated air pollutants (such as spray paint, oven cleaner, or other solvents), smoke inhalation during a closed-space fire, deliberate inhalation of heated fumes (such as in the smoking of crack cocaine), and trauma to the larynx.

If you've had contact with an environmental irritant, acute laryngitis will occur abruptly and will improve just as quickly when the irritant is removed.

Chronic laryngitis occurs when exposure to the irritant is prolonged. Common causes of chronic laryngitis include: allergies, smoking (cigarettes, cigars, marijuana, or anything else), use of inhaled steroids or other orally inhaled products, certain infections, voice misuse or abuse, and chronic coughs.

Obviously, treating laryngitis requires handling of the underlying cause and/or removal of the irritant from the environment.

Hydration and resting the voice are the primary methods of dealing with laryngitis. Avoid exposure to drying agents such as caffeine. Steam or mist humidifiers can help lubricate the vocal folds, and soothing cough drops can help preserve the lubrication of the larynx (I prefer the traditional Luden's). But resting your voice is the only sure way to accelerate the healing process. If you find yourself in this situation, take a nap. It's easier said than done, but honestly you'll feel infinitely better after you do.

If left untreated, laryngitis is thought by some physicians to lead to the development of hyperfunctional voice disorders such as muscle tension, which may contribute to the formation of nodules, polyps, cysts, and scarring. We certainly don't want that, do we?

## Natural Remedies

### How to Ease Your Tired, Sore Throat

There are a few really good remedies to take care of your aching throat. The object here is to hydrate your pipes, and the best, most consistent remedy is a mug of hot water, preferably tea temperature. A simple, piping-hot mug of water will keep you hydrated and slough the cobwebs off your vocal cords. The idea is to allow your vocal cords and all the muscles in your mouth and throat to relax and loosen up, and nothing does a better job than hot water.

Every **Sound Advice** client who enters a coaching or recording session with us starts with a mug of tea-temperature hot water. The difference from the beginning of the session to the end is often dramatic, whether their throat was aching and tired to start with or not. In addition, I insist that all of our clients carry their own bottle of (cold or lukewarm) water with them outside the studio to keep the pipes hydrated.

The hot stuff works wonders during a session if your voice is scratchy and irritated—or even just to keep you sounding stable and take as much effort out of your delivery as possible. It will come in handy take after take when you have a handful of scripts to get through. Just keep it plain. No additives, please!

Tea dehydrates. Slap a teabag on your face (even herbal tea) and let it dry—it'll tighten your skin. I rest my case.
Citrus juices are too abrasive, so stay away from them as well. The object, once again, is to keep you well hydrated. If you need the vitamin C, use a supplement.

The product we endorse most is called **Emergen-C Super Energy Booster,** which is a powder sold in single-serving packets. It's available at many grocery, convenience, and health-food stores. You add the powder to hot or cold water and drink it. Not only does this stuff taste good—it cures quite a few ailments, many worth noting in this chapter. **www.alacercorp.com**

Each packet contains either 500 mg or 1000 mg of vitamin C, 38 mineral compounds, and is high in potassium.  There's a sugar-free variety if you're avoiding sugar.

It will relieve a hangover, take care of a headache, ease sinus and allergy problems, derail a migraine, offset a cold or flu, pick you up when you haven't slept enough, and if you already have a cold, it may offset your symptoms long enough to get you through the session.

This stuff works wonders, even if you're simply fatigued, so it pays to keep it on hand—especially as the winter season carries its share of catch-able ailments past your door.

## Keeping a Cold at Bay

Emergen-C is half the components included in what I refer to as my "flu bomb." If you find yourself coming down with something, follow this to the letter: in a single glass, empty your favorite flavor Emergen-C and an orange **Airborne**. Add water, either hot or cold, but allow the ingredients to dissolve completely. Drink the entire contents. It tastes great and, if you caught the illness within the first 48 hours of your initial symptoms, it's likely you'll avert coming down with anything. (Or the duration of whatever is trying to take over will run its course well within a week.)

Follow-up is key: Repeat the "flu bomb" formula every four to five hours for at least two to three days. Then follow with one flu bomb in the morning and one before bedtime for the remainder of a week—EVEN if you feel fine.

To relieve the symptoms of common colds or allergies, make **Yogi Tea**. Take cloves, black peppercorns, 3-4 cinnamon sticks, crushed (green) cardamom seeds, and slices of fresh gingerroot. Boil the mixture in about two quarts of water for 30 minutes or simmer for up to 3 hours (tops). Lastly, add a strong black tea (either loose leaf or in tea bags). Freeze it or store in the fridge.

## Echinacea *with* Goldenseal

The combination of these two remarkable herbal supplements used in tandem to avert a cold or flu is legendary. And you may find this to be your preference in conjunction with your standard vitamins and at least 2,000 mg to 3,000 mg of vitamin C a day when attempting to stave off illness. However, without eating something rather substantial, echinacea can be hard on the stomach. Generally, when we're under the weather, we often got that way from lack of sleep and proper nutrition. So be sure to "feed the fever," but don't assume you have to "starve a cold," especially if you intend to take echinacea to shorten the duration of whatever ails you.

Further, it's important to note that you should not take echinacea and goldenseal for more than two weeks at a stretch, as your body will develop immunity to the benefits of these medicinal herbs.

## Zinc and Vitamin C

Zinc dries you up when you need it, while vitamin C has the opposite effect. C allows your sinuses to open up and self-moisturize when your eyes, throat, and sinuses are too dry.

If your eyes and/or nose are runny, try 50 to 60 mgs of zinc. It will allow you to get through an hour-long recording session, for example, without incident. Nothing shy of miraculous here. No wonder it's common to smear zinc (in cream form) on a baby's bottom to keep it dry and free of diaper rash.

At **Sound Advice**, you'll always find a small bottle of zinc within a few feet of our booths, no matter which studio you might be in.

## Bruises, Sprains and Aches and Pains

Here's a find: a natural anti-inflammatory and analgesic—possibly even a more effective replacement for Advil or Tylenol. It's called **Traumeel**, a natural remedy that's been around for more than 100 years. It comes in a cream, a gel, or in tablets, but I recommend the cream for the best results. For stiff necks and joints, as well as sprains and back pain, I swear by this stuff! It even reduces the pain and discoloration of bruises.

A small tube of less than four ounces goes a long way and can be found online or at most health-food stores.

## Sleep and Rest, or the Lack Thereof

Take it from someone who comes from a long line of restless insomniacs. There are essentially three remarkable remedies I have to offer to accomplish a good night's sleep. The greatest of these is **Cal-Mag** (a powder consisting of calcium and magnesium only) **by Peter Gillham's Natural Vitality**. Add boiling water to 1 to 3 teaspoons of this incredible powder. Drink it down or add a chamomile tea bag to taste. Point is: It works! And when you've not slept through the night for an extended period of time, that's a huge relief.

Taking **melatonin** every two weeks or so should also help you become truly rested and recharged as well. So this supplement offers long-term help. Make sure your room is dark to glean the greatest results.

The two vitamins that assist in a more restful sleep are **B1**, especially if you have nightmares, and **B6** if you have trouble falling asleep, not just staying asleep.

Exercise helps a great deal too. Although it's best if you accomplish this during the day rather than in the middle of the night, as some have been known to do.

For those who suffer from irregularity and lack of sleep, **Peter Gillham** also makes a supplement known as **Calm**, which contains far more magnesium than Cal-Mag and has proven remarkably effective on either/both of these ailments.

## Best Vocal Sprays

If you have a gig and you woke up with a cough or your feel the dreaded cold coming on (just to add to your drama) be sure to have this on hand for just such emergencies: Quantum makes a terrific product called **Thera Zinc Spray with Echinacea and Elderberry**. At the first sign of a cough, chest cold or runny nose, zinc works wonders, and *this product* is the best I've found, without question. It's incredible!

For a dry throat and a hoarse voice, try **Entertainer's Secret Throat Relief**. It's a well-promoted favorite among voice-overs and is worth trying out.

## The Best Lozenges

The best lozenge I've found when tackling a cold, sore throat, bronchitis, or any combination, is **Elderberry Zinc** herbal lozenges by Zand. It works wonders!  No sugar, but tasty and incredibly effective and fast.  They come in a variety of flavors, but this specific variety offered the best results.

**Cold-Eze** is another brand that works quite well, too, but has a tendency to kill the taste buds.

## Sinus Trouble

Scores of our clients have sworn by this old world remedy known as a **Neti Pot**.  It involves heating water and a simple saline solution, which you run through one nostril at a time.  This process offers the greatest relief of sinus pressure I've found, whether those issues are chronic or not.

## Simply Saline Neti Pot

ARM & HAMMER® Simply Saline® is an all-natural, drug-free way to clear nasal congestion quickly. It's ideal before bedtime or a few hours before a session because it helps open up and clear nasal passages. People who have issues with sinus and/or deviated septums have sworn by the Neti Pot.

## Cold Sores

Taking 1,500 to 3,000 mg of **L-Lysine** at the first twinge of a cold sore will avert the incident in its entirety and lessen an actual outbreak should you not be quick enough.  Of course rest and eating well in conjunction with a good week or two of no less than 1,500 mg of this mineral will lessen the malady dramatically.

## Upset Stomach and Indigestion

Ginger ale, such as Vernor's (The Original Ginger Soda), not only tastes great, it also settles the stomach.

If that's unavailable, some simple San Pellegrino water works wonders, as it has vital minerals and nutrients your body may be lacking.

For additional stomach irritation and nausea (even for kids and pregnant women):

**Ginger Syrup**. Peel and slice fresh ginger and layer the slices in a wide-mouth jar adding sugar between each layer. Continue to layer: ginger-sugar-ginger-sugar. Then add water to "float" the mixture slightly and cover. After 12 to 18 hours, drain, and the mixture is ready to be taken by teaspoonful. Store in your cupboard.  Make homemade ginger ale by mixing mineral water (such as San Pellegrino) in a one-to-one ratio.

Chamomile tea does the trick, too.  There's also the option of taking the random peppermint, or even peppermint tea.

## Diarrhea

**Bilberry Honey.** Grind up dried bilberry or blueberry in a coffee grinder. Add a half-cup of honey and mix. A tablespoonful might just do the trick. Store some on the shelf in your cupboard.

FYI: Herbs typically last for a minimum of two years. If you simply taste them and taste an herb taste, then they are still potent.

## Vitamins
There is something to be said for the proper combination of vitamins and minerals and how they are assimilated into your body.

That said, there are three brands of vitamins I can confidently endorse through experience.

The first is **Metagenics**. Many chiropractors offer this brand, but they can also be found rather easily online. I've seen many a friend, colleague, and client take a simple multivitamin, multi-mineral, and a 1,000 mg of C over the years when they are overtired, run down, or on the verge of catching something, and every one of them would inevitably say after a mere 10 minutes or so, "Hey, that was great! I feel dramatically better." The reason being: It's what their bodies lacked in the first place.

The second brand is simply Whole Foods' **365** brand. They're quite well made and will certainly do the trick.

The final brand, which you can pick up at Trader Joe's, Whole Foods, or any decent natural-foods store, is **Source of Life** vitamins. They have a wonderful multivitamin.

The goal, in any case, is to establish an overall sense of well-being and assist your body in healing itself from environmental stress, fatigue, and wear and tear. The fact remains that if you're sick and run down all the time, no one's going to want to have anything to do with you. It's your responsibility to maintain your health and vitality so that you're ready to deliver your best at a moment's notice.

If you discover, though, that you have a chronic condition beyond simple everyday maladies, you *need* to get a professional opinion (if not two)! PLEASE seek the help of a trusted physician right away.

## Women

Okay, in addition to ensuring you're getting rest and taking proper vitamins and exercising, there are scores of natural supplements that offer relief from the burden of becoming "over-40" (if you follow me), not the least of which is **Extra Strength Estroven**, available at any Trader Joe's or standard drug or grocery store. It's loaded with evening primrose oil, black cohosh, chromium picolinate, green tea extract, grapeseed extract, CoEnzyme Q 10, between 400 and 800 i.u. of vitamin E, 1,000 mg of fish oil, B6 and soy protein. All of these elements work well together in relieving hot flashes, irritability, lack of sleep, as well as a litany of those problematic issues that accompany this stage of life. (I strongly recommend you create your own mix, should you find the Estroven does not tame the beast within.)

Another great product is **R Generator**, a scoop-able powder supplement taken five days a week that offers a boost to your body's ability to create, maintain, and generate its own human growth hormone (HGH).

## Maintaining Your Youth; the +40s

The body makes HGH naturally on its own when we're young, healthy and at the top of our game. However, as we age the body gradually loses its ability to create this "youthful" hormone. But the more we can encourage our body to make HGH on its own, skin tone is better maintained, and we can experience greater vitality, increased metabolism, clarity of thought, more restful sleep, increased immunity, better hair and nails, etc. Athletes often get in trouble from getting injections of HGH; it's illegal in the States. Injections run thousands of dollars a dose, yet once you start receiving shots of HGH, the body will cease creating its own entirely. So the healthiest, least invasive, and only legal way to generate more HGH is a diet that would encourage its production and a supplement such as this.

Men gain the same increased health benefits from this product as well.

## Dehydration, Focus, and Concentrated Energy

Depending on the time of year and where you live, maintaining electrolytes can be an issue. If you become dehydrated from the heat or from adjusting to a new climate after a move, I recommend you let your body adjust by taking **ElectroMix,** which is made by the same company that makes Emergen-C. It's sodium-, calorie-, and sugar-free. It comes in lemon-lime and quickly gives you a sense of well-being so you can be at your best.

When I first moved to Los Angeles from Chicago, I was seriously stressed, barely slept, and felt extremely light-headed and out of sorts most of the day for about two to three months. It's a very different climate and I felt I was dehydrating. I started taking ElectroMix every morning, and it gave my body exactly what it needed.

It's wonderful for concentration as well, as it contains potassium, magnesium, calcium, and chromium—everything you need to sort out blood sugar levels and focus. Great stuff.

## The Smoking Section

It may seem odd, but a lot of voice talent smoke.

In fact, I smoked for the better part of 18 years, not that I'm proud of it. What's more, I was completely hardcore about it—easily two packs a day. Friends of mine who never smoked would light up when I did because they said I made it look good. I loved it.

So how did something that started out social become quite the opposite? Where did I go wrong? When did I become a complete and utter social pariah? And I loved everything about smoking.

Do I smoke now? Nope—not a puff. In fact, it turns my stomach a bit to even consider smoking, many years after I'd quit.

Was it hard? To begin with, sure. But I can honestly say it *wasn't* the hardest thing I've ever done. An awful lot of people will tell you quitting smoking is the hardest thing you'll ever do. Honestly, I have to disagree. I've had far tougher trials test my mettle.

Then there's the whole weight issue.

I'm 5'7" tall, and I weighed 118 pounds when I quit. What kept me from quitting for years on end was the justification that I *might* gain weight if I kicked the habit. That was my logic at the time, and it seems odd to even consider that now. Did I gain weight? Eventually I did, sure. Eight years later. Although after the first year and a half I gained what I now consider an obligatory 10 pounds, which I ultimately lost with my newfound *will of steel*. Granted, I'm not the waif I once was, but I'm certain that has more to do with turning 40 than quitting smoking years before.

The truth is *it's easy to quit*. It's far harder to *remain* off the smokes for good. I knew I could quit, at least for a while. I had "quit" dozens of times before. I just couldn't stay "quit." I kept falling off the wagon.

You have to become determined in your decision to quit—make it an active choice.

At least, that's what I thought at the time. It turns out I was right.

## How to Quit Smoking

The thing is if you want to play at the top of your game, you've got to stop playing through a handicap. Smoking is a major obstacle on so many different levels. Granted, there are a number of truly successful talent who smoke, no doubt about it. But if history serves us, they usually die from it.

When I was smoking, this notion never really put a dent in me. I figured that was what happened to the other guy—not to me, of course—until a month and a half before I quit, I went to my doctor with bronchitis. She shook her head when she saw me and said, "Kate, do you realize this is the fourth time this year I've treated you for bronchitis?"

To be perfectly honest, I *hadn't* realized it. I had no idea. Between you and me, I only went to the doctor if I was about to keel over. In fact, I thought, "Hmm... there were a couple of times when I had bronchitis and I didn't see her at all (gulp)."

She went on to say, "In fact, this is the fourth...fifth...no, *sixth* year in a row you've had bronchitis *at least* four times." At that point, she scribbled out a prescription for an inhaler. It was official, I thought—this was ridiculous. You see, that meant that every other month for at least six years I had had bronchitis and I hadn't even *acknowledged* it. Could that be right? (How embarrassing. Who did I think I was, Bette frickin' Davis?)

"Kate, if you end up with bronchitis again in a few months and you're still smoking, please, find another doctor, because all I'm doing is treating your smoking. At this rate, you'll have emphysema by the time you're forty."

179

All right, so I knew I had to rev up to quit. Fine, fine, fine. I never really thought I'd smoke my whole life anyway. In fact, I avoided dating guys who smoked—I thought it showed a lack of control on their part. And besides, they smelled. All the while, of course, I smoked a solid two packs a day.

Ridiculous, I know, but it's true—all true.

When I decided to quit, I realized that the game was to get *as much time as possible between me and my last puff*. When I did this, this *quitting* thing, it'd be a waste of time not to do it for good. I hate wasting time—to torture yourself for a month or so, then end up smoking as heavily as ever inside a week after succumbing to just a single puff.

Even worse were the scores of people I had talked to about quitting who told me, "Yeah, I quit for about eight years," as they'd puff down another unfiltered Camel. "All it took was one night in a bar over a beer, and here I am back at it again."

"After having even one puff, I was pretty much smoking about a half pack less than a month later," they'd confide to me as they took another long, hot drag from the cigarette they had bummed off me.

Anyway, I needed a plan. I figured I needed to get as much time as possible between my last smoke and me. Thus, I invented "the Game."

## The Game

"Wait five minutes and you won't want one"—became my mantra. Every time I wanted a cigarette, I'd tell myself precisely that. "Wait five minutes and you won't want one." I'd say it out loud. And keep saying it…a lot!

"Drink some water and just wait five minutes, and you won't want one."

Sounds crazy, but it worked! It got me through. Five minutes became a half an hour; a half an hour became an hour. An hour became an afternoon, and *eventually* a full day, and then a week. After a while I completely forgot about wanting one.

180

And a month became six months and six months became a year. If smoking is a numbers game, how many cigarettes are you consuming in a day or week or month; then it stood to reason it worked in reverse. The more time I could put between me and the last puff I had was the game I was playing.

"Just wait five minutes...." I'd heard alcoholics do this—that's where the adage to "take it one day at a time" comes from.

If saying you'll never smoke again for the rest of your life overwhelms you and is too much to confront (and it *always* was for me), it's easier to view what you're attempting to tackle in smaller, more manageable increments. Quitting smoking is a time game.

So, if a whole day is too much to confront, take it hour by hour. If an hour is too much, take it 30 minutes at a time. If a half hour is too much, take 15 minutes. If that's too much, try five minutes.

Personally, I never got as far as an hour—I kept to the five-minute increment pretty consistently until I was on the other side of it, which was about eight weeks altogether. (Not that any hard-core smoker can bear confronting even that. I know I couldn't at first.)

But I avoided drinking alcohol completely because I knew it would undermine my judgment—even after just one beer. I made sure I drank at least three to four liters of water a day and kept physically busy. And kept to my mantra, "Wait five minutes and you won't want one..." I wanted smoking behind me once and for all.

## Cautionary Tale

About two weeks after I quit I went out for a *single* margarita. One and *only* one, I told myself, and my friend who had "quit" smoking too. Anymore than that and I knew I would be vulnerable to completely losing it and blowing two good weeks of nonsmoking accomplishments.

Well, when all was said and done, I had finished the margarita and hardly tasted it—instead I had squirmed in my seat the entire time for want of my beloved ciggies. I found myself completely preoccupied with this guy at the bar who was—ooohhh, lookie there—he's smoking my brand! Look at him! He looks so happy! I couldn't take my eyes off him. I wrestled with myself for a good 45 minutes before removing myself from the scene entirely. I drained my drink and started for the door. Walking out, I passed him.

"You don't know how close you came to losing that pack of cigarettes tonight," I told him through a clenched jaw.

"Oh, would you like one?" he asked.

"No, I don't want *one*, I want the whole damn *pack!*" I joked.

At that moment, I realized, that was the absolute truth. One smoke would never satiate the urge I had brewing. I actually imagined inhaling the entire pack; suddenly, I couldn't take a deep enough breath. In fact, I couldn't fully breathe at all. My chest felt tight, my heart was racing. I gave myself another five minutes to get over it, but I was struggling.

An hour or so later, when I wanted to smoke again, and I reminded myself of that sensation of not being able to breathe, not being able to satiate the urge no matter how many "smoky snacks" I might inhale. No amount of smoke would honestly be able to scratch the itch entirely. My breath seemed shorter. I was clearly going through withdrawal, and I felt like crap. When was I going to feel good about this?! This must be what emphysema must feel like, I thought—until, of course, you eventually succumb to the disease. It was awful.

But I never succumbed. I got past it. That was more than 18 years ago. So it can be done. For good!

It's worth mentioning, prior to this very last time when I finally quit smoking, whenever I would cave and have "just one," I would find I wanted to smoke more than ever, as if to catch up for lost time or something. So, I made the conscious decision to stay the course. I already knew the traps. If you're addicted to *anything*, that's apparently what you ultimately have to do. Nicotine is no different. It's a drug.

It *feels* like *food* (most drugs do), which is part of the reason people can justify doing it for as long as they do. But it's not food. It's not sustenance. It's a *drug*, and if you smoke—you're addicted. If it's running you, you have to _decide_ to conquer it—or it will most certainly conquer you. Says so, right on the box. So the manufacturer is off the hook.

I might not have realized it at the time, but I had passed a real milestone that night. I actually made a conscious decision that when I _did_ go, smoking was not how it was going to happen. I told myself to wait another five minutes and _I wouldn't want one_. An hour or so later, I was asleep, and I had gotten through another day. And the next day was actually a whole lot easier.

That two-week mark was the toughest to get to and then surpass. Then the four-week mark and the six-week mark got a little easier, and another milestone. Eight weeks was another one. Yet the more time I could put between me and that last puff, the more faith I had that I could keep it up and continue.

## Will I Ever Feel Better?

Around the sixth to eighth week after my very last puff, I thought I would have felt better than I actually did. I still felt crappy physically. It was discouraging. It occurred to me at the time, "This is clearly why a lot of people go back to smoking at this point."

But I stayed with "the Game" and started working out, and sitting in a sauna a couple of times a week—it seemed like I needed to kick out the remnants that were still driving the urge.

Then (and I realize this sounds completely cliché), I literally woke up one morning feeling better than I had (it seemed) my entire life. I could inhale deeply, which I couldn't remember doing since I was a little kid.

I honestly didn't know how lousy I felt until I felt _good_. It was dramatic, and it may sound totally unreal to you if you've never quit smoking, but it's the truth.

The bottom line is, if you smoke and want to quit, you have to know that it's a big-time game. If you don't smoke for a whole afternoon, it feels like a big deal, right? By the same token, you usually feel like you've made miles of progress if you haven't smoked for a couple days—until you end up lighting up once again.

## How to Begin
### Simply Make the Decision to Be Smoke-free

If you seriously want to quit smoking, begin by being totally honest with yourself. Don't attempt to quit for anyone else. It's a personal goal. You have to challenge *yourself* continually to *put as much time as possible between you and your last puff*. Otherwise that small box of cigarettes will run your whole day.

But sooner or later, if you're a professional talent, you'll have to confront the fact that you're playing through your body. And if you smoke, you're making your body play through a handicap.

Believe it or not, I've heard numerous talent say, "I think I have more control over my voice if I smoke." To that, I can only reply, "How would you know? You have nothing to compare it with." The experiment's a bit one-sided, frankly.

It takes almost three months to clear most of the tar and nicotine out of your lungs alone. It all just boils down to another excuse to maintain the habit, though—it's just another justifier.

No one can make you quit. And you can't really do it for anyone but yourself. It has to be something you *need* for yourself, before it gets so out of hand that you find yourself on a respirator or going under the knife.

YOU have to decide. You have to make the decision that you won't smoke for your entire life. You won't be run by a little box that determines where you go, how much money you have on you, what your breath and clothes and hair smell like. And that's just for starters.

I want to encourage you to take your destiny into your own hands. You have to decide when you've hit your saturation point. Smoking *is* finite—you may as well make a conscious choice, while you can.

# II. Production:

**Performance, Auditions, and Demos**

# Chapter 11:
# The *sound advice* Approach

"For me… (my approach), it's improvisational.
But, it's real science."
—Denzel Washington

Technique training can be rather tricky. Especially when it's commonly thought in our field "there's no single approach considered more effective than another." We hope to challenge that. As we see it: Acting is acting is acting.

At **Sound Advice** we propose there are a handful of technical demands you must tackle with each medium, but basically the same demands are needed from you as a talent regardless of the medium.

The concepts we impart to you in this chapter are just a few of our own signature training, which we consider *the **Sound Advice** Approach*. A second book dedicated to this approach and primarily to performance will ultimately follow this publication. Until then,

187

our one-on-one coaching and this chapter will have to suffice. (We offer coaching through **Sound Advice** in either our Chicago or Los Angeles studios, or we can coach clients through the use of Skype and Source-Connect regardless of their location.)

Having coached more than 10,000 people to date, varying in ages from 4 to 89, I've managed to determine what I consider the common denominators of what the actor experiences and needs to know and do on any given job, and further, what those who have hired him expect and need. **Sound Advice** has offered me a fascinating opportunity to observe and define a few steadfast tools here that can only assist the entire production, regardless of the medium, if employed with consistency.

That said, there are a few **common misconceptions** in the way, right out of the gate, such as:
- Those who have hired you are after a single, perfect take
- You'll be required to do only a take or two and then you're done
- Those who hired you *know precisely what they want*
- You'll receive direction that will determine your delivery

Most of us have the idea that those folks on the other side of the glass on a voice-over session will be feeding us every nuance and notion. Now, this may be something of a lightning bolt striking from the blue, but you are not likely to get *any* direction at all! The direction you do get will be limited, if not flat-out confusing, which is why we've taken the time to define the limited vocabulary you may come across on a commercial session or shoot.

(See "The Most Common Direction: Defined" in Chapter 13, What's Expected of You As a Talent.)

Far too many actors kill a perfectly wonderful opportunity to play and create by trying to second-guess the director or producer. To heck with that—how do *you* think the spot should go? Don't think about it; don't tell us what you're going to do—just DO IT (there's a reason why it's called *acting*). Work it up in the lobby or the greenroom or some hallway just off the auditioning area, but whatever you do, play with it! Don't sit and wait for someone to come hold your hand and lead you.

Don't assume the copy (the script) is broken simply because you don't get it yet. If you don't get it yet, either read it out loud until you do or (here's a novel idea) ASK! If there's anything *to* get, I'm certain they'd be happy to tell you.

On the other hand, if you happen to know the grammar is incorrect or the sentence is actually saying something other than what the advertisers are truly driving at, by all means, *tactfully* let the powers that be know. But be sure *you* know that's truly the case before even opening your gob!

Ninety-nine percent of the time, there's no hidden message. The director is usually trying his hardest not to step on your talented toes by giving you a line reading—so give the guy a break. Get in there and have a ball. But if he has a suggestion you truly can't decipher, tell him to give you a line reading! It's not going to hurt anyone. It cuts to the chase, and everyone goes home happy. Maybe they'll invite you back to play with them again sometime.

You obviously have the stuff—you wouldn't be there if you didn't—so let the director see how you'd tell this story. If he has a specific idea, he'll guide you toward it—just listen and apply from there. And if the director needs a line to be said in a certain way, remember this: You're there to help. In the meantime, be decisive in your reads. Be bold. Have fun. Stretch the canvas, as I like to say. Keep it loose. And be willing to drop that attack and go in a completely different direction. THAT'S THE JOB!  We're all about service, baby.

You are truly capable of a *limitless* number of deliveries. Make it your mission at the onset of every audition and every session to discover just a few of them *on the spot* by means of play. *That's* what you're getting paid for.

You are *not,* on the other hand, paid to judge each delivery you make. Deciding for the director which take *you* happened to like best is rarely—if ever—welcome. Trust me, you don't have the best vantage point to make that call. There are a few big pieces to this puzzle that you are clearly missing.

Let it go. It's not your job to piece the whole thing together anyway. Your job is simply to stand and deliver in your most alive, animated, genuine way. *Capisce*? Obviously, you have brought to the table what it is they need to complete that detail of the spot, so get in there and play. And, please, have some fun with it, will you?

## Objective vs. Subjective Training

The training you receive from **Sound Advice** is unique in that it is purpose-driven. In fact, it's easy to attribute the success rate of our clients to this very objective training.

The truth is, most acting training is completely subjective, based solely on the whim of the coach or director. That is to say, most coaching is done without any specific purpose or intended result.

Frankly, if you don't know what you're trying to accomplish, then you're at a decided disadvantage. This could explain, in part, why so many talent go off and unnecessarily spin their wheels on random details that ultimately derail their progress and performance. It's this lack of results that ultimately frustrates them to the point of utter paralysis.

At **Sound Advice**, our goal is to remove as much *subjectivity* from your training as possible and replace it with ardent *objectivity*.
The primary focus behind our coaching is: If you know what you're striving for, if you know what to look for in the script—even if the producer, director, or copywriter aren't quite sure what the piece needs—you can then deliver a handful of strong creative options within the context of the piece, all of which will be uniquely yours.

This unique process was designed to replace that critical little voice in your head and allow you to concentrate on the adjustments you need to make with each take to deliver the most playful, most skillful performance possible.

Address what's expected of you in the field, in any medium (voice-over, television, film, or stage).

## Beginner, Intermediate, and Advanced

Every talent is essentially on the same level playing field when it comes to landing the work, which is precisely why we at **Sound Advice** don't conduct beginner, intermediate, and advanced classes. I don't believe in it. It doesn't exist in the field, so why would it exist in training, where we are trying to re-create practical application training for the talent? I consider everyone I work with a professional and expect them to act as such. If it doesn't exist in the field—it has no place in training.

There's no litmus test out in the field used to keep a newcomer from landing a principal role in a film over a career veteran. In fact, you're very likely to be cast opposite children who have far more experience than you and older talent who have never done a thing. If the talent is correct for the part, they make themselves available to the work and they're cast—there ya go. No beginning, intermediate, and advanced categories to go by. Think of it: If these classifications were in place when Laurence Olivier was working, he would have had no one to play off. It's ridiculous.

That said, while the industry is always in the market for new voices, the goal is certainly to become known as one of the tried-and-true. No matter your ability, you're either known or you're not. Certainly producers and copywriters will stick with the talent they've had a fair amount of success with when they are in a pinch. Wouldn't you, if your career depended on it? Of course you would. THAT'S the talent we all aim to become, regardless of your experience level. And you can achieve this with dedication and persistence. If you make yourself accessible to the work continually—not just for three months or six months or eight—and if you dedicate yourself to this as a profession, then you *will* work.

You can't compete if you don't rise to the occasion on a professional scale. You must have the proper materials to represent you well when you're not there. That means you must have a competitive demo that will rise above the din! And that means you must first be trained.

# Technique

Technique is the process you apply to achieve results in a performance or promotion. This term literally applies to *every* single aspect of this business—performance, promotion, marketing—it's a vital component to achieve any form of success.

Ironically, no one is interested in seeing or being made aware of your technique any more than any one wants to be made aware of your DNA. Yet, like DNA, it's the stuff that holds the whole delivery together. The difference is technique requires development in order for it to blend fully into the scenery and become a natural part of your professional fabric.

Generally, it's most commonly associated with performance. Method acting, Meisner, Linklater, and Lessac are some of the better-known modern techniques that make up so much of the American acting training palette. Well-schooled talent should be familiar, at least in theory, with these over the course of their career if for no other reason than to have a reference of them should the need arise. They all have their merits, to a greater or lesser degree.

As you might have guessed, when it comes to creating a process for running the business of your career, a bit more structure is required. Even the notion of incorporating order and routine into the mix is usually met with resistance by most artists. Yet without it, it's not likely their art or therefore their performance will endure.

And if it's true that great art endures because it continues to communicate, then I'd like to take that one step further. I tend to think art continues to communicate because it remains accessible— much like pop culture.

For art, like anything worthwhile, you must persist. In fact, in order to accomplish ANYTHING you must persist, but certainly that's especially true when it comes to your career.

If you fear selling out to commercial work, for instance, you're not alone. In fact, you are probably in the majority. This might account for the scores of talent that take a stab at a career as an actor only to give up a short time later, hanging their hat on the fact that they repel transferring their skills to another medium, namely commercial work.

You've actually conformed to this notion, you know, just as much as you may have conformed to the mass-pop culture you probably embraced as a child. In doing so, you have already succumbed to the first great artistic litmus test to which most talent give in: the notion that if you do commercial work you've sold out. It's beaten into all of us who have enjoyed an art- or theater-school background.

Ultimately, it's quite confusing, really. Commercials aren't cool, but pop culture should be embraced. Go figure.

We're also taught that an artist must forsake *everything* for his art, including pay, as long as it's for the love of the work. This is probably why so many young talent have the idea they are expected to accept *all manner of work* regardless of the dent in makes in their integrity or the hardship it places on their lives.

This is often the button that less-than-credible individuals will push when you inform them you really need to keep that shift at the restaurant rather than hand out promotional snacks at the ballpark for eight hours. Keep the day job if it pays more. That's the sensible thing to do. Even if you think that agent will never call you again.

Moral to the story: Choose your battles and aim higher—always!

There are times you should take a leap of faith, and it's not always clear when to seize those opportunities.

So many of our best-trained stage actors flounder for years in bad, or at best *mediocre*, local stage productions that (hopefully) feed the aesthetic soul but often nothing else.

These folks may develop their stage technique by flexing this muscle, but their ability to transfer those skills from one medium to another is almost always completely nonexistent.

Put a stage actor on a microphone in a recording booth and he's suddenly projecting with great volume to the back of the house when what's actually required of him is almost always far more one-on-one and intimate. The problem is a stage actor is used to his entire body being seen from head to toe. Making the adjustment from walking the boards to a mic in a small padded room is seldom easy.

Conversely, the radio personality who spends every day on a mic almost always tends to be very announce-y, attacking the mic exactly the same way on every single spot, whether it's appropriate for the script or not.

As talent, we tend to create our own individual technique, regardless of our background or level of experience. In fact, we are more likely to create a comfort zone out of muscle memory the moment we step in front of a mic, whether or not it happens to be a good habit.

This is precisely why at **Sound Advice** we've developed *The 10 Principles of Performance,* the technique we employ in all our one-on-one coaching, in-studio workshops, and demo production. The objective of the 10 Principles of Performance is to give every talent, regardless of training level or experience; precisely what to aim for on every single take, regardless of the medium. The principles allow you to be about as specific as you can get while keeping your imagination stoked take after take, performance after performance.

## A Time Art

A time art is best defined as an art that relies on time or moments for effect. All performance, especially if it's recorded, falls under this definition.

It's imperative you surprise yourself, take after take, and that each read be a little different than the last. Voice-over, like all acting, is a time art. You have a whole new moment with each take and within each take, with each line. With each moment you will have a thought that evolves.

Nothing in this world stays the same from start to finish. Things are either expanding or contracting, building or decaying. Nothing remains static.

This is an opportunity to create and discover with each take—all within the parameters of what's being asked of you—because the truth is you are capable of a limitless variety of takes. What's expected of you is just a few takes that relate to what the creatives are driving toward, and even surprising them a bit as well.

## Everyone Says I Should Do Voice-over

Just because you have an interesting, textured voice doesn't mean you know how to turn a phrase. Voice-over takes practice and training.

If you're simply interested in doing announce, you may be able to get by if you make yourself available to the people who are casting for that sort of work. In the more rural areas, more mainstream voices are generally required. In the bigger metropolitan areas, the more unusual, quirky, or textured voices tend to be in demand.

No matter what it is you do, you simply must persist until you find the audience for your sound or delivery. That's the truth. If history teaches us anything, that's always been the case. That means you must persist at working your abilities and define them in demo form so your demo can audition for you when you're not (physically) there.

But you need to develop your skills *before* you invest in producing a demo.

When we produce demos at **Sound Advice**, we record as much as 20 hours of commercial and narrative text. This is where our clients cut their teeth and gain practical experience. Then, we take time and care producing each of these spots and craft a demo that will go the distance professionally, for each individual talent.

But we do all this only *after* we have done a fair amount of *foundation coaching*, regardless of the skill level, so that we're on the same page and you know what's needed and expected from you on an actual session. If we did anything less, we'd be doing you a disservice.

You must be trained. I don't care if you already know how to act for the stage, or speak in front of an audience or on mic.

You must be able to back up everything you have on your demo with performance. If you can't re-create a read without the virtues of production, you should not even attempt to have it on your demo. If you can do it, but it takes some work on your part, you better get working! If you haven't kept your skills up, and you're not able to deliver a read you have representing you on your demo, you'll only disappoint the client, the director, your agent and, inevitably, yourself.

Training is a constant. You must continually work your chops. It's your job, no matter how far along in this profession you may have come or intend to go.

## Get Grounded

Before you even open your mouth in any audition or session, standing in front of the mic, plant your feet shoulder-width apart, with knees loose (this will help you ground yourself and avoid room noise—including the shuffling of your own feet).

Make sure your mouth is slightly slack, and your cheeks and tongue are relaxed and easy. Allow your mouth to hang open just a bit. Let all the muscles in your face relax. This will help you avoid creating mouth noise right from the onset.

Begin each take from a neutral place—relaxed and easy. Keep it simple from head to toe! Simply saying to yourself, "nice and easy" allows you a moment to focus before you begin.

The adjustment all talent should continually be making from one take to the next, even if the director is ecstatic and swooning all over you (which will rarely, if ever, happen), is to make the read a little easier and a little more fluid. That's it! That's the tweak of all tweaks. Ease and fluidity are *always* the goal.

## "Muscle Memory Delivery"

At **Sound Advice** we refer to a muscle-memory delivery as a read that is by rote and runs as if on a circuit. (It's not to be confused with the American Method actor definition of muscle memory.) In fact, what we refer to as a muscle-memory read is an impulse encoded into the muscles from the very first read. So if you've been worried you might have trouble repeating a delivery—fear not. Muscle memory will practically *ensure* you continually come back to your initial read over and over and over again—whether you want to or not! Left to its own devices, your delivery will run on automatic by pure virtue of muscle memory.

I would not consider a muscle-memory delivery to be something to strive for. In fact, it is quite the opposite, because what's needed and wanted from you as a talent is to deliver *a variety of reads*, within the parameters dictated by either the text or your interpretation or the intent of the director or writer or any combination thereof. So, basically, you must work *against* the muscle-memory read if you hope to deliver a few truly creative options.

To give you an example of just how ingrained muscle memory really is, consider this: If you were to take a bus three days in a row to the exact same location—wherever you sat the first day out, you are most likely going to try and sit in the exact same seat the second and the third day. If on the third day, someone is sitting in "your" seat, you're probably going to sit as close to your original seat as possible. In fact, you're probably going to feel a bit pissed off that guy has taken your seat. Now, it really doesn't matter where you sit on the bus to get from point A to point B, yet we develop this comfort zone from our first attempt, and we tend to cling to it whether it's necessary or not. There's comfort in familiarity, and we want to make it familiar immediately.

Well, familiar is one thing, repetitive is quite another.

I'm sure there is something to be said for this impulse. Without it we may not have lasted on this planet as a species. There's certainly something to be said for persistence—and that's all it really is: an impulse to persist. It just goes to show you—if you persist you will succeed, eventually.

In the meantime, our goal as talent is to deliver a few good options within the context of the piece. Whether we're talking film, television, or commercial voice-over, you are always expected to deliver a few options.

So at **Sound Advice,** we've made it our mission to make agility the routine. We attempt to make variety overcome muscle memory, of course; again, within the context. But sometimes you have to color outside the lines to discover what "too far" means. You may discover it's nearly impossible to go too far as long as your delivery is genuine.

If your delivery is simply running on the muscle-memory read, it's a by rote read and there is no real original thought connected with it. Muscle memory negates the moment, which is counterproductive. The sooner you acknowledge it and exercise your skills to work beyond it, the sooner you will truly be playing with real freedom and abandon that makes a valuable, spontaneous, clever, authentic read—which is just what's expected of us on every single take!

## "Stretching the Canvas"

*Stretching the canvas* is a **Sound Advice** term that refers to animating your delivery beyond what you'd consider appropriate from the very first take and delivering a performance beyond your natural defaults and comfort zone. To the character actor it means an outrageously broad, over-the-top interpretation of the text. To anyone else, it almost inevitably allows for an absolute bull's-eye of a take. This is a great exercise to discover a new delivery, especially when initially approaching very serious, often flat, copy and when you're trying to break out of a muscle memory delivery (a read that repeats again and again as if by rote).

You must allow yourself to *go way too far* in your first initial delivery, whether the script requires it, then drop that read and deliver the piece once again.

What you will have there is one of two things: a) a terrifically on-target performance with the correct estimation of energy included, which is what the director was truly after in the first place. Too often, when making their own adjustment from stage to on-camera or voice-over, talent downplay what they're doing and in doing so, come across as completely introverted. So what feels like an over-the-top read to you (the talent making this adjustment), may actually be exactly what the director is going for.

Or, b) some of that residual energy you used in the first over-the-top read will spill over into the second and give it more life and expression. Either way, there's loads of discovery in those reads because you've just played something you never heard yourself. Certainly, at first, it may feel like it's broken because you've just broken the muscle-memory mold on whatever delivery you kept coming back to (which was probably remarkably similar to one of your first three reads, way back when it was cold). You have to be that bold! By doing so, you'll find yourself on the brink of brilliance. So, play it. Stretch the canvas as far and as wide as you can. This is precisely how you will find something new and avoid playing every read by rote. (That'll snuff your creativity right where you sit before you've ever given yourself a chance.)

## Move Your Body

Even though you're just standing in front of a microphone, you have to express yourself with your whole body. You can't make your mouth do all the acting here. So, back up your sound with your body! That means gesture! Your body backs up your voice!

As a test, record yourself reading a piece of copy with continued gestures as you speak, then record yourself without. Which delivery do *you* prefer? Thought so. It's far more alive when you allow your body to back up your read!

So get moving—give it a pulse! You're paid to have a pulse!

## Cinematic Shorthand

As talent, we sometimes indulge ourselves with these "layers of internal monologue," which can impede the simple telling of the story and add a mechanical effect, complete with pauses for all those excessive mental movie thoughts and cues.

When we are directed to "tighten up the performance" we're required as actors to mentally edit out the excessive pauses designated to allow for all those mental cues.

199

Therefore, we refer to this as cinematic shorthand, which allows for a greater economy of performance that is more direct and to the point.

A *commercial* example of cinematic shorthand would be this short fictitious McDonald's ad:

> The on-camera scene depicts a young, frenzied assistant-type dashing to and fro on a busy city street while he delivers files and such.
>
> The voice-over comes in, "You're running around and you need to get lunch—*fast!*"
>
> We see our young assistant rub his stomach when a light bulb goes on above his head.
>
> "So, you drive through McDonald's for a hamburger, fries, and a Coke."
>
> We see a pristine, glimmering burger, fries and Coke turning slowly on a Lazy Susan. "Now..."
>
> We see our assistant receive his order in a perfectly tidy white Mickey D's bag at the drive-in window, then we see him post-lunch—a satisfied character, dabbing the corner of his mouth, smiling.
> "...Isn't that better?"
>
> The mnemonic *"I'm Lovin' It"* plays on a solo electric guitar to indicating the youthful target market.

We don't see the McDonald's crew in the kitchen making the burger or even the fellow eating the burger. Nope. The scenario is established at the top: young guy, working hard. The problem: hunger. The solution: McDonald's. The result: satisfaction. There you have it. That's the essence of cinematic shorthand.

## You Can't Tell Yourself How *Not* to Do Something

Before you even open your mouth to utter your first syllable—before you even set foot in the booth—know that there's already an internal monologue going on inside your little noggin. In fact, I can hear it all the way over here like some small child banging on a tin pan with a hammer and—what's that? It's assessing and coloring your every move.

That head of yours is going to keep chatting away whether you like it or not. The ultimate point here is that *you can't tell yourself how not to do something!*

Say it. Go on—say it out loud. You can't tell yourself how *NOT* to do something. It's fruitless. If you do, you are concentrating on how you *DON'T* want the spot to go and, as a result, that is *precisely* how your performance actually *will* go. Mark my words. I call it banana directing. As if you're telling yourself, "Whatever you do, don't think of a banana."

What did I tell you? You've got a big, bright, shiny yellow one dangling there in the ether, now don't ya?

Your brain doesn't register the "don't" when you're telling yourself how to do something. It only gets "banana." Same goes for performance—if you're directed to "Keep the beginning just like it was, but DON'T go up on the word *pupil*," you're going to have to tell yourself to *go down* on the word *pupil*. Reverse the flow, as it were.

How does that work? Well, nearest I can figure it, you don't generally tell a computer how NOT to do something. And what you have up there in your skull (you know, your brain) happens to be the most effective computer you've got at your access. Therefore, you have to tell it how you want the read to go—not the other way around! Whatever elements you want to employ into your delivery, be sure you run down your mental checklist prior to going into the next read, tell yourself what you *want* in the delivery and then just GO! Be decisive! That's how this whole performance thing *really* works.

What's that? All this seems a bit simplistic? Give it a try! Go ahead. I dare you. There's power in simplicity. Never underestimate it.

The reason this works consistently so well is simply because that's how your noodle operates. You have to tell it how to do something, not how NOT to do something.

Yes, I'm repeating myself—I'm trying to get a point across here. Some folks are only just coming out of the fog! Granted, this idea is a bit of a mental pretzel at first glance, but it's the truth. If I thought graphs and diagrams would help illustrate this idea I'd have put them in here, but they don't apply, so pay attention!

You'll want to keep this hot little tip in mind on your next recording session—especially when you find yourself doing take after take after take, and the entire experience starts to become something of a surreal event. How many takes of the word *if* can you do while giving it some variety *and* staying completely out of your head? Trust me. A session can become very weird in a heartbeat.

That recording booth can become something of a sensory deprivation tank if you're not careful. As talent, we're expected to keep our imagination alive and vivid and our delivery playful and new while giving the director/producer a variety of options, take after take. On any given session, we're not after *one* perfect read—we're after a few of them. So staying with it, being awake and current and "in the moment" (to quote those Method Actor types) is an absolute must.

# Chapter 12: Auditions

"When you go to meetings or auditions and you fail
to prepare, prepare to fail. It is simple but true."
—Paula Abdul

Auditions are an art unto themselves. The more of them you do, ideally, the better you get.

The fact is, no one is all that keen on auditions, producers and talent alike. It's nerve-racking for both sides of the production process; those casting are worried you're better on your demo or in the audition process than you will be on the job, and talent are just plain worried about what it is they don't know.

On one hand, some talent become expert auditioners but can't deliver when ultimately put to the test. They often harbor the erroneous notion that once booked they are expected to deliver a flawless performance in one single take after which the entire studio will explode into spontaneous applause and then they can go home. The only real difference between the audition and the session is the number of takes. A booking may require 5 takes, or it may require 55 takes. (It varies dramatically from job to job, and from director to director.) Whereas on the audition, we usually get only one or two takes regardless of the project, regardless of the medium.

Still others are only good once they land the job, but bridging the gap from unemployment to employment remains the eternal dilemma and demands they master the art of the audition.

I know, I know. I can hear all those young hopefuls, pining, "Can't someone just take a chance (on you) so (you) don't have to go through this ridiculous process." In a word: no. Creatives and talent agents alike look good only *if you do*—and if you don't pan out, they feel the brunt of your professional missteps even more directly than you ever will as a talent. (This explains the cold, harsh reception you're often met with when you first embark on securing representation, doesn't it?)

## A Numbers Game

Auditions are promo. And, for voice-over, they aren't and should never be the sole form of promotion, due to the simple fact that relying on a *single* talent agent from a *single* region to supply you with enough auditions is not a viable option. Statistics dictate that it generally takes between 150 and 200 auditions to book a job. If you're getting two to three auditions a week from the *one* talent agent you have then it'll take you *a year to land a single job*! You have to increase the odds in your favor. One of the great benefits of voice-over is that fact that you can (and should) secure numerous talent agents in a variety of regions across the country. With consistent, targeted promotions driving traffic to your voice-over demo Web site you can effectively be cast directly off your demo. You'll increase your odds by a significant margin if you do.

In order to land a job, for both voice-over and on-camera work, *auditioning* is generally required of nearly every rank and file talent. And to make the best use of valuable production time, headshots, voice-over demos, and on-camera reels (promo) are generally used in advance of your audition to determine whether you're the correct type, look, style, and personality required for the specific casting project.

Voice-over demos and on-camera reels can act as an effective substitute for an audition on occasion in large part because they are thought to be the best example of what you have to offer as a professional, and what sort of work you are seeking *more* of. So if your professional tools are not up to date or are low grade and makeshift, you may be keeping yourself from landing jobs you might be perfect for.

After submitting your promo you may be called in for an audition. The more auditions you do, the more you make yourself known, and the more familiar you'll become to those most likely to hire you.

However, if you only come to life when you're all alone, and clam up in front of others during an audition, or only respond in one- or two-word responses—then it's a deal killer.

EVERYONE experiences nerves. Surviving them is the key. Redirecting nervous energy into performance energy is done by allowing yourself to BE nervous, rather than fighting it.

The more you expose yourself to auditioning opportunities, the more comfortable you'll become, and the more realistic your expectations, the more you can be yourself and the more conversational and communicative you can be during the audition/interview process—and ultimately the greater your likelihood for booking the job.

Even with exceptional headshots, which will need to be reshot every 8 months to a year or so until you are nearly 30 years old (no kidding), with a remarkable on-camera reel, and an incredibly well-produced commercial voice-over demo—all auditioning for you in lieu of your presence—you still need to bring your very best performance consistently to every audition. The only way this comes about is from exposure. And that translates into logging in scores of auditions under your belt until your auditions and your overall performance become seamless.

## The _ONLY_ Difference Between the Audition and the Session

There's a lot to realize about auditioning, not the least of which is that there is very little difference between your audition and your actual performance. You must treat _every_ audition as if it were a booking. And the _only_ difference between the job (booking) and the audition is _the number of takes_ expected from you.

On an audition, it's extremely rare that you'd be given more than two to three attempts to deliver the performance you wish to submit. You're expected to be decisive and offer the _same_ performance energy, the _same_ uninhibited imagination and full-on

205

creativity—all the same performance goals that are expected and required of you on the job must be present *at the audition,* or you'll never get to the session.

> Every major job you ever landed, you booked because you stuck your neck out—not because you played it safe. You took a risk.

In some respects, your imagination and creativity are challenged *even more* so at the audition than on the session, simply because at the audition you have to make a great leap of faith as to what the production may require of you, or ultimately look like. Therefore, it's imperative you're committed and decisive in your choices to garner the greatest results.

Think about it—any major job you ever landed, you booked because you stuck your neck out—not because you played it safe. You took a risk.

This is the basis for all of our performance training at **Sound Advice** and the focus of our overall approach to acting.

## The Art of Self-Direction

Even if you've been pursuing your career ambitions for a few years, you still may harbor the misconception that you will be offered very specific direction, and that those auditioning you know exactly what they want.

We can't even count how many times we've heard (seemingly) seasoned talent say, "I just saw the commercial I auditioned for last week. Heck, I would have done that if they would have told me to do it that way!"

Chances are *no one* told the guy who booked the job to do it that way! He brought in a great deal of imagination and spirit of play with him when he auditioned for the job. THAT'S what booked that guy: a decisive, confident talent who made the text sound as if that's exactly what he was thinking/what he knows, and he has an honest point of view about it. Don't assume he was directed precisely what to do. Granted at the audition (just like you) he may have been given, "Just play it natural, with some personality."

You must learn to trust yourself completely by taking an 8,000-foot dive into a Dixie Cup. However, none of this is immediately intuitive. It takes repeated exposure to taking chances. And that begins with discovering how to effectively self-direct under pressure.

Auditions, by design, require you offer your own interpretation of the copy. So, rather than concerning yourself with, "What do they want from me?" Instead concentrate on "Here's how I think it should go!" Make definite decisions and commit wholeheartedly to that attack.

> Energy is interest.
> *If you are interested,*
> *you are interesting.* It's true in
> life, but it's especially true
> in performance.

Granted if you are actually given direction, you're required to be just as committed to that delivery as you were to your own a moment later—regardless of how different this attack might be from the direction you were initially headed.

Do yourself a favor and do NOT memorize your script! This will only paint you into one delivery that reads like a broken record and ultimately lacks spontaneity and inspiration. You're expected to create on your feet. So PLAY!

Developing these skills requires you work this muscle a great deal until you seem confident in what you are doing.

To book the job you have to step it up in terms of energy—not *speed and volume*, but actual *energy*. *Go further* than you think is truly required of you from the very first take and you will most likely hit a bull's-eye.

There's nothing safe in playing it safe.  In fact, it's a detriment. They'd rather pull you back than come at you with a whip and a chair.  That's a promise.

As valuable as theater training is to an actor, this is the one medium you will actually be given a fair amount of direction, but it's not likely you'll receive much direction in any other medium (voice-over, TV, film, commercial work, narration) beyond, "Can you go up on this word?" Or, "Can you go down on that one?"

In fact, the most direction you can count on will probably seem extremely vague and may even seem completely contradictory. These include a "softer confidence," a "wise innocence," or even an "intelligent stupidity."  Yes, each of these are actual directions given on real sessions, so careful what you wish for, you might just get it.

So, you could say the audition demands on-the-spot decision-making regarding your performance: You're expected to get off the ground from a very short runway.  On the other hand, at the booking, they expect stamina and many effortless, spontaneous deliveries from what could easily be a very long runway.

Since you can't book the job without mastering the audition, it's imperative you deliver your very best from the very start *always*, rather than ramping up into your performance as so many talent (sometimes indulgently) allow themselves.  This tends to become a performance habit that far too many talent bring into the session as well, if they do get cast.

Save yourself:  Read the script *out loud* at least six to eight times through. The script sounds dramatically different out loud than it does "in your head."

Try not to fall into the trap of finding everything you hate about the script, in fact, the opposite.  Find something you can *like* about it. Repelling the script or concept will not help you or your audition. Instead, ask yourself, "How do YOU think this spot should go?" What is it about this script, this line, this project can you really like? This can and will significantly alter your performance—for the better!

On the booking, whoever hired you (the creatives, the producers, the director) are all simply after a few *options* from you. This means you're expected to *deliver every take with a slightly different* inflection, while remaining true to the framework of what's being asked of you. The general idea is to remain creative and offer a handful of options, rather than mimic a broken record take after take.

You're capable of a limitless number of exceptional deliveries, and your aim should be to offer a handful of these exceptional reads, within the context of the project. Give them "fabulous" on one take and "remarkable" on the next. That's honestly the job of a professional talent, regardless of the medium.

## What Do They Want From Me?

Consistently you'll be asked to "be yourself." Those casting you want YOUR interpretation of the script. We want the most dynamic, spontaneous, "YOU" you can be!

Besides, most casting sources *know what they don't want* rather than what they do. (You may even hear, "They'll know it when they see it.") And as a result, many novice talent set out to determine what a client might want from them using deductive reasoning; they attempt to rule out all the don'ts rather than concentrating on the dos. Problem is: You can't tell yourself how NOT to do something.

For instance, DON'T think of a banana. Or DON'T think of a cat. It's an impossible proposition. Yet, a good deal of direction you may be given will be, "The first paragraph was great, but don't do what you did on the end. Do something else. And…rolling…"

This is where effective coaching comes in. You have to tell yourself what you *want* in the equation, not the other way around. At **Sound Advice**, we've been imparting how to self-direct and avoid this trap for nearly 20 years.

## How Auditions Are Held

How auditions are held refers to the manner in which casting is being done. This varies widely from project to project, commercial to film, on-camera to voice-over, let alone from one production company or casting agency to another.

Some initial on-camera casting calls will have you scheduled to be seen at a specific time and location. You'll sign in, read the rather vague direction ("The Real Mom" or "The Real Dad"), and you'll wait to be called with a burgeoning room full of people who either a) look exactly like you, or b) couldn't be more different from you. (Take your pick.)

Scripts and/or descriptions are typically available where you sign in.

When you do go in to deliver your audition, you may or may not be told where to stand. Look for a mark on the floor. It's usually shaped like a T. You'll slate your name and then be expected to go directly into your performance. Most casting agents and assistants guide you through this, as it behooves them to get the best possible read from each submitted talent, but it helps to know how it works for the exceptions.

On union auditions they *must* have the lines displayed in front of you on an easel, usually next to the camera or placed where they will ask you to look slightly off-camera. Often in initial commercial auditions you are not expected to have your lines perfectly memorized (sometimes the lines have changed overnight from the sides posted on the casting site) and it's acceptable to refer to the posted lines on the easel. Be familiar with the lines but able to change the lines you have rehearsed.

It is best to be better acquainted or memorize any lines for the callback. (Again, copy can change in an hour as the ad creatives' work becomes more intense as the actual shoot is probably in a few days.) On-camera callbacks will be in a room with the head casting director, and often the director, the producer, any number of ad creatives, and possibly even the client.

Often in castings where there are few or no lines, you will be asked a question and expected to answer to camera, sometimes about your own life experiences. "Have you taken a family road trip before?" or "Do you enjoy your garden and the outdoors? Why or why not?" This is usually to see your expressions and personality and where your improvisational skills are essential. It doesn't matter if you are a great gardener or not for the Home Depot Garden Club spot you are auditioning for—but it does matter that you engage, connect, and animate for the camera. You're paid to have a pulse. It's more important to animate the *concept* than the words on the page. This is true for on-camera and voice-over alike.

(See Chapter 11, The **Sound Advice** Approach.)

## Your Slate

A slate is stating your name at the beginning of your audition.  This is where your audition truly *begins*, not the moment you start to recite the text from the script.

Your slate usually is just your name, spoken in the *same* emotional tone or character of the performance you're about to deliver.

If your audition is on-camera, typically you direct your slate directly into the camera as if you are speaking to an individual person (unless you are told otherwise) and the rest of your performance is *slightly off camera*. And by slightly I mean generally 4 inches to 6 inches to either the left or right of the camera lens.  This is generally the case, especially if you are the only person on-camera.

For commercial on-camera, physical headshots and résumés are a rarity by today's standards.  However, you still should have them with you. All of your information is included on the online sites the casting agency is using to recording your audition.

Most commercial auditions begin with a video "snapshot" either from an iPad or a camera. You'll often hear, "Give me a big smile," or "Relaxed and neutral, please." They may want more expression than the headshot they brought you in with or a look with (or without) teeth.

After your slate they may ask you to hold still for a full body shot, then proceed to profiles. Profiles means you'll slate facing the camera, then (while maintaining the same confident, friendly smile) face right to offer your profile, then the same to your left, and occasionally your back.  This is all part of your slate and part of the client's first impression of you.

The moment you walk in the room you've already decided whether you've gotten this job.  Be prepared.  Be on time.  Be polite. And keep it confident.  Always carry yourself professionally regardless of your experience level and others will want to work with you.

## One Is the Loneliest Number

You rarely get the opportunity to see anyone else audition, especially if it's for a voice-over and you're auditioning from your home computer.  This may pose a bit of an issue when it comes to your delivery.  Be sure to let the script dictate your emotional tone and point of view, rather than offering repetitive performance habits that can stagnate your auditions.

Being all by your lonesome in front of your mic at home demands you continually challenge yourself, vary up your read and change up your attack.

Chances are great you'll give yourself too long a runway when you first start out auditioning from your home recording setup.  You'll likely overthink it, give yourself 40 takes, and then submit take 3 when all is said and done.

## Learning Curve

There's certainly a learning curve to developing your basic recording and simple editing of your auditions. Therefore, every opportunity that develops your self-directing skills, the better. So, once you have determined WHERE and HOW you will record your voice-over auditions from your mobile device, tablet or home computer, you'll need to develop your editing skills to record and edit your auditions.  These skills are NOT immediately intuitive!  It takes time and practice to offer an audition you can confidently deliver.   You don't want to advertise to talent agents you're available for auditions and then find yourself unprepared.  You want you new talent agents to confidently endorse you.   THEREFORE… we recommend our exclusive and practical service called **PRACTICE AUDITIONS.**

This is eight full weeks worth of exercises and challenges to help you hone your home-editing skills, while playing with the copy currently used today on many top auditions.

How it works:  We randomly e-mail you scripts throughout the week for eight weeks, most with pending deadlines just like you can expect from real auditions. For instance, you might receive two auditions on Monday, nothing on Tuesday, three on Wednesday, one on Thursday and nothing on Friday.

These won't be real auditions for actual jobs, but you should treat them as such. The object is to practice recording, editing, and returning your auditions quickly and well within their deadlines.

Our engineer will let you know whether you are too far off mic or too close, too low or too loud, and whether you sent it in on time. The more you do, the better you get and the sooner you can put your attention back on your performance, where it belongs. They are only meant for you to practice your skills from your home-recording setup. The goal here is to give you the greatest opportunity to deliver your very best—always.

## On-camera Casting
Sample audition e-mail from Casting Networks (via agent):

| My Representation: | Venture IAB |
| My Rep's Phone: | xxx-xxx-xxxx |
| Audition Time: | 12/15/20XX 11:20:00 AM |
| Role Name: | Female 1 |
| Rate: | SAG day rate, usage will be paid as SAG new media (negotiated). Usage is 6 months online only and will not exceed day + $1000. |
| Description: | Brunette, long hair, medium skin tone. Caucasian/Mediterranean. The women should be friendly and real. Definitely fun, great smiles and personable. Height 5' 4" - 5' 8" |
| Wardrobe: | PLEASE HAVE THE GIRLS COME DRESSED IN WHAT THEY WOULD WEAR TO A SKI LODGE, STRETCH PANTS, SWEATERS, BOOTS. |
| Casting Director: | LJ Casting |
| Audition Location: | XXXX |
| Audition Address: | Los Angeles, CA 90064 |

In larger markets (New York, Chicago, and Los Angeles), your talent agent will submit you via Casting Networks or Casting Frontier for commercial work, and usually through ActorsAccess for theatrical (film and television). After the casting director chooses and schedules you, they forward all available casting information to your agent. Some agencies first notify you via text you that you will be receiving an e-mail from the Casting Networks site, for instance, with all pertinent audition information. Such as: what the audition is for, date and time, location, what to wear, and casting director.

You're required to confirm as soon as possible, ideally, *within an hour*. The link for confirmation can be accessed via your computer or mobile device. If for some reason you see the text that you *do* have an audition (MOST likely for the following day), and are not in a place where you can access this—*give your agency a call to confirm as soon as possible*. Sure, they prefer the electronic confirmation as they are always pressed for time, but they require confirmation as quickly as possible.

## What to Wear

Certainly every job is different, and therefore various expectations as to what you should wear to on-camera auditions are project specific. So you'd serve yourself well to pay attention to details pertaining to wardrobe.

Whenever you're meeting professional contacts and there are no specific wardrobe demands (such as for voice-over sessions) aim to look like you belong in advertising: smart, stylish, a bit more hip, approachable and clean. In these instances, dressy-casual is always appropriate, especially if you're meeting producers, agents or various casting sources. These interview settings are a form of audition as well.

As for Mom and Dad roles, for instance, go online to view commercials that are stylistically similar to the commercial you're about to audition for. Pay close attention to what the actors are wearing. Notice the *colors* and cut of these clothes and how *normal* they appear. Do you have items in your closet now that would work if you were to audition for that role?

Avoid striped clothing. It does oddball things on-camera that will only distract from your performance and make you appear clueless to this fact. (An experienced talent would know this.)

Wearing *all (or mostly) black* or *all (or mostly) white* clothing messes with the white balance on the camera: If you're lighter skinned and wearing very dark colors or black, your skin will overexpose on-camera, and your face will glow as if you're radioactive. Your features and expressions won't be easily read, and your audition will be ineffective. And as wonderful as African American skin looks in all white, it doesn't play well on-camera. All white clothing will essentially make you appear so dark that your expression will be absent. So, vary up your wardrobe. If you wear a colorful T-shirt under a lighter or dark shirt or jacket, that should balance out most issues and the color will draw focus to you and your face.

You may discover you're being repeatedly called to play the same sort of roles, such as "upscale business types." You may find you need to supplement your audition wardrobe to accommodate a few key pieces. Retreat to your favorite resale shop and re-create the very same styles you'd find in higher-end stores for a fraction of the cost. If they aren't fitting as well as you'd like, a tailor is as close as your local dry cleaner. For a couple bucks, it's well worth it for a proper fit.

## Turnaround Time

Quick turnaround has become the standard in production today. Taking a day or more to confirm or deliver your auditions can and often *is* a deal killer. Make it your mission to respond quickly to your agents or they will replace you with talent who are far more dedicated and who offer more solutions than problems.

Most on-camera auditions for TV and film may schedule you one to three days in advance. While commercial auditions are typically held the next day.

Your ability to receive and respond quickly is the difference between working and unemployment.

## Confirm, Decline, or Reschedule

NO talent agent needs or wants to hear *what doesn't work* or how difficult all of this is for you. They need to hear *solutions* and whether they can count on you for this audition.

They require quick online confirmations. If you receive an audition from your agent through Casting Networks, you will be directed to a link to "confirm your audition and check for sides."

From there you will be offered the option to: **Confirm**, **Decline**, *or* **Reschedule**.

Please note that even though you have these three options, your agent expects (and wants) you to click **confirm** every time. You wouldn't have been included in submissions for this project if you had booked out. If you cannot attend, you should have booked out in advance. This can be a deal breaker with agents, especially if it happens again and again. It reflects poorly on them when you back out and adds undue stress that could be avoided.

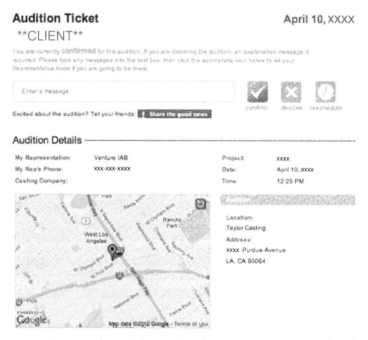

There are times when it's perfectly appropriate to **decline** an audition. For instance, you may have a *conflict* with the product the agent is unaware of. These are often listed on the audition notes

216

(i.e., *no conflicts with competing banks or fast food*), or you may have a personal (ethical) issue with the product or service. (See conflicts in Chapter 22, Industry Terms.)

Then again, you may have a booking the day of the shoot that can't be rescheduled. Regardless, you're expected to state why you're declining if you haven't booked out.

Clicking on the **reschedule** option is acceptable *only* if you are already booked for another audition, session, or callback on the same day and time. Or if something truly unforeseen occurs, such as a sick child, car accident, or illness. Crises do occur, however how well you manage and survive them (by not making them other people's problems) speaks volumes. Only *if it's absolutely necessary*, should you make a very brief phone call to your agent (lasting 10 to 15 seconds, tops) to ensure good communication between you when snafus happen.

If you absolutely can't make the time they gave you and you ask to reschedule your audition time, keep in mind the casting director may have you teamed you up with a partner or "family" and changing your time could mess up that schedule. Also, the auditions held *for your role or project* may be over by the time you can make it, so keep rescheduling to a minimum.

It's considered your responsibility to check your smartphone or e-mail hourly.

And though most casting takes place weekdays during standard working hours (Monday through Friday, between 9 a.m. and 6 p.m.), there are times when a weekend audition occurs. And, even though it's rare, you may even get an audition notice on a Sunday for a 10 a.m. call Monday morning.

Occasionally, auditions aren't going well and the casting agency has to act fast. They will contact the talent agents to call in a whole new crop of talent to deliver a fresh approach at the last minute. So, it's not out of the ordinary to get an urgent e-mail, text, or phone call from your agent asking you to drop what you're doing and head to an audition inside an hour. How well you weather these last-minute opportunities speaks to your preparedness. And as the saying goes, "Luck is when preparedness meets opportunity." And this certainly would be yours!

The best case scenario is when you're asked to attend a *callback* in record time. Perhaps the client is not pleased with the final choices and wants just a few more appropriate options. One of these precious few are going to get the part, it may as well be YOU.

It's understandable if you can't make some of these last-minute auditions, but whenever possible challenge yourself to make it. You can make a terrific impression with your agents, the casting directors, as well as the producers/clients if you are able to make it happen.

Probably the best way to prepare yourself for the unexpected audition is to have an "actor's survival kit" in your car at all times. Keep a small suitcase with neatly pressed business slacks, skirt, shirt or blouse, jacket, and nice shoes or pumps, as well as extra makeup, razor, or hair products, along with extra headshots and résumés. This little piece of sound advice could save the day and get you booked!

In Los Angeles, commercial casting is in peak season between January through June. Many top agencies suggest their most committed talent not take time off during those crucial months if possible. And even though television programming has changed dramatically in recent years and you may be auditioned at *any time during the year* for a TV pilot or series, pilot season is still generally considered between January through March, or (to some extent) even between September through November.

## Booking Out

It's okay if you can't make *every* audition. Just don't make a steady habit out of it. This is referred to as *booking out*.

There are perfectly legitimate instances when you need to inform your agent that you won't be available for auditions or accepting work, like being booked on another job, or travel and vacation. However, neglecting to do so will place undue strain on your professional relationship. Otherwise your agent will be under the impression you are always poised and ready to work.

Some agencies prefer you to book out with a simple e-mail with detailed dates and times, while others offer online options. Make it your business to become familiar with your agency's policies and preferences.

## Callbacks

It's rare to have a callback for voice-over. You either book it or you don't. However, on-camera auditions are almost *always* followed by callbacks, which further narrow the competition to only the most appropriate candidates. The cast is assembled from the callbacks.

Best advice: *Wear exactly what you wore*, and *re-create the energy and performance* you delivered at the initial audition. By the same token be prepared to adapt to the direction you may be given— even if it deviates dramatically from what you were doing at the original audition. The client wants to know you can take direction and apply it seamlessly and immediately. You're always expected to deliver options within the context of what's being asked of you. THAT'S your job as a professional talent.

## How to Audition for Voice-over

More than half of all voice-over auditions are recorded from simple home-recording setups, while the remainder is usually done at the local talent agency. Few, if any, are held at casting agencies.

When you first start recording your auditions from home, you're likely to record an excessive number of takes before settling on the take you want to submit. (Many end up using take 5 or 6, after recording as many as 30 or more takes.)

If the spot is 15 seconds or less, it's generally expected you'd submit at least *two, decidedly different deliveries* on the same MP3. However, check the *specs* (the direction) of the audition. They may want only ONE TAKE.

There are generally *three* things you never change: pitch, volume, or speed. Beyond that, a variety of inflections are consistently what's required of you, keeping in mind—when it comes to performance, there are no absolutes. The point is: As long as you're in front of the mic you must continue to create.

219

A talent agent will certainly interview and/or audition you before agreeing to represent you. Agents need to be reassured you can deliver what's promised on your demos. So, during your initial interview (either in person or over the phone) you will likely audition for him with material that is meant to be more of a challenge just to test your mettle. They may want to see how you respond under pressure.

Some local talent agents often prefer you come into their office for your voice-over auditions for the first six to eight months and to develop a professional relationship with you. Although most agents will happily e-mail you the script in order for you to record your audition at home and e-mail back as an MP3.

If the audition is a dialogue, expect the audition to be held at the agency. However, every talent agency has its own policies and requirements when it comes to auditions.

Certainly if the agency is in another state, you will be required to have your own home-recording setup and either have *access* to ISDN (digital patch) or have it at home—free of charge.

Should you be auditioning at your local talent agency, you may have as many as eight auditions to record at a time, which is why they are not as likely to give you more than one or two takes. They simply don't have time.

Arrive 15 minutes ahead of time to run your auditions out loud a number of times before you step into the booth to record. Your cold-reading skills and your ability to break down the script on the fly will certainly be tested.

The only direction you are likely to get *consistently* is, "Just be *yourself.*" Direction or specifics (also known as *specs*) vary from one production to the next. But by and large, they are looking for someone comfortable in her own skin, and you are simply expected to offer a natural, honest version of yourself.

## Cold Reading

Unless the audition is for film or TV, it's not very likely you'll get the copy (script) in advance of the audition. This is often the case for voice-over and commercial on-camera work. Therefore it's imperative you become a strong "cold read" and the best way to develop those skills is to read anything and everything *out loud.*

Once you have produced your demos and promoted them well, it's very likely you will be booked (hired) right off of them. This occurs more than 80 percent of the time for our **Sound Advice** clients who consistently promote themselves. When this happens you won't have the benefit of the audition to become familiar with the copy. The first time you hear the spot out loud will be in front of whoever hired you while you're *in* the booth *on* mic. So there's no underestimating the importance of building and maintaining your cold-reading skills.

If you're already a strong cold reader—wonderful!

During your first few reads, it's imperative you animate the read fully (or *stretch the canvas* as we call it at **Sound Advice**) to avoid taking too long to ramp up into your performance and to keep from falling into a stiff, robotic delivery that can become almost impossible to break out of after 10 or more takes.

(See The **Sound Advice** Cold Reading Exercise in Chapter 9, Developing Your Vocal Skills, for added assistance.)

## When Will You Find Out If You Got the Job?

It varies from job to job, but if you've been cast the producer will contact your agent, who will then, in turn, contact *you* to confirm the time and the location of the actual session or shoot.

The earliest you may be called might be an hour or two after your initial audition or callback (for on-camera auditions). You may get an e-mail or call from your agent a day or so after submitting your audition. Generally speaking, if you booked the job you would usually hear within 48 hours. You would not hear if you didn't get it, only if you did. Then again, you may hear a week or so afterward—every job is unique and there are no set standards.

## Getting Coached Before an Audition

Certainly many talent enlist the services of acting coaches for help prior to important auditions or especially callbacks. This may be extremely helpful provided:

a)      You've worked with this coach in the past, and they understand you and the medium you'll be auditioning for.

b)      As long as you don't practice, practice, practice one SINGLE delivery until you can't do it any other way.   You'll fall apart if they offer you direction that deviates even an inch.

c)      You may require coaching on developing the character, making the genre more familiar and in order to feel more comfortable and natural with the material.

Unless your coach has some inside connection with whoever you may be auditioning for, your coach may end up directing you miles away from what will actually be needed and wanted from you. This is always a chance you take in soliciting coaching prior to any audition.

## Auditioning for Practice

Novice talent often audition for projects "just for practice."  Or so they think.   However, even nonunion talent put an awful lot of people at risk by auditioning for jobs they have no intention of accepting.

NEVER audition for anything unless you intend to accept the job. No matter your experience level, you are *always* expected to behave professionally.

> Your demos will audition *for you*, and provided they are well produced and you promote them properly, you will secure work directly from your demos about half the time.

Otherwise your talent agent will get in trouble from the producer, the producer will catch it from the people she's working for, and all due to the fact that you just cost this production a couple of days casting and deliberating, which could easily force the project to go over budget. They'll have to get approvals on who's playing what all over again from the ten to twenty decision makers behind the scenes—while trying to make an impossible deadline all on a tight budget. People lose their jobs and valuable income due to this sort of thing, and all because you were "just auditioning for practice."

## Auditions Are Promo

You may have never have considered it before, but auditions are just *one* more form of promotion. Granted it's a remarkably important form of promotion—but it's only one. If you rely solely on auditions from only one talent agency in a single region as your sole source for employment, you'll be at a decided disadvantage.

It bears repeating, and may not be what you want to hear, but generally it takes between 150 and 200 auditions to book a job. So, if your agent includes you on three to four auditions a week (which is common), and there are (conservatively) 48 weeks of auditions during a single year, then it will take you a year to land a single gig at this rate.

You have to improve the odds in your favor, as well as increase the sheer number of auditions. First and foremost, for voice-over you must drive traffic to your voice-over-only Web site, where your demos can be heard. Continued direct mailings of your promotional postcards to the various producers your demos were designed to service creates name recognition, opens your employment opportunities in various markets and establishes you as a known and trusted brand in voice-over. It's Marketing 101.

Your demos will audition *for you,* and provided they are extremely well produced and you promote them properly, you will secure work directly from your demos. Naturally, you can't rely solely on your demo getting you booked either. Auditions, continued promotion, great talent agents, and multiple markets all play into establishing your small business as a working, professional voice-over and talent.

There are well over a hundred remarkable talent agencies registered on **Voicebank.net**. Your goal is to have effective representation in at least three markets. And certainly the more auditions you pump out there, the greater your odds of becoming booked. It's a numbers game. But, even if you deliver the best audition of all out of the 372 auditions submitted for the role—it doesn't necessarily mean you're the one they'll choose. We witness this in casting all the time.

Of course, if you turn in your auditions late or don't get back to your agent within an hour, all those marvelous skills you're sitting on will die with you.

The preferred method of communication among producers is mobile devices (smartphones and iPads). Therefore, your demo Web site must be easily viewed on these devices. If your site was created primarily in Flash (as so many are), it will be visible only on standard computers and not mobile devices. And adding an all-important QR (Quick Response) Code would be fruitless, as your site won't be easily viewed.

(See Chapter 16, Web Sites, for more details.)

QR Codes turn your postcards into interactive promotions. Besides, while e-mailing a direct link to your Web site is better than no promotion at all, they typically meet with a quick delete from the recipient. (Think about it. You do it all day long. Delete, delete, delete.)

The object behind repeated postcard promotions, ideally, is to get cast directly off your demos by their intended audience on fast turnaround projects, which most are today. If the adage "Luck is when preparedness meets opportunity," holds up—then this is precisely why you should commit yourself to continued promotions. Without it—out of sight, out of mind.

On a personal note: I'm cast directly off my demos better than 90 percent of the time. And my promotions have remained constant and consistent for the better part of 15 years. Whenever I have stopped for eight or ten weeks at a time, my bookings slow or stop entirely. When they begin again, my bookings resume. Funny that.

Also, it's worth noting if you have a Web site that requires more than two clicks to hear your demos, or (worse) a site that touts your various interests beyond voice-over (writer, juggler, actor), you won't instill confidence. Again, your Web site is a form of audition—it's representing you when you're not there. A site that shouts "I do EVERYTHING" may read to a professional that you're actually a wanna-be rather than a professional voice-over. For instance, avoid creating a site with your singing vocals, your dance, your recycling efforts, your stage acting, AND your voice-over. Save all the periphery activities for Facebook. Your Web site should concentrate on you as a professional voice-over _or_ you as a professional on-camera actor. (Again, see Chapter 16 for more details.) We want to _imagine_ what you look like in voice-over, but actually seeing you honestly isn't a selling point.

## Always Aim to Instill Confidence

So much of auditioning is confidence. Those hiring you want to know they can count on you to come through, but if you send up numerous red flags you'll continue to wonder why you aren't getting booked, and the various producers who really could and would hire you will take a pass on you because you appear makeshift and thrown together.

Even if you're only just beginning, it's imperative you carry yourself as the pro you intend to be.

You must to have drive. It's a certain combination of charm and determination mixed with a healthy dose of confidence, often beyond your experience level. That'll get you booked if you're in the same room with those auditioning you. Certainly, this stuff doesn't grow on trees.

For the most part you simply have to take a leap of faith and learn to trust yourself. This comes only from experience and repeated exposure to the work.

We encourage you to study up but trust your own creativity. Confidence is a muscle that needs to be exercised. The more you use it, the better off you'll be.

# Chapter 13:
# What's Expected of You As a Talent

"Sometimes I play things I never heard myself."
—Thelonious Monk, jazz pianist

As a voice talent, or an actor, keeping the delivery fresh and new is not only the goal, it's the job. In fact, there *isn't* one single, perfect read for any given line, script, or piece of copy. There are *thousands*. And that's just from *you* alone. The read is limited only by your imagination. Your mission, should you choose to accept it, is to deliver a few wonderful reads within the context of what's being asked of you.

This is true on the audition, on the session, and when you produce your voice-over demo.

Now that we've covered that first, most important point, here are a few guidelines to help define what's expected of you as a professional talent, which you're not likely to hear expressed anywhere else. It's generally assumed you know much of what we are about to impart.

## Time Is Money

To begin, when it comes to coaching: don't be early, don't be late, *be right on time*!

You're likely to be anxious yourself and can't wait to get started and figure, "Well, it's better to be early than late, right?" Not necessarily. It's actually just as problematic to be early as it is to be late.

This is a good habit to get into for future appointments with talent agents and other industry professionals, as well. If you show up early, you're going to make yourself comfortable and everyone else involved anxious, especially if it's a small office or a single- room location. Your early arrival could infringe on someone else's session or the completion of production that could set the entire schedule back. (Consider that the next time your coach or agent is running late.)

In that 10 or 20 minutes that you arrive ahead of schedule another 10 or 15 calls and a dozen e-mails, without exaggeration, could be completed. So, be respectful of their time.

Besides, your coach is your greatest professional ally to date. It's unfair to expect him or her to deliver more than initially promised without offering a proper exchange of goods.

Aside from that, you should treat every coaching session as if it were an audition, and every audition as if it were the actual job.

Arriving 15 minutes ahead of schedule for auditions and bookings is not only acceptable it's expected.

Consistently arriving early (or late for that matter) could be read that you expect more attention or leniency than anyone else and that you don't expect to compensate your coach for the imposition. Either way it's inappropriate. Even if your coach has an occasional delay, as she is in a far better position to make it up to you than you will be to her.

If you're late, call ahead, but *don't make a habit out of it.*

Of course, on occasion we all find ourselves in gridlock traffic or inclement weather. But by being late more than *twice* you'll likely discover three strikes and you're out!

If you discover you have to reschedule your coaching session, as with most other businesses, you are expected to offer no less than 24 hours' notice or you will be charged for the sessions. Time is money, and knowing that you are less likely to waste either.

This allows your coach the opportunity to reschedule someone else in that open time slot and avoid losing out on revenue. You want the coach to stay in business. Well, this is what it takes to do so.

If you're ill, you need to e-mail _and_ make a phone call as soon as possible. Chances are you have had at least some forewarning in advance of your coaching session—so hop to it.  If you're contagious, stay home, but again, be sure to call as soon as possible. Most coaches understand.

This is a business.  You're expected to behave as a professional, even if you're just starting out.

Most coaches are in the positions they're in because they have a certain level of expertise. If their experience with you leaves a bad taste in their mouth over something that could have been set right had you offered a solution or compromise to correct it or remedy the situation in some way, _every one_ would be better for it.  It's the professional and just plain polite thing to do.

In business as in life, we all make missteps; we experience setbacks, and overlook our responsibilities from time to time.  How you weather conflicts only tests your mettle.  Your ability to preserve and do your level best to maintain good business relations will dramatically impact your progress.  Granted you can't make everyone happy, but beyond proper representation, your coach is the greatest relationship you have in this business, so do your best to adhere to her needs and wants to garner the greatest results.

## Coaching

Coaching sessions, like auditions and bookings, can use up a great deal more energy than you might first expect.  They are typically meant to be a workout, to challenge you.

Try eating a crisp apple prior to your coaching sessions, bookings, and auditions. It will clean your palate, work the muscles in your mouth and tongue, and give you a little energy lift for added stamina.

229

It's not likely your coach will confirm you prior each session, so be sure to keep a proper schedule of your own. Call in advance if there is any question.

Ask your coach how late (or how early) she'll accept calls. Keep your calls to your coach during business hours, which is generally 9 a.m. to 5:30 p.m., Monday through Friday.

Bring a liter of water, a pen or pencil, and a highlighter with you to every coaching session. Bring your headshots, résumé, and demos, or any other promotional materials.

If you are prepared for your coaching sessions, you'll make a habit of being prepared for your auditions and bookings, too.

If the only time you work your skills is while you are actually *in front of your coach*—your career will begin and end at her front door. You will be giving those coaching you complete responsibility for performance skills and therefore for your career. This will demand longer, more arduous coaching sessions, *and lots more of them*, if you dedicate these sessions to "practicing" with your coach in front of you, which likely serve to frustrate you both.

You don't need to worry so much about "doing it right," instead focus on whether you are doing it *at all*! Everyone is busy to excess these days, *but if you simply apply yourself,* you are likely to obtain remarkable results.

When you first practice at home what you've learned from your coaching you're going to be wobbly. Nothing newly learned is immediately intuitive. It takes practice. That's why you're seeing a coach in the first place—to keep you on your course. Your coach will correct outpoints, but stay with it and you'll see results. With persistence comes success. It takes commitment and effort on your part.

Coaching gives you targets to apply and develops your performance skills. There should be specific objectives you're attempting to achieve. But, just because you are paying for coaching doesn't mean you are paying anyone to do the work for you, or that you're "buying a career."

Do your homework. Always arrive prepared and you'll get the most out of every coaching session.

*We can deliver this service via Skype, (video conferencing) or you can schedule an appointment through either of our studio locations, in Los Angeles or Chicago. Check www.voiceoverinfo.com*

## When You Record Your Demos

There are three ways you can produce a demo:

a) Produce it yourself
b) Hire a seasoned recording engineer
c) Or, hire a professional demo producer

Our best advice follows the saying "leave it to the professionals." You should *always* enlist the services of a professional *demo* producer.

A seasoned recording engineer experienced in producing a variety of *national caliber* commercials will offer a great deal to the production of your demo. But ensuring each segment sounds as if it were produced in a different studio, by a different producer, targeting the specific markets that suit you best is an extremely tall order and not the concerns or expertise of an engineer. You would still be responsible for your scripts.

And, frankly, if you were considering recording and mixing your demo tracks yourself, it's worth mentioning that even after nearly 15 years of producing for some of the top national brands, after just as many years as a professional voice-over, and after producing no less than a *thousand* demos was I able to objectively and, more importantly *successfully*, produce my own demo tracks. Lucky for me, at **Sound Advice**, I have an extremely astute and experienced team of professional demo producers and casting directors on whom I can confidently rely.

Be the talent alone on your demo.

Our **Sound Advice** demo clients typically coach with us, based on our assessment, for no less than four to six hours prior to beginning tracking for their demos.

## Direction on Your Demos

No one will direct every word or phrase you utter on an actual recording session therefore you shouldn't expect it on your demo sessions either.  Keep these recording sessions as true to actual bookings as possible for the best results.

The ability to self-direct as well as take a whole new tack within a take or two, if the client suggests it, is what direction actually is. There's an agility required here that can only come from experience, which is why coaching is essential to any and all skill levels of talent.

The demo producer you enlist the services of should have great knowledge of the styles even *within* the genre of voice-over you are producing a demo for (commercial, promo, narration, Spanish, and animation) and therefore have an overall intention of how to focus the direction of your demos.

Be sure to determine whether your demo producer will provide the copy for your demos.  Also, determine how many recording sessions you'll need, and whether these items are all-inclusive in their price, or whether they are additional.


## In Preparation of Recording Your Demos

### 1. Create a routine with our vocal warm-up

If you are not warmed up, your diction will be sloppy, your articulation won't be sharp, and you will not be ready to deliver your very best. Therefore, we insist you dedicate NO LESS than a half hour at a time, three to five times a week to doing your vocal warm-up <u>in front of a mirror</u>, and most importantly on the days you're tracking your demo. Making the warm-up part of your routine will build your dexterity, articulation, and stamina and your tracking sessions will help establish the most successful performance habits.

### 2. Study up!

DVR a few of the commercial, narrative, promo, and/or animated *styles* you intend to create for your demos. Follow the study as it is illustrated in Chapter 8, Determining Your

Commercial Strengths. These principles apply to every voice-over genre.

What makes a great voice-over great? How would YOU do it? These styles will be what you'll imagine when you record your own demo tracks.

### 3. Be decisive

Make decisions on your scripts, such as:

a) How loud or how intimate do you expect to be on each individual spot

b) What's the primary emotion; and does it change

c) What's your point of view (POV)

d) Determine the concept: honest, authoritative, personal, playful, quirky, bored, etc.

e) Picture it! Imagine what this spot looks like on-camera and the action in it

### 4. Score your copy

Don't worry about doing it wrong. Scoring your script doesn't mean it's set in stone. It just allows you to tell yourself what you want in the equation and follow through. If you score your copy, at least you'll have a rough idea of what you're looking for, which will give you just enough structure to allow you to feel safe and stable while allowing you to be decisive and agile enough to simply play!

Regardless of your skill or experience level, you're paid to *play*!

### 5. Read your scripts OUT LOUD

Do NOT memorize your scripts, instead read them for *understanding* every day prior to recording.

Read your scripts while on your feet and in front of a mirror so that you have a receipt point for your communication: YOU! Take the words off the page—and give them right back to yourself in the mirror.

Don't worry about how it sounds. NEVER try to perfect your read as if there's only one ideal delivery. Instead, surprise yourself—take after take. Reserve room to keep the read spontaneous. This will allow room for a whole new direction you may not have counted on and leave you agile.

Avoid reading your scripts only in your head because you can't honestly *hear anything in your head*. Hearing is kinetic. It's physical. You can only _recall_ things in your head. This is why we often find ourselves saying, "Wow, that sounded completely different in my head than it did out loud."

Also, be sure to look up any words you don't understand, especially all those you are unsure how to pronounce. Check out Merriam-Webster's dictionary online at www.m-w.com. You find there's even a pronunciation tool that's very handy especially when it comes to difficult narrative/industrial text.

## 6. Play with the text, rather than settling into a single read
Look for comparisons and contrasts in the script. This denotes point of view (POV) from the very beginning and allows for more vocal variety.

## 7. Get a good night's sleep

Be sure to take good care of yourself, and be sure to get a good night's sleep especially the nights prior to your recording sessions.

## 8. Manage your time wisely

Most recording sessions last about an hour to get the best results out of the talent. Give yourself plenty of time to arrive, get yourself grounded, and arrange your time so that you don't have to rush out at the end.

Additionally at **Sound Advice**, in preparation of tracking their demos, we recommend our clients listen to the CDs of their coaching sessions in their entirety, in chronological order. (We record each coaching session for the talent to use for future reference and to continue to glean the best results from coaching. Many **Sound Advice** clients listen to the prior coaching driving to their next appointment as an effective refresher.

You'll discover vital information that you may have missed prior, especially while you were being coached; you were processing concepts we were presenting to you at the time. There is no way you could have absorbed all that information the first (or even second) time you heard it.

And resist the urge to listen and criticizing your past deliveries. That's not why we recorded these coaching sessions. The idea is to discover a great deal of data you may have originally missed during these sessions and reacquaint you with concepts that will dramatically improve your performance.

**If nerves are a problem**: *try forcing the nervousness out of your system rather than resisting it.* Based on the same notion that when we're sad and we tell ourselves "not to cry," we end up crying, or "not to laugh" and we crack ourselves up, if you tell yourself, "I need to be way *more* nervous. My hands aren't nearly sweaty enough!" You will reduce your nervousness to a completely manageable level.

## At the Demo Recording Session

### 1. Get yourself a mug of hot water

Hot water sloughs the "cobwebs" off your vocal chords, while keeping you hydrated during the session. Apply hot water on the session, cold or lukewarm water before or after. But always hydrate, hydrate, hydrate.

### 2. Do NOT try to self-produce! Be the *talent* on the session

Don't comment on your reads, such as, "I didn't like that one," or "Ooh, that stunk!" It's NEVER appropriate to be self-deprecating, and it quickly becomes a difficult habit to break.

Besides you'll only succeed in undermining your future takes by concentrating on what you *don't* want in the equation rather than what you do. Further, you'll undermine confidence in yourself and how others view you.

The fact is as talent we're too close to make an objective call. And not all of your best work will feel comfortable. Some takes will seem awkward and strange. The director has the benefit of distance, a vantage point you simply don't have.

To succeed at *anything* you have to take a leap of faith.  This is one of those times.

Simply concentrate on your performance.  It's the sign of a professional.  Sit back and let someone else drive.

### 3. Have FUN!

Tracking sessions can be stressful (and frustrating). This is true of so many things that are worthwhile. So, you need to stay out of your own way.

What comes from numerous recording sessions, as we produce your demo at **Sound Advice** to garner the greatest results, you learn to shake off the day the moment you walk into the studio, and it does become easier and easier to do with experience.

There's certainly a learning curve here, but if you come prepared to work and do your best to stay out of your own way—you're gonna have a ball and honestly enjoy yourself! And that will reflect in your reads.

**CAUTION:** Should you neglect your responsibilities and leave it to your demo producer(s) to carve you out of stone at every session, you will be unfairly relying on their editing and production prowess. This will only serve to waste valuable time, energy and resources addressing issues that could have been addressed in front of your bathroom mirror.  Do your job.  You'll be very pleased with the results if you do.

## On the Job

While no two sessions, even with the same client, are exactly alike, there are a few common denominators that come to mind.

Don't wait for someone else to tell you how to play anything. YOU have to run your session. If you don't, it will run you over. Be decisive.

If they actually give you direction, they expect you to apply it immediately. Again, you have no idea what something will sound like unless you play it.  Be open to options.

Lastly, and most importantly—STAY OUT OF YOUR HEAD! (Go on. Get out of there!) Concentrate on *what you are talking about* and less on how you are saying it for the best results.

**Who will be at the session?**

Besides the engineer and his second (the guy who raises and lowers your mic and runs errands for the engineer—depending on the size of the studio), there will also be the copywriter(s) (who will double as the directors on a voice-over session), the producer (who also may lend a bit of direction as well), and possibly even the creative director. Occasionally, one or two account people from the ad agency will also make an appearance. It varies from job to job and from session to session.

The client himself may even be present at the session. In this case, you can almost always count on the session lasting an exceptionally long time. The client knows his product and has very specific ideas about how the product is perceived. These guys are corporate types who usually want their product taken very seriously, even when it's a game for a toddler. Best advice: Stay light and playful. You have to sound effortless, even when you're working really hard.

Then again, the session may only consist of you, the engineer, and the director/copywriter. But that director has to make a whole lot of people happy. Your job is to make the director and yourself happy. And you may only succeed at one out of the two, that's fine. Who cares if *you* were disappointed in the read—as long as the director's happy, you've done your job. Move on. Sometimes you're too close to assess the situation honestly.

While a bulk of the national commercial work is produced out of Chicago ad agencies, they may cast you no matter where you may live. The session may be a phone patch, and you may only hear any number of these people over the phone in your headset. If it's a digital patch, it will sound like they are all in the same studio with you.

(See Chapter 7, Advancing Technology, for a description and comparison of digital patch and phone patch.)

These sessions are extremely common, and you may never meet the individuals who cast you in person.

National commercial (network, cable, and Web) budgets typically exceed $350,000 to more than a million dollars for a single 15-second spot. (Ironically, this is probably three times the total budget for the half-hour show during which the commercial is being broadcast.)

## How long does a session last?

Plan on being at the session for an hour or two. This way if you're out of there in a half hour you'll be golden.

Technically, if you're booked on a union spot, they can keep you for up to an hour and a half per script on a radio spot and two hours if it's a national TV commercial. Nonunion jobs have no real parameters regarding the length of the session, or anything else for that matter. However, chances are you'll be in and out of there in about a half hour depending on the number of spots, what the booking is for, how prepared the producer and studio are to begin, and a number of factors that define the specific project.

Keep in mind, creating a commercial or a corporate industrial is generally "art by committee," and everybody wants to hear you do it their way, so that requires a few rounds you may not have originally counted on. Very often they simply don't know what they want until they hear it. So you'll accommodate the demands of the production. It's best if your focus isn't split thinking about whether you should have put another quarter in the meter because you thought you would have been out of the studio in less than an hour. Be prepared. Pay for parking, you can write it off and buy yourself some peace of mind.

## How many takes will I get?

On a commercial voice-over session, no fewer than five, and as many as it takes to get what they're after. That may mean 10. Then again, that may mean 50 or more. (Seems the shorter the piece the more options will be required.)

On an industrial voice-over, you may be required to voice as little as one paragraph, or there could be 50 or more pages. Since every producer is different, the process varies wildly from one job to the next. Generally, recording is done a paragraph or sometimes a page at a time. Typically you are asked to record two takes in a row. Once you've gotten through the entire script, they are likely to have you hang around while they compare the energy on your reads at the beginning of the piece, in the middle, and at the end to ensure a consistent read. They may have you rerecord the beginning to match the energy you had later on and a few lines they may have been unsure of.

Promos generally involve two to three takes, if that. This work is fast and furious. These producers want to get in and get out and get going. In fact, you are very likely to do these from your home studio.

Producing an animated feature is often spread out over the course of a couple of years. It's rare you have anyone or anything to play off while you're in the booth. The voice tracks are generally recorded first, the animation is then created from the vocal, and then the talent return to the studio for changes in the script or to the cartoon itself. So, the number of takes can vary widely. But on the average, every line is a *three-in-a-row*. (See Chapter 22, Industry Terms for the definition of a *three-in-a-row*.) The same is true for recording games.

### How much direction will I get?

Not much, if any.

Consistently, you'll hear many seasoned voice talent complain, "They had no idea what they wanted. I got absolutely no direction on that session."

To be honest, the only time you actually get detailed direction is onstage. It's rare you get much direction on a voice-over session (or any on-camera work, for that matter). So, unless you're not giving it your all, or you're way off the mark and they're trying, gracefully, to guide you back to Earth, or they simply want more variety, don't expect much direction.

For the most part, you are expected to arrive with a vivid imagination and the ability to self-direct, regardless of whether the job is a commercial voice-over, a film, or a TV series.

That said, when you are offered direction you're expected to apply the direction you're given _immediately and fully_ on the very next take. (That's often easier said than done.)

So direction is a double-edged sword, and the knife cuts both ways: You're expected to be creative and apply what you can given the specs of the audition and what you can deduce from the script itself. And when you're cast and on the session, you're expected to apply any and all direction you are given in the very next take or certainly shortly thereafter.

Again, your goal is to give them options within the parameters of the piece with each take. Imagine what _you_ think the commercial looks like and what you're talking about. Each new take will have a slight but effective adjustment, a slight change in inflection that keeps the read fresh.

Surprise yourself take after take, if you do you'll learn to trust yourself.

Don't worry so much about the quantity of takes, but rather, the quality of each. That's what matters most. Your job is to play. As a talent, we are quite literally paid to play.

**How does a voice-over session usually end?**

Usually, before the session is over, they'll ask the talent if there's anything else you'd like to try. If there is—then go for it. If not—don't sweat it. You did your duty for God and country, now get out of there and go home.

You'll fill out a W-2 form. Get a copy for yourself and then thank them for inviting you to the party. Leave them a postcard promoting your demo logo and demo Web site.

Be sure to ask the producer if you can obtain a copy of the spot via FTP or an MP3 once everything is produced. Be sure to do this in front of the engineer. The engineer will not release a copy of the piece without the producer's permission for legal reasons.

Ask the producer and the recording engineer for their e-mail to send a reminder to release the spots to you in a week or so.

This process, called *collecting your elements*, will save you a great deal of money in the long run when it comes to updating your next demo. If the spots you've done go into the ad agency archive it will probably cost you as much as $450 to $950 to collect each spot at a later date.

(To learn more, see Chapter 21, How to Collect Your Spots.)

### Your Part-time Job As a Working Talent

The adage: "You get out what you put in" certainly applies to your career.

Therefore if you dedicate a minimum of 20 hours a week to your career, what's considered part-time by any other business, you will stand a far greater chance of working FULL time as a talent. So, by all means, make it your aim to work part time as a voice-over.

How to divide up *20 hours a week* to make your career happen varies slightly based on:

> a) Whether you're just starting out and you've only just started coaching with us.
>
> b) Whether you're currently mid-production on your demos.
>
> c) Your demos are fully produced and you're ready to promote yourself.
>
> d) Or, maybe you've dropped the ball (which many of us have been known to do from time to time) and you need help sorting out the clutter to get organized, so you can effectively move forward.

Here are your weekly targets to help you accomplish your professional goals. This requires you consistently commit yourself to the task of becoming what we all want you to be: a steady working talent.

241

It typically takes TWO weeks to create a habit at anything.

**The FIRST 20-hour PART-TIME Checklist (Prior to Recording Your Demos)**

- Six to eight and a half hours of vocal warm-ups; 45 minutes to an hour of articulation exercises and a half hour of cold-reading four to five times a week, for the first four to six weeks that you are getting started.

- Two to three hours of one-on-one coaching a week.

- Three to six hours of improvisation or group acting classes that get you thinking on your feet and playing.

- No less than *two hours of research* such as reading and following the *Sound Advice Encyclopedia of Voice-Over*, our monthly **Sound Advice** newsletter, current events and blogs, to remain up to date on changes and trends in the industry.

- Three to four hours of studying the medium. In other words, DVR four or five of the top hit shows, or the shows you watch most, and observe the commercials playing during these programs to become more familiar with current commercial styles. (It's very likely they will be used as a reference at auditions and on sessions.) When playing them back, observe the list of specific questions outlined in Chapter 8, Determining Your Commercial Strengths.

**The SECOND 20-hour PART-TIME Checklist (Mid-Demo Production)**

- Five to seven hours of vocal warm-ups; 45 minutes to an hour of articulation exercises and a half hour of cold reading three to five times a week and making yourself familiar with your demo scripts. (This is vital regardless of your skill level if you expect to deliver at the top of your game!)

- Two to three hours of tracking (recording your demo tracks).

- Two to four hours prepping the graphics, ordering the materials you'll need to promote yourself.

- Three to six hours of improvisation or group acting classes that get you thinking on your feet and playing.

- Two to three hours of listening to your one-on-one

coaching and our podcasts.

- Three to four hours of studying the medium.  In other words, DVR four or five of the top hit shows, or the shows you watch most, and observe the commercials playing during these programs to become more familiar with current commercial styles.  (It's very likely they will be used as a reference at auditions and on sessions.)   When playing them back, observe the list of specific questions outlined in Chapter 8, Determining Your Commercial Strengths.

## The THIRD 20-hour PART-TIME Checklist (Post-Demo Production)

- Five to seven hours of the **Sound Advice** Vocal Warm-up: no less than 30 minutes of articulation exercises,   and a half hour of cold reading four to five times a week. (Keep it constant to keep your skills sharp.)

- Four to six hours of studying the medium.  In other words, DVR four or five of the top hit shows, or the shows you watch most, and observe the commercials playing during these programs to become more familiar with current commercial styles.  (It's very likely they will be used as a reference at auditions and on sessions.)   When playing them back, observe the list of specific questions outlined in Chapter 8, Determining Your Commercial Strengths

- Three to five hours compiling and getting your promo out to both AD AGENCY contacts and to potential TALENT AGENTS (both locally and nationally).  Promotion is ongoing and never goes away. It takes persistence and due diligence on your part. So don't let up. It will make your demo available to those most likely to hire you.

- Two to three hours of brush-up coaching sessions a week

- Three to six hours of improvisation or group acting classes that get you thinking on your feet and playing

- Three hours of:

    a) Rereading *The Sound Advice Encyclopedia of Voice-Over* in sequence (rather than jumping around as you may have done in the past).

    b) Reading the **Sound Advice** newsletters from the past six months to be sure you're up to date.

c) Reading related material as recommended in the back of this book.

- A minimum of two to six hours of auditioning a week by signing up for the **Sound Advice** *Practice Auditions*, the equivalent to an average of four to ten auditions a week.

If at any time you find you've dropped the ball and haven't been promoting or working your skills, you'll now have a game plan to begin again and to build up your part-time commitment to your career each week.  Just apply the first 20-hour part-time checklist.  That ought to get your game back up to par in no time at all.

Give yourself four to eight weeks to build your stamina back up and sharpen your performance agility so you're competitive and confident in your skills.

Our one-on-one coaching at **Sound Advice** is designed to help you deliver performances that are effective and valuable business habits that will forward your acting career. This is the fastest way to develop your professional product: YOU!  We offer these sessions via Skype, so we can coach you where ever you live provided you have a computer.

You now have a proper game plan to follow to realize your career, regardless of what stage you happen to be in the process of producing your demo tracks.  And you now know what you have to do to transition from being unknown to KNOWN as a professional working talent.

# III. Postproduction:
**Promotion & Getting Work**

# Chapter 14:

## Producing Your Demos & Various Promo

"Free advice is worth the price."
—Robert Half, American businessman

After months of preparation and hard work, you now have the master of your well-produced voice-over demo(s). Wonderful. You'll probably listen to it about 50 times in the first 24 hours.

This is an odd experience.

I equate it to this scenario: Let's say you landed a small role opposite Robert De Niro in the next Scorsese film. You have six scenes. After that initial shock and after going through the intense task of doing the job itself, after months have passed, you head to the premiere. You've heard at least *three* of your six scenes actually made the final cut, and you're very excited. You sit in the darkened theater with your spouse, your family, some friends, and there you are! It's an extreme close-up of just your eyes, nose, and a little bit of your forehead. Whoa! Odd. You turn away quickly as if you were a small child being force-fed lima beans or something.

In the meantime, your husband's eating popcorn and saying, "Oh my Gad! Honey, look...that's...wow, is this ever..." Okay, fine, got through that scene. The spouse is clearly no help here. He doesn't know what to make of the whole experience either. Next scene, let's say it's in a park. You recall what the set was like that day, who was where, what was said, what you were thinking. Fine. That scene—over. Your husband kicks the seat in front of him when the scene is over for effect and stares at you, grinning. You want to die. Last scene—cut in half, is not what you thought you shot. Over. You're left with having no idea really whether this film is any good. And you have no idea whether what *you* did was any good, either. The whole thing's a surreal experience.

Okay, well, on a much *smaller* scale, listening to your voice-over demo is a similar experience.

For example, when you play your demo for friends and family they will think you want them to criticize it when, in fact, you've played it for them purely for entertainment value. Your mother will be proud. Your father will think you paid too much. Your best friend will think it's too short. The guy at work will think he heard the spots on the air.

No matter how good it is, they will all be smiling, squinting, and shaking their heads and you'll hear them say, "That doesn't even sound like you," as if that were a compliment. Thank them just the same. As backhanded as it seems, the thing is, they simply see you as a sister or a neighbor or a daughter or a friend, and it's very difficult for them to see the forest through the trees.

As for you, your demo is going to sound different *every* time you hear it. Sometimes, it'll sound great—very professional, completely natural, all these spots could easily be well-produced spots airing nationally during the *Today Show*. Other times, you'll listen and it'll sound awful—you'll hear flaws you didn't hear the first 85 times.

You'll be convinced it can't go out as is. This is a nightmare. All this time and money invested and—you've FAILED! Good God!

You'll leave it alone for two or three days, listen to it again, and suddenly it'll sound wonderful again.

Okay, what's that all about? This is insane.

Welcome to life as a professional talent, my friend. This is why we have directors and (ideally) managers and why it's so important to surround yourself with people you can trust professionally: advisers who understand you, your goals, and the industry you're now in.

Tall order.  But then that's why we're here.

First off, it's important you acknowledge the fact that you're simply too close to the demo to judge it fully for yourself.

Get your demo into the hands of the talent agents who will, after some planning and promotion on your part, want to audition you to ensure you can deliver what you claim and who will, with any luck and persistence on your part, agree to represent you.

Your demos lead to auditions. Auditions lead to bookings. The more you audition and the more your demos are out there auditioning for you, the faster you will get a return on your initial investment and establish yourself in this field.

Commit yourself to becoming relentless in your pursuits. When you're not working your skills, you're promoting your demo. When you're not promoting your demo and auditioning, you're doing something to keep up your skills. This is _your_ job if you expect this to become your profession.

This is vitally important, especially now!

## Soliciting Feedback

Here's a rather novel idea for this or any business: At **Sound Advice** we *never* advise you to ask for feedback on your demo tracks, whether we produced them or not.

Think about it. If you're pro, why would you ever ask, "What do you think of my demos? Can you give me feedback?" to people you're intending to solicit work from? It serves only to undermine your professional authority. It inadvertently reads that you are unsure of yourself and you are likely a novice that lacks confidence and experience.

If you're a pro, and you *are* if you're presenting yourself as such with your demos to talent agents and producers alike, then you're expected to stand behind your promotional materials. This is true regardless of your experience or skill level. And only in the talent business is it possible for you to secure the principal role with little or no experience, while those with the most experience might play the smallest role. If you're right for the role, you're right for the role. The longest résumé is not what scores the job—YOU do. Therefore, asking for feedback unintentionally reads as if you are unsure of yourself, obviously a novice, and suggests you may not have much confidence.

Besides, if you are given feedback—what are you prepared to do with it? Start over?

You may have asked for feedback simply for a lack of anything else to say, or maybe you wanted praise for your remarkable vocal prowess.

Most agents or producers will offer feedback if they honestly feel the situation warrants it, but for the most part they'll listen and discern whether they can use you. In many instances, they'll offer feedback simply because you asked and they are trying to be accommodating. Yet, they're likely to forget what input they gave you or change their minds after hearing your tracks again at a later date. This happens more often than you might expect, and it honestly doesn't help you much.

To add to this, what if an agent comes back with, "Put the middle spot second and the second from last spot first" (which is at least specific input)? Even if you're willing to pay the studio/producer to accommodate these changes, you may not end up with a demo that's an improvement over what you've already presented. Additionally, another authority may offer you conflicting feedback that dramatically contradicts with what another professional source may have recommended. Keep in mind, the individuals who are offering you the feedback aren't in the studio while these changes can be made. Even very seasoned ears typically must hear the edit in the studio to discern whether the change is effective.

Of course, if you ask a competing demo producer for feedback, they're likely to criticize your tracks and tell you what *they* would do with your demos. The fact is, in lieu of you having any tangible experience or objectivity, asking for feedback will often only serve to confuse you, whether the advice is astute or not.

What matters above all else is what YOU think! Commerce is confidence, and your job is to instill confidence in those you hope will either rep or hire you. When you walk into an audition, and read as if you're unsure of yourself, then you will not land the job.

251

Since your demos are auditioning for you, the same theory applies.

Granted, you may want an objective assessment of whether your demos are effective. For this we recommend you head to Voicebank.net. Find talent agencies that have a lot of talent pursuing the same style of work you're attempting to land. Some won't be all that great, while others will sound remarkable. Listen to demos of talent of your gender, your relative age, your vocal range, and vocal quality if possible. How do your demos stand up?

Keep in mind your demos are held to the very same criteria advertising creatives require of their own demo reels. These are the very individuals your demos were created to draw work from as a voice-over, and they understand you may be creating spots for your demos in order to define who you are and what you bring to the industry as a talent. Each spot must seamlessly sound like broadcast quality.

Other than that, if a talent agent or any other industry professional has a recommendation for you they'll offer it without being asked.

Certainly everyone has an opinion, however few are objective enough to offer you the insight you might be hoping for should you solicit feedback, so it should be avoided.

Simply present your tracks with confidence and _without_ excuses. Stand behind your promo. It's the professional thing to do at all times. You really want to determine whether they can use you. That's the goal in sending anyone your demos.

Certainly you may doubt yourself when you're just starting out. That's natural. You have to take a great leap of faith to present yourself with confidence. Every opportunity will build from there.

> Asking talent agents, "Can you give me feedback on my demo?" inadvertently reads that you are unsure of yourself and you are likely a novice that lacks confidence and experience. Stand up for yourself and your professional promo.

## How to Determine Whether Your Demo Is Competitive

If you're completely unsure whether your demo is up to snuff, consider the following:

- On your commercial demo, do the spots sound primarily like authentic, national TV spots?
- Compare your demo to spots on TV and radio *that are done well*. Would you believe a bulk of these spots on your demo might be found on national TV or national radio?
- Do your demos show a range of vocal expression (not a huge turn of the emotional dial, but some movement should be included)?
- Is there imagery? Can you picture what you're talking about?
- Can you imagine what the commercial might look like?
- Do you approach the mic differently from spot to spot?
- *Does your own personality come through?*
- Are your reads *believable?*

If you adamantly feel your demo lacks any or all of these items, take it up with your producer and *redo* it! Or give us a call and we'll assess your concerns and devise a game plan for you.

## Producing Your Various Promo

In case you've been sleeping, it's imperative you drive traffic to your demo Web site. This is your most vital tool in making your demos available to those most likely to professionally hire or rep you.

> You could have a Maserati
> for a demo, but if it remains
> in the garage it won't get you
> anvwhere.

This is successfully done two ways: through repeated promotion of postcards that forward your name and Web address especially to ad agency creatives (people most likely to *hire* you), as well as continuous promotion to talent agents until you secure representation with at least three nationwide.

It's important to point out that ad agency creatives neither need nor accept headshots. The promotion defined in the following pages is a

253

unique feature afforded solely to voice-over talent.  And therefore a terrific opportunity for you!

## The Purpose of the Demo Postcard

Your postcards promote your Web site; your Web site promotes your demos. The more you promote, the more accessible you'll be to the work, the more you'll make your name known, the more likely you'll see a return on your initial investment by securing steady work in this business.

If you rely solely on auditions to secure bookings it will take you 150 or more auditions to land a job, according to statistics. You will be *more than doubling* your opportunities if you continually direct mail your promotional postcards to the various producers and contacts your demos are designed to service. Your goal is to make it easy for them to hire you.  This is done by repeated direct mailing your promotional postcards (prominently displaying your QR Code which leads directly to your site) to various ad agency creatives. This is the most direct way to establish name recognition, brand association, and ultimately encourage your primary target audience to listen to your demos from your voice-over-only Web site.

Promoting yourself is as much your job as a professional talent as maintaining your performance skills.  This continues to be the case even after you have achieved a certain status as a known and established actor.

The objective is to establish you as a known and trusted brand in voice-over.  That takes time, commitment, and momentum.

You will be sending a demo postcard to *the same professional contact every two to three weeks* for five to seven weeks *per mailing list*. This is what we refer to as a full mailing. It's very likely you have never promoted yourself to this many potential clients with any consistency—ever. We recommend you have 5,000 postcards printed. A thousand will be used to promote to the talent agents, the rest for repeated mailings to the creatives. This is how you truly establish yourself in this or *any* business.  You must continually make yourself known and accessible to those who require your skills.

Far too many talent fail simply because they sidestep this vitally important process, which allows them to drive their business rather than leave it in someone else's hands, or succumb to the notion they can't control any aspect of their business.

So, coupled with your direct mailings to the ad creatives in various regions, you will require enough postcards to promote yourself to talent agents nationwide, which will further fortify your opportunities to secure steady work.

If you follow the two forms of promotion we have laid out for you later in this book, you will need approximately 5,000 demo postcards for your first two to three months of mailings.

*Note:* **Sound Advice** *offers current regional mailing lists. The rates are subject to occasional or incremental increases. We don't recommend ordering mailing lists until after your promo materials have been produced.*

## Postcard Printing

Here are the two postcard printing services we endorse above all other options:

**Modern Postcard**
(800) 959-8365
 www.modernpostcard.com

**GotPrint.com***
(877) 922-7374
http://gotprint.net/g/pricing.do

* GotPrint.net requires a smaller postcard design prep of 4" x 6," rather than the standard 4.25" x 6".

After our rather extensive search, **GotPrint.net** has proven to provide the very best rates, greatest value, and best customer service we've found nationwide for both *printing your postcards* as well as *bulk mailing your promo*, should you prefer not to do all of that work on your own.  It's ultimately your call.

So if you're about ready to reorder your postcards, we strongly recommend you have GotPrint.net handle your mailings as well. They are also capable of offering a turnkey operation (as does

ModernPostcard.com), which helps you save time and effort. Their site allows you to calculate the postcard printing, as well as the approximate cost of bulk mailing.

## Our Suggested Promotional Postcard Order

We recommend the following:

> **SIZE**: 4″ x 6″
>
> **Paper/Material/ Substrate**: 16 point Dull Cover with Matte Finish
>
> **COLOR**: Color Front, B&W back  (Or color both sides)
>
> **Quantity**: 5,000 postcards
>
> **Proof**: Instant Online Proof
>
> **Cost**: approximately $155 (plus postage, and/or shipping & handling)

Regardless of whether you handle your promotional mailings yourself or if you enlist a bulk mailing service, you'll need to purchase regional mailing lists from us to do so. The contacts available on our exclusive mailing lists *are not available through any other source to individual talent.*

Additionally, our promotional mailing lists have a less than 5 percent margin of error when you initially purchase them. This is unprecedented in this or any industry, offering you the greatest opportunity to establish yourself with those most likely to hire you as a voice-over.

Ongoing promotional mailings (to those most likely to hire you) are essential to succeed in this field. It's the price of doing business. This form of promotion is not well known in our business, which would explain why so many fail. Relying solely on auditions *without continued promotion* reduces your success rate by a terrific margin. It's better than 90 percent of your job.

Order the most current mailing lists available anywhere off our web site designed to promote yourself directly to your target audience from our online **SHOP**.

Be sure to have 1,000 postcards sent directly to you for your talent agent submissions, for the occasional thank-you note, and for your personal promotion.

Promotional mailings to ad agencies should not be confused with promotion to talent agents. Talent agent submissions should still be done by you personally whenever possible, rather than through a service, to secure representation.

## Bulk Direct Mailing Plan

Our **Sound Advice** marketing plan is designed to offer the greatest value through direct mailings, which is laid out in detail in Chapter 19, How To Get Work.

Keep in mind the goal of continued promotion is to effectively establish yourself as a brand and to make your name and logo familiar to potential clients in relation to the field of voice-over.

Postage rates will continue to change, and our mailing lists are subject to random increases due to the fact we are constantly adding new contacts and altering them every month—so our lists increase all the time.

Promotion to the talent agents for representation is an entirely separate process and should NOT be confused with promoting yourself to the ad creatives, as illustrated here.

It's up to YOU (rather than the printer or graphic artist) to triple check *everything* to ensure all your contact information is correct prior to confirmation of your order.

Your return address will be needed on the top left or top center on the reverse side of your postcard. If it's on the very bottom, the zebra code the Post Offices place on postcards will cover up vital information. So avoid placing ANY information on the bottom third of the postcard, or it may end up in the dead-mail file.

Also, placing a line down the middle of the reverse side of the postcard may interfere with the zebra code data and inevitably cost you money, especially if they need to be returned, so leave that off as well. It's worth mentioning the post office will charge you at least 9 cents more per postcard if you do not use a bulk mailing service such as GotPrint.net, unless you follow the money-saving process we offer in Chapter 19, How To Get Work.

Example of the back of a demo postcard

We have often been asked about business cards. Although not essential, GotPrint.net offers business cards mirroring your postcard graphic, if you're so inclined.

## What to Include on the Demo Postcard

Beyond your logo, it's important your demo postcard include:
- Your e-mail*
- Your cell phone number*
- Your return address
- And, most importantly, your Web address and QR Code

*Your voice-over e-mail and cell number can be replaced with your primary agent's contact info, if applicable.

Adding a QR Code (Quick Response Code) turns each postcard promotion into a direct link to your Web site where your voice-over demos can be heard.

QR Codes can be scanned with a simple free app from any smartphone or iPad. Once scanned, that link to your site will then be bookmarked on the mobile device until it's removed at a later date.

Suffice it to say, adding a QR Code to the back of your promotional postcards offers you a far greater advantage of being heard than ever before and by your targeted audience. What could be better? QR Codes turn your postcard into an interactive promotional tool, provided your Web site wasn't designed solely in Flash, as Flash will *never* be read on iPhones and iPads and cannot be viewed on these devices. Another bonus about QR Codes is that they don't cost anything to create, and the app to scan them (QR Readers) is free to download as well. However, unless you are a major techie we recommend you leave it to the experts. We recommend you have Ron Martin of Ron Martin Web Design create your QR Code for you when he designs your site. You can contact Ron at ron@ronmartinwebdesign.com

So, given all of this, the value of direct mailing your promotional postcards has just increased by at least 80 percent over any other time in the history of promotion.

## Agent Info

If you intend to include your talent agent on your promotional materials, we suggest you keep it simple and only include ONE or TWO talent agencies and contact info rather than multiple. (This applies only if you currently have more than one talent agent.) If you include more than one, you'll only confuse your potential employer and clutter up an otherwise clean design.

If your talent agent's info isn't included on your promo, it's not the end of the world if the producer calls you directly. Just field him to your agent for bookings and rates.

It really doesn't matter if a postcard you send out has this agent's contact info on it and the postcard you send out two weeks later (to the same potential client) has an entirely different talent agency contact on it. We'd be dead impressed if anyone noticed it was a different contact at all. It really doesn't matter. What matters is whether the recipient can reach you and can find your Web site demos via QR Code with ease. That's far more vital.

And, believe it or not, if you include a talent agent as your contact, PLEASE be sure he has agreed to rep you *first*. Otherwise, you'll be burning your bridges before they're built.

## Reproducing Your Demo

Technology has advanced so dramatically in recent years, we've ceased advising clients to reproduce their demos in compact disc (CD) format. Considering downloads are the required and preferred method, you may as well save yourself some money and time.

CDs are nearly obsolete. However, if for some reason you may need a disc at a later date, we still recommend you have your graphics designed as a CD face. This will allow you the option of creating a tangible, physical version (rather than digital only) from your computer, or through one of the two following affordable sources.

Although this may change within the year or so, at this writing at **Sound Advice**, we continue to deliver your demos in both MP3 (which we e-mail to you) as well as in a CD master consisting of either AIFF or WAV files, the highest quality of uncompressed digital files possible in the event you might duplicate your demos on CD.

First and foremost, we recommend **Paul Mally** from **Top Dog Disc** in Chicago. His product includes CDs in C-Shells (our preferred CD option, if you're going to reproduce your demos in CD format).

Top Dog's rate includes a process called digital heat transfer, which refers to adhering your graphic onto the face of each disc. Your own graphic image is first printed on a clear, micro-thin Mylar ribbon, then that ribbon is applied to the top surface of a blank CD or DVD. Detailed color print resolution of 300 dpi (up to 600 dpi) is achieved through this process.

**Top Dog Disc**
**P.O. Box 46232**
**Chicago, IL 60646-0232**
**(773) 775-8393**
**http://www.topdogdisc.com/**
**Paul@topdogdisc.com**

25-49 pieces are $3 each
50-75 pieces are $2 each
Reorders of same master/design are $2

*Minimum order is 25 pieces. Pricing includes CD duplication, full color on-disc printing, and C-Shell case.*

Be sure to check with TopDog for current pricing and shipping costs.

The average turnaround no matter where you might live in the States is approximately seven to ten days. Simply e-mail Top Dog your CD face design, and mail him the CD master of your voice-over demos.

The second CD reproduction option we recommend after Top Dog is **Kunaki.com**. Kunaki will include a hard-plastic-style jewel case, and more information can be included on the tray inserts if you wish. The price is low and the product is perfectly good for its purpose.

They only operate online and can be contacted via e-mail. Check out their Web site for more details on their services and prices.

## C-Shell CD Cases

If you must reproduce your demo in CD, we suggest you employ a simpler one-piece, soft plastic CD case called a C-Shell, rather than packaging your demo in the typical, rigid, square, jewel-box- style CD cases commonly used in the music industry. C-Shell-style CDs are far more practical because they create a cleaner, more aesthetic look and are more affordable in every way.

## C-Shell Labels

We recommend adding a 3"x 2" label to the back of the C-Shell with your logo, contact info, and QR Code. In fact, whether you reproduce your demo in CD format or not, we recommend you have these labels created for a variety of promotional reasons. For example, these labels can forward your brand logo and QR Code by attaching them inside thank-you notes, as seen in Chapter 18, How to Get an Agent. These labels will appear on the flipside of your C-Shell CD case and will contain your logo, your name, cell phone number, e-mail address, and QR Code.

Actual size 3" x 2" (C-Shell) label

A *single-color* 'C-Shell label' (as we call them at **Sound Advice**) can save you as much as $150 over printing these labels in full-color. That's substantial. Single-color labels are perfectly fine and more economical. (Adding various colors never end up the shade you had initially hoped, so keep it simple.)

We suggest you order a roll of 500-count 3" x 2" printed labels from **BizPrintExpress.com** to place on the backs of your C-Shells. They run about $65 for 500 labels. We recommend you order black print on a white field. They arrive in a box, 500 on a roll, and unlike labels printed from most home computers, these labels will not smear and save you on using up all your ink!

## BizPrint

Web site: www.BizPrintExpress.com
E-mail: orders@bizprintexpress.com
They ship all over the USA and Canada.

# Chapter 15: Graphics

"Information about the package
is as important as the package itself."
—Frederick W. Smith, Founder and CEO of FedEx

Presentation is EVERYTHING. Especially to anyone in advertising or the talent business, so it's vitally important that your demo Web site and the postcards you promote your site with look as good as your demo sounds. The more appealing and professional your promotional materials appear, *the more likely you are to elicit a profitable response.*

Most demos out there are remarkably below par production-wise, but that is only half the reason they fail. The rest of the story lies in the outward appearance. If your graphics are not conveying contemporary aesthetics to appeal to the most progressive audience or just as bad, if they are flat-out boring or drab, you're likely to be overlooked or written off as unprofessional no matter how extraordinary your demos may be.

> Great graphics create great interest. This is precisely why the artwork on your promo is *as* important as your performance and the overall production values on the demo itself.

Besides, why would anyone bother to listen to your demos, if at first glance your presentation is less than appealing? Would you purchase anything from a grocery store without any experience with the product that was in a less-than-desirable package? Of course not! You could pummel the market with your demos, but if it looks like a dog it will be a very tough sell. The fact is it takes a relatively small amount of effort on your part to rise above the din.

It's imperative you consider the target audience in advance of producing your demos: Commercial producers, copywriters, and creative directors, are all in *advertising*. It's important that you offer and meet the basic aesthetic standards if you expect to be taken seriously and to generate an interest among ad agency professionals.

## Establishing Your Brand Identity

The primary function of a graphic artist is to create a versatile, memorable logo, known as an *identity*. The object is to establish you as a professional brand. Your continued promotion of this appealing brand is to entice others to listen to your demos. This means incorporating color, form, but most importantly making your name known and synonymous with voice-over. And even more specifically, define what you do best. *Your graphic should look like your demo sounds.*

Our most sound advice when it comes to your graphics: Identity and branding are defined conceptually by describing *what* the subject represents. For instance, if the subject is *fences*, describe *what* this represents: home, ownership, pride, security, tradition. Get it?

So then, if the subject is you as a voice-over, describe yourself to your graphic artist conceptually, such as *quirky, youthful, wry, approachable, contemporary.* Describe yourself in five to six words that best define how you are most likely to be perceived professionally as a voice-over.

Also, it's not necessarily what graphic elements you *like* most that counts instead it's *what represents you best conceptually as a brand.*

These tips should assist you a great deal, as most talent are often too close to discern how they are perceived commercially to ensure their graphics represent the marketing focus of their demos.

## What You'll Need Designed

- A graphic logo that establishes your brand identity to be used on the following:

  - A standard, two-sided 4.25" x 6" postcard, with your QR Code added to the back, to promote your name, your logo/identity and your demo-*only* Web site.

  - A Web page dedicated solely to voice-over. NOTE: Your Web site will NOT likely be designed by your graphic artist. These are separate skills. Your graphic must be created first before enlisting the services of a Web designer.

  - A CD face featuring your logo/identity.*

  - A 3" x 2" C-Shell label displaying your logo, demo tracks, QR Code** and your contact information.*

*Considering CDs are nearly obsolete, at this printing we still recommend you have the CD face designed, should the need arise so you can burn a disc and print these elements from your home computer. We also recommend you continue to have the C-Shell labels designed as we have promotional suggestions for them beyond using them for CD C-Shells.*

**QR Codes are generally created by the Web designer (we recommend hiring Ron Martin—see Chapter 14, Producing Your Demo & Various Promo Items and Chapter 16, Web Sites) and are added only AFTER your graphics have been designed, approved and your Web site is up and operable. So this is the very last element added to your designs. However, it's important your graphic artist accommodate for it in advance of completing your designs.*

# Friends Don't Let Friends Design Their Graphics

*"Naw, not me and Joe, we've been pals since college.
We're friends to the end."*
—Famous last words

When meeting with a graphic artist to design your graphics, there are a number of things you *must* know right from the onset.

First of all, there is NO FREE LUNCH! If a friend or relative tells you they'd "be happy to design your artwork for nothing," *or for a deal,* take my word for it, it's going to take a very, *very* long time to complete. And that's a promise. Run, don't walk, in the other direction! Why? Because you will easily add about six to eight months onto the entire project.

Here's why: Everybody's got to pay the bills, and frankly, paying jobs will get done first for just that reason. Besides, God forbid you want to make changes or modifications to the initial design that was done for you gratis. Your friend, or cousin, or brother-in-law figured they could throw a microphone over your name and a mouth and call it a day. Hiring a proper graphic artist keeps it all professional.

And just because your graphic artist (friend) works for an ad agency doesn't mean that he's a valued player there. Your graphic artist-friend may even feel this is his opportunity to really express himself. Frankly, how he sees you may not suit you or your demo commercially. Are you prepared to reject his graphics after all that?

> It's not worth having a
> "cheap attack" on your graphics that is
> bound to become a bone of
> contention between friends.

But wait, there's more. With the advances and availability of technology today budding graphic designers are turning up on every corner. The problem is that while your friend or relative who's designing your graphics may have great taste and a keen eye for style and color, he may have trouble converting your graphic from one format to another. His technical skills may be limited. In fact,

268

at Sound Advice we've observed this issue to be the most common obstacle talent stumble over when it comes to their graphics.

No matter how great the graphic is or how cool the graphic artist may be, if you can appreciate this guy's work *only* on his computer, or painted on some rock or sketch pad some place because the only format this graphic artist is familiar with is completely antiquated, you are going to have one helluva time trying to reproduce that thing as your graphics anywhere else.

Keep in mind proper promotion is the goal of having a demo with professional graphics created in the first place. It completes the package if you are going to be taken seriously.

Again, you're presenting yourself as a professional to people in *advertising*. Why would you have a cheap attack on the *advertising* to advertisers? That defeats the purpose.

As anything, if you want something done right, leave it to the professionals.

## What You Can Expect From a Graphic Artist

It's a little-known fact, but it's NOT your job as the voice talent to come up with a design to give to your graphic artist to create.

Your objective is simply to give the graphic artist *suggestions* on promotional strategy, nothing more. For example, "I think anything from Design Within Reach suits the style and mood I'm looking for. It's sophisticated and urban. That's the direction we're directing my demo to go."

If you are a young adult between the ages of 18 and 25 years old, look at the art direction that Land of Nod, Prius, CB2, and Apple use for their promotional campaigns as inspiration. Observe the use of color, form, and text. If you're a 35+ suburban mom (or at least this is how you're being marketed, these are the primary roles you'll get most), consider what they are putting out there in magazines for this market in *Real Simple*. West Elm, Piperlime or Crate and Barrel catalogs are great sources of inspiration. If you're an earthy, "real" sort of guy, look to Honda, Dodge, Jeep, Home Depot, or Lowe's for design and identity inspiration. Skew your suggestions to suit how you will most likely be perceived, first and foremost when talking branding and identity with your graphic artist.

The most difficult aspect of your graphics is the fact that they might somewhat contradict with your own personal taste. If you put on a uniform to go to work—is that who you are personally? Maybe, maybe not. If you dress for a part you're auditioning for, that may require wearing clothes that your mother might prefer to see you in, but if it weren't for the audition, you wouldn't be caught dead in them. There's something of corollary here when it comes to your graphics immediately defining your brand and making your name known and associated with a certain feel or emotional tone. We want your graphics to say at a glance who you are type-wise and in a cool way. We want to evoke interest. It's *more important* you appeal to your target audience and to further define who you are commercially, than what you like most personally. Ideally we're achieving both, but that's simply not always the case. Keep that in mind when you see the first preliminary options offered by your graphic artist.

If you want to offer more inspiration or suggestions for fonts, logos, color, and design layout, go through the grocery store and observe the packaging. Go through a cosmetics section of a department store or take a stroll through Best Buy or Target and really look at the logos and packaging of well-known products. What grabs your attention most and why? Is there an element of this design that you could incorporate into your graphics? Point out those elements to your graphic artist. "The font from this and this and this appeal to me and I think suit me." Tell your graphic artist who and what you identify with most. That's the best way to art direct your graphics rather than offering up an idea that's so specific it might never play out as well as it did in your head. Observe how the name of the product is incorporated into the overall graphic. Interesting stuff. And right under your nose all the time.

Fight the urge to come up with a concept that is obvious or literal, such as your name half in and out of a box. Get it? Out of the box?! (Trust me, it's been done. And done, and done.) Anything too literal or too obvious often says little if anything about you. A strong graphic design stands on its own and says a great deal more than a forced concept any day.

Look through your potential graphic artists' portfolios for samples of past design projects. Point out the fonts, shapes, color, and mood that best conveys who you are from his past work. Determine which, if any, apply to your demo and appeal to you most when it comes to fonts, form, and color.

If you hire him, you will be expected to pay an initial deposit, usually half up front to begin work.

With your initial communication (often over e-mail) determine whether the graphic artist will contact each vendor to reproduce your graphics (postcards, Web design, etc.) or whether you will be handling these items yourself. These responsibilities vary from graphic artist to graphic artist, and their rate will often reflect their degree of responsibility.

(Refer to Chapter 14, Producing Your Demo & Your Various Promo, for reliable vendor options we recommend.)

Most graphic artists create three or four rough designs. You need to establish when you can expect to see the first roughs. A week? Two weeks? Set the date so you have a target to avoid unrealistic anxiousness on your part.

From there, you will choose the one you prefer most and tweak the design further to your liking. But keep it simple.

Unless you have a truly remarkable idea that comes to you in a bolt from the blue, *leave the designer alone to create a few ideas until you meet again*. You don't want to force his hand to such a degree that you stilt any of his creativity.

Again, you are not required to come up with the graphic concept. Let the artist present a few things. If you give the graphic artist too much direction, you will probably succeed only in painting him into a corner with a very forced graphic idea that will, more than anything else, equally frustrate the both of you. That doesn't make for the best final result.

All the vendors **Sound Advice** recommends (for printing your postcards, Web design, etc.) create the best possible product at the best possible rate, yet each requires a separate and completely different format for the specific graphic they are to reproduce. Our goal is to have consistent clarity and color from one vendor to the next so that we have a seamlessly designed promotional package. This is done with ease, provided your graphic artist is on the ball not a total novice.

The issue is this: With the accessibility of programs that allow every layman to record from his home computer, design graphics from his home computer, and create Web sites from his home computer the true professional is often lost in the process. Everyone's an expert— and yet no one is. Leave it to the professionals if you expect to come off as a professional yourself. Period.

## How to Art Direct Your Graphics

Creating an effective logo (or "identity") to define you, your demos, and your professional brand can be a daunting task, especially without previous experience.  Over the years, we have observed there are generally two camps when it comes to novice art direction on demo graphics: those who fret because they don't know what to tell their graphic artist to do, and those who know *exactly* what they want.  In either case, we're here to offer some sage advice on how to get the most out of your graphics experience.

First off, you need to consider what the primary goal is, which is to establish your brand to a rather specific audience: advertising creatives. So, you have to consider what appeals to them. You want your identity to appeal to their aesthetic sensibilities.

Given that, you need to avoid the obvious, such as including mouths and microphones circa 1940–1950 on your graphics. It's poor advertising and it's been done to death, besides it doesn't say a thing about you and what you bring to the table as a talent.

Other obvious items that can and should be avoided:

- If your name is Rhodes, please don't include a literal road in your graphic
- Avoid symbols that mean something only to you and no one else
- Please avoid catchphrases, such as if your last name is

Peele "a voice with a Peele!" or "Bob Boyce, the voice of choice." This is as obvious as it gets and tells us nothing about you, except that you're hokey and rather old school. Graphics like these can sandbag perfectly remarkable demos

With every promotion your demos are bringing the store to your audience. We want them to walk in. Great graphics give them a reason to! The aim is for your graphics to define who you are with the logo. It's about making your name known and associated with voice-over.

When working with a graphic artist, here's what we suggest you do:

1. Whenever possible, look at other designs the graphic artist has created and use these as points of reference. Tell the graphic artist, "I like the fonts you used on these designs." "The color-story (color combinations) you used on these are great, and I'd like to see something like this."

2. If the graphic artist has very little to show you, or if you found a few magazine ads and/or Web sites with images, graphic shapes, logos, colors, and fonts that you feel suits you, forward them to your graphic artist as references. Do this gingerly. Three to five references would be plenty. Again, it's not your job to design your graphics, especially in your head! Use tangible references for tangible results.

3. Whenever and wherever possible be sure to *hire a professional graphic artist* rather than a relative or friend for the simple reason there is no free lunch, and you want to maintain your relationship. Of course, friends and family want to help, but they have bills to pay too, and it's for this reason paying gigs will always come before your graphics. Besides, should you need or want changes or if you mandate a timeline, you're likely to hear, "I'm doing you a favor!"

If your graphics remain in limbo indefinitely, then your ability to generate an income from your demos will be dramatically diminished. And that's a problem. So keep it professional and go with a graphic artist you can do business with.

4. Now, sit back and let your graphic artist create a couple of things. He will likely create three or four roughs. You may love one of the images offered right from the start or like the overall design on image #1 and the fonts used in the logo from image #3. Fine. Ask to see that combination and work from there.

Remember the onus falls to you to ensure *all of your contact info* is spelled correctly, the return address is correct, and the numbers are all accurate—NOT the graphic artist. So, be sure to triple check EVERYTHING before signing off!

## Graphic Artist vs. the Illustrator

There are distinct differences between these two artists.

A *graphic artist* takes existing graphic elements and incorporates them into a unified design to communicate a graphic story. An effective graphic design will convey a memorable identity. Just as typing defines you as a talent, your graphic design will define who you are before anyone even hears your demo. The graphic artist incorporates the design in a variety of formats for each vendor (such as the postcard printers) in order to reproduce each promotional element.

A graphic artist sometimes designs artwork from premade elements such as assorted fonts and clip art or images that may require a licensing fee.

An illustrator creates an original drawing, cartoon, or painting and very rarely completes the work by adding the graphic elements such as your name and so forth to the artwork. Generally speaking, if you hire an illustrator, you will still need to hire a graphic artist to complete the design. An illustrator simply creates the original work, while the graphic artist creates the logo identity and balances out these components in their respective formats to complete the project.

## Graphic Artist vs. Web Designer

Typically, your graphic artist and Web designer are not one and the same. This is a common misconception if you are about to create your first *professional* site and you've never had a logo promoting you as a brand before. Therefore, your graphic artist will need to provide your Web designer with the graphic elements necessary to build your Web site.

Experienced Web designers need to know how to write the code necessary to allow your graphics to look as good as the postcard promoting the site itself. That's not necessarily an easy thing to pull off.

Further, the Web designer needs to consider and understand the variety of platforms and Web browsers that may view your site and have the skills to create a site that looks consistently professional in all of them. Also, don't assume if you can see your site from your laptop, you can view your site from a mobile device, such as an iPhone, Blackberry, or iPad. The Web designer you employ is of no use to you if they are unable to do this. Never assume they can. You want your wonderful graphic to look amazing from all of these sources (and it looks really, really good) and all the links and MP3s work properly as well.

Considering your target audience prefers their mobile device to a standard computer, your Web designer should also create a QR Code for you to add to all of your promotional materials (postcards and C-Shell labels). QR Codes turn all your promo into direct links to your Web site. You'll then e-mail that QR Code to your graphic artist to complete all of your graphics. This will be the last thing you'll do.

If you're doing this "on the cheap"—never assume your site looks the same on all of these platforms without testing it yourself. *Test* everything especially before sending the QR Code to your graphic artist. Test the site and QR Code on your iPhone, iPad, and a variety of browsers off your standard computer.

(For more details on designing your Web site and QR Codes, see Chapter 14, Producing Your Demo & Various Promo, and Chapter 16, Web Sites)

## The Best Example of a Professional Graphic Artist EVER

At Sound Advice, we have worked with and recommended graphic artist **Jennifer Harrell,** founder and CEO of **Wyville USA** more than any other we have ever worked with for a very good reason: She's the absolute best! And we're not the only ones who think so. Her skills and experience in mass media marketing is extensive, which makes her a wonderful example of how to do it right. Jenn's eye for detail, contemporary designs, and mass appeal make her highly sought after to create identities for major national brand campaigns by numerous advertising agencies. Her designs are classic, clean, and powerful. And we've included a small handful of her designs for few of our voice-over clients in this chapter to assist you with your pending graphics.

### Jenn Harrell, Wyville USA
e-mail:  wyvilleusa@earthlink.net

If you are producing your demo through Sound Advice, we'll be happy to recommend one of our current graphic artist options, including Jenn Harrell, Wyville, USA. All of our graphic artist recommendations create compelling designs, they know the drill as to what a voice talent needs created for the most effective promotions and, of course, the variety of formats necessary to reproduce your designs.

## What Makes a Graphic Great

The goal of your graphic above anything else is *to make your name known*, related to voice-over, and to be inviting enough to get your demo heard. A well-crafted logo, or identity, will establish name recognition as you continually market yourself to those most likely to hire you. Therefore, the mission of your graphics is to *make a logo out of your name.*

Your logo is the unifying element that generates an interest in who you are and what you bring to the table as a professional. The design on your Web site and promotional postcards doesn't have to mirror each other, but it needs to forward your logo as a brand.

Ideally, your design/logo will continue to represent you for a good five to six years or more depending on your age and provided the style doesn't become outdated or misrepresents how you're perceived.

You may choose to update your design in the future in a different color story. For example, instead of yellow, red, orange, and white, the next version of your graphic may be in blue, green, yellow, and white, yet in the same design. You can get a good deal of longevity out of great graphic in this way.

Again, the primary mission is to generate an interest and create name recognition as well as help define your professional personality.

## What to Avoid

Your name may be at the forefront of a design, but if the font is too elaborate or difficult to read, the graphic will fail.

You may love the graphic element, but if your name floats on top of the design and doesn't have unified appearance, there will be a disconnect in your graphic.

Avoid making a literal icon out of it if your name is Fox or Glass or Peach or something. They're uninspired and *unintentionally* resemble an advertising campaign misplaced during the Korean War. Avoid the obvious, whenever possible.

The truth is you don't need a lot of random verbiage muddying up your graphics. Avoid descriptive terms, such as, "versatile, witty, sophisticated," as well. The rule here is: SHOW us with your demo—don't *tell* us. Besides, these terms are subjective and can be limiting. And they read as amateurish. Let your graphic say who you are conceptually rather than being so literal.

And no headshots included on your graphics, either, unless you are over 70 or under 16 years old. Because we don't want to know what you actually look like as a voice-over, we want to *imagine* what you look like. Headshots are for film, TV, and print. Keep your on-camera promotion SEPARATE from your voice-over.

No caricatures either—far too reminiscent of a state fair in Iowa. So assuming this isn't what you're aiming for, avoid it.

# What If You Hate Everything Your Graphic Designer Presents

This is a tricky one.

It's not common with the graphic artists we recommend, but it does happen from time to time, even with the most experienced graphic artists and the most easygoing voice-over clients. An open, businesslike communication is the *only* way to handle the situation. DO NOT roll over and play dead. You will have to live with the consequences if you do.

If none of the designs appeals to you at all, be professional and honest with your graphic artist right away. Leave emotion out of it. Everyone wants to be blown away from the initial images, but this rarely happens.  So take a breath. Don't ask everyone you know whether they like them or what they think.  That never helps and will serve only to confuse you further.

Leave the images alone for a couple days and then come back to them.  Look over the designs and focus in on what you *like* about them not what you *don't*.  Do you like your first name on this one and your last name on that?  Do you like the fonts used in this one, and shapes or stripes in that? Great, you can start there when you speak with your graphic artist.  It will yield far better results regardless where this relationship ends up. Do you like the background on this one, but the rest don't do it for you? Let the graphic artist know you'll need to see a few more options. And start again with offering tangible suggestions, such as "I'd like to see one option that's similar to the packaging on Method products from Target," and "Can I see something that echoes the style of what Audi currently has on its Web site?"

Give them three to five tangible options such as this with regard to color, font, and form.  That will help them and, ideally, that will help you. It's usually not a problem and considered part of the cost, unless you paying them an hourly rate or they are doing all this for you for gratis. Determine whether he would be willing to create three or four more roughs for you.

If none of them appear dynamic or professional enough after that, cut your losses. The graphic artist will usually keep the deposit for the work they put in and you should begin again with another graphic designer.

This is standard operating procedure among professionals.

However, if your graphic artist accommodates numerous changes much beyond these, they may require an additional sum. It would be perfectly appropriate to ask how many options and changes are deemed acceptable, as unlimited changes is *never* acceptable, whether you're happy or not.

This is often a very subjective dilemma, however the fact remains the graphic artist delivered a product. The number and magnitude of changes he may be willing to deliver from his original quote should be discussed *before* you incur a greater expense than your budget might allow. Or before imposing excessive demands beyond a professional comfort level. It can be a rather slippery slope. When in doubt, ASK!

Most professionals respond best to professional behavior, and everyone is far more likely to get what they're after in the end if you take the high road. Allow the graphic artist to take your lead and run with it.

## *Before* Signing off on Your Graphics

The onus ultimately always falls to YOU whether or not things are spelled correctly, whether your QR Code links to your site effectively, and that all the numbers and your return address are correct. So be sure to TRIPLE CHECK each and every detail on every single element the graphic artist asks you to approve. Be sure ALL the contact information on each promotional item is correct.

Also, be sure every piece of promo has your contact information on it, including your cell phone, Web address, QR Code, and e-mail address.

(Follow the details in Chapter 14, Producing Your Demo & Various Promo, for suggested return address and contact information.)

# Demo Graphics Samples

The following examples of exceptional voice demo graphics were designed by Jenn Harrell of Wyville USA. We've worked longest and more extensively with Jenn than any other single graphic designer, so we thought her designs would offer you the best illustration of truly effective branding.

Please note the Web site is taken directly from the postcard design, however Wyville USA defers to our recommended Web designers for this service.

(See Chapter 16, Web Sites, for more detail.)

We've included the basic art direction we offered for each of the following graphics.

Notice we didn't tell Jenn precisely what to do.

These graphics were successful because we described *who each talent is conceptually and the mood (or moods)* we're trying to convey with each identity in order to entice someone to listen.

Your demo needs to *look like you sound.* Most talent are far too close to this to effectively art direct their own graphics. (But then few are as skillful as Jenn Harrell when it comes to creating your brand identity.)

1. Jami Considine. Our art direction: 25-to-35-year-old female, cheerful, refined, bright, playful.

2. Phil O'Brien. Our art direction: 35-to-45-ish, direct, genuine, smart, colorful, with a bit of wit.

3. Eva Breneman. Our art direction: 30-to-40-year-old sophisticated female, articulate, authentic, refined.

4. Bill Greene. Our art direction: 30-something, grounded, earthy, natural, real.

5. Steve Graham. Our art direction: 30-to-40-year-old guy. Progressive, lower-end voice, sophisticated, yet earthy.

6. Steve Cannon. Our art direction: 40-something, approachable, real guy, whimsy.

7. Frances Miller. Our art direction: Young, professional, contemporary, approachable.

8. Me. Our art direction: I was looking to entice back my retail voice work (Sears, Macy's, etc.), so I told Jenn, "Imagine walking through Macy's makeup aisles. So whatever that conjures up!" 'Nuf said. It came out better than I could have ever imagined.

1.

2.

3.

4.

5.

6.

**7.**

**8.**

# Chapter 16: Web Sites

"The Internet is like alcohol in some sense. It accentuates what you would do anyway. If you want to be a loner, you can be more alone. If you want to connect,
it makes it easier to connect."
—Esther Dyson

Potentially the greatest promotional tool you have available to you, aside from your voice-over demos and headshots themselves, is your Web site. In fact, the primary source with which your completed demos are presented and promoted is your voice-over-only Web site.

According to current standards, a Web presence far exceeds the usefulness of a CD to present your demos. Regardless, the adage "Luck is when preparedness meets opportunity" applies here, which is why we continue to recommend you have your graphics created as a CD face as well. In this way you can still create a CD from home should you find you need one on short notice.

(See Chapter 15, Graphics, for more details.)

## Your Domain Name Is Not Your Web Site

It's important to note that your Web *address* and your Web *hosting* are two distinctly separate entities. Far too often we hear at Sound Advice from our somewhat novice, albeit enthusiastic clients as we begin their demo production process, that they've already secured their Web site. "I've got my name already! It was cheap! It only cost me $10!" Unfortunately, this can pose a problem when it comes time to establishing Web *hosting*. And here's why: Your Web address is NOT your Web page, nor is it the location where your page will ultimately reside. It is simply a name that points TO your site, it ISN'T the site itself.

Once your site is *created*, it will then be hosted at a virtual location on the Internet, such as Dreamhost, HostMonster or Go Daddy. That hosting is typically secured for a year at a time.

However, if you have secured your Web *address* (your domain name) for only a year at a time, as many people do, and you have done so four to six months *prior* to establishing your *hosting*, then your address will *expire* four to six months in advance of your hosting—rendering your site completely inaccessible with that specific address once it has expired. It will appear to you that your site has simply vanished.

It still exists on the Internet at the location where it's hosted, however without that all-important Web address, it will not be readily accessible.

Now, I know what you're thinking, "Why don't I just renew my Web address for $10 again?" If it were only that simple.

You'll be contacted a good 30 days in advance of the expiration of your *Web address*, whereas you always have the option of placing your *Web hosting* on an auto-renewal basis. Of course, placing your domain name on auto-renewal would save a lot of trouble as well. However, many individuals neglect to do so and accidentally allow their domain names to lapse, figuring it to be a small fee to pay to renew. However, there's a far greater problem that's about to rear its ugly head.

## If You Inadvertently Let Your Domain Expire

You may have assumed since you owned your domain name originally (and it's your name after all) no one would want it and you could casually take your time and even let it expire only to renew it at a later, more convenient date. This is a common misconception especially for those who aren't all that tech or Web savvy. Unfortunately, picking up what you let expire may prove far more convoluted and costly than you might have ever imagined.

First of all, your domain name is NOT the same as your Web hosting. They are two separate and distinctly different things. Your domain name LEADS to where your Web site is actually located (host) on the Internet. So, while your Web address may have expired, if you established your Web hosting independent of (often months AFTER) purchasing your Web address, they will be on two distinctly and different renewal cycles and will need to be renewed separately as well.

Now, that may sound simple enough, but it poses quite a few problems when it comes to maintaining your Web presence and promotion, especially if you secured each for only a single year at a time. When promoting yourself as a voice-over you're promoting this domain name as your primary contact with which to locate your demos online.

Think of your domain name as a virtual phone number that leads us to where your demos can be heard and your brand identity can communicate who you are and what you do best as a professional. But if your domain name expires independent of your Web hosting, your Web site will still exist online, however there's no address in existence with which anyone will be able to reach your site.

To add to this, once your domain name expires, you only have a brief grace period of between 15 and 29 days to renew. In some instances (depending on who you used to secure your domain name) it may take up to a full year before an expired domain name might be openly available again. Which is precisely why at **Sound Advice** we encourage you to secure your domain name at the SAME TIME as your Web hosting is being established.

In fact, here at **Sound Advice** the sequence we recommend for establishing your Web site is as follows:

> a) Have your graphics designed FIRST, then forward your approved graphics to the Web designer.

> b) The Web designer (in our case, Ron Martin ron@ronmartinwebdesign.com) creates your Web site in a format that can be easily seen on mobile devices as well as laptops and desktop computers, establishing your hosting, and THEN securing your domain name (with the

corresponding e-mail) to include on all of your promotional materials.

It's not the end of the world if you secured your domain name five minutes after your first coaching, well in advance of even producing your demos. In fact, you can have dozens of domain names leading to the very same Web site. However, the issue lies when you've established a *particular* domain name on all of your promotional materials leading the recipients of your beautifully choreographed promotions absolutely nowhere, which ultimately renders your promo useless. And all this often unbeknownst to you if you were unaware of the fact that your domain name evaporated into the ether because it was created six to eight months prior to your Web hosting, just as an example.

All of this is certainly a cautionary tale unto itself, but sadly there's more to this story. Buckle your seat belt.

It's likely you registered your now-expired Web domain name on Go Daddy or some such site for only ten bucks. The Central Registry (the global governing source for all things dealing with Web addresses, as meager as that may be) mandates a fee of approximately $100 to renew any expired domain name, even if it once belonged to you, provided you contact them PRIOR to the address becoming openly available (again, it's elusive as to how long this grace period may be), and provided a cybersquatter doesn't snatch up this domain name ahead of you.

According to redalkemi.com, "Cybersquatting is a malpractice done by (CYBER CROOKS) who use (your) domain name with a bad intent to capitalize on the name and market value."

But why would they want to buy YOUR name? In plain English: MONEY. The cybersquatter will offer you the opportunity to purchase your former domain name for a ridiculously inflated price hoping it means enough to you to buy it back because you've established this domain name as your primary lifeline for your small business.

It's a cold, cruel Web world out there. No doubt about it.

So, if you don't reregister your domain name with an Internet registrar PRIOR to this domain name effectively expiring, anyone can purchase it. Cybersquatters typically use automated software tools called bots (I know, I know, totally sci-fi, but it's a fact). These cyberbots search for domain names and snag them the instant the Web address lapses, making it impossible for you to renew your own domain name without first paying these crooks up to $500 or more to get it back. They're counting on the fact that your business relies on this Web address and that your clients know you by this route, and you're desperate to get it back.

It's as if your phone number had an expiration that you were unaware of, and after it expired these unscrupulous characters took it over and offered to sell it back to you for more than *100 times* what you paid for it. In fact, that's precisely what this situation is like.

Your promotional momentum will have been brought to a screeching halt until this is all sorted out, which it can be, but not without some concerted effort and expense, especially considering CDs have all but been replaced with downloading your demos off the Internet and accessing your demos on your voice-over-only Web page.

We can't impress upon you enough how important it is to pay attention to your Web and domain renewal e-mails and to be sure to RENEW your Web address well before it expires. That's the best way to avoid all this drama and allow you the greatest opportunity to sidestep disaster. And if you're in doubt, contact Ron Martin for Web assistance. He's a remarkable resource who's reliable, where others are not. It's his business to establish, design, and help you maintain your Web site.

## There's a Solution for Every Problem

There's a solution for every problem, and there's a hat for every head.

An entirely new Web address would have to be secured to effectively access your site again. This would also require rewriting the code on your site to accommodate the change that would ultimately impact your e-mail address. Most e-mail addresses are typically edited into the flash element on your site, making them a hyperlink, which requires a professional Web designer to alter, costing you even more. In other words, none of this is a quick and easy fix. But wait—lest we forget to mention the necessity of reissuing all of your promo to reflect the *new* Web address AND your new e-mail! So, much for a quick and cheap "Web address," eh?

Our suggestion: When and wherever possible, secure your Web address and hosting AT THE SAME TIME, rather than months apart. And whenever possible, do so for a good ten years at a time to avoid any interruption of service or promotion. If that's not possible, be sure to maintain your site(s) with consistency as it is likely you are only just getting started in this field and you want to avoid interruption of promotion of your greatest professional tools: your voice-over demos and/or headshots and on-camera reels.

Beyond that, our best parting advice (and to quote *Futurama*), "Don't date robots!"

## What's in a Domain Name

If your name is taken (or someone already has that Web address and/or e-mail), then a simple www.joetalent**vo**.com not only makes sense, but it's far easier to remember, too. Again, this gives potential employment opportunities a simpler task of locating you and will further associate your name with voice-over.

If, for example, your Web address is www.joetalent.com your e-mail should echo that, to further promote the Web address, such as joe@joetalent.com rather than use something complicated like razzledazzle123.com, for instance. In fact, we strongly encourage you to avoid numbers entirely. They tend to complicate the situation rather than simplify. Besides, it makes matters easier, too, when interested parties Google your name.

These elements are all part of promoting your brand and identity in this field.

## How to Create the Most Effective Site

We wholeheartedly recommend Ron Martin to design your Web page.

Utilizing Ron will ensure your Web page will be easily accessed on multiple browsers, as well as on mobile devices (i.e., cell phones, Blackberries, and iPads). That may seem like a no-brainer, but I assure you it's not. These are key factors as to whether your site will be truly accessible, and are details consistently overlooked by the novice Web designer.

His Web site is: ronmartinwebdesign.com/sound-advice-clients. You can e-mail him your graphic design and he'll create a workable Web page dedicated strictly to your voice-over.

He can even create your QR Code for you, if you're not all that tech savvy, as well to convert your postcard promotions into direct links to your demo Web site. And if you require an on-camera Web page(s), he is able to create that as well.

## Web Page Etiquette

It's important *nothing* on your Web page make a sound until you click on it to do so. It's just bad manners and violates the etiquette of proper Internet protocol, which is completely off-putting and should be avoided. It's annoying when something goes "boing-boing-boing" or "swoosh" or creaks like a squeaky door when you scroll over it. Ick. Don't do that. Again, NOTHING should make a sound on your site until the visitor clicks on it to do so. This can be completely off putting when you are listening to music while you are surfing the net, as so many people do, because it creates a cacophony of noises between your demo and whatever they are listening to.

Your Web page should load within three to four seconds and allow the visitor to click on your demos *immediately*. If a visitor has to click more than *twice* to hear your demo—you've already lost him. And we can't have that.

Your Web designer needs to incorporate your MP3s into your site in such a way as *to not open an additional window* in order to hear your demo tracks.  This way visitors to your site can listen to your demos while continuing to look at your super-cool graphics, your name, and your contact information.

## New Web Technology

In recent years, many people have taken advantage of Adobe Flash elements on their Web sites.  Flash gives the Web site some animation to add visual interest to the page.  And until recently, Flash was the most common way of incorporating animation in a Web site.

The problem arises when a potential client tries to view your site on his smartphone (iPhone, Blackberry) or iPad, if your site happened to be designed primarily with Flash. It should be noted your site will be viewed by various producers from their mobile devices more often than from a standard laptop.

Flash is NOT mobile-device- or iPad-friendly and it never will be, per *Apple*.  So that potential client ends up looking at a big, *blank* page because these mobile devices can't run Flash.

Mobile devices can read HTML with no problem, however, but designing Web sites in HTML is something of a throwback.

Fear not, there's a solution!  The newest version of HTML (HTML5) can add animation/video type elements without incorporating Flash to your Web site but won't cut out mobile devices like the iPhone or iPad.

So, if you already have your site up and running, we strongly encourage you to add a mobile-friendly version to your site, such as an HTML5 version. We're not suggesting you throw the baby out with the bathwater, we're simply saying you should *add this version to it*.  This way anyone who wants to check out your demos online can do so easily, regardless of what they're using to access your site. Again, your target audience (various producers, creative directors, and copywriters) will most likely view your site from one of their mobile devices than from any other online source.

If you're having your site designed for the first time, we suggest that you have your Web designer use HTML5 for any animation elements for the most versatile site possible.

## QR Codes and Your Web Site

In addition to ensuring your site can be seen on mobile devices, promoting your Web site by including a **QR Code** to your promotional postcards makes your promo interactive.

QR stands for Quick Response. Quick Response Codes have revolutionized direct mailing and promotion. They are quick to create. (IF you are a techie! If not, stay out of it. Leave it to the professionals.) QR Codes are simple to create and easy to scan from virtually any mobile device or tablet (iPhone, iPad, or Android).

Your Web designer should create your QR Code for you to add to your promo in order to drive substantially more traffic to your demo Web site, but ONLY if your site can be viewed on these devices. (Once you have your QR Code, it needs to be sent back to your graphic artist to add to your postcard and C-Shell label.)

(See Chapter 7, Advancing Technology, and Chapter 19, How to Get Work for more information regarding QR Codes.)

## The Importance of a Voice-over Only Web Page

It's important to keep your voice-over and on-camera Web sites independent of each other, as we discovered from extensive surveying, due to the fact that few, if any, potential hiring opportunities for voice-over want to _see_ what you look like. Instead they want to IMAGINE what you look like. So we suggest you have a link to your voice-over Web page from your on-camera Web site, if you have one, but NOT the other way around.

To illustrate this point, have you ever seen what George Jetson or Fred Flintstone looks like in real life? Unless you know them personally, this would likely be a dramatic departure from your reality. If you saw Ronald McDonald out of costume and makeup, you'd be disappointed. The fact is voice-over creates an image in the listener's imagination. The objective of your Web site is to maintain this illusion by keeping the on-camera Web site independent of the voice-over-only site. Combining their purpose only confuses the issue.

There are only a handful of exceptions to this rule:
- Children and young adults (18 years of age and under)
- If you are more than 70 years of age, and sound like it
- If you are already established as a talent and known for your on-camera personae, such as Seth MacFarlane (creator of *Family Guy*), Nancy Cartwright (the voice of Bart Simpson, among many, many others), or you're a known film star such as Mike Myers, Eddie Murphy, or Cameron Diaz, to name a few
- Your voice-over Web site should be a *single*-page site, featuring:
    - Your voice-over demos (MP3s ONLY)
    - Your graphic logo, that furthers your name as a brand (which may be repeated on your on-camera Web site, if applicable)
    - Your contact information, and that's it!

No bios, please. You will spend hours creating these and only your family and very few of your friends will actually read them in their entirety. Your résumé is required ONLY if you're pursuing stage or on-camera work, rather than voice-over. Also, please avoid random cross-referencing of other interests or professions such as painting, directing, or screenwriting, for instance.

Further, on your voice-over only site, your demo tracks should be available *only* in the form of MP3s. Not as AIFF or WAV files—*just* MP3.

(See Chapter 7, Advancing Technology, for further details.)

If you are pursuing on-camera work, you should have a single-page site that concentrates promoting you commercially and theatrically (film and television).

Your on-camera Web site should include:

- A professional graphic logo that forwards your "brand" and makes your name known
- Your headshots, including at least two, but no more than eight professional looks, but ONLY if they are incredible shot and really look like YOU and the work you're attempting to secure professionally
- A brief, but current, on-camera reel, if you have one
- A PDF of your most current résumé
- Your contact information, as well as any talent-management or talent-agent contact info
- A link that leads directly to your voice-over ONLY Web page

## Separation Anxiety

We can't impress upon you how important it is to keep these two sites separate. Again, our extensive surveying at **Sound Advice** revealed those looking to hire you for voice-over don't want to know what you look like, they want to *imagine* what you look like.

Therefore avoid using photos or even illustrations of yourself. To add to this, if your image is serious and your demo lighthearted (or vice versa), your image would contradict the effect you've set out to create with the demo track. Instead, you should have a separate page devoted totally to your theatrical pursuits (film and television).

Any promotional plan, in order to be effective, relies on a *single-minded* approach. Don't try to accomplish a zillion things with a single site. Therefore, you should NOT be trying to secure on-camera or stage work while simultaneously focusing your efforts on voice-over with this Web page. Know your audience. Your demos are designed to target commercial producers and potential talent buyers interested in hiring you for the specific genre of voice-over you do best.

If you are pursuing on-camera work *as well as voice-over*, the objective is to have an overall site that features your headshots, your résumé, your on-camera reel and has a direct link to your voice-over only Web page. That voice-over-only page can be accessed independently of the on-camera site. However, we don't recommend your voice-over page have a link that returns you to your headshots. Again, no one looking to hire you wants to know what you look like—they want to IMAGINE what you look like. This is a critical point and can't be emphasized enough. It can be a deal killer. Target your efforts.

Additionally, you will have two separate Web addresses for each site. For instance, if you are pursuing voice-over solely, your Web address should be your name, such as Susietalent.com, or Susietalent**vo**.com. If you are going after both on-camera and voice-over, we still recommend two separate domain addresses.

Granted if you already have Susietalent.com for on-camera, you could add a simple Susietalent.com/VO, however, with an attempt to maintain that those looking to hire you for voice-over are primarily interested in what they imagine you look like, rather than actually seeing what you look like.

Before you run off and establish your *Web address*, it's important to point out three things must be addressed when creating your Web site(s):
- The Web design (as opposed to the logo design)
- The Web *hosting*
- The *domain name*, and in that order

You may be under the impression it doesn't matter which order you secure these three vital elements. In that case, I'd suggest you read this chapter all over again, 'cuz you missed something. There's an order of importance designed to save you a great deal of time, money, and effort.

# Chapter 17:  Headshots and Résumés

"Opportunity is missed by most people because it is dressed
in overalls and looks like work."
—Thomas A. Edison

A good headshot and résumé is the common calling card of a professional talent pursuing on-camera or stage work.

In fact, you *can't* land commercial representation from a talent agent without first having a really good headshot and a decent résumé. The headshot, like your voice-over demo, is your first opportunity to let the agent know whether you are up to speed as a talent.  It's a dead giveaway as to whether you know what you're doing in this business. It defines you—it types you.

One casting director put it this way, "Your headshots are a marketing tool.  They must sell your type."

A talent agent will either be interested in you from what your headshot communicates and will become engaged enough to want to call you in or not.  Pure and simple.

A bad headshot, like a bad demo, will turn a talent agent off in a heartbeat. It's a career killer. There's absolutely no excuse for a bad headshot, because it exhibits a complete lack of professionalism if it's not up to the industry's current standards.
So, please don't have a cheap attack when it comes to your headshots. This is one of those times where you should really spend the money. The investment will pay you back in aces if you do.

Again, if you aren't in the ballpark, you can't play ball.

You want to be wise in your choices of photographer, shots, reproduction, and distribution. It's the difference between working and NOT working.

## Do I Need a Headshot to Land Voice-over?

You *don't* need a headshot to land voice-over work; you need a headshot to *land on-camera* work and to land an agent who handles more than just voice-over.

Not everyone pursuing voice-over is also interested in pursuing on-camera work, but since such a substantial number are, we felt it necessary to include our best advice regarding headshots in this volume. And if you're interested only in voice-over work, at least for the time being, many local talent agents will probably ask you if you're interested in pursuing on-camera, especially if that agent happens to handle *both* voice-over and on-camera, as many do.

Nevertheless, should you decide at a later date you'd like to pursue on-camera work, this section should be helpful. Keep in mind sending a talent agent a headshot implies you are interested in being submitted for such work, so only do this if you actually intend to accept the work.

But don't feel you have to pursue on-camera. If you're interested solely in voice-over work, that's perfectly acceptable and completely up to you. It's your career.

## How Do I Look?

Consider this: Agents, casting directors, producers and directors will be viewing your headshots online. Therefore, in the end, they will be viewing a thumbnail-size JPEG of your headshots.

So, to be the most effective, your main shot must be "you" coming at the camera *head-on*, with all of your best personality and emotion penetrating the shot. It's imperative your headshot look like YOU, the person walking into the audition.

Given the size of your headshots as they are viewed online, they should, for the most part, be tighter than a three-quarter shot (in which most of your body can be viewed). Ideally, most of your shots will have you framed from the middle of your chest on up, or from your solar plexus on up is in frame (slightly more than head and shoulders).

It's standard to have a variety of different looks/headshots. Three to five final looks are more than enough, again provided (and we can't say it enough) the shots look like you. Any more than that is overwhelming and unnecessary.

Once you are chosen for a theatrical audition from your headshot online, from either an agent, submission, or from any number of the online casting services, many casting directors prefer you arrive at the audition with the very same headshot in hand for recognition sake. (Branding.) Bring the headshot that won you the audition. It obviously got you in the door.

For commercial auditions, you will receive an e-mail from an online casting site, which will reflect the audition details, any sides (scripts) to be downloaded, your stats, and will feature the shot they chose of you that got you this audition. Unless noted, you aren't likely to need to give them a headshot for these auditions.

However, there seems to be a bit of a split among casting directors on this point. Some contend they'd like to see other looks as well. To be safe, lead with the shot that got you the audition, and be sure to bring all three to five of your headshots to the audition should the need arise. Again, they're your marketing tools, and you're definitely in the market at the audition. Better to be prepared than left shorthanded.

What we're striving for as your finished product, when it comes to your headshots, is three to five looks (the person walking in to that casting session) that represent you best for the work you're best suited to land. They should all be in JPEG form (the MP3 equivalent of a headshot) so you can submit your headshots online, or via e-mail, and printed out as an 8x10 headshot with your résumé attached to the back.

It may seem elementary but it stands mentioning: color headshots, rather than black and white, are the standard.

## Leave It to the Professionals

Be the talent on the shoot, not the stylist, not the makeup artist, and especially not the photographer. Be yourself and let everyone else do his job. As a talent, *your* job is to remain engaged and interested. You are on the job throughout this shoot.

Be free enough to follow the direction the photographer gives you.

Play as many attitudes as you possibly can. Shots with all smiles are a bit too static and can appear forced and affected after a while.

Let us see that you're thinking something or feeling or playing something—and make that something *interesting*. Play a scene from your last production or your favorite movie or do a monologue. Exaggerate it! Tell a story, do stand-up. Go for it. Entertain yourself and you will find your audience.

Don't be in a hurry to get out of there. Make yourself comfortable and don't rush the shoot.

Most importantly: Express yourself and choose shots that look like YOU!

## Looks

What you're striving for as the all-important, final product when it comes to your headshots is a small handful of looks. For instance: a commercial shot, a theatrical (film and television) shot, and one to three of the following that most applies to you:

The Professional    The Mom / The Dad        The Comic/Quirky

The Girl Next Door   The Blue Collar Worker   The Regular Guy

The Athlete    The Romantic Interest/Lead        The Hero/Heroine

The Sexy Vixen/Stud    The Down-Trodden      The Bad Guy/Gal

The Upscale          The Intellectual         The Natural-Earthy

The Rugged    The Student    The Surfer-Slacker   The Innocent

## The BEST Photographers

To be honest, there are only a few photographers we can confidently recommend, simply because quality counts. So, don't scrimp. The success of your career absolutely depends on it. Headshots are an investment.  Treat them as such.

Most professionals shoot on digital today rather than film, but there are still a few purists, even in the few photographers we endorse. As long as their shots are exceptional, and they make you feel at ease at the shoot, you're more likely to get the greatest outcome.

## In Chicago

**Zoe McKenzie Photography** has to be my *very* favorite in Chicago and the Midwest. Photographer Sandy Sager shoots remarkable color shots that rival ANY I've seen—*anywhere*.  Sandy named her business after her daughter, Zoe. She is cost-effective, professional, and produces terrific results. Discuss her process with her staff beforehand as well as what you hope to achieve. You're sure to get a few looks that will get you noticed and last you.

Be sure to insist they DO NOT RETOUCH your shots in advance of your viewing them, even if the studio offers this service as a favor. I promise you, this is NOT what they do best.  You want your shots as is, rather than tampered with.  If there is a slight modification to be made through retouching, you need to have control of that option rather than have anyone dictate that change prior to your approval.  If you find your shots have been tampered with PRIOR to your viewing, insist on receiving the unadulterated versions to run past your agent and/or professional acting coach, manager, or adviser.

(See Reproducing Your Headshots in this chapter)

### Zoe McKenzie Photography
Photographer: Sandy Sager
(773) 852-1189
E-mail: info@zoe-photo.com
www.zoe-photo.com

### Janna Giacoppo Photography
Studio Manager: Julia Fields
Chicago, IL
(312) 437-5555
E-mail: info@jannagiacoppo.com
www.jannagiacoppo.com

## In Los Angeles

### Paul Gregory Photography
(323) 848-9682
E-mail: paulgregoryphoto@mac.com
www.paulgregoryphotography.com

### Theo and Juliet Photography
(310) 973-7315
E-mails: juliet@theoandjuliet.com, theo@theoandjuliet.com
www.theoandjuliet.com

### Vandiveer Photography
(323) 630-0344
E-mail: mail@jvimages.com
www.stunningheadshots.com

### Denice Duff Photography
(818) 769-0707
E-mail: deniceduff@sbcglobal.net
www.duffimages.com

## In New York

**Kristin Hoebermann Photography**
 (212) 807-8014
www.hoebermannstudio.com

**Andrew Brucker**
 (212) 724-3236
www.andrewbruckerheadshots.com

**Peter Hurley**
Chelsea Arts Building
 (212) 627-2210
www.peterhurley.com/photography/actors-headshots
*Peter also has studios in Los Angeles* (310) 363-0020
*and Dallas* (214) 377-0062.

**Chia Messina**
 (212) 929-0917
www.chiamessina.com/actor-headshots

## Before and During the Shoot

You will meet with your photographer well in advance of the shoot to ensure you're both on the same page and so you can give her a deposit, which is typically required to secure your photo shoot.

Cancellation fees always apply, so learn what your photographer expects and requires ahead of time. It's usually listed on her Web site.

Let the photographer know what your goals are. Most professionals suggest their own makeup artists and rates.

Use examples of your photographer's existing work as to the looks and styles you're interested in having shot. Ensure your photographer considers those shots are correct for you.

Bring plenty of water and whatever it takes to keep your energy up, including friends, if the photographer is okay with that. Again, determine this well in advance of your shoot.

Refer to the list of looks included earlier in this chapter to help you articulate what you're after and to help the photographer better convey what her professional viewpoint may be on the subject.

Be sure to arrive the day of your shoot on time, well rested, and ready to work! If you prepare well ahead of time, this shouldn't be a problem.

Your headshots should show you have a thought in your head; you have expression, can animate yourself, and simply be yourself comfortably. They should convey your personality naturally. An affected (unreal, forced) personality is off-putting and obvious. You should feel comfortable and safe to accomplish the best results. Provided you've enlisted any one of the professional photographers we've listed in this chapter, you'll be in extremely capable hands.

## Costs
Headshots can run between $450 and $1,200 for a shoot, depending on how many rolls, shots, and/or desired looks and, of course, depending on the photographer.

Makeup artists and reproductions will of course incur additional costs.

## What to Wear, What to Wear

Bring a variety of clothes. It's better to have way too much to choose from than not enough. It always seems to be the last piece you threw into your garment bag is the one the photographer likes best.

During your initial meeting with your photographer you need to discuss if they will choose what you're wearing. Some do, some leave it to you and offer modifications as you go. Determine this ahead of time.

Each recommended photographer offers great suggestions and information on his or her Web site. Read as many of them as possible for the best advice. They typically suggest do's and don'ts regarding colors, materials, and prints. Most suggest layering for a more interesting look that generally works best on camera, provided that suits you. You may be a minimalist—simple tees, jeans, and bare feet, perhaps, might be perfect for you. Just be sure to offer more than only one or two options.

Nudes are never appropriate for headshots. And bathing suit shots are for models, not actors.

If you are "cut out of marble" as the saying goes, and want to show off your six pack, it's perfectly appropriate for men to have a few shots sans shirt, provided the shot has more to do with your personality and simply highlights your hard-earned physique.

Tailored, well-fitting clothing, rather than garments that are too tight or too baggy will work best. Most dry cleaners offer tailoring services for a small charge. It's worth the expense, as these items often become your auditioning wardrobe. The better they fit, they better they look.

DON'T dress in costume. If you're going after a specific type, which you certainly should, then "suggest" the role through clothing. Imply the type or role through emotion and thought. The same holds true at the audition. (However, most auditions will specifically ask for wardrobe demands.) No lab coats or scrubs or cop costumes in your headshots. No fireman, construction worker, or chef hats, and no UPS, maid, or army uniforms. They are too specific and such shots are considered outdated. (Again, the same goes for the audition. Imply these roles, unless otherwise requested for each audition. Instead, concentrate on the emotion and mindset and convey these roles as an actor, rather than showing us you know how to play dress up.)

Bring a variety of shoes. We carry ourselves differently in different shoes. Heels, loafers, tennis shoes (as long as they're CLEAN), business shoes, or even barefoot! Whatever makes you happy, and as long as they offer you an option in terms of how you carry yourself. Just be sure they look neat and tidy and relatively new, should they ultimately appear in the shot.

If you've never treated yourself to a manicure/pedicure, I suggest you do so the day before your shoot. This goes for guys, too. (In fact it may even go double for guys!) There's a cheap nail salon nearly on every block in most cities nationwide. You won't hesitate to remove your shoes if you do.

We want your face and your build to be the focus of the shot, but if your hands and feet end up in the shot and they are distracting for the wrong reasons, or should they draw unwelcome attention away from you and your face, you can't have that retouched quite so easily.

Look at this shoot as an opportunity to build your on-camera wardrobe. You're expected to have a variety of looks for commercial auditions, corporate industrial (if applicable), television, and film.

Go over to the Gap, the Limited or Banana Republic and either buy or, at the very least, observe in detail what the mannequins are sporting from head to toe. There's your standard commercial look. If money's tight, the Salvation Army or Goodwill are great options. Many talent find their best audition clothes from discount places, including hospital scrubs and lab coats.

Frankly, they may not even be what you might normally consider as your style, but they may be the "soccer mom" or the "average guy at work" look that you will be considered for, provided you offer these options in your headshots.

## The Makeup Artist

Go with a makeup artist your photographer recommends most. They've likely worked together before and will work together to make you look great. Don't have a cheap attack at this point.

*All* women should count on securing a good makeup artist, even the most natural, earthy types. The goal here is to put your best foot forward without losing who you are. Make sure, in advance, they will style your hair as well.

Some men may find they need one as well. We strongly encourage it.

As for teenage girls, there is NO question—a qualified makeup artist is an absolute MUST.

A good makeup artist will save you a great deal of money on retouching, no matter how great the photographer may be. Another good reason to hire a proper makeup artist is the hot tips you will inevitably pick up that could make a world of difference for you on future shoots and every day.

A proper makeup artist runs between $125 to $150 for men, and $175 to $225 for women, and is generally tipped about 20 percent on top of that. Consider bringing cash, but checks leave you with a record. Either way, ask for a receipt.

If you want more than one look with your hair, be sure to let her know *ahead of time*. Discuss in advance any changes she may do with your hair, how long she will be at the shoot, and how much time she may need prior to beginning the shoot (it's usually about an hour or so). The goal here is to have her make you look *very* natural, not made up and out of your element.

Don't be insulted or surprised if she informs you she will not be around for the whole shoot. She isn't necessarily there to be your stylist—unless you hire her for that too. That would be above and beyond the call of duty. If she does stay and helps style you during your entire shoot that would certainly call for another big fat tip! Again, discuss ahead of time what she feels is the extent of her commitment.

## Men and Facial Hair

Guys with beards, mustaches, major sideburns, or even the five o'clock shadow can and *should* shave at the shoot, if you want shot with and without. Do 50 to 100 shots with facial hair and a roll or two WITHOUT. We want a few looks here, and if that means tacking on an extra roll or two to accommodate the goatee and the adjustment without it, so be it. Just be sure to discuss this with the photographer well in advance of the session. Ask the photographer's advice.

Just be careful not to rush and cut yourself. This is another reason to enlist the services of a makeup artist and find out if it may or may *not* be something she is willing or able to provide.

On the other hand if you *are* your mustache—then *be the mustache*, I guess. You still want to be comfortable, but consider opening yourself up to a change. At the very least, be sure it looks clean.

As for toupees, shots with AND without will certainly give you a wider variety of options, and we are after options here. Women with longer hair would likely do a variety of styles as well.

## Glasses vs. Contacts

If you *always* wear glasses, then by all means wear them in your shots. If you sometimes wear contacts, try some shots with and some without.

## Music That Moves You

Provide music (and even people) that inspires you to move and brings out the *real* you.

Do NOT remain static during the shoot—move your body. You are NOT a bowl of fruit—try not to become a still life during the shoot. Move your body!
Have fun!

## How Many Rolls?

Plan on getting *no less* than 200 shots taken, regardless of whether your photographer shoots film or digital.  Trust me, you'll only just be getting comfortable after the first 60 to 75 shots.

Even if you're already an established talent, let's assume you're not accustomed to being the subject of a professional photography session. It takes some time and attention to relax and get really comfortable. All the more reason to plan on having *at least* 150 to 200 images shot, with the intention to choose approximately 10 to 12 looks. You may reproduce only one or two of these images en masse, but this is the goal.

## How Long Will the Shoot Take?

The length of a shoot depends on many factors, but generally men should expect to be here for two to three hours, and women for three to four hours.

You may be in makeup for an hour or so. You have to account for wardrobe changes, retouching your makeup, possibly restyling your hair, and changing locations and backgrounds a few times over. Take your time.

Discuss the length of the shoot with the photographer when you meet for your initial consultation.

Arrive with ample time to prep, in order to give yourself time to decompress and relax.

Give your shoot the time it is due and don't be in a mad rush to leave because you have to head to work or some such thing. Give yourself at least an hour after your shoot. It is work, after all. If you're rushing to get out of there your shots will reflect your anxiety to finish.

## Framing the Shot
The most effective headshots these days are facing forward, coming at the camera head-on. They often are head-and-shoulder shots, rather than extreme close-ups. A good medium shot, like that of a business professional, works well, too.

Primarily your looks should be **medium** to **medium close-ups**, as these shots communicate who you are quickly and effectively as thumbnail shots on online casting sites, which are your lifeline to on-camera work above any other source.

That said, peppering your shoot with a few good three-quarter looks (waist up, or thereabouts) will help vary up the series of shots you're posting online to promote you for film, television, and/or commercial work.

## Common Misnomers
Far too often stage actors choose headshots for theater that are too tight a shot to allow you to recognize who the actor is—even if they are standing in front of you. It's ironic really, considering stage is the one medium in which the audience views the talent from head to toe. But that extremely tight headshot ends up in the program, and only on the rarest occasion does it honestly look like the actor we just saw playing Biff in *Death of a Salesman*.

Most casting directors contend actors should *never* pick their own headshots, primarily because actors tend to choose the shots that convey themselves as they wish to be seen, rather than as they actually are. Generally, actors are often the worst judges of their own headshots.

You may love your eyes in this shot and your hair in that one, and the one "everyone" (your mom, your best friend, your dry cleaner) continually gravitates toward may be your least favorite. Frankly, your personal preference may not hold much weight in this department, I'm afraid. If you're getting a response from the shot— it's effective.

Keep in mind *you're not after one single perfect shot*. You're after a few looks from your headshots session. Be sure to give yourself some room. Precious few are completely comfortable and experienced in front of the camera, even if they've done dozens of jobs.

## Friends Don't Let Friends Shoot Their Headshots

DO *NOT* enlist a neighbor, relative, or friend as your photographer unless she happens to be a professional HEADSHOT photographer! That's *HEADSHOT* photographer. Regardless of how skillful your friend may be at shooting landscapes, realtors, kittens, or food, unless headshots are truly her area of expertise, we DON'T advise it!

What's that? "But she's *really* good! And she's not going to charge me. She wants to do me a favor!"
Trust me, I've been to the buffet, my friend, and it's true, there is no free lunch.

We can't stress what a waste of time it is to do anything but what is included in this chapter.

*Please* leave it to the professionals who already know the drill. Otherwise, it'll cost you time and it'll inevitably cost you money as you'll have to redo your headshots all over again if you expect to land work—and that's precisely why you're having your headshots taken! With that you'll add considerably to your overall frustration, and it can cost you your professional reputation. Save yourself, please, and simply follow what we've laid out for you here. All you'll be doing is delaying the inevitable.

## How Many Shots Should I Blow Up?

Usually within a week of your shoot the photographer will e-mail you link to a site where you will be able to view your headshots from your home computer, in most cases.

Each photographer has their own specific form of delivering the proof sheets or disc with all the shots from your shoot. It's best to determine this during your preliminary meeting with your photographer.

Narrow it down to your top eight to ten best looks, and blow those up to 8x10s. How do these shots look as JPEGs online? It is now somewhat unusual to go to a commercial on-camera audition with your hard copy headshot.

Many headshot photographers offer two clean (dust-free, repro-ready) 8x10s with every 100 shots, but don't limit yourself to only those few prints that come with the price of the shoot. Again, aim for eight to ten looks.

With all the online casting services available, three to five final looks are more than enough. According to some Los Angeles casting directors, some post far too many. The three to five you settle on should all have accompanied 8x10's for you to bring with you to auditions.

## How to Choose the Best Shots

This was one of the best pieces of advice ever passed on to me.

Don't ask *too* many people for their opinion when choosing your headshots—it'll only confuse you. Just ask one or two PROFESSIONAL people in the field, not friends, neighbors, or family members. No one who will be likely to have difficulty seeing you professionally; no one who might be more *subjective* rather than *objective*.

## Borders

The white border around your shot may be added by the photographer or by the photo reproduction house and may vary depending on the shot. The shot will require, at the very least, a one-inch border on the left, right, and bottom of the shot and about a half-inch border on the top. Nothing less than this border is really appropriate. In fact, your border may be as deep as three inches below the shot, half an inch on the left and right, and one inch on the top. It should appear balanced and include your name.

See examples on the headshot reproduction photo labs' Web sites listed below for specifics.

Your name should appear clear and concise in a font that reflects the emotional tone of the shot (playful, sophisticated, casual, etc.).

You can justify your name to the left, right, or center it depending on the composition of your shot. If your shot has more of you on the right side of the frame, justify your name to the far left for balance. If your image has more of you in the left side of the frame, justify your name to the right for balance.

## Comp Card

Some less scrupulous sources try to sell novice talent on getting a comp card, which is a compilation of shots. However, unless you intend to model full time you honestly don't need it. Comp cards are expensive and typically sold to parents trying to position their children for print work in catalogs and the like.

A simple Web page with three to five appropriate headshots is far more effective and all that's really needed.

Combining looks on a single headshot is outdated and says more about indecision, rather than versatility. It should be avoided entirely.

## Lithographs vs. Photographic Paper

For reproducing your headshots, *lithographs* are less expensive than reproducing your shots on photographic paper and allow you to print your résumé directly to the back from your home computer as needed.

Headshots reproduced on photographic paper are more expensive than lithos, but stapling the résumé (facing outward so it's easily read when you flip the headshot over) is perfectly acceptable as well. But, be sure to cut each résumé down from 8½x11 to 8x10 before stapling each to the back of your headshots.

Does photographic paper look better than litho? Sure, *slightly better*, but not by a huge margin, certainly nothing worth mentioning.

Certainly, most photographers would prefer their work be submitted on a better grade of paper than litho, but the purpose here, let's not forget, is to have them widely *distributed*.

When you reproduce your shots, regardless of whether your shots are lithos or photographic paper, be sure they have a matte finish, *not* glossy!

## Reproducing Your Headshots

No matter where you live, you can't go wrong with the following options to reproduce your headshots.

### Argentum Photo Lab
Los Angeles, CA 90028
(323) 461-2775          www.argentum.com

### ABC Pictures
Springfield, MO 65803
(888) 526-5336          www.abcpictures.com

### Fotek Photo Lab
West Hollywood, CA 90046-6724
(323) 512-0274          www.fotekphotolab.com

### Ray's Photo Lab   (Ray the Retoucher)
Los Angeles, CA 90028
(323) 463-0555

### Ray's Studio City location
Studio City, CA 91601
(818) 760-3656

## Digital Files (JPEG)

If your last shoot was on film rather than digital, and you're very *happy* with your shots, have your favorite shots scanned and made into JPEG files.

Besides reproducing your headshots, having your primary headshots available in a digital file format known as a **JPEG** is also required. Casting directors require JPEGs of your headshots to view headshots on their computers and to e-mail your shot to directors or producers, as needed.

You'll want your JPEGs to be no more and no less than **72 dpi** (dots per inch; the standard computer screen resolution) to e-mail them easily.

JPEGs that are 300 dpi (or more) are higher-resolution files used by professional printers to print/reproduce headshots. They're good for you to have on hand as a safety for reproductions or requests from producers and casting directors.

Your agent will require JPEG versions of your headshots as well. As long as your headshot is in a JPEG file at 72 dpi, and your headshot looks like the person walking in the door (namely YOU), then you should be in fine shape.

(See Chapter 7, Advancing Technology, for more details on this file format.)

### Making Your Shots Last
If you're between the ages of 16 and 28, a good rule of thumb is to count on getting new headshots every eighteen months or so. If you're 28 to 35, maybe every two or four years, provided your shots look like the person walking in the door.

Other than that? Again, it's relative. If the look continues to work for you—great. Don't change a thing. If not, take your stack of 8x10s over to your agent, have him help you pick one, reproduce it, and work *that* shot for a year or two.

The clean prints the photographer will blow up for you will be all set for reproduction, because these shots are meant to be your master shot. Just pick one and send it off to the reproduction house to be mass-produced. Simple.

Don't get caught in this trap: Far too often, talent think, "Oh, I'll go back to the photographer and blow up another headshot or two later. Next year."

You know what? I've been doing this a while. I've known only *one* guy to do it. In fact, most people end up going through the whole shooting process *all over again* rather than picking out another shot or two. And then they often lollygag for about a year or so before even doing that. So, save yourself and cut to the chase. It'll save you scads of dough in the long run just to choose a good ten looks and blow them up.

And, yes, each additional look (each additional 8x10) will run you about $20 apiece because they have to be flawless and completely dust-free for reproduction—but trust me, they're worth every penny. They'll last you. This is a very necessary cost if you expect to land work, and it's worth it if you invest in shots with a reputable photographer.

Be sure there are no scratches or defects of any kind on these shots—that's NOT what you're paying $20 a shot for. You may reproduce only one or two of these shots at a time. Meanwhile, you'll keep them in a photo box for safekeeping, where they will remain flat and dry for years to come.

## Do Your Homework
Visit the recommended photographers' Web sites mentioned earlier in this chapter for individual rates and each of their professional recommendations. Even if someone is on the opposite coast, or two thousand miles away, these pros offer outstanding advice on every aspect of getting your headshots done to the very best result.

You'll learn a great deal and walk into your shoot prepared.

## Résumés
It's important to note you should NEVER fake your résumé.

When you get right down to it, the world is smaller than you might first suspect. Your résumé is expected to be an honest account of your skills and experience. Falsifying your credentials will inevitably backlash on you so avoid it. Besides, if you're called to do something you say you're expert in, and you clearly can't deliver what you promised when auditioned, you will have shot a sizable hole in your professional reputation.

317

It doesn't hurt to mention, no one really cares *how much or how little* you have on your résumé, unless you've actually worked with the likes of Martin Scorsese or the ghost of Laurence Olivier.

A résumé is a point of reference and a necessity required of ALL actors for stage, commercial, and theatrical work. However, commercial casting directors and producers require a résumé only *if it pertains to the demands of the production they are currently working on,* but never for voice-over.

If those casting are looking for talent who are expert jugglers and can roller skate, play a concert piano, or are strong improvisers, they should, at a glance, find these things on your résumé.

A résumé gives those who don't yet know you a better idea of the sort of work you have focused on thus far, regardless of how meager that may be. With some due diligence your résumé will increase in no time at all.

## Your Standard Résumé

The following two Web addresses have the best basic samples of résumé s to follow.
http://www.diyactingresume.com/image-resume5.gif
www.equeryonline.com

Never include your physical address on your résumé. But be sure your Web address, cell number, e-mail, and a space to add your talent agent's contact info is included to ensure casting sources can reach you quickly and easily.

NEVER *glue your résumé to the back of your headshots!* Use a single staple *in each corner* to adhere your résumé to the flipside of your 8x10 (facing outward, so that when the headshot is turned over the résumé is face up). No one will think less of you if it's stapled, I promise you. This is uniformly accepted.

Print out only 20 or so résumés at a time, because it's very likely your résumé will change as you continue to pursue and land work.

Adding a QR Code that leads to your voice over demos is a nice additional option on your résumé. You can add a QR Code that leads to your on-camera acting Web page or to your

ActorsAccess page where your on-camera reel can be found (along with additional headshots). Just be sure not to clutter your entire résumé with QR Codes. (Two should be the limit.) They should be big enough to notice, but small enough to not overwhelm the rest of your pertinent information. If you have more than one, try color coding them. (Perhaps blue for voice-over and green for on-camera to keep it simple.)

You may even include a brief description with your QR Code on your résumé, such as "Scan my QR Code to hear my voice-over demos." Not a bad idea.

Again, this isn't mandatory, but a nice option to your résumé.
Most commercial agents will require only digital versions of your headshots and résumés. As you update your résumé and pictures, be sure to keep your agent manned with your most current résumé and whatever he needs to submit you for work. The same goes for each casting Web site you're registered with. Be sure to keep these sources supplied with your most current promotional materials as they change.

As long as the information on your résumé is correct and current, all is right with the world. The onus is on you whether everything is spelled correctly and aligned properly.

## Do I Need a Résumé for Voice-over?

It's really not necessary for you to have a résumé solely for voice-over. At **Sound Advice**, we contend your *demo* is your résumé, because, to a producer or potential client, the demo is all they are concerned with and represents what you do best. The idea is show me, don't tell me.

That said, you may be asked for such a thing, but it's likely to service a busy regional talent agency in a smaller market. It's better to oblige the agency this minor detail, should they ask for it. Clearly, having some point of reference for each individual talent on file and at their fingertips is what they are going for. Not a bad idea, so why not?

But don't feel you absolutely MUST have a voice-over résumé. Most voice talent don't have résumés, so DO NOT include it on your

319

Web site, should you find yourself compiling one for your local agent.

Here's a simple example, should the need arise, which you can edit to suit your own situation. Keep it to a single page.

*Example Résumé*

## Joe Talent
Voice-over
Cell #: 555.555.5555
Web: www.joetalentvo.com
E-mail: joe@joetalentvo.com

Client List/Experience

| CVS Pharmacy | Joe Blow's Auto | McDowell's |
|---|---|---|
| Sears | Cisco | Lucky Kitty |

Corporate Announce Experience

| Silly Serious | Narrator |
|---|---|
| Corporate Training Film | |
| Patten Industries | Principal |
| Quarterly Report Podcast | |

Related Experience

WBBI-FM, Tommyville, Maryland, Morning Drive, Spring 2004 – present
WXYZ-AM, Detroit, MI, 1996 - 2004

Training and Education
- Commercial Voice-over Technique and Promotion, Kate McClanaghan
- Commercial Audition, In-Studio Voice-over Workshop, winter 2009 to present, Big House Casting & Audio
- Commercial On-Camera, Technique, Audition and Voice-over, one-on-one coaching, Glenn Haines

Professional Assets
Able to deliver high-quality MP3 auditions from home studio; experienced announce; exceptional work ethic, steady promotion always in motion; great attitude, continually working and developing vocal skills.

Scan my QR Code to hear my demos!

320

# Chapter 18: How to Get an Agent

"Acting is the physical representation of a mental picture
and the projection of an emotional concept."
—Laurette Taylor

Down through the ages, every would-be talent has said to himself at the start (or possibly even somewhere in the middle of his career), "I need an agent." What often followed was typically a series of humiliations that would have tried the patience of Job and would explain why so many talent pack it in after a few months and often drift away from their dreams and goals.

Securing proper representation is key to building your career and achieving your goals as a professional talent. And while it's important to listen and heed the professional preferences your agent may require of you, it's important to exercise your own common sense, good judgment, and courteous professional behavior. These skills will serve you far greater than anything else. Ultimately it is *your* career, therefore it's imperative you own it and own up to it.

You must also run it. Contrary to what you may have dreamed, imagined, assumed, or been told.

Considering it's likely you're only just starting out as a talent and may lack the benefits experience brings, or you're starting over and at a loss as to what may be required of you in the industry today, we offer you the keys to running your career in the following pages. May you be wiser and better prepared from what you learn in this chapter, and may your career benefit greatly from applying these promotional processes.

All of this takes dedication, and some of it may not be what you want to hear or what you might have expected, but if you apply yourself and dutifully follow what you find here, you will have far more control over your destiny than you ever may have ever imagined.

First of all, to be clear there are _two_ separate and distinct forms of promotion:

  - One to the various **producers and ad agency creatives**
    most likely to hire you as a voice-over
  - And the other to the **talent agents** to secure    representation

But, before we get into detail as to what you need to do, it's important to define…

## Why You Need an Agent
It may seem rather elementary to have to explain why you need an agent, but in recent years an awful lot of doubt has been cast on the subject from sorted sources, especially over the Internet, that have had little, if any success in securing proper representation.  Well, allow me to shed a little light.

There are two primary reasons why you need a talent agent:
> a) To offer you greater access to acting jobs
> and voice-over work _that best suits you_
> b) And because an effective agent has the
> experience and ability to determine what
> the job is truly worth and acts as an
> authority on your behalf

A talent agent determines what a job is worth based on what it will be used for and for how long.

What an effective talent agent does, whether the project is union or not, is to submit you and determine what the job is worth. This is based on what the finished production will be used for (i.e. television, cable, radio, trade show, Internet, voice-over, on-camera, etc.) and how long it's expected to be used. These are the primary elements that determine the value of the project in relation to the talent's pay.

You may have imagined the length of the final audio determined the value of the project. And this has honestly never been the case. Especially considering a 30-second national commercial might have a budget that's typically eight to ten times more than the entire budget designated to produce the half-hour TV show during which the spot is playing. Or you may have thought what you're paid is based on how long it takes for you to do the job. This can be the case, depending on what the job is for, but not always. Again, this is why you need an agent.

The degree of difficulty varies from job to job and talent to talent. You want an agent who has experience with the sort of projects you're most likely to land and knows what these jobs typically pay from past experience.

Agents are only human. Therefore, like so many of us do, they occasionally say things and offer suggestions on whim, especially when it comes to marketing and promotion.

They truly want to help, and while you may be hanging on their every word for advice and counsel, it's often subjective. If you asked them about the same random promotional item six to eight months later you're likely to hear a dramatically different response.

The agent must service their production clients' needs in relation to the talent on their roster. They need talent they can rely on before, during, and even after the production. Knowing what industry standards dictate while offering a versatile yet reliable talent pool is how a talent agency makes itself valuable to casting agencies and producers.

Many regional (smaller-market) talent agents, outside New York and Los Angeles often assume many of the responsibilities typically designated to a manager, such as: offering you career advice, suggesting where to take classes and get your headshots done, or offering you feedback on your demos and on-camera reels when you first sign with them.

## A Word to the Wise
Prior to having a formal process to follow to promote yourself to the talent agents, most talent generally spend between $50 and $100 on headshots, and about $850 on creating what typically amounts to a "demo of a demo" with the express idea that "Once I land some work I'll get proper headshots and produce a really competitive demo." This could easily account for the terrific failure rate and the soaring frustration level a vast majority of novice talent encounter when first starting out.

Headshots for on-camera work and voice-over demos are simply the price of doing business. So if you don't mean business, by all means—don't invest. These two key forms of promo immediately define a talent's professionalism or lack of it. Without the effective promotional tools, even the most connected, most aggressive talent agent will _not_ be able to include you on projects they may consider perfect for you and your "raw, natural talent". These are the all-important tools of the trade required to submit you to producers and casting sources who might otherwise agree to audition or even book (hire) you—provided what you offer appears useful and defines you.

Far too many talent send their would-be talent agents long-winded cover letters, with inappropriate headshots and/or demos, and typically they do this—only once. They may "follow-up" with a phone call about a week later, only to be abruptly thwarted by an overworked agency receptionist, stating, "The agent will contact you if he's interested." CLICK. Consider this is a lesson in _How Not To Get An Agent_, as it will only serve in wasting your time and money.

Securing an agent requires tenacity. This is the business of being a working actor, or certainly of an actor _who intends to work_. The process we've laid out for you below is required if you intend to make yourself accessible to the work.

This process has replaced what was once referred to in the industry as "making the rounds." If you've made the rounds in the past with little if any success—you need to read and follow this section THOROUGHLY.

If you have been successful making the rounds in the past, then you already have an agent you're happy with. You're probably working steadily, and all's right with the world. If this is the case, this section will update you on how a talent would secure representation today and how to pursue representation in multiple regions nationwide as a voice-over.

There are very specific professional tools required of you as a talent in order for a proper talent agent to utilize your skills to their fullest. They are vital for submitting you for auditions and securing work. A talent agent is the bridge between you and the work. They will represent you professionally, determine your value to the producers, and inform you of the job demands.

Your aim is to instill confidence and elicit a positive response from at least one or two *local* talent agents, and perhaps another two to three agents nationally, if you're pursuing voice-over.

Be sure to follow the eight-consecutive week process completely. If you do, you will land that all-important element in every successful career: professional talent representation.

## YOUR Job

The fact remains you are expected to arrive fully realized to a talent agent if you expect to work. That is to say, you are expected to be a complete package: your demos must be up to date, your headshots and résumé are of professional caliber and define you well. Don't leave it to their imagination; they have enough work to do. Demos and headshots promote that you are ready to work and able to deliver. An agent can't submit you for work, or represent you properly, if these promotional materials are working against you. Your promo is expected to define what it is you do best and what you want more of.

Beyond that your job is to give your agent solutions rather than problems, especially when it comes to your schedule, how quickly you respond to texts, emails, or calls, and your ability to deliver a consistent, effective performance when called upon at a moment's notice are key. Continually rescheduling auditions or repeatedly booking out are absolute deal killers. An agent can't overcome or handle these issues for you.

Your job is to make it easy for those representing and hiring you to do so. It's just good business.

## Who Does What

A **casting director** does not *represent* you as a talent. Instead, a casting director is hired by the production company, the director, producer, or the ad agency because they have experience with the specific work being cast, understand the project demands with regard to the talent required for the project, and have access to a wider variety and number of appropriate talent than what a single talent agency would offer.

Fewer and fewer casting directors specialize in voice-over today, unless it's for animation, games, TV, film, or on-camera commercial work.

A casting director contacts a talent agent in order to reach you for auditions. You promote yourself to casting directors every couple of weeks for on-camera work (if applicable) once you have a talent agent.

In some regions, **talent agents** have taken on many of the responsibilities of casting directors, however they aren't paid for the privilege. They make nothing from you until you're hired.

A talent agent isn't a manager, either. If they were, they'd be paid to mold and shape your career, recommend specific classes, pick your headshots, and make between 15 to 25 percent (or whatever the specific agreement is between you) from every job you book, and in some cases receive a monthly stipend until you start securing steady work.

Talent agents generally *want* to assist you like a manger, but to be perfectly honest it's not their job and they're far too busy submitting you for work, determining the value of the gig, and establishing relationships with casting directors and producers. Besides, it's extremely rare and unlikely to have a manager for voice-over.

Most successful **managers** can be found in Los Angeles or New York handling only a precious few talent at any given time: They handle kids only, or specialize in film or television because their industry connections work primarily in these areas of the business. Managers typically have relationships with a handful of talent agents and may even assist you in securing representation with a proper talent agent. That said, many talent agents don't care for the added input of a talent manager and prefer to forgo this sort of situation entirely. So having a manager is not necessarily a benefit when you are just starting out.

In most cases, you need to manage your own career and secure proper representation with talent agents through consistent and professional promotions.

You're expected to promote yourself to the talent agents as a *complete* package, as someone they can confidently send out on auditions, and forward your demos and headshots (if applicable) to producers without hesitation.

## Your Target Audience

Knowing who you are attempting to service with your skills as a voice talent is imperative *prior* to promotion in order for your promo to be effective at all. And while it's true you need a talent agent, the talent agents aren't the individuals who hire you—the **various producers**, **creative directors**, and **copywriters** (known as *creatives*) are. In fact, your target audience above all else are the **producers**. *They* are your potential clients.

When it comes to your voice-over demos, if you're making the client happy by fulfilling a need, it stands to reason you'll make the talent agent happy. Therefore your demos (your promo) must serve the needs of various producers for commercials, or corporate narration, or any of the industry genre.

(See Chapter 3, The Purpose of a Voice-over Demo, for more detail.)

While promotion to the talent agents requires one approach, promotion to the producers entails another. Each is a process continuously required of you and necessary to establish yourself, make yourself known, forward your brand, and encourage employment.

Promotion to the creatives is ongoing. It's not done once, or even once a year, or once in a while. It's your on-going job if you expect to work with any regularity. Otherwise, out of sight, out of mind— out of work! Does it require an investment of time and money? Yes, without a doubt. There isn't an existing business that doesn't require this of its proprietor. So, stop thinking of this business as anything less than what it is—a business. The upside is it puts the reigns of driving your career in your hands. Therefore it falls to you to steer it.

> Promotion is a continual and
> ongoing process. Embrace it.
> It's your job.

Promoting yourself to talent agencies is an on-going process as well and continues until you've secured a capable agent in your immediate region, as well as representation in *at least* two to three additional markets across the country. This requires you continue promoting yourself until you're confident you have representation with tried-and-true, time-tested talent agents you're confident are offering you the best possible opportunities to the work you're most likely to land.

It's worth mentioning, far too many talent rely exclusively on their agent as their sole source to securing work and auditions. This proves effective for less than 2 percent of all talent for any extended period of time and certainly puts you at risk of barely or rarely working at all.

Each of the two forms of promotion defined in this chapter and Chapter 19, How to Get Work, to the talent agents *as well as* to the creatives, are processes that takes time and attention. It's up to you to continually maintain them.

## Promotion vs. Oblivion

Perhaps you held off from promoting yourself because you were afraid you would "bother" the agents or your potential clients. If so, weigh these two options out for yourself: on one hand, complete oblivion. No one knows you, and they never will without promotion. You'll never realize your ambitions or goals. And your potential will die with you. On the other hand: You're worried sending repeated promotions of your demo(s) and other promo will be a bother. Considering most talent literally waste years floundering, doing absolutely nothing to secure proper representation or promote themselves to potential clients, you have to admit this beats the alternative.

Okay, that's it. Get off the couch and go bother somebody, will you?

At least you now can take matters into your own hands and effectively manage your career. And this is precisely how you do it!

## Common Misconceptions

There isn't a single, successful small business in existence that requires little or no effort, investment, or attention. Promotion is a constant. Even once you achieve success promotion is required of you to generate further business.

Movie stars who stay home instead of promoting their films aren't movie stars for very long. You must continue to promote or you won't work. And like most small businesses this requires you establish yourself as a brand, which can take three to five years to do—like any small business.

You'd think this idea would be elementary, yet a common misnomer continues to keep scores of talent who have great potential from ever achieving even a moderate amount of success, and that is the erroneous notion that once they achieve some success they will then promote themselves properly. They have it completely backwards. I'm convinced it's this very idea that has managed to cement thousands upon thousands of would-be professionals into utter oblivion.

The fact is, even those with only a modicum of ability when first starting out will develop and become better and better by applying themselves to the task, often through promotion. It's these talent who find themselves well-established in this business in a few short years.

## How to Get an Agent

Even if you have the benefit of nepotism, or a well-connected friend, much of what you'll discover in the following pages defines better than 90 percent of your job as a working talent if you hope to continue in this business beyond an initial meeting with a possible talent agent regardless of your experience level or past success rate.

The following is the most-effective promotional process available anywhere and will always be required of you to effectively secure representation from talent agents that offer plenty of auditions, submissions, and bookings.

This promo process is designed specifically to secure representation from talent agents. Follow it consistently and religiously to glean the greatest results. It's established and has advanced the careers for scores of talent, and it's meant to do the very same for you.

NEVER wait to promote yourself directly to ad agency creatives (producers, copywriter, and creative directors) PRIOR to securing a talent agent. You can and SHOULD begin making yourself known to those who might hire you whether you have an agent or not. Your goal is to generate momentum and interest. That's the whole point behind promotion. You want to establish yourself as a brand and make yourself accessible to the work.

With that thought in mind, it should be noted: Promotion is a matter of math and momentum; it must be done a LOT and to many (thus the math), and by doing so your career will generate a return.

## The SOUND ADVICE 8-Week Promotional Process of Pursuing Representation from the Talent Agents

The objective of the following **8-Consecutive-Week Promotional Process** is to secure proper representation from a handful of talent agents *in a variety of regions nationwide*, not just locally.

We suggest you pull all your materials together two weeks or more in advance of sending them out. Be sure to keep the list of all the talent agents you're promoting to, what was sent and when, and whether you received a response—even if it's a rejection.

BE SURE TO INCLUDE YOUR CELL NUMBER, YOUR E-MAIL ADDRESS, YOUR WEB ADDRESS, AND (*UNLESS YOU'RE SENDING A DIGITAL SUBMISSION*) YOUR QR CODE IS ON EVERY CORRESPONDENCE!

TRIPLE CHECK all your materials to make sure your contact info is correct.

The following promotional process includes the correspondence you should include each week. You can copy the notes verbatim or vary them slightly, but be consistent in getting them out EVERY week! Do your best to see to it that each week's promotion arrives to their recipient midweek (Tuesday, Wednesday, or Thursday). In fact, most marketing experts claim Tuesday is the best day for your promo to be received in order to garner the greatest results.

Aim for your promo to arrive on the same day each week throughout this promotional process. Otherwise you may inadvertently end up sending the agents two pieces of promo at the same time. Instead, each week's promo should promote you as a talent, your brand, your demos, and a single idea should be communicated each week. It's drip, drip, drip, rather than sending everything all at once.

## The Overall Process of Securing Representation

Except for the first week, you can do the following in any order you like, provided *something* goes out each week for eight consecutive weeks. It should be noted, that following this process might need to be done three or four full rounds (or more) until you get the sort of representation you're truly after, such as an agency in your own area or at least two or more in other regions.

**Week #1**: Send your demo(s) in an e-mail in MP3 format.
SUBJECT: Your Name, Seeking Representation
"I'm interested in representation. Looking forward to meeting you at your earliest convenience."

If you are a union talent, be sure to mention that. Beyond that your demo(s) offer an effective example of what you do and what you want more of.

NOTE: *Some talent agents prefer digital submissions only. Knowing the preference of the agency shows you have done your homework. Check their Web site to see if they have an online submission option first. In lieu of that, it is perfectly acceptable to call the receptionist at the talent agency and ask what the agents' preferences are for submissions. Just keep your call brief and to the point! In the last few years, many, (but not all) talent agency Web sites will list their submission policies and preferences.*

**Week #2**: This is a brief note sent on the back of one of your demo postcards.
"Please access my Web page to hear my demos. I look forward to meeting you very soon regarding representation."

This correspondence can be printed on an address label and placed on the back of your promotional postcard, especially if your handwriting isn't all that legible or presentable.

**Week #3**: This correspondence consists of good stationery that could appear to be an invitation to a party. It IS, after all, an invitation. It's an invitation to YOU!
"I'm eager to learn whether you have my type in your talent pool."

Let's face it, that's the million-dollar question. That's really what you want to know. Can they use you?

These submissions should appear professional, tasteful, and just a little bit hip/contemporary to appeal to the recipients. Again, be sure to include your cell number, e-mail, AND Web address.

**Week #4**: Send an e-mail with a hyperlink to your Web address.

NOTE: *Do not make the mistake of sending a mass e-mail to all the talent agents at once. Just one talent agent at a time to each individual agent and/or their assistant. OR, at least if you do, be sure to BCC (Blind Carbon Copy) everyone you're e-mailing to in order to keep your correspondence personal and private. Besides mass e-mailing all the agents at once opens them up to viruses and the possibility of being phished. (Talk about a deal killer.)*

SUBJECT: Your Name, VO submission
"I'm interested in representation for voice-over. Looking forward to meeting (or speaking with*) you at your earliest convenience."

*If the talent agent is in another state*

(Be sure to TEST out your e-mail in advance to see what it looks like and to make sure your links work properly.)

**Week #5**: Another postcard with a note is sent.
"I've recently updated my demo tracks. Looking forward to meeting you regarding representation."

**Week #6**: Another card using your C-Shell labels. (See sample below.)
"Looking forward to meeting you soon regarding representation."

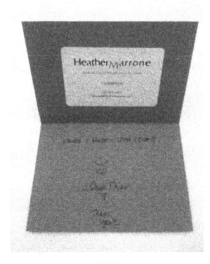

**Week #7**: E-mail with link to your site.
SUBJECT: Your Name, voice-over

"I'm very interested in working with your agency. Please access my demo tracks from my Web site. Looking forward to meeting you some time soon."

**Week #8**: Another postcard
"Please access my Web page to hear my demos. I look forward to meeting with you very soon regarding representation."

YOUR ULTIMATE MISSION: Continue this process repeatedly UNTIL you secure the type of representation you are truly comfortable and happy with. THAT'S the goal.

Now, by week 3 you will feel like all of this promotion is falling on deaf ears—let me assure you IT'S NOT!! KEEP GOING!! You will never accomplish anything if you stop now.

And it may be a tough pill to swallow, but the truth is it may take at least THREE full rounds (yes, 24 consecutive weeks or more) of this process to secure the sort of representation that works best for you. Frankly, that's a small price to pay when you consider most talent literally waste years doing absolutely NOTHING but expect someone to come along make something of them. Ironic, really.

This is YOUR responsibility.

The fact remains that even though last summer the very same agent didn't need you and may have said, "Thanks, but no thanks" (or he didn't respond at all), three to four months later he may be more receptive to you due to changes in the market, a change in his talent pool (someone similar to you may have left), or there's been a change in management that may alter his perception of you.

This industry changes dramatically every four to six months, so a fresh approach may yield greater results only a few short months after "giving it your all" last year or the earlier part of this year. Stay the course. DON'T GIVE UP!!

## Additional E-mail Submission Letters
Increasingly we're finding numerous talent agents across the country prefer digital submissions and are encouraging you to send

e-mails only. Be sure to include your Web address in the signature of your voice-over related e-mails. This will allow your e-mail recipient to click directly on your Web page.

Considering e-mail offers the recipient the opportunity to opt out of repeated e-mails, demo postcard promotions remain the most effective opportunity to forward your brand logo and are strongly encouraged in order to accomplish your objectives.

Again, follow the once a week submission over 8 consecutive weeks process until you receive the response you're looking for.

**WEEK #1**: Subject: Your Name, voice-over
Hello, Bob (agent)…
"I'm interested in representation. Please find my demos included in this e-mail."

Your name, cell, an MP3 of your commercial voice-over demo, and a hyperlink leading directly to your voice-over-ONLY Web page.

**WEEK #2**: Subject: Your Name, voice talent
Hello, Bob (agent)…
"Please find the direct link to my site and demos in this e-mail. Looking forward to meeting you soon!"

Include your name, cell, and a hyperlink leading directly to the voice-over-ONLY Web page in your signature.

**WEEK #3**: Subject: Your Name, VO
Hello, Bob (talent agent)…
"I'm interested in representation. Please find my commercial demo enclosed in this email."

NOTE: It's not uncommon to become discouraged by Week #3. Hang tough. Your materials are _not_ falling on deaf ears, no matter how much it seems that may be the case. You've only just started. Keep with it!

*Here's another option, an e-mail version of your demo postcard and VO Web-page graphic that is a hyperlink that leads directly to your voice-over-only web site. This will further promote you as a voice-over through promoting your brand identity, whether the recipient clicks on this e-mail to peruse your demo Web site or not. It still forwards your brand and you as a voice-over.*

**WEEK #4**: Send a postcard. On it write:
"Looking forward to meeting you at your earliest convenience. Best wishes!"

Don't forget to include your **QR code** (which leads directly to your voice-over only web page) when printing your postcards.

**WEEK #5**: Subject: Your Name, voice-over
Send another e-mail version of your Web site/postcard or simply another e-mail submission.

**WEEK #6**: Subject: Your Name, seeking representation
"Hope to become a welcome asset to your talent roster sometime soon. Best wishes!"

Include direct links to your site and MP3s of your demos.

**WEEK #7**: Subject: Your Name, VO
"Looking forward to learning whether you have my type in your talent pool."

Always be sure to include direct links to your site *and* add MP3s of your demos.

**WEEK #8**: Subject: Your Name, voice-over
"Looking forward to speaking with you regarding representation at your earliest convenience."

NOTE: It's important to stay the course, stay positive, and *continue promoting* until you secure the representation that suits you best. Even if you repeat this process three or four times or more in its entirety.

## QR CODES

QR Codes, or Quick Response Codes, designed to lead directly to your Voice-over only Web site, can and should be used on your promo items sent to your would-be talent agents. (See *QR Codes* in Chapter 7, Advancing Technology.)

### Thank You Notes

Use good stationery, thank you notes, and envelopes, when promoting yourself to talent agents. All promo should be eye candy, or it's not really promo.

Shop around for some exceptional-looking (and feeling) stationery. I like textured envelopes, such as homemade paper. They're tactile. They're interesting and they are notoriously known for getting a response. They tend to look like an invitation to a really fabulous party or reception. It should be an invitation. It's an invitation to YOU!

Check out a truly wonderful stationery store: Paper Source (paper-source.com). They have numerous locations all over the country and online. Bonus: They will happily send you samples.

### "No Thanks"
If you are sent a response from a talent agent saying, "No thank you at this time." Respond with a brief thank you note right back. In most instances you will resubmit to this agent again in six to eight months.

The downside of e-mail submissions is recipients can opt out of receiving them, which is why promotional postcards will not evaporate altogether. The frequency has certainly changed significantly over the last couple of years, but nothing quite creates an impact like the tactile opportunity that direct-mailing affords.

## Agents in Multiple Regions

Union agents are licensed by the state. Therefore, should you become exclusive (or signed) with an agent, you would be contractually obligated against accepting auditions or further representation from any other talent agent in that same region or state, according to the policies established with that agency. However, you may secure representation from talent agents (and therefore accept work) from talent agencies in other states or regions.

However, as a word of caution: Talent agents do not relish being pitted against each other. Such as: "My agent in Baltimore never does that." Doing so will only service in alienating your agent. Instead, keep your dealings with them private and individual. Discussing policy with one agent and comparing notes with another should be avoided.

Think about it. Would you want your agent telling you how wonderful they thought their other talent was that happens to be the same type as you? Would you want them telling you that another talent is making them scads of money? Or how much they wished you were more like them? Of course not. That would be very rude and would place unnecessary stress on your professional relationship.

So, even if your talent agent asks you outright about other agents that rep you—politely change the subject. DO NOT GO THERE! This is not a topic of discussion beyond, "We prefer you only have representation with no more than two or three agents total, provided they are in other regions." Fine. You may be asked what other agents you're registered with, which is fine but that should be the extent of the conversation. Leave it at that.

## Pursuing On-Camera Representation

If you're not only interested in pursuing representation for voice-over work, and you're looking for representation for on-camera as well, it should be noted many talent agents handle both. However, some agents might focus their efforts only on on-camera, or vice versa. Every agency is different.

Most on-camera agents require you live in the same area they're located for them to represent you.

Do your homework. If you live in a major metropolis, contact your local union office for a list of the talent agents they recommend.

Beyond that, if you're pursuing on-camera work, be sure to post your headshots on ActorsAccess.com, CastingNetworks.com, and FrontierCasting.com. Ideally, four to six of your best headshots should be included on each of these sites. These sites offer various on-camera opportunities, while listing talent agencies that you can pursue in a similar manner as we have laid out for you in this chapter for voice-over.

## Auditions and Booking Out

Regardless of whether you're auditioning for a union or a non-union project, you should never audition "just for practice." Audition only if you plan on accepting the role. Agents, casting sources, and producers are all basing their professional reputation on the fact that should you land the job, you will happily accept it. Otherwise, you will only add time, expense, and unnecessary stress to the production, and that's a certain deal killer.

(See Chapter 12, Auditions, and *conflicts* and *availability* in Chapter 22, Industry Terms.)

If more than one of your talent agents sends you an audition for the same job, you MUST audition only ONCE! The best rule of thumb is: Whichever agency sends you the audition FIRST is the agency you will audition through. You must take a pass from the other agent. It's awkward at first, but it does happen.

No need to state, "Sorry, Paradigm, my agent in NYC, sent me this audition already. You got to me too late! Better luck next time!"

Instead, a simple, "Thanks for thinking of me, however I've already auditioned for this campaign/spot. So, I have to take a pass this time. Best," It happens occasionally. Let it go.

It will only read as unprofessional if you audition through more than one talent agency for the same spot and will only serve to cancel your future opportunities with BOTH talent agencies and the potential client as well. Why? Because it confuses the issue for the producer as to how they'll get a hold of you. Plus they'll think you don't know your job. So avoid it.

We recommend you secure no more than five agents in five different regions as a voice-over, provided you have the facility to record your auditions from home or have access to a professional studio. Or you field the client to us (or a studio of equal value) to track (record) the production.

More than five agents and you'll have tough time managing your career. (For some that may be too many, others not enough.) Some agents request you limit yourself to three or less. But it's really up to you. This is your business.

Best rule of thumb: Know thyself! If you're overwhelmed you won't be good to anyone, least of all yourself. Keep it simple.

If you know you won't be available for auditions or a possible gig, you must "book out" with your talent agents. Otherwise, your agents will figure you're available and call you in, only you won't return their calls and e-mails, and you'll end up making everyone miserable, including yourself.

Every agency has its own policies and procedures for booking out. Usually this is required in writing simply by sending an e-mail a week or so in advance of when you expect to be unavailable. Some talent agencies require you do this online.

Be sure to check with your agency to determine the preferred policy and procedure for booking out.

If more than one of your talent agents sends you an audition for the same job, you MUST audition only ONCE! The best rule of thumb is: Whichever agency sends you the audition FIRST is the agency you will audition through. You must take a pass from the other agent. It's awkward at first, but it does happen.

No need to state, "Sorry, Paradigm, my agent in NYC, sent me this audition already. You got to me too late! Better luck next time!"

Instead, a simple, "Thanks for thinking of me, however I've already auditioned for this campaign/spot. So, I have to take a pass this time. Best," It happens occasionally. Let it go.

It will only read as unprofessional if you audition through more than one talent agency for the same spot and will only serve to cancel your future opportunities with BOTH talent agencies and the potential client as well. Why? Because it confuses the issue for the producer as to how they'll get a hold of you. Plus they'll think you don't know your job. So avoid it.

We recommend you secure no more than five agents in five different regions as a voice-over, provided you have the facility to record your auditions from home or have access to a professional studio. Or you field the client to us (or a studio of equal value) to track (record) the production.

More than five agents and you'll have tough time managing your career. (For some that may be too many, others not enough.)

Some agents request you limit yourself to three or less. But it's really up to you. This is your business.

Best rule of thumb: Know thyself! If you're overwhelmed you won't be good to anyone, least of all yourself.

If you know you won't be available for auditions or a possible gig, you must "book out" with your talent agents. Otherwise, your agents will figure you're available and call you in, only you won't return their calls and e-mails, and you'll end up making everyone miserable, including yourself.

Every agency has its own policies and procedures for booking out. Usually this is required in writing simply by sending an e-mail a week or so in advance of when you expect to be unavailable. Some talent agencies require you do this online.

Be sure to check with your agency to determine the preferred policy and procedure for booking out.

# Chapter 19: How to Get Work

"Business has only two functions
—marketing and innovation."
—Milan Kundera

Here at **Sound Advice**, we have extensively surveyed scores of your target audience for whom your demos have been produced, and what we've discovered is: Talent who consistently mass promote work the most. Those who don't have a *much* tougher time establishing themselves in this field and maintaining steady work.

Auditions are promo, too, however they simply aren't the *only* promotions you should be relying on. Nor should you rely solely on one talent agent to generate all your opportunities, especially in voice-over.

Continual promotion is elementary for _any_ business to succeed. It's Marketing 101. Lack of proper promotion explains why so few talent work with any regularity or accomplish their career goals.

Every single promotional piece you send out is essentially auditioning for you when you're not there: So any and all promotion is an opportunity to make yourself that much more accessible to the work. The more traffic you drive to your site with postcards and links, the greater your opportunity for auditions and bookings.

So much of your work as a talent is a numbers game. And by numbers, this means you must send numerous promotions out, numerous times, to many, many creatives.

Still, many very well-meaning professionals may be quick to offer you their two cents as to why continued postcard mailings promoting your demo Web site, "isn't at all necessary." This could explain why so few talent work with any regularity. Promotion is a given for any other business. It only stands to reason this goes double for the entertainment industry.

So, regardless of how much you may respect the individual discouraging you from properly promoting yourself (especially as we have laid out in these chapters), your career will atrophy without consistent promotion.

## How to Promote Yourself to the Producers

Well, here it is. The most important part of the trip: getting your promotional postcard mailings out. It's imperative to note that these promotions are for voice-over promotions only. If you're promoting yourself for on-camera, we recommend you follow Option TWO (defined below) and only to local casting agencies.

The simple fact is that although you may have the greatest skills, the most remarkable demos, and the most appealing graphics and Web site in the business, without consistent and repeated promotion little if anything will come of them. And we can't have that!

It is a proven fact the following process, done frequently and in its *entirety*, increases your opportunity for employment exponentially, and you will find you'll have a great deal more control over your career. So, this process could be considered *the most important step* you can take to establish, relaunch, or maintain yourself in this business. The only way you can do it wrong is to not do it at all or to use outdated mailing lists, which creates undue waste, frustration, and costs.

This promotional process is designed to effectively establish yourself as a voice-over with various producers across the country, but most especially with advertising agency creatives for commercial work. Better than 78 percent of our **Sound Advice** clients attribute the following promotional process to their ultimate success in this field. Your small business as a working talent relies on it, it's the price of doing business in this or any business and will lead to your ultimate success provided it's done completely and with consistency.

Don't fool yourself into thinking, "Once I'm making money, I'll promote myself." That day will NEVER arrive, because the logic is completely backward.

It stands to reason repeated promotion will establish your name and your brand identity in the industry. Promotion drives traffic directly to your voice-over demos and from there you will secure work. This is rarely done with a single postcard mailing. It takes dedication, and if you promote yourself, you WILL work. It may not be right away, but with some tenacity and due diligence you're bound to see a return.

This doesn't mean two or three full mailings over the course of a year will necessarily garner direct results either. It may. But the real aim here is to establish yourself as a brand in relation to voice-over. That requires two to three years of due diligence. And that due diligence has to be targeted, consistent promotion to those most likely to hire you.

## The SOUND ADVICE Regional Mailing Lists

An exclusive feature we maintain and update with great frequency at Sound Advice is the seven regional and specialized mailing lists consisting of targeted creative contacts. As voice overs, and all other forms of freelance talent, you would not normally have such specific and targeted access to those most likely to hire you. Yet, given our casting and production expertise, we do and pass this extraordinary access to you. However, these creative contacts ONLY accept direct mail promotions. (They, like you, consider unsolicited email to be spam. And no one appreciates spam!)

These contacts move around a great, great deal. People come and go from one agency to the next, from city to city. They move up, move over, go freelance, switch ad campaigns, and transfer their skills to corporate industrial or documentary or what have you.

Considering it takes at least seven impressions (promotions) to the same individuals before they acknowledge or "bite", it is imperative repeated promotions are made to the same contacts again and again.

You're essentially promoting yourself with your promotional postcards (with direct links to your demos on your voice over only Web site) to a huge swarm of people that never remain in one place for very long and are continually expanding.

Of course, nothing in this industry remains static for long and neither should you. It's the difference between making yourself known and falling into (or remaining in) oblivion. And the latter is not an option.

So, if you become dormant after sending out a single promotional mailing, then you need to pick up the reins all over again. And there's no time like the present. GET GOING!

## The SOUND ADVICE Overall Direct-mailing Process

Promoting to the creatives at ad agencies is best done two regions at a time. Should you concentrate your efforts on the East Coast and the Midwest simultaneously, for example, this is done most effectively by sending postcards to the same individuals every other week for five consecutive weeks in a row, thereby driving interest and traffic to your demo Web site.

In other words, each week of this ad agency promotion proceeds as follows.

There are two effective options:

OPTION ONE:

       Week one: Postcard
       Week two: Skip a week
       Week three: Postcard
       Week four: Skip a week
       Week five: Another postcard

OPTION TWO:

       Week one: Postcard
       Week two: Skip
       Week three: Skip
       Week four: Postcard
       Week five: Skip
       Week six: Skip
       Week seven: Another postcard

It's best if you follow a full mailing by starting another promotion to two more regions (such as West Coast and Chicago), if the first full mailing went to the Midwest and the South, for example. A continued rotation of mailings, alternating regions as you go, keeps you current with various producers with each mailing.

Utilizing the same mailing lists beyond 8 to 10 weeks will likely result in an excessive amount of returns. We strongly recommend you use your mailings within a week or two of their purchase to ensure a less than 5 percent margin of error.

## Oh, Bother!

You may have had the passing notion that you might be "bothering" the various producers with your continued promotions. Yet, keeping yourself from promotion will only serve to secure your anonymity and force you to remain in oblivion.

> The fact is industry professionals are more likely to book you based on familiarity. And familiarity is best accomplished through repeated promotions.

Otherwise, out of sight, out of mind. They can't book you if they don't know you. Given you don't have the luxury of face time with potential clients in today's voice-over market to establish relationships and develop a rapport as you do with on-camera auditions, your repeated postcard mailings allow you the opportunity to make these connections.

Additionally, we do not advise cold calling, texting, or forwarding your headshots to our voice-over mailing lists. Headshots should be sent to casting directors, rather than producers and creatives.

## QR Codes: Direct Links to Your Demos

Ah, technology. Who knew the future would arrive so soon and bring with it the very thing every professional marketer has dreamed of since watching *The Jetsons* on Saturday mornings as a kid. They're called QR Codes, short for Quick Response Codes, and it's very likely you've seen them included in ads in magazines and on posters as you walk through the airport.

QR Codes can be scanned with a simple app from any smartphone or iPad. They can lead directly to your voice-over Web site. That link to your site will then be "bookmarked" on the mobile device until it's removed at a later date.

But wait, the plot thickens! Considering today creatives rely more on their mobile devices than on their laptops (as nearly any self-respecting businessperson would) it stands to reason you now can promote and communicate with them on these terms to greater effect than ever before.

According to industry data, ad agency creatives (your targeted audience and potential clients) are far more likely to be receptive to scanning your QR Code from your promotional postcard than if you were to send them an e-mail with a direct link to your site. In fact, statistics show less than 8 percent of e-mailed site links are ever accessed. And yet greater than 80 percent of all sites scanned via QR Codes are not only accessed, but are accessed repeatedly—up to ten times during the four weeks that follow first scanning the QR Code. Now, that's a dramatic promotional improvement!

It's also worth noting: The average QR Code is generally kept on the mobile device for up to three months...just in time for your next postcard mailing to that region. How opportune! Again, out of sight, out of mind.

So, given all of this, the value of direct mailing your promotional postcards has just increased by at least 80 percent over any other time in the history of promotion, making the future far more optimistic. Seize the day!

## Where the Work Is Online

There are numerous online casting options these days, the most important of these are: **Voicebank.net** for voice-over auditions of every type; **CastingNetworks.com** primarily, but not exclusively, for commercial on-camera auditions; **ActorsAccess.com** primarily for theatrical (film and television) auditions, and **CastingFrontier.com** mostly for commercial work.

Until you are included on these sites, you honestly don't exist to those casting talent throughout North America and much of the U.K., whether that work is union or not.

Managing your own postings on these sites offers you far more control over your destiny than you ever had in the history of the entertainment industry. And that's a fact. It can be overwhelming at the onset, but buck up. What you discover in the following pages will help you expand your employment opportunities the more you expose yourself to these sites.

## Voicebank.net

Beyond continual promotion to various producers and your ongoing quest for proper representation (until you're truly satisfied with the number and caliber of auditions you are receiving), you must also pursue online opportunities. People casting voice-overs tend to go where there are *numerous voices* and the site they search more than any other source is **Voicebank.net**. (www.voicebank.net)

The majority of professional, national voice-over auditions are held on Voicebank every day.

You want to make sure your agents include you on their Voicebank.net Web page after agreeing to rep you. If one of your agents continually includes you on quality auditions, but has yet to include your demo under his Voicebank listing, then be sure to ask him to please do so. It might be a slight oversight on his tech's part.

You can post your demo on Voicebank *independently* prior to having the representation you're most comfortable with, but we recommend you continue to pursue representation (as we have detailed for you in Chapter 18, How to Get an Agent). Your opportunity to book increases greatly with proper representation, and the agents worth pursuing are all found on Voicebank. Voicebank.net is *the* primary online source for quality voice-over projects. Whether the agents you're with are included on these auditions is another matter altogether, and whether they are including you in those auditions is yet another.

You have the option of posting your demos independently on Voicebank without yet having an agent. Again, it's an option, however we recommend you secure representation from a professional talent agent rather than attempting to rep yourself. Besides if you were a producer and looking for voice talent, wouldn't you search where there are many voice-overs rather than dealing with talent one at a time? Exactly. So would we.

While Voicebank may very well be the premiere online voice-over casting site for the majority and the very best opportunities out there (which it is), there are always various opportunities that arise from sources the world over that should not be overlooked. These opportunities will continue to spring up, but care should always be taken to protect yourself from predatory types that are undoubtedly lurking in deeper, darker waters.

Even with completely reputable representation, there are no guarantees that you won't find yourself in the precarious position of being left unpaid or some such unfortunate situation. Yet, if you're promoting yourself without the support of a reputable talent agent, you are less likely of establishing continued, reliable employment in this business.

(See Chapter 12, Auditions, and Chapter 18, How to Get an Agent, for further details.)

## Securing a Premium Link on Voicebank

Once you have representation for voice-over with an agent or two listed on Voicebank.net, we recommend you secure a Premium Link.

A Premium Link adds a red star alongside your name wherever your name is listed on Voicebank. The idea is to draw more attention to you and your name. A Premium Link makes a hyperlink out of your name that's a direct link to your voice-over Web page where the listener can happily hear your remarkable demos. You pay a monthly fee for this privilege, but it's well worth it, so we highly recommend it.

You don't have to pay to be included on Voicebank, provided your talent agency does. But adding this feature only draws attention to you amid many other voice-overs on your talent agent's Voicebank page. It allows you to stand out in the best way.

## Actors Access

What Voicebank is to voice-over, Breakdown Services is to film, television, and commercial *on-camera* work. The difference is that even without an agent's representation, you can sign yourself up to **Actors Access** (actorsaccess.com) in order to be considered for work, whereas with Voicebank it's far more advantageous for you to be registered with a talent agent who is *already* subscribing to this service. So these sites achieve the same ends (casting talent), but they go about it somewhat differently.

For on-camera actors, Actors Access is the primary online source to generate auditions, and therefore to secure work. This site is adjacent to Breakdown Express (breakdownexpress.com), and both are offered by Breakdown Services, which most professional casting sources in the country utilize for film, TV, and commercial work. Casting directors post breakdowns (synopses of the characters contained within scripts) via Breakdown Express, and actors view these breakdowns through Actors Access (hence the name). Talent agents submit their talent for each project through Breakdown Express. The casting directors choose whether they want to accept submissions from actors or agents, then view the submissions of headshots, résumés, and even on-camera reels.

Therefore your headshots have never been more vital. If they don't look good online as a thumbnail image (roughly the size of your thumb) and at a glance, you'll have a tough time getting chosen.

Posting your headshot/résumé and on-camera reel (if you have one) on Actors Access allows you audition opportunities you would never have exposure to otherwise. This is the primary on-camera site for auditions of every caliber.

It's *free* to post two headshots, a profile, and résumé. And headshots and résumés can be updated quickly and conveniently at *anytime* for no additional charge. We recommend you include four to six looks, provided they look like you and are professionally shot.

Breakdown Services offers a variety of features that most actors really do need, such as an online video reel, as well access to sides (sitcom and movie audition scripts), and the ability to submit extra headshots to suggest different looks. Each extra is fee-based but well worth it.

According to one agent, even if actors shell out the money for the extras, "They'll probably end up spending less money than they would on ordering more hard-copy headshots." So while you don't *have* to spend a dime on the extras, it would be well worth your time to promote yourself there and invest less than $100 to boost your on-camera career.

"Actors are missing the boat on auditions because they *aren't* registered [with Actors Access]," said one seasoned agent. "Casting directors and producers don't want to look at pictures, they want it right there on their computers."   Visit **breakdownservices.com** or **actorsaccess.com** for more info.

## CastingNetworks.com

Commercial casting has never been easier for you, the talent, or the casting agents since the expansive use of **CastingNetworks.com**. Formerly NYCastingNetworks.com and LACastingNetworks.com, this service requires you post your headshots, résumé, and demos on the site for nominal fee.  And we can't recommend it enough that you do so—immediately!

It's unlikely you'll be able to secure commercial on-camera work, without utilizing CastingNetworks.com as it's the primary commercial on-camera casting service utilized in the industry today.

Here's what their site states:

> "Casting Networks gives talent more access to potential auditions than any other service. It allows a Casting Director to instantly see who is out there and what they have worked on. If a talent is serious about working in the commercial industry, they need to be on Casting Networks!" says Casting Director, Gabrielle Schary.
>
> This seamless system was the first to successfully shift the industry from paper to digital by empowering users with online tools that save them both time and money.
>
> All of Casting Networks expertly designed tools are built specifically for the users' needs. The Casting Networks' Interactive Résumé gives Casting Directors everything they need to have a comprehensive preview of the talent they are casting.  It includes a talent's professional photos, digital Polaroids, audio clips, and video. Casting Networks' Web Builder enables talent to create a custom link to their profile for use on business cards and in their email signature.
> For unrepresented talent, Casting Networks' Talent Scout is a free service that connects them to agents who are seeking new talent.
>
> Casting Networks' pricing starts at $25 for a one-year membership and includes two free pictures (a headshot and a digital Polaroid), a profile, and a résumé. There are also additional features available such as Photos Unlimited, Media Hosting, and Video Unlimited. Casting Networks is dedicated to providing talent exposure and opportunities for less than what they pay for their weekly Starbucks addiction!"

To learn more about Casting Networks, or to sign up, visit CastingNetworks.com.

## Promotions to Casting Directors

If you're pursuing on-camera work, you should make it a habit to send your demos, headshots, and your current résumé, or a link to your Actors Access page to the local casting directors once a month via e-mail and once a month via snail mail (two weeks apart). This is necessary.

Your goal is to establish yourself as a brand/type they find appealing. They should be able to identify immediately where they would cast you, so your promotion should quickly and easily help define what context they would hire you: film, commercial, television and which genres best suit your casting within those media.

Keep these promotions simple and professional. Ideally, you are promoting a _single_ idea, such as voice-over, or a new on-camera reel, or a link to a clip from a commercial you recently booked, or brief scene from a short film you were featured in. (Provided that film was produced well! Otherwise, avoid it.) So, rather than sending ALL of these items all at once, promote _one_ of these items at a time. Remember all promotion is drip, drip, drip. It's gradual and continual. It establishes who you are and what you do best—the sort of work you intend to secure.

Avoid forwarding odd, non sequitur emails (like those jokes of the day) and provocative, illicit messages should be avoided entirely.

## Safety in Numbers

Besides Voicebank, your voice-over demos should be found (or mutually linked) to sites where there are _lots and lots of reputable voice talent_, such as our sites: voiceoverinfo.com and bighousecasting.com (provided your demos were produced through **Sound Advice**). Otherwise, maintaining your voice-over demo Web page is the online equivalent to stuffing a note in a bottle and tossing it out to sea. You don't want your site left off on its lonesome. That's not how the Internet works. There are far more opportunities in posting your demos (or links to your site) wherever *numerous* voice-overs can be found. That's going to help you get booked directly off your demos.

The aim here is to attract as many sources to your site as possible. If you don't take full advantage of these opportunities, the odds simply won't be with you. Whenever the Internet is involved, the old real estate adage applies it's: location, location, location.

Make that your mantra. There are numerous sites continually popping up online. Do some research as to what's current. You always want to be included on your talent agent's Web sites, as well, if they have them.

The more, the merrier.


## Your SOUND ADVICE
## Pay-to-Play VO Sites Game Plan

It's imperative your demos are included on as many sites as possible where *numerous voice talent are cast*, not simply through your talent agent on their sites, or strictly through voicebank.net. So much so, we now have a specific game plan designed to assist you in securing work from these sites as soon as you have a professional demo.

With the introduction of various Pay-to-Play (P2P) sites, such as **voices.com** and **voice123.com**, nonunion talent now have greater opportunities than ever before from these casting sites devoted to posting voice-over auditions from across the country and around the world for a broad range of productions. These sites often offer free introductory opportunities, but are most effective when you register for a yearly subscription (usually for about $395).

While there are various Pros and Cons to utilizing these sites, we do suggest, once you have your voice-over demos, register with one or more of these sites and complete the profile describing your greatest assets and abilities to increase your rate of return on your demos and auditions.

(See Chapter 7, Advancing Technology to determine the Pros & Cons of Pay-to-Play sites.)

## Our Exclusive P2P Game Plan:

#1) Check out the two biggest (primarily nonunion) P2P sites, voices.com and voice123.com, to determine the process for each and to determine whether they have any free or low-cost introductory offers you can start out with:

> a) Study various talent profiles to determine key elements you may want to echo on your own P2P site profile (*or* be sure to avoid)
> b) Complete your own P2P site profile and be sure to upload your demos on these sites as well

#2) Commit to first auditioning for every *appropriate* project paying $75 or more for the first two to three months you are on these sites. (What's considered appropriate is almost impossible to say without having the details of what the final production will be used for and for how long. Do a gut-check before accepting a rate. If the potential client only offers $25, it's probably best to pass.  There will always be another job.)

#3) Don't record the entire script.  This is your best assurance they aren't using your audition as the final without paying you.

#4) Once you have booked five to ten projects or more over the first couple months, increase your personal pay criteria to only auditioning for projects which pay $250 or more.

#5) Then again, after another six to eight months, and after seeing some steady improvement in your rate of return, raise your personal pay criteria once more to only auditioning or being considered for projects that pay $500 or more.  (It's always nerve racking to 'up the ante', so to speak.  But remaining in the low paying jobs will not increase your bottom line, and will not serve to challenge you professionally.  If you expect to get paid like a pro—then you must BE A PRO.)

#6) During this entire process with the Pay-to-Play sites, *be sure to continue to pursue representation from talent agents from across the country* following our exclusive 8-consecutive week process. It may take three to four FULL cycles (8-weeks at a time) to secure representation with various talent agents you feel good about.

Until you have established and built relationships with three to four effective talent agents in three to four regions, you MUST continue to pursue representation, otherwise you will have to:
  a) Continually determine what each project you voice is worth
  b) Concentrate your efforts solely on nonunion projects offered on these P2P sites
  c) Maintain work standards that demand greater and greater demands from you with less pay than talent agents would offer

#7) No double-dipping! Just like having multiple talent agents, you DO NOT audition more than once for a project and from multiple sources.  So, if a talent agent sends you an audition for a project you already auditioned for from a Pay-to-Play site, you must PASS on that audition.  Auditioning for both will only serve to confuse the producer as to who they should contact to book you and undermine your professionalism with both the producer and possibly your new-found talent agent.

#8) Plan on utilizing the Pay-to-Play sites for a maximum of three years only.  Your goal is to work toward securing union work through your talent agents.

The objective is to continually raise your game, skill-wise and income-wise, however, there's a ceiling to the benefits these sites offer.  They are a perfect entrance and supplement to this very vast industry, provided you have a game plan.

Now you do!

## The Social Networks
In addition to postcard promotions, and Voicebank and so on, including your Facebook and LinkedIn activity to your general online promotions can only add to your possible employment opportunities.

Most people seem to use Facebook for friendship, family, and personal contacts, (although Facebook's promotional business purposes are becoming more prominent).

LinkedIn is usually viewed as more of a professional site for businesses.

There is a lot of crossover, though.

So, be sure to promote your demo Web site two or three times a month through your Facebook and LinkedIn pages.  Your friends will help forward you to *who knows where*, which can only help your overall promotional efforts. And while businesses are required in today's working world to maintain a presence on Facebook (for this very reason), LinkedIn is generally for connections and colleagues you know professionally and at least peripherally in a business manner.

Your demos or your Web site may very well meet an unexpected opportunity. So including links, demos, logos, and the like are required of you on a monthly basis.  So never let up.  Pick a day out of each month for Facebook, and another two weeks later for LinkedIn.

Twitter can always help as well. Keep it brief and professional. Send a link to your voice-over Web site. Do this two to three times a month. Where you end up will likely be miles from where you started. Consider it a start, even a year from now.

Remember: When you're online, you're in public! Keep it professional. Keep it clean. You'd be surprised what might come back to haunt you. The Internet, to a great extent, has a shelf life. Whatever you put out there stays out there for a good long time. Make it something you can live with.

## Parting (or "Starting") Thoughts
You now know what makes up better than 90 percent of your job: *promotion*.

This process (direct mailing your demo postcards) works *extremely* well, but you must be tenacious. Tenacity is a quality vital to ANY talent if they expect to succeed. It's targeted and relentless. So keep that ball in play. It will propel you farther than just about anything else. Even farther than innate talent or experience. Skills, like a muscle, can atrophy with lack of use!

Besides, God forbid, the ONE agent you happen to develop a wonderful rapport with suddenly up and joins the Peace Corps instead of remaining your agent for the rest of his natural life. Having this process, you have the opportunity to take the reins and *run your career*. Your career no longer is left to the mercy of others.

So, please, by all means… continue…

# Chapter 20: How Union Work Works

"All labor that uplifts humanity has dignity and importance
and should be undertaken with painstaking excellence."
—Martin Luther King, Jr.

This chapter is a *basic* reference intended to help you familiarize yourself with the most important union to your professional career, the newly merged SAG-AFTRA.

Many policies, rates, and procedures will always be subject to change (which they are expected to do in the coming year or so). Therefore, we advise you either to call or consult SAG-AFTRA directly for details pertaining to your particular situation. Be sure to ask to be directed to the information they offer you *in print* to ensure you have the correct information and in order to properly cite the specific reference. Avoid basing key career decisions on hearsay. (*"That's what I was told over the phone."*) Even if you supposedly heard it *directly* from someone at SAG-AFTRA. It's a bad habit to get into, besides one or both of you might get the details wrong.

Certainly, when it comes to voice-over, many talent may choose to remain nonunion and do very well pursuing that work, however we strongly encourage every talent to aim to become a union talent. The main reason is this: The opportunity to support yourself as a professional is far greater if you are union, as we hope you discover from this chapter. Although it would be impossible to answer *every* question, our hope is this chapter will serve as a quick point of reference. Keep in mind any of this information is subject to change at a moment's notice, especially when dealing with numbers. Numbers always change.

So, here are a number of frequently asked questions covering some of the finer points of union work and policy.

## 1. What are the unions' jurisdictions?

The unions we concern ourselves with as professional talent in North America are SAG-AFTRA, ACTRA, and AEA.

**SAG** stands for Screen Actors Guild. **AFTRA** stands for American Federation of Television and Radio Artists. As a newly merged union, together **SAG-AFTRA** determine the valued rate of pay and work standards for film, national television (in other words, network such as ABC, NBC and CBS), cable, radio, industrial (corporate production), IVRs, animation, Internet, and games.

**ACTRA** is the acronym for the Alliance of Canadian Cinema Television and Radio Artists, the Canadian union for professional actors. This is the union that represents talent in Canada for radio, film, all television work, cable, and the Internet. It is much like SAG-AFTRA.

Please note for an American to work in Canada, you must either have a work permit or belong to ACTRA.

**AEA** stands for Actors' Equity Association. Equity deals strictly with American stage work.*

*Considering the concentration of this book is primarily on recorded mass media and how to transfer your live performance skills to recorded media (we don't address live spokesperson work either), we will only touch upon AEA. While stage actors who are, or aim to be, AEA are <u>certainly</u> working actors, our focus in this publication is on expanding your skills to commercial work, film, industrial, Internet, and television. Our goal is to educate you to the greatest opportunities available to you in order to remain employed in this business with as much frequency as possible. Our* *hope is that you will have more opportunity to better subsidize your passion for stage, stand-up and/or Improv, by concentrating your efforts securing work in commercial, industrial, TV, and film. The objective here is to generate enough capital to support yourself in your field, while making enough to support your labor-of-love projects that feed your aesthetic heart.*

## 2. What is my union status?

Everyone has a union status, even if you're not in the union. Currently, you are one of the following:

>a) Nonunion
>b) TAFT-HARTLEY (or *SAG-AFTRA*-e) for SAG-AFTRA
>c) A "must-join" for SAG-AFTRA
>d) SAG-AFTRA, not in good standing
>e) SAG-AFTRA, in good standing

If you are nonunion, you can (and should) audition for union jobs. As long as your talent agent has access to union work and is willing to include you on union auditions. You'll then have the opportunity to secure your first union job and ultimately become a union talent. But once you join the union (SAG-AFTRA) you cannot accept nonunion work.

If you are already an Equity (AEA) member, you essentially have Taft-Hartley for SAG-AFTRA status and may join the union directly upon securing your first SAG-AFTRA job. (However, check with the union to confirm this policy hasn't recently changed.)

## 3. What is the difference between being "in good standing" and "NOT in good standing"?

In order to be *in good standing* with the union your dues must be paid up to date. You can audition for union work *only* if you are in good standing with the union and your dues are current.

## 4. How do you join the union?

To join the union you must have worked under a SAG-AFTRA contract, earning SAG-AFTRA wages, either for one day as a principal or three days as an extra (offering you three "vouchers" and a Taft-Hartley or SAG-AFTRA-e status).

Contact your local SAG-AFTRA office to make an appointment to join; you will be asked to show proof of your work as described above and to pay the initiation fee of $3,000 (national rate) plus the first six months' dues of $99.

(See How

## 5. How much does it cost to join SAG-AFTRA?

At present, a one-time fee of $3,000 is necessary prior to the scheduled session that would initiate your SAG-AFTRA status. This fee includes your first dues. Base dues are $198 per year.

Your specific dues also includes 1.575 percent of how much you make per year (up to $500,000) and are paid in November and May of every year in order for you to remain in good standing with the union.

If you continue to audition for union work and you're not in good standing, you'll have to bring your membership up to current before accepting a union job.  This includes any past fees you may have incurred before accepting future work, or you will jeopardize your union status overall.

## 6. What's Taft-Hartley?

The first 30 days after securing your first union job as a principal performer under either SAG-AFTRA jurisdiction, or working up to three full days as a SAG-AFTRA extra, for example, you are considered Taft-Hartley for the designated union with which you worked. During that 30-day Taft-Hartley period, you may accept as many union jobs as you wish without being required to join that union. You will enjoy all the benefits of union, such as residuals, working conditions, and the client must pay within two weeks or will owe you an additional fee.

## 7. What's a "must-join"?

As of the thirty-first day after that initial session, your union status changes. You will be considered a "must-join" until you secure your next union job. Once you land that next job, then you must join the union and pay your join fee, which includes both your initiation fee and your initial dues.

Once you become a must-join DO NOT accept union auditions unless you intend to join the union. If you can't afford to join you will cause a great deal of trouble for the entire production if they want you but can't have you.

## 8. If I join SAG-AFTRA, can I accept a role in a nonunion production?

No. *Rule One* of membership in SAG-AFTRA requires union members to work only for companies that have signed a collective union signatory agreement.

## 9. How much do you get paid?

 "Scale" is the term designated to the lowest rate you can make as a union talent. This rate varies depending on the usage, but suffice it to say, all nonunion work is based on scale.

A scale session fee (the pay you get for simply recording the spot) for a union TV on-camera commercial is $758.40. For a union radio spot, scale is $278.60 +10. (The "+10" is the talent agent's 10 percent, so that his fee is not taken out of your $278.60 session fee.) Scale for local television session fees run $401.50.  Rates for on-camera commercial work run $758.40 per day.
(See the chart further into this chapter.)

Industrial    on-camera    has    two    categories    (CATs)    for Narrator/Spokespersons:

Industrial voice-over runs $401 for a CAT I contract and $437.50 for CAT II for the first hour, plus $117.50 for each additional half hour.

The lowest union pay rate is a 'demo rate'. A scale "non-air commercial demo" runs $236.00.

(Yes, this business pays you to record *demos*. Not YOUR demo, mind you, but demos for products and services an ad agency is attempting to service or secure as clients. They usually create demos to test commercial campaigns on audiences to determine whether they find the campaign, product or service interesting or effective.)

It's extremely rare to book a demo for radio. Demos are typically produced prior to creating full-blown ad campaigns that cost thousands and thousands of ad dollars. If you record more than one spot at that session, or they edit what you read or shot into multiple versions, you will receive multiple session fees.

All this said, the production you just booked might never air. If it doesn't, you still receive your session fee for doing the job.

If it does air, you receive additional pay called "residuals," or "resids" for short. Residuals account for a bulk of a talent's income, and allow the average working actor to cover his basic living expenses, as well as maintain his small-business expenses such as: ongoing training, production of demos, headshots, Web sites, and promotional costs.

The terms or classifications given to the types of job you may be auditioning for or landing, such as "featured," "costar," "recurring role," "series regular," and "guest star" are no longer used in union contracts today for scale (minimum rates). Yet you will still hear these terms used by your agent, casting sources, and producers and are actually based primarily on the duration of the job. See the chart for clarification.

## 10. How are residuals paid?

This is the single most difficult question in this business to answer. The reason being talent and talent agents alike are not privy to production company and ad agency media plans for fear the clients' competition will attempt to undercut their promotional strategy. (Which they most certainly would!)

So, network television (ABC, NBC, CBS, and Fox) is paid on a sliding scale. Network airplay is the greatest amount of residual income generated of all media formats. It is paid on 13-week cycles, with four 13-week cycles in a year.

For example:  On a typical national product, such as the Swiffer Sweeper, two full 13-week cycles, could easily incur as much as $45,000 to $65,000 in residuals, just from playing on network TV alone. So, this commercial would have to play during Oprah, a few standard daytime dramas, the evening news, *Access Hollywood*, *The Office*, and during Letterman, for example. And that's just the voice-over. You can pretty much double that amount for on-camera work.

Residual cable use is paid on a flat-fee basis, which means you get paid at the end of the cycle, unlike network, which pays you every time it airs. With cable, the more markets in which the ad airs—the Northeast, the Midwest and so forth, the more residual income is generated. Cable-subscriber count per market determines the residuals incurred. Cable pays a fraction of what network pays, by and large. That said, the residual pay here is nothing to sneeze at; you're still looking at about $20,000 to $65,000 for the same example as mentioned above, yet during the most popular shows on TV Land, Bravo, or HGTV.

Internet currently is a flat-fee buyout overall, so it doesn't pay residuals. Residuals are what allow talent to break even, earn P & H (pension and health), and generally keep their heads above water.

## 12. Why can't my agent tell me how much I will make from a commercial, for instance, from my residuals?

No one, *including your talent agent*, can tell you definitively what you will make on your commercial residuals until it's actually paid. This is because when it comes to commercials, this information is kept confidential between the ad agency and the corporate client. This way their marketing strategy is kept from their competition.

Best rule of thumb: Count your money only once it's in the bank. In the meantime, dedicate yourself to continually challenging yourself to delivering the best possible final product and being the most valuable talent you can be.

## SESSION FEES/USE RATES   *selected categories*

### BROADCAST TV
*Agreement Effective through April 2016*

| SESSION FEE | |
|---|---|
| For each spot recorded. A like amount is paid each 13-week renewal cycle for USE or HOLD | $472.00 |
| LA or Chicago Alone 13-week "Wild Spot" use rate | $758.40 |
| Additional "Tags" (2-25 in body of spot or at end) | $140.40 |
| PSA (public service announcement) (w/SAG-AFTRA waiver) 1-Year Use Rate | $472.00 |
| "Non-Air Demo" Fee | $236.00 |

13-Week "Program Class A/Network" (Each Airing) Use Rates

| 1st USE | 2nd USE | 3-13 USES | 14 USES OR MORE |
|---|---|---|---|
| $472.00 | $112.65 | $89.60 EA. | $40.70 EA. |

### NETWORK TELEVISION CODE
*Agreement Effective through June 30, 2014*

| PROMO RATE | |
|---|---|
| 7-Day Rate for on- and off-camera performers in Television Program Promotional Announcements airing on TV or Cable | $240.00 |
| Additional Promo "Tag" Rate (at beginning, middle, or end) | $93.00 |
| Value Added Promo Rate (Product Mention Within) | $410.00 |

### CABLE TV
*Agreement Effective through April 2016*

| 13-Week "Commercial" Rate | |
|---|---|
| Minimum RATE for UNLIMITED airings in a 13-week cycle. A like amount is paid each 13-week renewal while in USE or on HOLD (Holding fee) EXCEPT MADE FOR CABLE ONLY where there is NO holding fee. A higher RATE could be paid based on a combined total of Cable Subscriber units. The maximum amount of units is approximately 2000=$1,833.50 per 13-week cycle. | $472.00 |

### RADIO
*Agreement Effective through April 2016*

| SESSION FEE | |
|---|---|
| For each spot recorded. A like amount is paid | $278.60 |

| | |
|---|---|
| each 13-week renewal Cycle for USE or HOLD | |
| **LA or Chicago Alone 13-week "Wild Spot" Use Rate.** <br> A "Wild Spot" is for UNLIMITED use in as many cities, on as many stations for any number of airings. When your "Wild Spot" airs you are paid the Use Rate based on the number and size of those cities. | $378.35 |
| Additional "Tag" Rate (at Beginning, Middle, or End) | $108.75 |
| "DEMOS—copy Tests for Non-Air" Fee | $181.15 |
| 4-Week "National Network" Use Rate | $721.55 |
| 13-Week "National Network" Use Rate | $1,426.30 |
| 13-Week "Regional Network" Use Rate | $860.70 |

## ANIMATION
*Agreement Effective as of July 1, 2013*

| | |
|---|---|
| **SESSION FEE** <br> This Session Fee is paid for up to Three Voices in a single program or segments of programs over ten minutes in length. Programs 10 minutes and under have a session fee of $804.00. If more than Three Voices, you shall be paid an additional $209.00 per voice. Residuals are based on Producers optioned payment schedules. | $889.00 |

## CORPORATE/INDUSTRIAL/NONBROADCAST AND E-LEARNING
*Agreement Effective through April 30, 2014*

| | |
|---|---|
| NARRATION <br> (1st Hour Spent in Your Recording Session) <br> CAT 2  $437.50 | $401.00 |
| NARRATION <br> (Each Additional Half Hour Increment of Session) | $117.50 |
| OFF AND ON-CAMERA NARRATOR <br> SPOKESPERSON (1st Day) | $891.00 |
| NARRATOR        SPOKESPERSON        (Each Additional Day)   (CAT 2 $597.50) | $490.00 |

## NEW MEDIA/INTERACTIVE
*Agreement Effective through June 30, 2014*

| | |
|---|---|
| **SESSION FEE** <br> This Session Fee is paid for up to Three Voices in a single program or segments of programs over ten minutes in length. If more than Three Voices, you shall be paid an additional $269.75 per voice. | $809.30 |

| Voices used on any On-line or Network platform or used as a 'Lift' to another program, add an additional 100% of the original rate in each case if the rights are acquired within one year of initial release and 110% after such period. Residuals are based on Producers optioned payment schedules. | |
|---|---|

## AUDIOBOOK
*Agreement Effective as of July 1, 2013*
*All Rates are Per Hour (in studio) or Per Side, whichever is higher*

| NARRATOR/ANNOUNCER | $192.50 |
|---|---|
| ACTOR (1 ROLE) | $169.75 |
| ACTOR (2 ROLE) | $339.25 |
| ACTOR (3+ ROLES) | $510.75 |

## ADR WALLA
*Agreement Effective as of July 1, 2013*

| SESSION FEE<br><br>This Session Fee is paid for Recognizable Voices of Five Lines or More in a Theatrical Film, MOW, TV Series, or Pilot. Residuals are paid based on each airing either Network, Syndication, Cable or Foreign, and Video or Multimedia release. These residuals are activated using the same formula as on-camera performers. The voice performer is placed on the CAST LIST. | $872.00 |
|---|---|

## 13. Are there any differences between Spanish-language and English-language commercials with regard to the minimum session fees or working conditions?

No, the minimum session fees and all working conditions for Spanish-language commercials are exactly the same as English-language commercials. All provisions of the contract apply. In addition, if the producer wishes to also hold the Spanish-language performer exclusive to the advertised product in the English-language market, an additional 50 percent of the session and use is paid to the performer.

## 14. What are the differences between Spanish-language and English-language residuals?

For Class A or program-use residuals, Spanish-language performers receive a "per cycle" payment rather than a "pay-per-play" structure. The four major Spanish-language networks, Galavision, Telemundo, Univision, and Telefutura are paid either as program use or Wild Spot, depending on the media buy. For Wild Spot residuals, the television markets are weighted differently than in the English language market to account for the cities with large Hispanic populations. For example, Miami has a unit weight of 4 for the English market and a unit weight of 17 for the Spanish market. All cable use payments for Spanish-language commercials are identical to English-language commercials.

## 15. If performers are asked to translate the script at a session or an audition, do they get paid more?

Yes, an additional 50 percent of the session is paid to any performer asked to provide translation services.

## 16. What is a SAG-AFTRA signatory?

A SAG-AFTRA signatory is an advertising agency, production company, or producer that has signed a SAG-AFTRA agreement requiring them to adhere to the working conditions and methods of payment. These parties are ultimately responsible for your pay—not only for the initial session but also any pension and health payments and future residuals you may incur from this same production.

*(Under certain circumstances, such as some industrials, a paymaster may also be a signatory.)*

A signatory must been given the okay by the union to become such.

According to dv.com: "Production companies that want to work with actors who are (SAG-AFTRA) members must first become signatories of the (SAG-AFTRA) Codified Basic Agreement. This means that the production companies must sign a contract with SAG in which they agree to abide by (SAG-AFTRA's) rules and regulations."

## 17. How does a producer or production company become a signatory?

This is not, and should not, be a talent's concern, except as much as you simply want to make sure you get paid.

Instead, it's likely your agent will ask, "Who's the Signatory on this job?" when he firsts gets a call for an audition.

However, you may want to work on an indie film. This can be trial by fire. If that's the case, you need to avoid getting burned. You need to know what your job is worth. (This is a job, regardless of the budget. It is worth something.) Additionally, it's perfectly appropriate to encourage, if not insist, the producer or production company employ a signatory or become one if you are SAG-AFTRA talent and you want to work on this project.

Suggest to the producers to contact SAG-AFTRA for more information.  They are extremely helpful and can assist in getting this done.

## 18. What are the designated rates for low-budget SAG-AFTRA film contracts?

The following are the variety of categories of agreements SAG-AFTRA offers.

**Student Film Agreement**. This contract is only for students currently enrolled in film school. The film must be made for $35,000 or less, limited to a 20-day shooting schedule and 35-minute edited length. Salaries and other monies may be deferred pending any sale, distribution, or release of the project.

**Short Film Agreement**. The film must be made for less than $50,000 with a maximum running time of 35 minutes. SAG-AFTRA principles must be paid at least $100 a day, but the salaries are deferred.

**Ultra-Low Budget Agreement**. The film must be made for less than $200,000. Actors must be paid a minimum of $100 a day (not deferred), plus pension and health plan contributions.

**Modified Low-Budget Agreement**. The film must be made for less than $625,000. Actors must be paid a minimum of $268 a day/$933 a week plus pension and health plan contributions.

**Low-Budget Agreement**. The film must be made for less than $2,500,000. Actors must be paid a minimum of $504 a day/$1,752 a week, plus pension and health plan contributions.

Detailed summaries of these contracts can be found at: www.sagindie.org/contracts2.html.

## 18. What is a SAG-AFTRA paymaster?

A paymaster is a payroll company hired by the production company or ad agency to assume the payroll obligations for the job. This includes paying your salary and making proper deductions, handling pension and welfare contributions, keeping track of residuals, and processing unemployment and annual W-4 forms or 1099s.

## 19. Can I work on a job if the paymaster is a signatory but the ad agency and the production company are not?

If the job is under an industrial contract, yes. If the job is under a commercial contract, no.

When the job is commercial, the paymaster cannot be the only signatory. The production company or ad agency must also be a signatory. The paymaster can handle the payments, but the production company or ad agency remains responsible for all-future cycles and uses. An industrial is different: industrials are usually one-shot payments, not cycles, so the union allows the paymaster to be the only signatory.

## 20. How do I know if my employer is a signatory?

Ask! The responsibility ultimately falls to you to ensure that a company has a proper signatory once you are union. Doing so only ensures that you will get paid. If you are in doubt, this can be checked on the SAG-AFTRA Web site. There is an online section as well as contact numbers for inquiries.

## 21. Can a SAG-AFTRA signatory hire nonunion actors, too?

On any SAG-AFTRA job, all actors must be union members, unless the union contract specifically permits the use of nonunion performers or allows a waiver (called a Taft-Hartley Waiver) to the signatory.

All actors on a union job must be paid union wages unless the union contract permits a certain ratio of union members to nonunion members. That ratio can include things such as using a certain number of nonunion extras.

## 22. How do I get a SAG-AFTRA voucher?

Typically the first AD (assistant director) is allotted a limited number of vouchers during the course of a union production, based on the size of the production budget. If not enough union talent show up to fill the EXTRA vouchers the day of production, the first (or second) AD can dole them out to non-union talent in exchange for a days work as a contracted background performer.

Once you have earned three union vouchers (for three days work on any given SAG-AFTRA project, you become SAG-AFTRA-eligible.

(See *How to Join the UNION* section at the end of this chapter for more details.)

### 23. So, do I need to sign a contract at every session?

You do if it's union.

Come to think of it you should have some sort of agreement even if it's nonunion. Spell out the particulars of each agreement in advance. This is why most nonunion agents use vouchers to verify when and where the session took place and what it was worth.

You must sign a W-4 at the session, on the day of the job. Keep a copy for your records, your agent usually gets a copy and the producer gets one as well.

### 24. Who is responsible for supplying the talent contract on the day of the job?

The producer on a commercial.

They typically supply the necessary paperwork for commercial, film, TV, and industrial, that means you will fill out a W-4. Your contract will include the length of the session, the number of spots you actually shot or recorded, and where your check will be sent (to your agent or to you) and so forth. DO NOT SIGN IT IF IT IS INCORRECT.

Instead, call your agent and verify the particulars, then bring it to the producer's attention so she can correct it, initial it, and THEN sign it. Typically, talent write "exempt" from withholdings (on line 7) and include their 36# (also known as the FEIN number) if they're Incorporated or an LLC. (This is highly advisable to legitimize your business write-offs including parking, travel, wardrobe, union dues, and promotion costs, including all of your promotional materials.)

## 25. What does it take to become eligible for medical/dental benefits under SAG-AFTRA?

SAG-AFTRA offers two levels of benefits: Plan I and Plan II. There are three ways to qualify for coverage: Covered Earnings, Days of Employment, or a combination of age, service, and Covered Earnings. The manner in which you qualify for coverage determines the level of Plan benefits you will receive for eligible coverage.

You become eligible for 12 months of health coverage when the Plan reviews your Covered Earnings and Days of Employment. This occurs approximately six weeks after the end of Base Earnings Period. This six-week period is needed for employers to submit reports of your earnings and for the Plan to process these reports. The 12-month Benefit Period begins on the first day of the calendar quarter after the date that the Plan determines that you are eligible for coverage.

You cannot qualify for Plan I and Plan II simultaneously. You will be eligible for the Plan for which you first meet the requirements.

In order to maintain your Earned Eligibility without interruption you must continue to meet the minimum Covered Earnings, Days of Employment, or Age and Service requirement during your established Base Earnings Period every year.

| SAG-AFTRA Minimum Health Plan Eligibility Requirements | | |
|---|---|---|
| Eligibility Commencing | Plan I | Plan II |
| January 1, April 1, July 1, or Oct 1 | Earn no less than $30,750 Base Earnings | Earn $15,100; or 76 days of employment; or $10,900* if you are at least 40 yrs of age with 10 yrs of Earned Eligibility |
| These minimum requirements may increase each year. The Trustees have set a target increase of 3% per year, however they will determine the actual size of the increase based on an annual review of the Health Plan's financial condition. | | |

*These rates and dates are current as of this writing. See the SAG-AFTRA Web site for more details or possible changes. www.sag-aftra.org
For the complete 2013 Health Plan summary visit:
http://www.sagph.org/html/healthspd2013.pdf

## 26. What is "fi-core" and why do people take it?

Fi-core is short for financial core.

This is a basic provision allotted to any union member in the United States who may, by law, be required to join a particular union. The right to opt for such status stems from a 1988 Supreme Court decision in Communication Workers of America vs. Beck.

It allows a union member to become a dues-paying nonmember by allowing that individual to take financial core.

The idea here initially was if a union member disagreed politically with the union they had to join for financial reasons, then that member has the right to exercise this option.

Taking fi-core makes dues-paying nonmembers of union members. In other words, these nonmembers essentially can legally work BOTH union *and* nonunion jobs, while remaining eligible for the "core financial benefits" of SAG-AFTRA.

However, by officially resigning from the union by paying only the base annual dues ($198), a fi-core talent essentially withholds the portion of their dues that goes toward such activities as political campaigns and contract negotiations.

A fi-core talent cannot hold office or vote in union elections.

A number of professional talent have used financial core without having any political conflict coming into the equation. If a talent lives in a rather remote area or in a location where the work isn't abundant for union jobs, he may want to accept the jobs available to them in that area. "Right to work" states such as Texas and Florida prefer their talent to be fi-core to open them up to more opportunities.

Twenty-two states are right to work states, the rest are not. The remaining states are referred to as a "closed shop."

According to Wikipedia: "Right to work" is a provision of the Taft-Hartley Act (which went into effect in 1947, under Truman), which prohibits trade unions from making membership or payment of dues or "fees" a condition of employment, either before or after hire.

Those right-to-work states are: Alabama, Arizona (established by state's constitution, not by statute), Arkansas (established by state's constitution, not by statute), Florida (established by state's constitution, not by statute), Georgia, Idaho, Iowa, Kansas, Louisiana, Mississippi, Nebraska, Nevada, North Carolina, North Dakota, Oklahoma (established by state's constitution, not by statute), South Carolina, South Dakota, Tennessee, Texas, Utah, Virginia, and Wyoming. If your state is not listed here, you live in a "closed shop."

We're including these states here, because you may live in one of these states, or you may secure representation with a talent agency in one or more of these states as a voice-over while residing elsewhere. Agents in these areas generally expect you to accept work.

Opponents of right to work argue that the laws prevent free contracts between unions and business owners, making it harder for unions to organize and less attractive for people to join a union. For these reasons, they often refer to non-right-to-work states as "free collective bargaining" states.

Wikipedia goes on to say: "Proponents of right-to-work laws point to the Constitutional right to freedom of association, as well as the common-law principle of private ownership of property."

Clearly it's a terrifically controversial issue.

Union-franchised talent agents do their best to stay out of it and many maintain a strictly need-to-know basis—and for the most part, they simply don't need to know.

Believe it or not, you are not obligated or even required to inform your talent agent (or potential agent) if you are fi-core. Certainly, they need to know if you can accept union (or even nonunion) work. But YOU are expected to keep yourself in good standing with the unions to accept any form of union auditions or work whether you are fi-core or not.

It's far more profitable to remain in good standing with SAG-AFTRA—regardless of where you live, and whether you happen to take fi-core or not.

Where financial core gets sticky is deciding when exactly then do you make the leap over to the big kids' table if not when you join the union? I mean, aren't you officially considered a professional once you join the union? And how do you deactivate financial core, should you choose to?

The fact is: You have to reapply to be reinstated in the union(s) from which you took fi-core, and then that union has to allow you back in. In most cases, this would like require paying another initiation fee as you did when you first joined.

The fact is fi-core is frowned upon by the unions, which is why you will hear very little, if anything, about it from them. It's viewed as undermining the collective impact of having a union.

Every talent is scared to death they'll never work again. We're freelancers who have to drum up the work for ourselves for the most part. Certainly that's a very scary notion before you've given yourself the opportunity to back it up with any experience. But don't cave in from it. Rise to the occasion.

## 27. When does a union talent become "vested"?

Becoming vested means earning enough income through any given union in America, which thereby affords you to be paid a pension. That pension is based on your overall earnings.

You can become vested one of three different ways:
1. By earning 10 Pension Credits.
2. By earning 5 Pension Credits without a permanent break in service and satisfying union requirements of activity.
3. By attaining normal retirement age and earning Pension Credits at or after normal retirement age.

Pension Credits are units that measure the amount of time you have worked in employment covered by the plan. Pension Credit is earned based on your Earnings Credit or your days of covered employment. Pension Credits are used in determining your eligibility for benefits as well as the amount of benefits payable under the plan.

*For more details, visit SAG-AFTRA Web site, www.sag-aftra.org*

## 28. What's honorary withdrawal?

Honorary Withdrawal or Suspended Payment, according to SAG-AFTRA is: If you are not actively seeking employment under SAG-AFTRA's jurisdiction and have been a member of the union for 18 months, you may request inactive status.

Requests must be made in writing to membership services. Be sure to include your SAG-AFTRA ID and signature. If your request is granted, you will not be eligible to vote on union matters, and you will not receive union publications.

You will, however, continue to receive any residuals due to you, and you may reactivate your membership at any time in order to audition or accept work.

## How to Reinstate Your Union Status

Inactive status must be maintained for one year in order to avoid incurring past-dues obligations. Members seeking reinstatement from Suspended Payment status must pay dues owed at time inactive status was granted in addition to current dues and fees. Once reinstated, a member must maintain active membership for one full year from the dues period in which the reinstatement occurred before becoming eligible again for inactive status.

If you changed fields and no longer choose to pursue professional acting after you've joined the union and you don't expect to pursue the work any time in the future, you may take honorary withdrawal.

Doing so relieves you from paying dues every May and November and keeps you from falling behind and becoming a member not in good standing. However, you CANNOT accept ANY form of work: voice-over, film, TV, Internet, industrial, or otherwise. You are considered retired from the industry.

Should you change your mind at a later date you will most likely be readily accepted back into the union from which you have officially withdrawn.

# How to Join the UNION

In order to join SAG-AFTRA, you must first become ELIGIBLE. This can be done a number of ways, for instance:

#1 Secure employment on a SAG-AFTRA production in a principal role. This might be for a film or television production. It can be done on a *bona fide* SAG-AFTRA web series as well. However, not every role in any given web series, film, or production qualifies to offer every nonunion talent involved in the production eligibility status. Further, the series must be properly registered with the Union well in advance of production and follow the various demands necessary. (Please note: a Web series can be very difficult to validate with the union, and ultimately may not be acceptable for eligibility after submission.)

#2 Land a SAG-AFTRA principal role in a commercial. This would occur if you're a featured talent, whether that be on-screen or as the featured voice-over.

#3 Complete three (3) days of work as a background performer on a production that is legitimately under a SAG-AFTRA contract. (This is referred to as the 'Voucher System' because after each day of work the talent is awarded a 'voucher', which legitimizes their effort toward becoming SAG-AFTRA eligible.)

#4 Once a performer is a paid-up member of an affiliated performers' union (ACTRA, AEA, AGMA*, or AGVA*) for a period of one year and has worked and been paid at least once as a principal performer in that union's jurisdiction, the talent is then eligible to join SAG-AFTRA.

It's important to note any one of these aforementioned eligibility options must be accepted by the union in order for a talent to qualify to become (eligible with) SAG-AFTRA.

The very first union job is followed by a 30 to 45 day grace period. During this period the talent may accept additional union jobs without having to join the union, yet receive all the benefits of union standards, including pay, for those projects. Once that grace period has lapsed, the talent is then considered *TAFT-HARTLEYed*, also known as SAG-AFTRA eligible (SAG-AFTRA-e), otherwise known as a "Must-Join". Meaning the next union job the talent is hired on, after this 30 to 45 day period, he or she must actively join the union.

Once the talent is eligible under the conditions stated above, it's best to contact your nearest SAG-AFTRA office to determine the amount of your joining fees.

All new members pay a one-time-only initiation fee, plus their first (semiannual) dues at the time of joining. The national initiation fee rate is currently $3000.00 (initiation fees may be lower in some states). Annual Base dues are $198.00. In addition, work dues are calculated at 1.575 percent of covered earnings up to $500,000.

It's ultimately the performer's responsibility to determine the validity of each qualifying job he's hired on. (After all this is *your* career.) However, it's up to the Union to determine whether the employer was legitimate or not, and whether the qualifying employment was actual production work. Each application and proof of employment is fully investigated by the Union for validity and left up to their discretion to accept or reject.

It's worthwhile to contact the Union about your eligibility status. If your file is not on record or incomplete, you may submit one of the following documents as proof of eligibility:
• Original paycheck stubs.
• Original activity print-out or report from the payroll company that states your name, social security number, the name of the production company, the title of the production, the salary paid in dollar amount, and the specific date(s) worked. The payroll company must submit this document directly to the SAG-AFTRA Membership Services Department.

Background vouchers and copies of paycheck stubs are not acceptable as proof of work. Submitting these types of documents will only delay verifying your SAG-AFTRA eligibility.

*AGMA: American Guild of Musical Artists

*AGVA: American Guild of Variety Artists (circus performers, Las Vegas showroom and cabaret, etc.)

## Parting Thoughts on the Subject

Always consult with your local union office if you're ever in doubt and to better assess the situation of the given project in question to ensure you are afford the greatest benefits.

It's important to note you are ultimately responsible for your career. Not the unions.  Not your agent, coach, or manager.  Not the producer, director, studio, ad agency, or production company. Should you work on a union job and later discover you were upgraded on that project to a role that was worth more than you were originally offered or paid, you have only 90 days in which to set the record straight.

And if you sign off your rights, you are then agreeing to the flat fee offered as payment in full.  All the more reason we advise that you secure proper representation with a capable talent agent who understands what the job is truly worth.

It's YOUR career.  Run it the best you can.

There are times you'll need to compromise, and times when you should stand up for yourself.  All you can do is try to choose your battles wisely. You'll make mistakes from time to time, as will your advisers.  You don't learn a thing from playing it so safe that you are painted into a corner.  The fact remains every project has its own unique demands and specifics that ultimately determine what that job is worth, whether that job is union or not.

# Chapter 21: How to Collect Your Spots

"Unless you are prepared yourself to profit by your chance, the opportunity will only make you ridiculous. A great occasion is valuable to you in proportion as you have educated yourself to make use of it."
—Orison Swett Marden, writer

How do you get a copy of the spots you've done?

Good question.

First ask yourself, "Are the spots you booked *worth* tracking down _and_ adding to your next demo?"

You shouldn't include every spot you've *ever* landed on your demo just because you got paid to do it or because it aired. When you update your demos you should include only the work that best displays your greatest assets and abilities. (The type of work you want more of.)

As the adage goes, "You eat a peck of dirt a year." In other words, there will be a percentage of the spots you book that will be absolute rubbish and have no business ever seeing the light of day again—especially on your demos.

Still, you do want to make a habit of collecting your elements (the spots you've booked). This will serve to help you avoid chasing down perfectly good commercial spots to use the next time you update your demos.

Most talent don't even think about securing a copy of their work until they're ready to update their demos. Of course, by that time, collecting your spots often winds up taking a great deal more effort and time than you may have ever dreamed and costing quite a bit of money. Those commercials you landed have more than likely been archived, and retrieving them is a costly venture (often as much as $450 to $950). Yes, even if you were paid to voice these spots, you have to pay for your own copy if they've already been archived. It's a rather convoluted process to determine which spots you're looking for and where they might be located.

To begin, you'd have the awkward task of tracking down the producer, who is certain to be on another project by now, especially if it's been a year or more since you recorded the spot. Considering the session probably lasted all of a half hour or so, you may even have a tough time remembering his or her name. To add to this, no one wants to be bothered about a production that was completed ages ago.

May I suggest an alternative? There is an *easier* way—provided you use a little forethought prior to your commercial booking.

## Ask the Producer

While at the session, ask the *producer* if you can receive a copy of the spot(s) you just voiced (or shot). Do this *while you are filling out your W-2 forms*. Most producers will agree to release a version to you once the spot has been fully produced—unless the spot is a demo. In that case, the producer may not be at liberty to release it until the spot has been fully approved by the client to move forward. This may occur with some new products as well. For these sessions, producers usually have you sign an agreement saying you will not discuss the product with anyone prior to its release. This does happen from time to time and is why a producer will be unable to release a copy to you. A recording engineer cannot release a copy of the spot to you without the producer's okay for this very reason.

The producer is the authority and ultimately the primary individual whose permission you must have to receive a copy of the commercial. So, be sure to ask the producer for a copy *in front of the engineer*—you're very unlikely to get those two in the same room again (or even on the phone) after the session is over. This will expedite the process considerably, if you have to go through the studio to obtain a copy of the spot.

## "E-mail Me a Link to the FTP"

Most producers will find this the easiest way to accommodate your request: e-mailing you a link to their FTP site. FTP, which stands for file transfer protocol, is standard in most businesses today. The same is true in production.

At the session be sure to ask the producer *and* the recording engineer for their e-mail addresses, so you can contact them *within a week after your booking* to receive a link to where the finished spot can be downloaded. This is referred to as "e-mailing a link to the FTP site."

(For more FTP details see Chapter 7, Advancing Technology.)

Technology has made it easier than ever for us to collect our elements (our spots) and there is no easier way (*for everyone involved*) to obtain them than this.  If you want to obtain a copy of your spots for FREE, this is how it's done. Just keep it brief and unobtrusive.

Example e-mail:

> Hey, Charlie (producer)—
>
> Great working with you on the Kraft spot last Wednesday.
> I'd like to include it on my updated voice-over demo.
> If you could forward me a link to the FTP site, or an MP3 of the
> final, I would truly appreciate it.
> Wishing you well and hope to work with you again sometime soon.
> Best,
> Tommy Talent, www.tommytalentvo.com

FTP makes it possible to send links to *large* files, so you will be able to download a *full-quality* (AIFF or WAV format) version of the spot(s).

If you still haven't received an e-mail back from either the producer or the engineer after two or three weeks, and more than four e-mails, your e-mail may be blocked by the studio and ad agency spam filter. In this case, pick up the phone and call the recording studio. You asked the producer in front of the engineer, so you shouldn't have a problem getting the recording engineer either to e-mail you an MP3 of the spot or a link to the FTP site. Give him the date and info on the session and you'll most likely have it within a day or so.

Be polite and persistent, *but not a pest*. If you still haven't gotten it, you may have to contact the producer directly at the ad agency. You should have it within a day or so after that.

Stay on it until you get it. It will be well worth it to track precisely what you're booking, whether you use them on your next demo or not.

## Once You Receive a Copy of the Spot

Create a folder on your computer desktop of the spots you have done and collected. (*Be sure to back everything up on a storage device.*)

It's up to you—not the producers, the engineers, or the studios, or anyone else to get a copy of the spots you've landed.

The nice thing is that this process is far easier and less intrusive than ever before, even if your producer is in another region altogether.

### Oops, I Forgot!

If you haven't secured a copy of your spot at the session as we've suggested earlier, ask your agent who the producer was. Do this within a few days of the session whenever possible. If it's more than a month, you may have missed your opportunity.

You may have to contact the ad agency directly. Keep in mind producers are busy folks, and it's not their job to serve you. They're doing you a favor sending you a copy of the spot you've done.

Even if you have to leave him a message, ask the producer to release a copy of the spot to you. Leave your e-mail and cell number. Supply the date of the production, the title of the spot, the product or service, and the studio you recorded in. Then contact the studio letting them know you're trying to acquire a copy of the spot you did.

It's a bit of a hassle on your end, and will take a bit more intention on your part, but it can and should be done.

## A Word of Sound Advice

Don't make the entire recording session about "how can I get a copy of this spot." You should collect your spots (known as *collecting your elements*), but first and foremost, be sure to concentrate on delivering the very best possible product in the booth at the session. What good will those collected spots do you if you've delivered a poor performance? It's worth far more to build a strong business relationship with everyone involved than be a self-serving, short-sighted individual.

This process is the easiest, most efficient way to secure your elements, so proceed professionally and you'll have some remarkable options to add to your demo the next time you update your demo tracks.

No producer really wants to be bothered tracking down your spots at a later date, so do your best to collect them as soon as possible after the session. The producer is focused on finishing the job and doing it well. If he's confident his needs are being met, he is more likely to be obliging to yours.

# Chapter 22: Industry Terms

> "For me, words are a form of action,
> capable of influencing change."
> —Ingrid Bengis

This chapter details industry terms and related information relevant to the work.

For example: Your agent just called.

She has you **on hold** for Payless and **check avail** for a number of **customizations** for Glade. She needs to know your **union status** and whether you've gone **exclusive** with that other local talent agency you've been getting auditions through lately.

Confused?  Well then, read on, MacDuff, read on!

To clarify, according to the American Heritage Dictionary, the definition of the word **dictionary** is:

*A reference book containing an alphabetical list of words, with information given for each word, usually including meaning, pronunciation, and etymology.*

It also defines a **glossary** as:
> *A list of often difficult or specialized words with their definitions often placed at the back of a book.*

And an **encyclopedia** as:
> *A comprehensive reference work containing articles on a wide range of subjects or on numerous aspects of a particular field, usually arranged alphabetically.*

This is precisely why this reference is considered the latter rather than the two former. After all, if the shoe fits, it must be a duck.

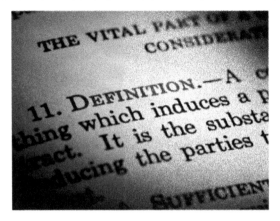

**A**

**a-b-c**    When you *a-b-c* a line on a voice over session or shoot you'll be expected to read the line apart from the rest of the delivery three times in a row on a single take, leaving a slight break between each read for editing purposes. You are expected to say the line *with a slightly different inflection* each time while remaining within the parameters of what's being asked of you.

This is usually done when a line is flubbed or unvaried from take to take, or to allow the actor a fresh approach to a phrase, a sentence, or a section of a script.

Occasionally you are expected to match an existing take with an *a-b-c*, but generally the delivery works best if you aim to vary it slightly each time.

This is also known as a *three-in-a-row* or a *three-wild*.

(See *matching, three-in-a-row,* or *three-wild*.)

**actorsaccess.com**

Currently the premier Web site where on-camera actors post their own headshots, résumés, reels, and voice-over demos to be considered for work.

Actor's Access is managed by *you*, the talent, and offers you access to numerous casting sources and projects registered on breakdownexpress.com, especially for film and television projects.

(See Chapter 19, How to Get Work.)

**ACTRA**

The acronym for the Alliance of Canadian Cinema Television and Radio Artists. This is the union that represents professional talent in Canada for radio, film, all television work, cable, and the Internet, much like SAG-AFTRA does in the States.

For an American to work in Canada, he must either have a work permit, belong to ACTRA, and/or belong to SAG-AFTRA.

**AD**

1. Assistant Director
On a film set, an AD is an Assistant Director, the person who expedites and coordinates a great many details for the director. Depending on the size of the budget there can be a first AD and a second AD. These are typically the people you report to on a set.

2. Art Director
In advertising, AD is the abbreviation for an Art Director. An art director defines what a commercial is going to look like for commercial TV and commercial print. Though AD's are probably the *least* likely to handle casting for voice-over or on-camera jobs, they are the individuals who create the look and style. They create the storyboards you may see at auditions (and occasionally for voice overs) to help illustrate the action and look of the commercial or campaign.

**ADR**    This is an abbreviation for <u>A</u>utomated <u>D</u>ialogue <u>R</u>ecording or <u>A</u>utomated <u>D</u>ialogue <u>R</u>eplacement. ADR is also known as looping.

Once a commercial, television program, or film has been shot and edited, vocal tracks may be added either to replace poorly recorded vocals in a scene or to add a voice-over narrative to the image. In either case, the actor will have to go into the recording studio and view the already- edited film (or video) and apply a few takes of the voice-over to the picture, which will be played back simultaneously on a monitor in the recording booth. For large studio productions and big-budget projects, this work is generally done on an ADR stage, rather than in a booth using the same type of microphone used to record the production audio. The objective is to better match dialogue tracks.

A good example of this would be what Meryl Streep's character had to do to replace a fumbled line in her movie within a movie in *Postcards From the Edge*.

ADR is recorded on a soundstage designed for just that purpose, which is acoustically engineered for recording dialogue in sync to picture.

(See *looper*, *loop group*, *looping*, *walla*.)

**AEA**    Abbreviation for Actors' Equity Association, the union that represents stage actors, known simply as Equity.

**AFTRA**    The acronym for American Federation of Television and Radio Artists.

In 2012, union members voted to merge SAG with AFTRA forming one union, SAG-AFTRA.

SAG-AFTRA represents professional actors in recorded media in America for film, radio, *national* television, cable, new media, and Internet.

One of the key reasons for writing this reference was to keep talent informed as the recent changes and updates in the industry, including this major, very welcome change with our union.

(See Chapter 20, How Union Work Works.)

**AVO**
(Pronounced "ay-vee-oh.") This is the abbreviation for an <u>A</u>nnounce <u>V</u>oice-<u>o</u>ver. Often used as a pronoun, as in, "Are you the AVO?"

**above the line**

This is a term used in both advertising and filmmaking referring to the budget allotted to fixed costs for producers, directors, actors and writers.

The 'line' in this term defines the difference between fixed expenses in the budget (above the line) from those for the rest of the crew (referred to as 'below the line'), which are for the most part crafts people whose costs typically vary. For instance, if a scene is cut from the script, potentially, you don't have to build that set, light it, shoot it, paint it or dress it, and so on.

Recently, added incentives are offered to film and television production in some states if local talent are hired (above the line) for smaller roles such as under-5 (roles consisting of five lines or less) and for featured guest stars, for example, rather than hiring actors from New York and Los Angeles.

(See *below the line* and *under-5*.)

**ad lib**
An ad lib refers to adding your own spontaneous lines and/or action to the piece that differs from the

393

original script. The term comes from the phrase "adding liberties."

To *ad lib* is to improvise, or to make up on the fly.

Ad libbing is often required, if not *expected,* of a talent on an audition and on a booking.

It's always *your* job to make the material sound spontaneous without discarding the concept, but rather adding to it.

(See *improvisation.*)

**affect**     (verb) To put on something; as in "to affect a phrase"; to put a change on a word, phrase, sentence, or delivery.

(See *spin.*)

**agent**     According to SAG-AFTRA, "a talent agent solicits employment, submits talent for employment and/or negotiates compensation and terms of conditions of employment for the performer."

Union talent agents receive a 10 percent commission for their efforts and expertise, while nonunion agents typically receive 15 to 20 percent. An agent's rate of pay is determined ONLY by the work you land on voice acting jobs, acting jobs and various productions.

Talent agents are licensed by the state in which they operate, much like realtors    regarding real estate state law.

(See Chapter 18, How to Get an Agent.)

**air**      (*verb*) When a project airs, this means it's being broadcast over television,   cable, radio, or over new medium (NM).

Just because you booked and shot/recorded a job does NOT mean that piece will necessarily air.

On a union job, you're always paid a session fee, in the event the project or spot does not air. This way you will have been paid regardless.   The best-case scenario is it does air, in order to offer you residual pay (known as *residuals*) that results in the bulk pay of a working talent.

(See *residuals*.)

**analog**      Analog refers to the method of audio recording and processing used by reel-to-reel tape. It's the precursor to digital recording and processing.

For recording, tape is not as versatile a medium as digital and requires more antiquated machinery. However, analog recordings have a favorable warmth, which mixing generally attempts to re-create. The celebrated sound quality of analog can be approximated digitally.

**animatic**      An animatic is a "video storyboard," typically employing some minor animation, thus the name.

When testing or creating a demo for a commercial, which the ad industry does a great deal, an animatic is often employed to better illustrate what the actual commercial will ultimately look like once it's shot. It is a series of storyboarded images with some subtle movement added.

(See *demo* and *photomatic*.)

**arc**        In a script or development of a character in a story, there is generally a climax known as an *arc* at which point the story culminates to its height.

The term arc is in reference to the plot thickening, whether that build or change be sweeping or minute.

**articulate**        As a verb, to articulate is to define or express an idea. It's also an adjective—an *articulate* speaker, for example. This refers to diction and the ability to speak clearly, easily, and effectively. Articulating an idea, a thought, a concept.

**atonal**        An adjective describing a voice without tone, or without sound. This occurs occasionally to all of us when portions of the words or sounds you're speaking are not fully audible. The result is an atonal quality.

**audition**        An audition is essentially an interview in which you demonstrate the suitable skills, personality and confidence to offer the best possible performance for the specific project. In order to land a job, *auditioning* is generally required of nearly every rank and file talent. And to make the best use of valuable production time, headshots, voice-over demos, and on-camera reels (promo) are generally used in advance of your audition to determine whether you're the correct type, look, style, and personality required for the specific casting project.

Voice-over demos and on-camera reels can act as an effective substitute for an audition on occasion in large part because they are thought to be the best example of what you have to offer as a professional, and what sort of work you are seeking *more* of. So if your professional tools are not up to date or are low-grade and makeshift, you may be keeping yourself from landing jobs you might be perfect for.

After submitting your promo (such as your headshots and voice-over demos) you may be called in for an audition. In fact, auditions can be considered your very best promo. (Just not your *only* form of promotion.) The more auditions you do, the more you make yourself known and the more familiar you'll become to those most likely to hire you.

The only difference between the audition and the job itself is the number of takes. You have a very short runway at the audition and are required to deliver your best quickly and concisely, while on the job you generally have a longer runway—what's required of you is *options within the parameters of what's being asked of you.* The *audition* requires decisiveness and confidence; the session demands stamina and agility.

(See *booking* and Chapter 12, Auditions.)

**availability**    At an audition or a callback you will be asked whether you're available for the date of the shoot or recording. If you aren't, *you shouldn't audition. Never* audition for anything unless you intend to accept it and you intend to make yourself available for the job. That's common professional conduct whether you are union or not.

(See *check avail.*)

# B

**background**

Also known as extra work, the *background actor* provides the human element to the background of the scene in a film and TV series. The actor's likeness is not featured or the focus of the scene or shot, but instead considered to be human atmosphere.

When performing as an extra, the actor is not required to speak or make sound. The background sound of crowds, restaurant, courtroom, baseball games, and assorted scenes is added in postproduction using what is known as ADR, or loop groups: extra work for groups of voice-overs with improvisational skills.

(See *ADR*, *extra*, *loop group*, and *looping*.)

**beat**
1. A pause. A brief break in the delivery or read.

2. In writing, film and acting, scripts are often approached "beat by beat," meaning section by section, defined in large part by the actor, director, or writer as needed.

These sections can be defined within a scene, commercial, monologue, film or TV script and are loosely determined by a change. Beats are generally identified in a script by an event, a decision, an idea, a thought, a "bit," a realization, an exchange, a departure, a build, a decline, or some other turn of events.

Breaking a script into beats allows you, as an actor, to *establish the narrative thread*, then *further it* with the following beat, and then ultimately *complete the "story"* with the third or fourth beats, even if the script is a brief commercial. Beats offer a beginning, a middle, and an end.

Simply put, a beat is one full thought or idea conveyed in a script.

**below the line**
This is a term used in advertising, television production, and filmmaking referring to the budget costs for crew such as the Line Producer, Assistant Director, Location Manager, Boom Operator, Costume Designer, Grips, Gaffers, Graphic Artist, Make-Up Artists, and various crew members.

The 'line' in this term defines the difference between fixed expenses in the budget (above the line), such as producers, actors, directors, and writers from those for the rest of the crew (referred to as 'below the line'), which are for the most part crafts people whose costs typically vary. For instance, if a scene is cut from the script, potentially, you don't have to build that set, light it, shoot it, paint it or dress it, and so on.

(See *above the line, grips, gaffers* and *under-5.*)

**billboarding**   An old-school term that refers to adding emphasis on a particular word or phrase especially on a commercial voice-over.

Also known as "putting a spin on it," "finessing" a word or phrase, or "putting a button on it."

**bit rate**   Sometimes written bitrate. It is the amount of information or detail that is stored per unit of time of a digital recording. It's comparable to the frame rate of video, e.g. 24 frames per second or 30 frames per second. The higher the frame rate, the more detailed motion the video can capture with each moment that goes by.

For MP3s, bit rate is measured in kbps (kilobits per second). The higher the bit rate, the higher quality the MP3 (and the larger the file size).  Since the lowest bit rate would sound awful, and the highest bit rate would defeat the purpose of using a compressed format at all, it's best to choose a bit rate somewhere in the middle. 128 kbps and 192 kbps are generally accepted standards.

(See *MP3.*)

**blocking**   The physical movement the actor is directed to do either on stage or on  set.

Blocking can also refer to the physical movement of the camera.

**blue screen**  Also known as *green screen*, or Chroma Key—to key in color.  Blue screen is used to shoot in a studio against a large blue (or green) backdrop to allow a computer-generated background to be superimposed on the final image during postproduction. The actors are required to imagine the set they are on and be aware of the limitations of their movements.

Acting in front of a blue screen is commonplace with advancements in special effects and CGI (Computer Generated Imagery). Blue screen requires the actor utilize his imagination fully—much like during voice-over.

(See *CGI.*)

**booking**  The job itself. Getting a booking is landing the job (i.e., the gig, the brass ring, the goods).

**book out**  If you know you won't be available for auditions or the gig itself, you must book out with your talent agents—give them the dates you are unavailable. Otherwise, they'll think you're available and call you in. You'll end up making everyone miserable, including yourself!

Booking out can be done by e-mail or online a week or so in advance of your not being available. Check with your agency to determine their preferred policy and procedure for booking out.

(See *conflicts* and *availability*.)

**branding**  This is a term used in marketing and advertising with regard to defining or upholding a distinctive trademark or name, which will immediately associate or identify a product, service, person, or manufacturer with a very specific concept or notion.

Branding refers to establishing a product line so well it ultimately becomes iconic in popular culture.

Coca-Cola is traditionally the most notable form of successful branding to date. Even when Pepsi held their "Pepsi Challenge" campaign many years ago, Coke drinkers who chose Pepsi over Coke in the blind taste test remained loyal to Coke and never even considered switching brands.

(See *type*.)

**breakdown**   A list of each character in a film, television show, or commercial with brief description of each.

## Breakdown Services

Also known as *BreakdownExpress*.com. This is the premier site to which casting agencies and similar sources subscribe to organize and call in talent who have listed themselves on ActorsAccess.com.

Talent post themselves (headshots, résumés, reels) on Actors Access so casting sources can find them.

Talent agents and managers will require you to post yourself and keep your materials up to date. This is primarily, but not exclusively, used for film projects.

**business**   *Business* is a term referring to the physical activity of an actor onstage or on-screen.

Stage business or physical business, as it may be referred to, can be what an actor is doing with his hands, feet, with a prop or gesture.

Business is not blocking. Blocking deals with physical direction and movement through the space the actor is in.

(See *blocking*.)

**buyout**        When a talent gets paid a set fee in lieu of residuals. Nearly all non-union work is paid with buyouts.

**by rote**       (See *rote*.)

# C

**CD**            1. This is an abbreviation for a compact disc.

However, an MP3 version of your demo for e-mail or electronic submission (also located on your voice-over-only Web page), has all but replaced the need to reproduce your demo on compact disc by today's standards.

2. In advertising, a CD is the acronym for Creative Director. The creative director is in charge of the creative focus of the commercials produced for a particular ad campaign. This person understands the overall concept of the campaign and directs the copywriters and producers in the creative process. Preproduction usually begins with the creative director designating which copywriters will be submitting scripts for the campaign and which producers will be assigned to the production. The creative director has the senior position on the production from the start. Once the production gets rolling, he is ultimately responsible for making sure the producer and copywriter get the job done. They represent the overall creative portion of advertising, as opposed to the account side of advertising, which ultimately makes sure the clients' needs are met.

3. Informally, CD may also stand for casting director.

**CD-R**          CD-R is an abbreviation for Compact Disc Recordable; a writable compact disc.

**CGI**           This is the acronym for Computer-Generated Imagery. CGI refers to graphics created and animated on a computer often for film, television, or commercial work.

Without CGI, the *Lord of the Rings* trilogy would have been lacking a bulk of the animation that furthered the story of Middle Earth.

**Co-Ed**     According to SAG-AFTRA, "Generally, these are productions for non-broadcast use, including in classrooms, in stores, or DVDs shown in corporate offices or dealer showrooms. They can also be instructional content shown on websites or on new media platforms. Behind-the-scenes footage or b-roll footage also falls under the Co-Ed Contract."

**C.S.A.**     These initials follow some casting directors' names on film and television credits. It stands for *Casting Society of America*.

The goal of this group is to eventually unionize casting directors in the United States, in order to create national standards for casting directors while earning them pension, health, and dental benefits, as well as establishing national rate standards for a variety of casting options.

Currently, there is no union for casting directors.

(See *casting director*.)

**CU**     This is the abbreviation is for a close-up shot used in commercials, television, and film. The script will indicate the use of a close-up by including CU before the description of the shot.

A close-up is generally from the actor's neck  up.

(See *ECU, LS, MCU, MS*.)

**CW**     In advertising, these are the initials for a copywriter the person who writes the commercial script known as copy.

In commercial voice-over, the copywriter is typically the individual who will direct you during the recording session.

**call board**      A backstage bulletin board that contains information about a stage production: contact sheets, schedule, rehearsal time changes, etc.

**callback**        After the initial audition you may be called back for a second or third audition. These are referred to as callbacks.

They liked what you did at the initial audition, so they want you to return     and do it again. *So, don't change anything at the callback unless you are directed to do so!*    In fact (if it's an on-camera audition), be sure to *wear* the exact same thing you wore at the original audition.

You'll rarely have a callback for voice-over, though there are no steadfast rules on any commercial or film. Every single experience is unique unto itself.

**cans**            A slang term sound engineers have for headphones.

**casting director**

A casting director or casting agency contacts a number of talent agencies, typically by utilizing one of the online casting services such as Voicebank.net, Castingnetworks.com   or   Breakdownexpress.com. The talent agents, managers, and in some cases individual talent themselves, submit talent for specific auditions based on the list of designated specs.   The casting agency then chooses the talent they feel are most suitable for the job, schedules them, and runs the auditions for the director and producers.

Generally speaking, the final casting decisions are ultimately made by the producers, directors, and commercial clients through the focus offered by the casting director.

Casting agents provide the service of guiding the production with their expertise and ability to articulate the project demands to the talent, while offering industry insights to both the production side of the project as well as the talent side with regard to performance. Additionally, they specify the work demands of the actor, the rate of pay based on the budget, and the general work regulation standards that apply to the specific production.

Most casting directors specialize in a specific area, such as only animation, only film, or primarily commercial on-camera.

The casting director is hired by the production company, ad agency, director, or producers. (They do not "rep" talent. Talent agents and managers rep talent.)

(See *C.S.A.*)

## Casting Frontier

This site is on the order of Casting Networks.com as one of the two primary online casting services geared almost exclusively toward auditioning commercial on-camera.

Most agents will require their talent to post their own headshots, current résumé, and on-camera reel(s) on this site in order to properly submit them for auditions.

Actors can also use this tool to view casting notices, especially, but not exclusively for commercial auditions.

**Casting Networks**

Formerly known as LAcasting.com or NYcasting.com. This site is on the order of CastingFrontier.com as one of the two primary online casting services geared almost exclusively toward *commercial* on-camera auditions.

Most agents will require their talent to post their own headshots, current résumé, and on-camera reel(s) on this site in order to properly submit them for auditions.

Actors can access this site as a tool to view casting notices and useful articles and tips, especially, but not exclusively for commercial auditions.

**cattle call**     An audition that calls for vast numbers of talent and types and often makes you feel like cattle being herded.

You generally won't see a cattle-call audition for voice-over, but you   may for on-camera and stage.

**cheat out**     To open yourself up by turning slightly *toward* the camera or audience allowing yourself to be seen or heard better.

**cheat toward**

If the actor is slightly off mic, he will be asked to cheat toward the mic or come in a bit closer. This is usually the slightest adjustment that can make a tremendous difference whether the talent is heard and understood.

**check avail**  At every audition you are generally asked whether you are available the dates of the shoot.  If you aren't— DO NOT AUDITION FOR THE JOB!

It's generally understood if you audition for any project you will accept the job if you are booked.  So it stands to reason if you *aren't* available the dates they intend to record or shoot—you can't accept the role. So, save your reputation and do everyone a favor, be sure you're available in the first place.

Additionally, if you have been put on "check avail" by your agent this is a very good sign *you may* have gotten the job.

After you audition for a job, if an agent calls to "check your availability" for a particular day and time, *you could very well book* the job. Though it's not a confirmed booking—*yet*.

Until you are officially booked, a **check avail** is a loose version of being placed *on hold*.

For union work, being put *on hold* means they intend to use you, they're just not quite sure where or when the shoot or recording will occur. The good news is that if they release you from an *on hold*, they must pay you for the session. For nonunion work, they can release you from being on hold and are not obligated to pay you.

(See *availability, booking, hold*, and *released*.)

**check in**   It's your responsibility to stay in communication with your agent. This requires you understand how they prefer you check in with them, and every agent is different.

One thing they all have in common: out of sight, out of mind.

Send them an e-mail. Keep it brief and keep it upbeat.

As your agents get to know you better and how you carry yourself professionally they will eventually call you in with greater consistency.

(See Chapter 18, How to Get an Agent, and Chapter 19, How to Get Work.)

**cinematic shorthand**

This term is exclusive to **Sound Advice**. The concept is based on the idea actors generally craft their performance (and learn their lines) by creating mental cues for themselves with thoughts and mental images. When they play through the scene or script, these "mental cues" play out much like a mental movie reminding them what to say and when.

This train of thought becomes part of the delivery whether the actor is aware of it or not.

*Cinematic shorthand* refers to an economy of performance the talent may offer by taking out the pauses between statements, possibly adding unneeded business or weight to a delivery. Thus there is something of *shorthand* of the mental movie one uses to recall their lines and play through a scene.

(See Chapter 11, The **Sound Advice** Approach.)

**close-up**          (See *CU*.)

**cold read** or **cold copy**

Any unrehearsed reading of a script is considered a cold read.

Every time you audition, and you haven't seen the script prior, it's a cold read.

Voice-over, as most acting, requires you become highly adept at cold reading. If you are booked directly off your demos, the first time you read the script out loud it will be in front of those who have hired you. In other words, you'll be given *cold copy*.

(See Chapter 9, Developing Your Vocal Skills.)

## colloquial dialects

*Colloquial* refers to regional or familiar dialects. And while everyone has an accent, when asked at an audition to have "no discernible accent" the object is to have a neutral quality, rather than a dialect that denotes a specific quality or region.

Still, everybody comes from someplace, so there's really no getting around it to some extent. Further, most people find themselves adopting specific forms of regional expressions particular to their experience and influence.

The thing is, having a distinct colloquial accent may limit what you might be called in for, especially if you're not working in the region your specific dialect is exclusive to.

But then, having a distinct dialect hasn't hurt Tommy Lee Jones, Holly Hunter, Arnold Schwarzenegger, Rosie Perez, or Rosie O'Donnell's careers any.

A great many talent attempt to tone down their dialects without proper training. Certainly a great deal can be said for vocal training and dialect modification, which all of these talent most certainly had done.

Of course, the importance of committing fully to their delivery by being extremely direct about what it is they are communicating, and the fact that each of these talent have a great deal of drive clearly played a role in how all of these people became celebrities.

(See Chapter 9, Developing Your Vocal Skills.)

## commission

The fee an agent or manager gets for being the liaison between the talent and the work, as well as for negotiating the contractual agreement between the talent and the client.

If the talent agent is a union-franchised agency, they are held to specific requirements and can only take 10 percent for voice-over and 15 to 20 percent for print. Nonunion agencies can take more and often do.

Most nonunion work, however, is buyout, where you're paid one flat fee.

A manager's commission is based on the specific agreement between manager and performer.

**composite**  A postcard print that has more than one look printed on it. These cards are two-sided and used almost exclusively by models to show a variety of looks such as glamour, casual, high fashion, and perhaps even a magazine-style look for print.

Also known as a *comp card*.

**conflict**  When auditioning you are typically asked whether you have any conflicts. What they are actually asking you is, "Do you have any commercials currently running that are in direct competition with this product or service?"

If you do, you do not audition for the job as you have a conflict.

For example, if you have a Ford commercial running, you would have a conflict with Honda or any other major car company.

Even if the commercial for Ford that had aired in the past isn't currently running, but you're receiving "holding fees" for it every 13 weeks until you are officially released, this too would be considered a conflict.

Additionally, a conflict could also mean being previously scheduled for another booking at the same time the project you're auditioning for is scheduled to shoot or record.

Lastly, you may have thought a conflict meant having a problem with the product, job, or service. Well, you're right. It does. If you do have a *personal* conflict with a product, job, or service, do everyone a favor and DO NOT AUDITION FOR THE SPOT! You'll end up getting the job and you'll make everyone involved miserable, *especially yourself.* And you could very well destroy your own professional credibility.

Instead, tell your agent you have a conflict with the job and to please inform those holding the audition you're unavailable for the audition. It's far more responsible to be true to your integrity.

**contact sheet**

After you've done the shoot for your headshots, the photographer will give you a contact sheet, which has every shot he took of you on it in miniature. From it, you'll choose which shots you want blown up to 8x10. You usually get one 8x10 look per roll (or 3 to 4 shots per 200 digital shots) included in the cost of the shoot.

Many actors e-mail a link of the digital contact sheet to the talent agent to help them decide.

(See Chapter 17, Headshots and Résumés.)

**conversational**

One of the single most commonly used directions you'll hear in the business is "be more conversational."

411

It simply means make the read sound more natural, more easygoing; as if everything on the page is what you think, and you're thinking out loud.

**copy** The script. The text. The piece. The spot itself.

**corporate** A voice-over demo (or on-camera reel) geared strictly to training, technical, medical, sales, and a variety of nonbroadcast work. These demo tracks are targeted specifically to meet the needs of corporate clients.

Also known as an industrial, narrative, corporate industrial, corporate narration, or nonbroadcast demo.

(See *industrial*.)

**craft services** The beverage and snack table on set is called craft services. I have no idea why.

**creatives** The people who work on the "creative side" in an advertising agency are known collectively as creatives. They are copywriters, producers, associate producers, art directors, production business managers (PBMs), and creative directors.

As these people see it, we're all in the same business. For example, when you are in front of them on a commercial voice-over session they're probably thinking, consciously or not, "You're in my world. My world is advertising, therefore—*you* (the voice-over) must be in advertising."

And if you are booked on a commercial job then you ARE in advertising.

There are essentially three divisions of advertising today: the creative side, the account side, and the PR and marketing side.

**crescendo**     According to Merriam-Webster's, "the peak of a gradual increase climax."

Also known as the *build* or *arc* of a scene, story, or commercial.

(See *arc*.)

**cue**     1. A cue can be the line in the script *just before your line*.

*For example:*
    Frank: Oh, sure. I knew that.
    Todd: All right then, if you say so.

So, Frank's line cues you if you're playing   Todd.

2. A cue can also be the last thing you hear from the director or engineer before you roll on a take, so you know they're ready to film or record you. "Stand by...and rolling" is a cue as well.

Every engineer or director will cue you differently from job to job. These usually happen rather quickly, so it's important that you're ready to *play* (work) even prior to being cued to start.

3. On a set, if an action is required to be shot, you may hear, for instance: "Cue the swans!"   And the swan wrangler would then let loose the honking menagerie.

**custom demo**  This isn't a voice-over demo at all—it's an *audition*. This term has been coined by low-budget online voice-over marketplaces. When a client asks a talent on these sites to submit a *custom demo* for a job they're technically asking for an audition using their script in its entirety. This opens the door for voicing work that you may not be paid for by unscrupulous sources.

**customizations**

Some national products have a need for a customized commercial to distinguish where the product might be available and therefore promote both the store and product at the same time. This is often done with voice-over. These spots are called *customizations*.

For example, you may be asked to voice the whole body of the spot and then do about 150 customizations, such as, "Available at all Benny's, PJ's and Jolly Kitty's and wherever boots are sold." Or how about, "Right now at Benny's when you buy a gallon of milk, all Goofball Boots are half off!" The spot may require as many 500 or as few as 5. It varies according to the job. Regardless, it takes a great deal of concentration, stamina, and spirit of play just to keep the ball in the air during these sessions.

The union pay on customizations is extremely lucrative. So much so it may seem like a good day in Reno, but keep in mind the skill level required to do them well. It can be a mountain of work that can easily become a very surreal and a torturous event if your chops aren't up to the task. You'll earn *every* penny.

# D

**DAW**          The acronym for Digital Audio Workstation.

The term used when referring to audio recording software such as Pro Tools.

**DGA**          The abbreviation for the Directors Guild of America, the union that covers professional directors.

**dpi**          The abbreviation for dots per inch. This term refers to the resolution of a printer or graphic file format, such as a JPEG file (the file format headshots are needed in).

The greater the dpi the greater the resolution and ability to blow up the shot with clarity and detail.

(See Chapter 7, Advancing Technology, and Chapter 17, Headshots and Résumés.)

**dailies**  The screening of footage on a film shot prior to it being edited, typically viewed the day (or week) it was shot.

**delivery**  The performance. Also known as the "read" or the "take."

(See Chapter 11, The **Sound Advice** Approach, *indicating, matching, read, stretching the canvas,* and *take*.)

**demo**  1. A demo is a professional illustration of what you do best, and what you want more of.

Demos are geared toward the specific market you intend to work in. That includes professional *demonstrations* of the type of work you're best suited to land. It is virtually impossible to secure repeated voice-over work without the use of a proper demo.

You must be able to re-create *everything* you have on your demo without reservation.

2. The term demo also refers to a type of booking used to test a commercial campaign. For instance, the ad agency may be attempting to secure a new account with a commercial client, such as Jif peanut butter. The ad agency would create a commercial campaign to pitch to the would-be client by producing a demo of the commercial.

415

You'd be hired to voice the demo, which would technically be a paid booking. The demo may receive an *upgrade* at a later date, which means the spot would air and you would be given additional pay.

A commercial demo booking for voice-over pays half of what a union scale session fee pays, which is still a very good rate.

(See *animatic, session fee, upgrade,* Chapter 3, The Purpose of a Voice-over Demo, and Chapter 20, How Union Work Works.)

**device**        A device is a premise; a tool employed in the creative process, either in the delivery for the actor or in text for the writer designed to further the concept.

**dexterity**     *Dexterity* refers to performance and vocal agility; the abilities that are not immediately intuitive to a talent but are developed over time with practice and attention.

Dexterity is necessary of every talent in order to deliver the direction that is offered at a moment's notice.

(See Chapter 9, Developing Your Vocal Skills.)

**diegetic**      This term refers to sound and music in a film or TV show where the sound element is *audible to the characters* in the scene (e.g. the phonograph in *The Glass Menagerie*; the sound of Darth Vader's light saber). If the sound or music exists within the world of the characters it is said to be diegetic.

If the sound cannot be heard by characters in the scene, and occurs outside of or separately from the world of the characters (e.g., the score in *Gone With the Wind*), it is said to be non-diegetic. This term can apply to sound effects, dialogue, or music.

Diegetic sound matters to an actor for two reasons:

a) If you are booked as a member of a loop group to voice the background sounds on a film or TV series, you will essentially be creating diegetic sounds for restaurant scenes, courtrooms, or whatever is needed for the project or series.

b) If you are doing background work (also known as extra work) you are never expected to make any sound while on set. This allows for greater control over the production elements in post. Extras silently gesture as if they are speaking to each other, but in fact they are not.

**digital patch**     Digital patch refers to either ISDN or Source-Connect, a technology that digitally connects two recording studios using either two designated, digital phone lines or broadband Internet.

Using digital patch, the talent is in a studio in one location while those who have hired the voice-over are in an entirely different studio, perhaps thousands of miles away. The two studios essentially patch with one another digitally.

(See *ISDN*, *phone patch*, and Chapter 7, Advancing Technology.)

**digital watermark**
(See *watermark*)

**direct mail**     Making yourself known to potential agents and production clients by repeatedly sending a simple, direct-mail promotional postcard to the same individual with your Web address and QR Code prominently displayed on it increases the likelihood you will work steadily if done consistently.

Direct mailings establish you as a brand, making your name known and associated with voice-over. It also greatly increases the opportunity for your demos to be heard by those most likely to hire you for voice-over.

(See Chapter 19 How To Get Work for more details on how to promote yourself and how to apply direct mail to your promotions.)

**donut**  Industry term for a radio spot that has music, sound effects, or other production elements at the beginning and end of the spot, with silence or a low music bed in the middle where a voice-over will fill the hole with live voice-over.  Hence the name *donut*.

**dry read**  Your first (cold) read through of a script, typically without direction.

(See *cold read*.)

# E

**ECU**  The abbreviation for an <u>e</u>xtreme <u>c</u>lose-<u>up</u>. A camera shot for commercials, film, or television.

The script will indicate ECU whenever this shot is required.

An <u>e</u>xtreme <u>c</u>lose-<u>up</u> is generally from the middle of the actor's chin to the middle of the forehead or tighter.

(See *CU, LS, MCU, MS, proximity effect*, and *two-shot*.)

**EOD**  Abbreviation for <u>E</u>nd <u>o</u>f <u>D</u>ay, as in "We need this audition back by EOD."

**EXT.**  An exterior shot.  A scene shot outside.

**ear prompter**

An ear prompter is a device that lets you prerecord your script lines so you can listen back to them while performing live or on-camera without cue cards or teleprompter.

Developing ear prompter skills requires you listen to the script you've recorded in advance, and you repeat back the text seconds later, while listening to the next part of the recorded text as it plays back through your earpiece.

This work is generally used for evening news anchors and to deliver long industrial film copy or for live trade show presentations.

Traditionally, the ear prompter device consists of an earpiece that looks like a hearing aid attached to a microcassette recorder. There are also wireless ear prompters that use a transmitter loop to radio the recording from the player/recorder to the actor's earpiece. The benefit of such a device is that there are no wires to conceal in the actor's hair or clothing.

**electronic submission**

When you e-mail an agent or potential employer your demo MP3s or headshots, this is a digital or electronic submission, also known as an e-submission.

**elocution**

According to Merriam-Webster's, elocution is "the art of effective public speaking."

Whereas Dictionary.com describes it as "the study and practice of oral delivery, including the control of both voice and gesture."

**energy**

One of the most common forms of direction offered talent, yet most talent will either speed up their delivery or get louder or both. Instead, after much survey and experience at Sound Advice, we've discovered energy is *interest*. *If you are interest*ed, *you are interest*ing.

So, when a director asks for "a little more energy," you need to be more "interested."

**Equity**          (See *AEA*.)

**establishing shot**
An opening shot that establishes location and/or mood.

**exclusive**     When you *sign* with a talent agency, you are then considered exclusive at least for the state or region your agent is in. Meaning this agency represents you for a specific aspect of the acting industry, such as voice-over. This means all the work you land for voice-over will be negotiated by that talent agency, solely, according to the stipulations of the specific contract.

(See *signed* and Chapter 18, How to Get an Agent.)

**Extra**          Extras are now typically referred to as back-ground actors. These are the actors on a set that provide the atmosphere.

*Extras* may be referred to as background performers, or simply background.

(See *loop group, principal,* and *walla.*)

**extreme close-up**
(See *ECU*.)

# F

**FX**      An abbreviation that refers to special effects or sound effects.

(See *SFX*.)

**FTP**      This abbreviation stands for File Transfer Protocol, which essentially means "how to transfer a file." Large files can be transferred from one place to another easily by using an FTP site.

It's useful for distributing digital files that are 10 megabits or larger and too large to send via e-mail (such as full-quality audio or video).

(See Chapter 7, Advancing Technology, and Chapter 21, How to Collect Your Spots.)

**fifty-fifty**      Two actors sharing equal space in the frame; usually denoted as *50-50*.

(See *two-shot*.)

**first refusal**      If your agent gives you what is called first refusal, it means if another paying job comes along in the meantime, your agent will call up the first job's producer and let him know you're wanted elsewhere—unless the first job would like to firm up your booking *first*.

It used to be, if you auditioned for something and were put "on hold," there was a good chance you had the spot but you *could* get released, and if you did get released that was the end of it.

(See *hold* and *iced*.)

**financial core** (Also known as *fi-core*.)

This is a basic provision allotted to *any* union member in the United States who may, by law, be required to join a particular union. Financial core allows a union member to become a dues-paying nonmember.

Many union talent instate fi-core, as it is most commonly and casually referred to, in order to legally accept both union and nonunion work.

(See *honorary withdraw*, and Chapter 20, How Union Work Works.)

**foley**
Jack Foley invented a process of creating sound effects for movies back in the 1930s and therefore coined the term Foley work. Essentially, this means creating sound effects, such as "heavy boots trudging over gravel," that lend more credibility to the overall piece.

You've probably seen specials on television where the Foley artist is busy turning the sound of crunching corn flakes into a frost-covered battlefield or something. It's a very intriguing profession and takes a tremendous imagination to create some of the outrageous things they come up with. When done well, their work blends seamlessly into the production, so that the listener/viewer doesn't notice the Foley work at all.

**foreground cross**
Action in a scene in which an extra or actor passes between the camera and the principal actors.

**format**
*Format* refers to different forms of media storage, such as MP3, JPEG, WAV, AIFF, or PDF.

The standard format for your voice-over auditions and demos is MP3.

(See Chapter 7, Advancing Technology.)

**freelance**   1. If you're freelance, this means you're multi-listed, or represented by more than one talent agency (as opposed to being signed exclusively with just one).

2. Freelance also refers to the fact that every talent is a freelance artist. In other words, unlike other professions, we don't have the benefit of relying on some other source, outside ourselves, to generate business.

As freelancers we are ultimately responsible for creating our own business and therefore our own careers.

(See *multi-listed.*)

**from the top**   To start over from the beginning.

# G

**gaffer**   The head of the lighting department on an on-camera shoot.

**gesticulate**   To express yourself through physical gestures. The reason we're including this term is simply because you can't leave it to your mouth to do all the acting during a voice-over. You'll end up developing a great deal of vocal tension (and therefore mouth noise) with each additional take if you do.  So be sure to put your whole body into your delivery.  By doing so you'll add ease and fluidity to your performance rather than the opposite.

(See Chapter 9, Developing Your Vocal Skills.)

**gimme**   When a friend or industry contact hires you outright for a job, without an audition, this is referred to as a gimme—it was *given* to you.

Should an agent secure a job for you, again without an audition, this too could be considered a gimme. Somebody *gave it* to her and she's now *giving it* to you.

**golden time**     Golden time is overtime, after the 16th hour, paid in units of one full day per hour. It is contractually referred to as *16-Hour Rule Violation for Extra Performers*.

(See *background* and *extra*, and Chapter 20, How Union Work Works.)

**grips**     Members of the film crew responsible for moving set pieces, lighting equipment, dolly track, and other physical movement of equipment.

**graphic artist/graphic designer**
This is the artist who designs your voice-over brand-identity graphics to be used for your Web site and postcards.     Generally the graphic artist utilizes predesigned lettering and images by combining them to create an original brand design.

(See *illustrator* and Chapter 15, Graphics.)

**green screen**     This is the same thing as a blue screen.

(See *blue screen*.)

# H

**hard sell**     A commercial voice-over delivery style that is extreme, over the top, and sell-y. The hard sell read is forced, often boisterous and pushing the product to the masses as if the announcer's life depended on it. This style of voice-over delivery is utilized primarily in small markets by smaller, regional vendors.

Who the announcer is speaking to is typically lost or diluted by speaking to everyone all at once; speaking to the masses, rather than offering a delivery that is more personable and one on one.

Many smaller, more regional clients will be the first to direct you to emphasize each and every single word when demanding a hard-sell delivery from you.

While there is a glut of this sort of work available in smaller markets, there are a great many bad habits voice-overs typically adopt from repeated bookings of these projects.

This form of delivery borders on offensive and is the polar opposite of what is generally required of you for a bulk of national-caliber voice-over work. In fact, you are likely to be asked on most sessions, both union and nonunion alike, to avoid the hard-sell read entirely unless it's a parody.

Instead, you are primarily expected to simply sound natural or sound like yourself; a relaxed, honest, real, not announce-y delivery is of great value consistently, and yet can be the most difficult performance to deliver.

(See *soft sell*.)

**The Harold**   A long-form improvisational game developed and created by improv innovator Del Close.

Based on the concept that *the Rule of Three* is the scaffolding of all scenes and performance, the basic idea is as follows:

Six improvisers are split into three groups (or teams) of two.

After taking an arbitrary word or concept suggestion from the audience that will be loosely woven into the improvised scenes of the Harold as a whole, the first group of two step up and establish a scene, giving it a loose beginning, middle, and an end.

This is followed by the next two teams of two establishing their own (seemingly) independent scenes, that incorporates the suggestion, as well as added elements from the scenes that has played out previously.

Then we return back to the original pair for a second scene where they either continue their initial story or play out action that could have played out prior to their first scene. (They do not necessarily play the same characters as they had in their first scene.) Once again, this second scene will incorporate concepts and elements from the scenes that preceded it from the other teams scenes as well— while, again, loosely forwarding the original suggestion.

The other two teams follow in suit with each of their own second scenes.

And the Harold is completed as the three teams resolve their improvised stories, continually forwarding their own story while incorporating elements and concepts from their counterparts work, yet remaining independent and fully completing the demands of the scene and story.

Long-form improvisation requires a great deal of mental stamina, as well as the ability to truly pay attention and listen to your improvisational teammates, while remaining loose enough to think on your feet and simply create.

Many commercial copywriters, television, and screenwriters develop their ability to effectively and creatively weave a story by utilizing improvisation and most especially by learning how to play the Harold.

Actors and writers alike develop invaluable professional skills from learning to master the Harold.

(See *improvisation*, *Rule of 3* and Chapter 11, The **Sound Advice** Approach.)

**headphones**  The device you place over your ears that allows you to hear your delivery when recording voice-over. Also known as the *headset*, *ears* (as in "Put on your 'ears' "), or *cans*.

Everyone's different when it comes to their use, or lack of use, but you do need to communicate with the control room and to monitor the performance you're putting into the mic. Some talent like to have one ear on and one ear off. Others hate to wear them at all.

If you find you're concentrating too much on *how you are saying what you're saying* rather than *what you are talking about*, try removing your headphones for a few takes. Just be sure to let the engineer and client know what you are doing, so you don't miss any direction they may have for you.

The best rule of thumb, keep your headset on for the first few takes to *establish where you are placing your performance* and to determine your level; *your volume*.

(See *proximity effect*.)

**headshot**  A headshot is the common calling card for talent intending to be considered for on-camera work.

Online casting services require JPEG versions of your headshot. These have all but replaced reproducing headshots especially for commercial work. However, you are still required to have a variety of professional looks and at least two or three hard copy versions on hand for theatrical (film and television) work and to secure professional representation.

Headshots are standardly reproduced as an 8x10 and occasionally reproduced as a 5x7.

The résumé should be attached to the back of the headshot (facing outward) by simply stapling all four corners, or printing the résumé directly to the back of the headshot from your printer.

Regular electronic submissions and snail-mail promotion of your headshots to casting directors is commonplace and highly encouraged to make yourself known and available to the work.

You never need a headshot for voice-over. In fact, according to survey, it's preferred by potential clients they imagine what you look like as a voice-overs, rather than actually see what you look like in a headshot, so we recommend you keep these two forms of promotion entirely separate from one another.

(See *contact sheet* and Chapter 17, Headshots and Résumés.)

**high shot**     A shot taken from above the subject.

**hip-pocket**    When a talent agency reps you on a trial basis, by oral agreement rather than signing you to the standard exclusive contract, this is considered hip-pocketing, meaning they'll keep you close and attempt to get you work.

**hold**
If your agent calls and says, "You're on hold for Comet cleanser," or "You're on hold for a part on *The Mentalist*," chances are very good you've got the part, but you aren't actually booked yet.

(See *booking, check avail, first refusal,* and *iced.*)

**honey wagon**
The term designated to the portable toilet facilities on a location set for the performers and crew.

# I

**iLok**
This is a unique flash drive used a great deal with editing systems such as Pro Tools, Source-Connect and FinalCut. Technically, it's a USB hard-drive key.

According to their site, "Software publishers use the iLok to provide secure protection for their software. When running iLok-protected software, it looks for your license on your attached iLok.

(See *Pro Tools* and *Source-Connect.*)

**INT.**
Interior shots; scenes shot indoors, whether on location or on a set erected on a soundstage.

**ipDTL**
ip stands for Internet Protocol and DTL stands for Down The Line.

This is a very promising Web app created by British-based tech company In:Quality designed to replace the extremely expensive, rather antiquated technology known as ISDN, the industry standard used to connect one studio with another for professional voice sessions and various radio broadcasts.

ipDTL is potentially the simplest, most cost-efficient option to be introduced to date to patch voice talent with producers from nearly anywhere in the world provided both parties have Google Chrome, stable Internet access, and at least one of the two parties has a subscription to ipDTL. At this writing, this App is yet untested, but has the potential to record high quality, possibly "better-than-ISDN" audio, according to their site and various online enthusiasts, using your basic broadband connection.

ipDTL doesn't rely on expensive proprietary hardware and pricey phone lines like ISDN. Yet, like ISDN and SourceConnect (the most popular broadband patching option thus far), ipDTL offers a professional grade option for audio recording, which delivers a similar experience as being in the same studio as the client, even though they may be across the country or half the world away. Like these two previous options, the client sounds as if they are in the Control Room while you are in the booth.

(See *digital patch*, *ISDN*, *Source-Connect,* and Chapter 7, Advancing Technology.)

**ISDN**          This is the abbreviation for Integrated Services Digital Network.

Originally used for businesses to access the Internet securely, ISDN was initially developed to offer two services: digital phone and broadband Internet— hence the name, *integrated services.*

ISDN (commonly referred to as a digital patch) is commonly used in professional recording studios to connect a talent in a studio in one location with a director/producer/client in an entirely different location often thousands of miles away. The remote studio can record the talent without any loss in quality.

And, to the talent (as well as the client), it sounds as if everyone were in the very same studio.

This technology has made voice talent available to work in markets they previously had not had access to. And its frequent use has changed *everything* in this business, expanding opportunities for every branch and style of voice-over imaginable.

(See *digital patch*, *phone patch*, *Source-Connect*, and Chapter 7, Advancing Technology.)

**ISCI (code)**     (Pronounced *"isky"*.)

First, ISCI stands for Industry Standardized Commercial Identifier. The ISCI code is used worldwide to identify commercials aired for TV stations, networks, ad agencies, post-production, and all related entities. This code can be found on paychecks and all professional paperwork pertaining to the commercial.

Should your spots end up in archives, you would need an ISCI code to identify the specific commercials to retrieve them.

**IVR**     This abbreviation stands for Interactive Voice Response, as in a car, or Intelligent Voice Routing, as in phone prompts.

According to Dictionary.com, IVR is "a telecommunications system, prevalent with voice-mail systems, that uses a prerecorded database of voice messages to present options to a user, typically over telephone lines. When used in conjunction with voice mail, for example, these systems typically allow users to store, retrieve, and route messages, as well as interact with an underlying database server, which may allow for automated transactions and data processing."

**iced**  If you've been iced, fear not, you're not dead. However, you're not *booked* either, but you are incredibly close.

If your agent calls and puts you *on ice* for that Maxwell House commercial you auditioned for, you are *not* to schedule any other auditions and bookings for the time they give you, as there's a very good chance you will be on the Maxwell House booking on that day at that time, though it's still being firmed up.

But until you hear otherwise, that day and time is reserved, *provided* you're already free.

(See *check avail*, *booking*, *first refusal*, and *hold*.)

**illustrator**  As opposed to a *graphic artist*, this individual creates an original cartoon, drawing, or painting. An illustrator rarely adds graphic-design elements (such as your name and contact information) however, a graphic artist would.

An illustrator would have to be hired in addition to a graphic designer to create an original design for a brand identity or logo.

Further, an illustrator will NOT convert the entire design into any other format for reproduction or alter the image to suit a graphic design, as most illustrators don't typically do graphics. Those are entirely separate skill sets.

(See *graphic artist* and Chapter 15, Graphics.)

**imaging**  This is short for *station imaging*; promotional spots for RADIO *only*. These spots are generally done by radio personalities or radio veterans and used to define the image of a radio station or a branch of stations.

This type of work is technically not handled by talent agents in most markets, although some agents in New York and Los Angeles will represent talent who are well known for it. But, honestly, it's rare. The reason being (and if you have any extensive radio experience you probably know this already) you'd make more money pursuing this line of work on your own.

(See *demo* and Chapter 3, The Purpose of a Voice-over Demo.)

**improvisation**

To improvise means to spontaneously create a performance on the fly, typically without a script. The abbreviation is improv.

In essence, everything you *ever* do as a talent (commercial work, film, television, and stage) should have a strong sense of play about it, which is based firmly in improv.

Improv allows you to think on your feet and flesh out your imagination, and we strongly recommend you continually develop these skills. You'll bring a greater imagination to your performance and greater overall confidence as well.

We are paid to play in this business. So get busy.

(See *ad lib.*)

**indicating**    When an actor is *indicating* during a performance, he is considered to be *overacting*.

This can be detected when an actor is trying too hard and thereby giving too much emphasis to nearly every single word in the script. Doing so indicates the actor is self-conscious, and too busy editing and observing himself. The result is completely losing the narrative thread, rather than establishing it, and ultimately the actual meaning of the line or scene.

(See *delivery, matching, read,* and *stretching the canvas.*)

**industrial**     A voice-over or on-camera job created for non-broadcast, used to train or inform employees for an internal company video, trade show or convention presentations, Web site tutorials, sales demonstrations for point-of-purchase (in-store) to illustrate sales policies or in-house office procedures, for instance, to name a few.

Industrial work is also known as narrative, corporate, corporate announce, corporate narration, or even as nonbroadcast.

In voice-over, an industrial demo specifically targets corporate clients who generally hire the talent directly from this demo track without an audition a majority of the time.

Industrial voice-over constitutes approximately 40 to 45 percent of all voice-over production.

(See *demo, Co-Ed.,* and Chapter 3, The Purpose of a Voice-over Demo.)

**inflection**     According to the Cambridge Advanced Learner's Dictionary, an inflection is "the way in which the sound of your voice changes during speech, for example when you emphasize particular words: *His voice was low and flat, with almost no inflection.*"

The goal with each new take is to effectively offer a slight but noticeable change in inflection, allowing for a fresh and spontaneous delivery without dramatically altering the pitch, volume, or speed of the performance.

(See *matching*.)

**insert**  A shot relevant to the scene, but filmed separately and inserted in post. Often a close-up shot of hands, feet, or specific physical business.

**in post**  When something is referred to being "fixed *in post*," it means corrections of the scene made during the editing the process in postproduction.

Whenever possible, you want to correct the problem while you are still in production (while you are recording/shooting) rather than in post to ensure the best final results.

(See *postproduction, preproduction, production*.)

**intimate**  Referring to a quieter, more personable type of delivery.

An intimate delivery is almost as if you're whispering into someone's ear, and we're hearing your thoughts as if they are our own.

**iso booth**  Short for isolation booth, pronounced "ice-oh booth" otherwise known as a vocal booth or whisper booth.

# J

**jewel case**  The old-style hard plastic CD case, prone to chipping and breaking when sent through the mail.

**JPEG**  A JPEG is a digital file format that is used to e-mail and reproduce images, especially photographs.

When you have your headshots taken digitally, each shot will be a JPEG file. This is the file format you'll use to view your headshots on your computer.

The term JPEG stands for Joint Photographic Experts Group.

(See *dpi* and Chapter 18, Headshots and Résumés.)

# L

**LS**        This is an abbreviation for a long shot. A long shot is, more or less, a full-body shot of the actor or actors or location in film and television.

(See *CU*, *ECU*, *MCU*, *MS*, *proximity effect*, and *two-shot*.)

**laryngitis**        Inflammation of the larynx (voice box) that can result from many causes, of which the specific cause should be identified for a correct diagnosis and proper treatment.

The result of laryngitis is the voice sounds strained and horse, and at least a week of rest is required to recuperate full vocal ability.

(See Chapter 10, The Health Department.)

**latency**        Latency refers to a short period of *delay*, usually measured in milliseconds, between when an audio signal enters and when it emerges from a system.

It sounds like something of an echo, because what you're hearing is not instantaneous.

This can (and often does) occur during sessions when *patching* with one studio to another.

(See *ISDN*, *patch*, *phone patch*, and *SourceConnect*.)

**legal**         At the end of many commercials, for everything from banks to medications, a mouthful of fast-read disclaimers are added to unburden the client of any legal obligation.

For example, "Void where prohibited. Must be 18 to enter. No one under 21 admitted without parent or guardian. May cause watery eyes, itchy nose, and violent convulsions. Member FDIC." These are known in advertising as legals.

**level**        The actual volume at which you intend to deliver the read.

When you're in the studio and about to record the very first track of the session, the engineer will ask you for a level.

The engineer is concerned with how loud or soft you'll be during the recording. Setting the correct level is his job, but he needs your help to do so.

(See *mic technique*.)

**lift**        A lift is taking a segment of the video and/or audio from any production and repurposing that performance for additional usage. For instance, taking the voice-over from a TV commercial and using it for the radio commercial as well would be a lift. Or using the TV commercial online in addition to the radio and TV, each of these would be a lift as well. If any part of the your performance, whether on-camera or voice-over is *lifted* to be used for any additional forms of usage you would be paid for a stipend for each form of usage. This is the case whether you are a union or non-union talent.

(See *usage*.)

**line-reading**   When someone prompts you how to say the line by saying it himself for you to mimic.

It's generally considered bad form to give an actor a line-reading, as many talent feel you are stepping on their creative toes—therefore, most directors will fall all over themselves trying to avoid doing so.

**listed**     If you are listed with a talent agency, then that agency has agreed to represent you. Listed means you are registered, but NOT exclusively.

The agent you are listed with will call you for auditions on a freelance basis and usually only after they have called their exclusives first. This is usually the period in which they get to know what you're like to deal with professionally and personally and how well you do on auditions. You may land work for this agent, but he may retain a freelance status with you for a year or more. The agent will still negotiate your contract for a job and call you in on work they believe suits what you do best—based on your type.

(See *agent*, *exclusive*, *freelance*, *register*, *signed*, and Chapter 18, How to Get an Agent.)

**location**     Any place, other than the studio, or studio back lot of a film production company, where a film is being shot.

**logline**     The pitch line used to sell a film in its most boiled-down, simplest terms in one active sentence, focusing on the concept, main character and main conflict, ideally in 25 words or less. (In fact, the more concise, the better.)

For example: "Jaws in Outer Space" to describe the film *Alien*.

**long shot**     (See *LS*.)

**look**
A look, when it comes to headshots, provides those casting with a faithful reflection of you, your age range, and type and is focused on the aspect of the industry in which you are looking to work.

You will successfully accomplish this provided your headshots represent a good variety of the sort of work you're best suited to pursue (such as commercial, television, film, or industrial). You'll want to make sure your headshot shoot offers variety of looks in a variety of settings with numerous wardrobe changes.

A look may also be how you're expected to dress for an on-camera audition, such as dressy-casual, young mom, or even high-end corporate professional.

So, *look* is a term that may be used to define type.

(See *type*.)

**looper**
A talent who records background group vocal tracks for film and television for crowd scenes such as in restaurants, school hallways, courtrooms, etc. Loopers are employed through casting professionals who run and manage loop groups, almost primarily in Los Angeles. Talent are hired at union day rates to add crowd or individual ambience to on-camera work.

These are very coveted positions because they pay both session fees and residuals and offer a great deal of repeat business, so they can be the equivalent of landing a recurring role on a sitcom.

Loopers are hired because it's far easier to control the sound of a finished piece when extras are shot silently and the loop group adds a far more controlled, desired sound in post.

This is also known as walla work because in the early days of recording, it was thought that group background sounds could simply blend into a wall of mumbles by simply stating, "walla, walla, walla."

Today, loopers are recorded in groups of as few as 3 to as many as 30, all recorded at actual level.

Voice-over experience and improvisational skills are a must to become an accomplished *looper*.

(See *ADR*, *loop group*, *postproduction*, and *walla*.)

**loop group**  Loop groups are used to add restaurant, classroom, courtroom, and general crowd sounds or human ambience to a film or television soundtrack in postproduction, which is why this work is almost exclusively indigenous to the Los Angeles area.

This work could be referred to as voice-over extra work, or even closer to the truth, *human foley* work because you'll watch the scene and record appropriate banter that plays as background.

It's worth mentioning this work pays the full SAG-AFTRA day rate.

A few well-know loop groups include: LA Mad Dogs, Barbara Harris' Loop Group, David Sharp's Totally Looped Group, David Kramer's Looping Group, and Loop Troup.

(See *ADR*, *foley*, and *walla*.)

**looping**  On film and television, when a line has been recorded incorrectly (or flubbed) by a principal but the shot is perfect, *or* when the swearing needs to be replaced for network television or certain cable station broadcasts, the on-camera actor is brought into a recording studio to loop the corrected verbiage to picture. The actor must match her lip movements in the picture as closely as possible. This process is called looping. This is also known as ADR.

Looping may also be done, in either film or television, if a voice-over track is an integral aspect of the production and must be in close sync with cuts in the picture. A good film example would be *American Beauty,* in which Kevin Spacey's character is recapping the events that lead up to his death. A good television example is *The Wonder Years,* where the adult version of the lead character, played by Daniel Stern, described the events of his childhood while Fred Savage played the younger, on-camera version of the lead role.

In the booth, the actor views a time-coded version of the scene over which her voice will be looped.

Again, from veteran ADR/looping aficionado, Ann Anderson, "Principal dialogue has to be looped if it wasn't recorded cleanly.

"For example, if a plane drones overhead while a scene is shot, the actors may have to redo some lines during postproduction. Actors sometimes flub lines, and if there's no time for a retake, the line will be looped."

If the actor isn't available (postproduction goes on for weeks after a picture is shot), loopers do a sound-alike.

(See *ADR* and *loop group.*)

| | |
|---|---|
| **lot** | A motion picture studio, buildings, or grounds. |
| **low shot** | A camera shot from beneath eye level. |

# M

**MCU**    This is the abbreviation for a Medium-Close-Up shot as used on film, television, or commercial scripts.

MCU indicates, relatively, a shot between the middle of the actor's chest to above his head. This is probably the single most common shot used.

(See *CU, ECU, LS, MS, proximity effect,* and *two-shot.*)

**MMORPG**    This is the abbreviation for Massively Multi-player Online Role-Playing Game, the term for an online computer game in which a very large group of players compete and interact with each other in a fictional world. Popular examples include *World of Warcraft* and *EverQuest.*

Most modern video/computer games use voice-over to give their characters greater emotion and animation.

(See *NPC.*)

**MOS**    MOS stands for Mit Out Sound and means *without sound.* It's pronounced em-oh-ess.

The term MOS may appear on film, television, or commercial scripts to indicate that the scene will be *shot without* recording dialogue or any other sound. We may see characters speaking with each other in the scene, but we won't hear what they are saying. The final product, in a scene that is MOS, may have sound effects or music playing over the action, possibly accompanied by voice-over.

Generally, with MOS, you're asked to improvise a short scene. For example, walking into a restaurant, giving a wave and then you're joined by your wife and two kids in one big, happy family shot.

Another definition that's not as common as it used to be, from television news, is M.O.S., referring to the Man on the Street.

**MP3**    Technically, MP3 is a digital audio file format that compresses the size of the original full-quality file by about 10 times (or more), resulting in a small file that is easy to deliver via the Internet while maintaining high-quality sound. These resulting small files are known as MP3s. MP3 is short for MPEG-3, which in turn stands for <u>M</u>otion <u>P</u>icture <u>E</u>xperts <u>G</u>roup, audio layer <u>3</u>.

(See *format* and Chapter 7, Advancing Technology.)

**MS**    This is the abbreviation for a medium shot as used on film, television, or commercial scripts. MS indicates, relatively, a shot of the actor from the waist up. This is one of the most common shots used.

(See *CU, ECU, LS, MCU, proximity effect,* and *two-shot.*)

**MacGuffin**    According to wikipedia.org, "a MacGuffin (or McGuffin) is a plot device that holds no meaning or purpose of its own, except to motivate the characters and advance the story. The device is usually used in films, especially thrillers. The term MacGuffin was invented by Alfred Hitchcock, who made extensive use of the device in his films."

Hitchcock referred to it as the item "the spies are after," but the audience knows just enough about to further the plot.

As an audience, we are satisfied not knowing the *full* story—just that there *is* a story. The MacGuffin is often the motivation of the nemesis, that's a mystery to the audience but not considered mysterious. In many ways, the MacGuffin is put to use in commercial story lines all the time, and not just for suspense.

**making the rounds**

A phrase used with regard to making your self known to the local talent agents and casting directors. *Making the rounds* refers to stopping into each agency on a biweekly basis and leaving promotional (on-camera only) materials with the receptionist.

This is seldom done with talent agents in general any more, however it's highly encouraged you practice this for on-camera submissions to casting agencies in Los Angeles, where these practices are welcome.

Determine each individual casting agency's submission policies in advance of promoting yourself to meet the specific needs of those most likely to hire you.

(See Chapter 18, How to Get an Agent.)

**manager**

A talent manager specializes in one or more aspects of the talent industry and then effectively directs and guides his clients' careers. Managers help define the actor's most employable options in relation to the actor's professional goals. This is done through headshots, training, how they dress, how they're styled, and a great deal more. (Of course, the talent themselves must invest in these professional upgrades to their careers.)

A manager has established professional contacts or makes them on the actor's behalf and in many cases will secure work for the talent, as well introduce him to talent agents.

A talent manager can earn a monthly stipend until their clients (actors) are more established and earning a steady income. At that time, the agreement is usually 15 to 25 percent of the actor's income.

(See *agent* and Chapter 18, How to Get an Agent.)

**mark**　　The exact position(s) given to an actor on a set to ensure that he/she is in the proper light and camera angle; generally marked on the ground with tape or chalk.

**master shot**　　A camera shot that includes the principal actors and relevant background activity; generally used as a reference shot to record the scene from beginning to end before shooting close-ups, over-the-shoulders, etc.

**matching**　　The term used when you are trying to recreate the timbre, emotion, inflection, phrasing, volume/proximity, and tempo of a delivery, to make a slight adjustment or to correct a minor error in the initial read.

Also, if at a session the client preferred a specific take and simply wants to change a line or phrase they may have you punch in the corrected line. This requires you match the original delivery as much as possible.

The truth is there are only three circumstances in which one specific delivery is required from you:

a) When you are understudying a stage role. According to Actors' Equity, you are expected to re-create the original actor's performance as closely as possible.

b) When you are in a professional touring company of a stage production (such as *The*

445

*Producers* or *Hairspray*). These productions are very strictly choreographed to *match* the original production—to the letter in every way because a very specific product is being presented, and the original show is the blueprint for the touring company. Additionally, these productions are often heavy "tech" shows, and straying from the program could increase the risk of injury to cast and crew.

c) When adding or correcting a line in a voice-over or on-camera production (known as ADR or looping).

Other than that, matching is *not* the desired goal of a performance; it's only a tool and nothing more.

(See *ADR*, *looping* and Chapter 11, The **Sound Advice** Approach.)

**media** or **medium**

1. Media is another name for the press. For example, "contrary to what was highly publicized in the media."

2. Media also refers to recorded media format, such as CD, CD-R, or an MP3 file.

3. Lastly, media refers to the art form you are working in as an actor, such as film, or television, or voice-over, or stage.

Much like a painter may work in watercolor as a medium, if that painter expanded to oil and sculpture then there would be a variety of media that artist was capable of working in.

The plural form of this definition is *media*, and the singular is *medium*.

4. Mass media refers to communication that reaches masses of people, such as Internet, television, film, and radio.

**medium close-up**
(See *MCU*.)

**medium shot** (See *MS*.)

**mic technique** The ability to effective place your performance on mic. This is not typically an intuitive action. *Mic technique* takes time to develop effective control over your volume and agility.

(See *level*.)

**motion capture**
Also known as "mocap" (pronounced *mo' cap*). This is a performance animation process that has become commonplace in numerous productions for film, games, animation, and commercials.

According to the book *Understanding Motion Capture for Computer Animation and Video Games* by Alberto Menache, motion capture is "The creation of a 3-D representation of a live performance."

Another name for mocap is "performance animation," which takes the emphasis off the capturing of data for animation for film and games.

**moving shot** Any shot that employs a moving camera, whether handheld or on a dolly, vehicle, or crane.

**mnemonic** (pronounced new-*mon*-ick) A recognizable tone or tune associated with a service, product or station.

For example, NBC has had its traditional three-tone mnemonic for as long as it's been on the air.

A mnemonic creates an audible memory associated with a brand or service and makes the spot and therefore the brand memorable.

**mouth noise**   Unwanted mouth pops and snaps in a voiced delivery are commonly called mouth noise.

Mouth noise occurs when you make your mouth do all the work during your performance, so all the performance tension is focused on your mouth coming up with the delivery, rather than animating the read by allowing your body to back up your voice.

To lose mouth noise: *You move your body!* Imagine sticking your hand out a car window and catching the drag. Make a figure eight with one hand; have the other on your hip.

It may sound silly, but it takes your attention off your mouth and it allows your body to back up your voice.

Mouth noise (tension in your mouth) occurs when you give your mouth complete responsibility for creating the read.

(See *gesticulate* and *safety.*)

**multi-listed**   A term referring to a talent who is registered, and therefore commercially represented, with more than one talent agent.

For example, you may be represented by a number of talent agencies for commercial, television, film, and voice-over if you are multi-listed.

(See *exclusive, registered,* and *signed.*)

**multiple camera**

The use of more than one camera in shooting a scene, all rolling simultaneously.

**muscle memory delivery**

A term exclusive to **Sound Advice** meaning a performance that, when repeated with each additional take, plays almost identically the same with little or no variation or creativity. In other words, a read that is by rote and runs as if on a circuit.

Muscle memory delivery dictates that however you read the script the first time out, you're most likely to return to that original delivery again and again—not because it's the best read you have in you, or the only read you have in you, but because you didn't die! It's a comfort zone created the first time you do anything, let alone read a script out loud. Muscle memory delivery is an impulse encoded into your muscles from your very first read.

So if you've been worried you might have trouble repeating a delivery—fear not. Muscle memory will practically *ensure* you continually return back to your initial read over and over again—whether you want to or not. Left to its own devices, your delivery will run on automatic by pure virtue of muscle memory, and the necessary spontaneity and freshness will not be present either.

Our definition of this term is closer to what kinesiology (sports medicine) refers to as muscle memory and should not to be confused with the American Method definition of muscle memory.

It's a talent's mission to deliver a variety of vocal deliveries within the perimeters of the project, and usually the only thing stopping you to do so is *muscle memory*.

(See Chapter 11, The **Sound Advice** Approach.)

# N

**NDA**     The abbreviation for <u>N</u>on-<u>D</u>isclosure <u>A</u>greement, also known as a confidentiality agreement.

**NPC**     The abbreviation for <u>N</u>on-<u>P</u>layer <u>C</u>haracter.

This is a character in a role-playing computer/video game whose actions are not controlled by the player.

(See *MMORPG*.)

**narrative**     1. A voice-over demo targeted to the market to service industrial, corporate, or broadcast.

2. In film, a narrative story line is one with a traditional beginning, middle, and end, as opposed to a more presentational or specific formulaic style.

(See *Co-Ed*, *industrial* and *nonbroadcast*.)

**narrative thread**

The through line of the story, concept, or idea playing out in the script and forwarded by the actor.

During the very first beat of the story or commercial, the narrative is established (how the story will be told). Connecting one idea to the next, forwarding the narrative device is generally referred to as *furthering the narrative thread*.

(See *beat*, *Rule of 3*, and Chapter 11, The **Sound Advice** Approach.)

**national**     A commercial that is broadcast nationwide on network and cable television. In commercial work, nationals earn higher pay from residuals than any other form of media. In fact, national commercials account for the greatest income rank and file talent earn as well as the greatest contributions into union coffers toward pension and health (P&H), than any other aspect of the industry including from film or television due to the sheer volume of work.

(See Chapter 20, How Union Work Works.)

**new and improved**

On a national commercial, advertisers can only call a product "new and improved" for six months. After that, the ad must be modified to a "non-new" or "sustaining" status, if the campaign is to continue.

You will be hired and paid additional session fee(s) to voice these "sustaining" spots.

**new media**    New media is defined as any and all media that can be found on the Internet, such as a video on You Tube, or anything interactive, such as games, Twitter or, Facebook.

According to SAG-AFTRA, "Initial pay is negotiable under the SAG-AFTRA New Media Agreement. There are no minimums under this contract; however, state and federal minimum wage laws still apply."

(See Chapter 20, How Union Work Works.)

**nonbroadcast**

Another name for industrial, corporate, or narrative voice-over and on-camera work.

(See *corporate*, *Co-Ed*, *industrial*, and *narrative*.)

**non-new**    Once a national commercial campaign has exhausted the use of its "new and improved" status, the "non-new" or "sustaining" spots may run, and for a number of years (best-case scenario).

(See *new and improved*.)

**nonunion**     Union talent have professional guidelines that are designated by the Screen Actors Guild (SAG) and the American Federation of Television and Radio Artists (AFTRA), now one union, known as SAG-AFTRA. If you are not associated with this union, you're considered to be a nonunion talent (if this is the case for you, this means you have "no union affiliations").

(See Chapter 20, How Union Work Works.)

# O

**OC**     The term used on a film or television script when dialogue is delivered o̲ff-c̲amera.

**OK-30**     This provision was established by SAG in 1999 to help would-be union members make the transition to union a bit more gradually. It allows for a talent who had *recently* had his Taft-Hartley status expire to call his local union office and request an OK-30, which would extend the 30-day Taft-Hartley grace period another 30 days. During this extended 30 days, the talent again, like under Taft-Hartley, is allowed to land more union work without having to actually join the union by paying the initiation fee and first union dues.

(See *SAG-AFTRA, Taft-Hartley*.)

**off book**     Having the lines from the script memorized.

Until you are *off book*, you must read from the script or sides to perform.

(See *sides*.)

**off mic**  If you are off mic, you may be directing your sound too far to one side of the microphone's pickup area, or the microphone may be set to the incorrect height for you. While some scripts require you to play off mic, generally you'll want to stay on mic.

(See *level* and *proximity effect*.)

**on call**  When an actor is *on call*, he or she is expected to be available for any call time.

**on hold**  (See *hold*.)

**on ice**  (See *iced*.)

**open up the shot**

To angle one's body more toward the camera—as with actors facing each other in a scene.

(See *cheat out*.)

**over-the-shoulder**

A shot over the shoulder of one actor, focusing entirely on the face and upper torso of the other actor in a scene; generally shot in pairs so both actors' expressions can later be edited together.

**overlap**  To speak or otherwise vocalize over another actor's line.

(See *stepping on lines*.)

# P

**P2P**  The industry slang that stands for '*pay-to-play*', as in 'pay to play sites'. These are sites you pay to promote your demos on in order to be considered for voice-over work. Some sites include: Voice123.com, Voices.com and VoiceBunny.com, to name a few.

**POV**        The abbreviation for p̲oint o̲f v̲iew.

A POV shot is a camera angle taken from a character's perspective.

This term also refers to a voice-over delivery that is personable, direct and one-on-one; it's said to have POV.

**PSA**        The abbreviation for a P̲ublic S̲ervice A̲nnouncement.

**pan**        A camera shot in which the camera moves horizontally on a fixed axis, surveying an area.

**patch**        Any connection with a studio other than the one you are recording from is considered a patch.

The ability to patch in to a studio from another region using ISDN, Source-Connect, Skype, or phone patch allows voice talent to secure work they might have otherwise not had access to.

Patching with a studio in another region is a common occurrence in every busy professional studio.

(See *digital patch, ISDN, phone patch, Source-Connect*.)

**per diem**        The Latin term meaning 'per day'.

*Per diems* are fees paid a performer on location shoots to compensate for expenditures on meals, wardrobe, travel, etc., not provided by the producer.

An agent is best suited to negotiate an actor's per diems. The more of these on a shoot, the greater the unit pay for the job.

(See Chapter 20, How Union Work Works.)

**perpetuity**        [pronounced: pur-pi-**too**-i-tee]

Dictionary.com's definition, that applies to working actors, is, "Endless or indefinitely long duration or existence; eternity. (Often preceded by *in*)."

*In perpetuity* is the term used in some acting contracts to confirm the client has unlimited usage of the recorded performance by agreement. Whatever you were paid is not and never will be subjected to any additional fees or compensation. EVER.

**phone patch**  A device in a recording studio that allows a standard *phone* line to *patch* with a client in outside location.

A common use for phone patch is a client will call in to listen and direct a voice-over session over the phone. An effective (and clearer) substitute for phone patch is Skype.

(See *digital patch, ISDN, Skype, Source-Connect,* and Chapter 7, Advancing Technology.)

**photomatic**    A photomatic is a photo  storyboard incorporated into storyboarded images employed to better illustrate the overall art direction or look of the commercial or production, thus the name.

Photomatics are used infrequently in commercial testing today, but they are employed to better illustrate what the actual film or animation production will ultimately look like once it's produced.

(See *animatic.*)

**pick-up**    On a voice-over, after you've flubbed a line, you leave *a little bit of space for an edit* and then pick-up the line *before* the flub. You don't have to start all over again at the top. You just pick-up the line *prior* to the phrase or word that went screwy.

For on-camera, a pick-up is essentially the very same thing.

**pilot season**　　Pilot season refers to the time of year the bulk of pilots are cast and shot during any given calendar year.

Even though television programming has changed dramatically in recent years and you may be auditioned at *any time during the year* for a TV pilot or series, *pilot season* is still generally considered the busiest production period and takes place from January through April, especially in Los Angeles. The bulk of most *episodic* production tends to take place from August through the beginning of November.

(See *audition*.)

**playing status**

Playing status refers to a performance that denotes social stature.

Such as:
　　a) Playing authority, confidence, or dominance.
Or, the opposite:
　　b) Playing vulnerable, somewhat awkward, and real.

(See *improvisation*, and Chapter 11, The **Sound Advice** Approach.)

**'plosive 'p's**　　(See *p-pop*.)

**plus 10 (+10)**

A union talent agent gets paid a 10 percent commission on *your* total income on any given job you may have booked through him.

Sometimes an agent will actually negotiate his commission on top of your rate. This is referred to as plus 10. This way, his commission is added to your total rate rather than taken out of your session fee.

**podcast**    A term that is an amalgam of Apple's "iPod" and "broadcasting" is a method of publishing audio or video files to the Internet, allowing users to subscribe to a feed and receive new files automatically by subscription, often at no or low cost. Many TV and radio shows are available as podcasts.

**point of view**  (See *POV.*)

**postproduction**

The phase of filmmaking or commercial production that begins after the film has been shot. It includes scoring, sound and picture editing, titling, dubbing, adding the voice-over, and releasing or airing the final.

In post, the entire project (ultimately) comes together. The scenes are edited and mixed with music, sound effects and so forth to create a cohesive, professional finished product (ideally).

**p-pop**    A term used to describe an over expulsion of air or sound on a mic. This sudden release of explosive breath causes a popping distortion on a recording. It can occur with an f-sound, a v-sound, a b-sound, but most commonly a p-sound. Thus the name.

**premise**    A premise is the central idea in a story or script. Also known as *a device.*

(See *device* and *Rule of 3.*)

**premium**    Promotional items, such as pens, pencils, mugs, hats, chattering teeth, T-shirts, and even hot sauce, etc. sent out by talent to promote the talent conceptually

457

and literally. Usually the premium includes the talent's name and logo to create name recognition.

**preproduction**

Preproduction refers to the preparation phase of a commercial, film, or television production prior to shooting or recording. During this period, the budget and time line to complete the project is established, the cast is secured, the script changes are determined, and the crew is assembled. Preproduction allows as much opportunity for troubleshooting as humanly possible.

How things will be shot or recorded are decided and put on a time line in preproduction. The more preproduction, the better prepared everyone involved with the production will be (ideally) and the greater the likelihood of having a successful overall production.

**principal**
A principal is the lead character on a TV series or film or one of the featured players on a commercial or an industrial.

**"Print!"**
Uttered by a film director when the shot is to his or her satisfaction.

**producer**
The person ultimately responsibility for the budget and for forwarding the creative vision of the project and final outcome of the film, commercial, or television show.

**production**
The phase of filmmaking, or commercial production, that has already been cast and is now in the process of being shot or recorded.

**promo**
1. A promo can be a promotional ID for a radio or television station, much like the famous promo James Earl Jones did for CNN some time ago: "This is CNN."

2. A promo may also be a local spot describing an investigative series featured that week on your local news show, such as "Gangs. What your kids know that they're not telling you. Details at 11."

The commercials promoting TV shows are known as promos.

(See Chapter 3, The Purpose of a Voice-over Demo.)

3. In radio, promos are the weekly advertising, created by the station talent. Radio talent generally need to write, voice, and produce between 150 and 200 promos a week just to keep "the lights on."

(See Chapter 4, Radio, Radio.)

4. Promo also refers to the *promotional* materials you must continually send out to solicit business as a working talent.

(See Chapter 14, Producing Your Demos & Various Promo Items)

**proscenium arch**

An architectural element separating the performance area from the auditorium in a theater.

The arch functions to mask stage machinery and helps create a "frame" for the stage action.

It could be said that this was one of the first great advances, or technologies incorporated into the acting profession.

**Pro Tools**  A DAW (Digital Audio Workstation). It is the most standard professional recording/editing/mixing system.

There are simpler versions for the less technically inclined to edit from their home computers and devises, such GarageBand, Twisted Wave, and Audacity.

**proximity effect**

A technical term describing a physical phenomenon: the exaggerated bass response that occurs when a sound source is especially close to a directional microphone.

**punch-in**     When a line or phrase needs to be replaced in a chosen take or voice-over occasionally a talent may be asked to punch-in the corrected phrase. The engineer will play the take back for you minus the segment they want you to correct. Your job is to correct the line while matching the emotion, tempo, volume, and proximity of the original delivery.

Generally, the engineer will play the cue line, followed by a blank space for you to drop in the take, three times in a row, allowing for spontaneity and variety in terms of inflection within the framework of what's being asked of you.

(See *matching, three-in-a-row*.)

**put on avail**     (See *check avail*.)

# Q

**QR Codes**     QR Codes stands for Quick Response Codes.

Usually a small square two-dimensional matrix bar code used as a mobile tagging device. QR Codes can be scanned with a simple app from any smartphone or iPad. They can be designed to lead directly to your Web site for more effective interactive marketing and promotion. This link to your site will then be bookmarked on the mobile device.

(See Chapter 7, Advancing Technology.)

# R

**RTFM**
A well-known recording-engineer abbreviation that stands for <u>R</u>ead <u>t</u>he *Frickin'* <u>M</u>anual.

**reaction shot**
A shot of a character, generally a close-up (CU), reacting to another character's dialogue or situation seen in the previous shot.

**read**
1. (noun) A read is a performance, whether it be an audition or a booking. It's another word for the delivery, or the take.

Example: The read she gave at the audition was exceptional.

2. (verb) How you read as a talent refers to how you come across as a type, as a professional, and as an individual. This speaks to how you present yourself and how you behave.

(See *delivery* and *take*.)

**recalls**
When extras or secondary roles are required to return to set the following day, these are referred to as recalls.

**reel**         An on-camera demo reel actors have to give casting directors, producers, and directors to offer a better idea of what they do best and what they want more of as a professional film, commercial, or TV actor.

A reel should be a compilation of the very best of your on-camera work. It should be composed of professional work you've actually done.

Each segment on a reel should be well-produced and -shot; each scene should begin with the height of the action and the height of the emotion.

The total length may vary from as brief as 45 seconds (with only a single, remarkable scene) or up to 3 minutes total. Just like a strong voice-over demo, it must be professionally produced and display the sort of work you are most likely to land and hope to continue to land.

**reference base**

A reference base is a concept that comes from improvisation, which refers to the pool of knowledge and/or experience a talent draws from to relate to or play a scene.

If you haven't any reference to the subject, then the subject will appear foreign to you. It's nearly impossible to speak confidently about something you know nothing about.

As a talent you should continually be building upon your reference base.

(See *improvisation*, *Rule of 3*, *yes...and*, and Chapter 8, Determining Your Commercial Strengths.)

**regional**     A commercial that runs in a specific market, such as only in the Chicago area, or solely or in New England or the greater Phoenix region.

**register**          1. (verb) When you submit your headshot /résumé and demo to an agency, and an agent there *agrees* to represent you, you are officially registered with that agency. However, being signed and being registered are two very different things. If you're registered, the agency will represent you. If you're signed, then you are represented *exclusively* through that particular agency.

2. Register (noun) also refers to a vocal quality that deals with pitch and range, as it would with a musical instrument. Vocal register is often determined spontaneously by emotion and point of view.

(See *exclusive, multi-listed, signed,* and Chapter 9, Developing your Vocal Skills, and Chapter 18, How to Get an Agent.)


**released**          1. If you are placed on hold or check avail and the client determines they no longer require your services, you will be *released* from the project.

2. While on a booking, you are not obliged to leave until you are officially *released* by either the producer (on a voice-over), or the Line Producer, 1$^{st}$ or 2$^{nd}$ AD on a film or on-camera shoot.

(See *availability, booking, check avail,* and *hold.)*

**representation**

Your talent agent represents and submits you for work to producers, copywriters, directors, and casting agents. He does this by negotiating your (pay) rate and establishing the provisions of your contract. This is how he earns his 10 percent commission on your earnings.

(See Chapter 18, How to Get an Agent.)

**repros**          Printed reproductions of your headshots. To ensure the best results, a JPEG file (of no less than 300 dpi or dots per inch) is recommended.

(See Chapter 17, Headshots and Résumés.)


**residuals**       Pay *in addition* to the initial session fees for the usage of your work in a commercial, film, or television program for broadcast and rebroadcast.

(Also known as *resids*.)

Residuals can often be the most sizable income you can make off the work you do as a professional talent.

Residuals are available only through union jobs for commercial, television, and film work.

(See Chapter 20, How Union Work Works.)


**retail**           A commercial for a department store, such as Sears, JC Penney, Kohl's, Marshall's, and TJ Maxx.

**reveal**          Usually the arc or climax of the story, script or idea.

Also, revealing what the character feels or thinks defining the viewpoint and situation of the character.

What a person might never reveal in real life is generally revealed in the actor's performance—regardless of the medium.

(See Chapter 11, The **Sound Advice** Approach.)


**reverse shot**    The shot that covers the performance of an actor in the scene, from the point of view of a second actor who has already had his performance recorded from the first actor's point of view.

**Right-to-Work states**

Those states that do not honor certain union provisions.

According to the National Right-To-Work Legal Defense Foundation (nrtw.org), "a Right-to-Work law secures the right of employees to decide for themselves whether or not to join or financially support a union."

Each state has its own statutes regarding this issue and should be researched online or at your library or through contacting SAG-AFTRA directly.

The Right-to-Work states include states include: Alabama, Arizona, Arkansas, Florida, Georgia, Idaho, Iowa, Kansas, Louisiana, Mississippi, Nebraska, Nevada, North Carolina, North Dakota, Oklahoma, South Carolina, South Dakota, Tennessee, Texas, Utah, Virginia, and Wyoming.

The remaining states are considered "closed Shops." Nearly half the country falls under Right-to-Work, which more or less renders the unions, in our case SAG-AFTRA, somewhat useless.

(See Chapter 20, How Union Work Works.)

**room noise** or **room tone**

The ambient sound of a room or space.

At some point as an actor on a set, you will likely hear a crew member call out: "Quiet for room noise!" Everything and everyone around you will stand still and quiet for a few minutes. The reason is that on each shoot, the production sound mixer/recordist needs to be able to record a solid minute or so of uninterrupted *room noise* or *room*

465

*tone* to use, if necessary in post.

Each space, each room or set has its own tone.  It's the way a space sounds.

The dialogue editor will use this to edit quiet moments into the dialogue track of a movie's sound track. This will match properly only if the room tone recorded that day is preserved.

**rote**     According to *Merriam-Webster*, by rote is a "routine or repetition carried out  mechanically or unthinkingly."

If your delivery is delivered simply by rote, then it has no original thought behind it.

**Rule of 3**   The Rule of 3 is a performance and literary device that allows the actor (or writer, respectfully) to craft the script into beats and gradually build their performance (and story).

This is a principle (exclusively taught and incorporated into an acting approach by **Sound Advice)** that proposes the Rule of 3 is the "scaffolding" upon which all performance, communication, and story hold up best.

The idea is that every script and every communication is best conveyed performance-wise when utilized through one of three formulaic performance options by employing the Rule of 3.

Simply put, utilizing the Rule of 3:
- You *establish the narrative thread* (the story being told) in the first beat
- Repeat or *further the narrative thread* in  the second beat
- And then *complete or conclude the story* in the third beat

Also known as *the Rule of 3* (or *4,* respectively), as <u>every</u> script/performance can be broken down into 3 *or 4 beats*, and each beat in turn contains 3 or 4 "fragments" in themselves.

<u>The three formulas of *Rule of 3* are</u>:
1) Establish the device (or premise) in the first beat, repeat the device/premise in the second beat, and the change (or arc) occurs on the third.
2) Establish the device (or premise) in the first beat, repeat the device/premise in the second beat, continue to further the device/premise, and the change (or arc) occurs on the forth beat.
3) Establish the device (or premise) in the first beat, repeat the device/premise in the second beat, the change (or arc) occurs on the third, return to the initial device/premise in the forth beat.

Originating from comedy and improvisation, this concept applies to any and <u>all</u> scripts and performance, regardless of whether the project is a commercial, film, TV, stage, stand-up, monologue or whether the project is *comedic or dramatic*.

This device allows you to break the script down quickly and "eat the elephant bite by bite" rather than attempting to swallow (the script) whole.

The Rule of 3 *demands a gradual build*, and determines meter, timing, rhythm, and *phrasing*.

Denying or ignoring the Rule of 3 (or 4, respectively) is on the order of attempting to deny or ignore gravity. It's there whether you like it or not, and you'll fall on your fanny should you ignore it.

(See *beat*, *improvisation*, and Chapter 11, The **Sound Advice** Approach.)

# S

**SAG-AFTRA**     In 2012, union members voted to merge SAG, which stands for <u>S</u>creen <u>A</u>ctors <u>G</u>uild, with AFTRA, which stands for <u>A</u>merican <u>F</u>ederation of <u>T</u>elevision and <u>R</u>adio <u>A</u>rtists, forming one union, SAG-AFTRA.

SAG-AFTRA represents professional actors in recorded media in America for film, radio, *national* television, cable, new media, and Internet.

(See Chapter 20, How Union Work Works.)

**SFX**     The industry abbreviation for *sound effects*.

**safety**     The take (or takes) recorded as backup to the delivery or recorded performance.

Once a few takes have been shot/recorded, it's customary to get a couple of takes as *safeties*, in the event a plane was flying over and bled into the tracks or the talent had a slight hiccup or gurgle that wasn't initially detected, or any number of possible unwanted flaws that may have crept into equation and slipped below the radar—just to "be on the safe side."

**scale**     This is the minimum standardized pay rate determined by SAG-AFTRA per job and/or script designated to session fees. (Nonunion buyout rates are generally based on scale.) Additional pay in the form of residuals is paid to the performer for the broadcast and rebroadcast of his likeness, image, performance, or voice.

(See *buyout, residuals, SAG-AFTRA*, and *session fee*.)

**script supervisor**

The crew member assigned to record all changes or actions as the production proceeds.

**segue**	The transition from one thought to another, from one scene to another, or from one spot to another on a voice-over demo or on-camera reel.

**session fee**	A session fee is the basic pay rate the talent will be paid, under a SAG-AFTRA contract, for delivering the performance. Additional pay in the form of residuals is paid to the performer for the broadcast and rebroadcast of his likeness, image, performance, or voice, or compensation accounting for these fees in a form of a buyout is generally paid due to the fact that the original performance may not ultimately end up in the final production. Session fees ensure the talent is paid for the session, whether the project airs or not.

	(See *buyout, residuals,* and *SAG-AFTRA.*)

**settle in**	The actor approaches the mark and, instead of stopping abruptly, slows the pace and eases into the mark. This is referred to as settling in.

**sides**	The scene(s) or pages of script an actor is expected to prepare for an audition or a day's work. Generally, sides consist only of your character's lines and cues.

**signed** or **sign with**
	If you are signed with a talent agency you are registered exclusive with that agency, which means you are represented solely by that particular talent agency in that specific region. This may be for voice-over alone or for theatrical (film and TV) or for any and everything as a professional talent depending on the specific provisions of the exclusive contract you signed.

	(See *agent, exclusive, multi-listed,* and Chapter 18, How to Get an Agent.)

**sizzle**	A sizzle is a low-grade demo used by businesses to bypass paying demo rates as designated by SAG-

AFTRA. Sizzles are used to entice buyers to sell their products without delegating a basic budget to the production.

According to LogoDesignWorks site, a sizzle reel is a type of demo reel used as "a public relations video, and a promo, as well as about twenty other names. This is a short video, usually no more than five minutes in length that is used to get a message across about your business's brand. These videos have a variety of uses. First, they can be used for business-to-business communication. This allows businesses to get an idea of what your business is about in a short amount of time. Second, they can be released to more public entities as part of a press kit or a plea for funding. Last, they are often used to draw in customers, especially when posted on YouTube or a social networking Web site."

In terms of pay rate for a talent, sizzles are generally considered to be a grade below a demo, as there's no designated rate associated to them.

**Skype**  A free downloadable application that allows for video phone calling between subscribers by utilizing basic broadband Internet service.

Skype is a reliable substitute for phone patch and offers those *patching in* a clearer, cheaper, and more effective option over phone patch.

(See *patch*, *phone patch*, *SourceConnect*, and Chapter 7, Advancing Technology.)

**slate**  Anything that serves to identify the content of the recording is considered a slate. Every voice-over audition begins with the talent slating her name. This is an opportunity to make your name known and in many cases, how to pronounce it! So *please* be clear, pleasant and distinct.

You can even say, "Hi, my name is..." if you like. (In fact, it's preferred in many cases.)

On a voice-over *recording session*, the engineer will always slate each take as it is recorded before giving you a cue. (Example: "McDonald's, take 379...rolling.")

In film and video, the slate is designated with the clapboard that displays the name of the project, the shot number, and the take number.

**soft sell**    A sales style that is considered a casual and friendly approach. A commercial delivery style that is the opposite of hard-sell.

(See *hard-sell*.)

**Source-Connect**

This is a brand name for a plug-in that allows its users to connect to each other's studios over the Internet, allowing a producer in one location to record a talent in a remote location. Source-Connect is the standard digital patch utilized in most parts of the world, except (currently) in the States which still relies heavily on ISDN.

It serves as an affordable alternative to the cost of ISDN.

(See *ISDN*, *patch*, *phone patch*, *Skype*, and Chapter 7, Advancing Technology.)

**specs**    An industry slang term for *specifics*, referring to the brief direction given the project and specifically each character.

For example, the specs on the average commercial audition might be "a natural-sounding 25- to 30-year-old, 'non-announce-Announce.' "

471

The specs are the closest thing to direction you're likely to find on a commercial audition.

The ironic thing about the "specifics" is they are often extremely vague.

*Specs* often include current pop-culture references.

**speed**　　The correct speed at which a film camera is required to run film for a time depiction of action, usually 24 frames per second.

In the days when film cameras were still hand-cranked, a cameraman would need a second or two of furious cranking to get the film "up to speed" before the director could call "Action." Nowadays, a cameraman will say "Speed!" immediately after hitting the switch to roll the camera.

**spin**　　Adding a slight finesse or a unique turn to a word or phrase is the same as putting a spin on your read.

(See *affect*.)

**spot**　　A commercial. A piece. An ad.

In the early days of radio, when ads were performed live on the air, talent were said to be performing "on the spot," and the name stuck.

**stand-in**　　A person who stands in the position of a lead actor after the scene has been blocked, while the lights and camera moves are being finalized for the shot. A stand-in will be the same height, coloring, and body type of the actor he is standing in for, wearing an outfit identical to the actor.

**station 12**　　This is the SAG-AFTRA office responsible for enforcing child labor laws.

(See Chapter 5, Kids and Young Adults.)

**stepping on lines**

When an actor begins delivering a line before another actor's lines are finished, whether deliberately or not.

**storyboard**

The rough drawings of an on-camera commercial, film, or animation created to give the talent (and everyone else on the production) a better idea of how the piece is supposed to go when it is fully produced. The storyboard also allows a voice-over to know when she is expected to come in with the images on the screen.

(See *animatic* and *photomatic*.)

**stretching the canvas**

A term exclusive to **Sound Advice** that refers to dramatically animating the read far beyond what might honestly be required of the project from the very first take, then dropping this device on the following read.

The idea is to give yourself a lot more room to create right from the start, rather than ramping up into your performance.

This is based on the notion you should never hold back. And like the artist Jackson Pollack, you should "stretch the canvas" and slap some paint around. Don't be afraid to make a mess. There's nothing but discovery in it. So challenge yourself to "go too far" from the very beginning of your performance to garner the greatest results.

(See Chapter 9, Developing Your Vocal Skills.)

**strike**          To remove props and/or set pieces from the set, or to dismantle the set.

**studio teacher**

Set teacher or tutor, hired to provide education to young performers; also responsible for enforcing child labor laws.

**stunt coordinator**

The person in charge of designing and supervising the performance of stunts and hazardous activities.

**submission**     To promote yourself by submitting your promo (postcards, e-mails with links to your Web site, a talent agent, casting director, or ad agency creative.)

A submission is also what your talent agent or manager may forward a casting source, producer, or director on your behalf to entice work.

(See Chapter 18, How to Get an Agent.)

**super**          Text seen on the screen in a film, television production, or on a commercial that is laid out graphically over the action (or superimposed, thus the name) or on its own with a black, white or color field behind. A voice-over may coincide with the super, or the super may appear on its own.

On a commercial script, the video is described in detail on the left half of the page and the audio is described on the right. This way everyone involved with creating the production can easily determine whether the actor speaks along with the super or over the images or not.

A *super* can also be referred to as a *card*.

# T

**Taft-Hartley**     The 30-day grace period after landing your first union (SAG-AFTRA) job.

You'll get all union benefits on that spot (such as getting paid in two weeks, work standards must be just so). For the 30 days *after* your first union session, you may work as many union gigs as possible without joining the union (paying the initiation fee). However, once that 30-day period has lapsed, on the *next* union job you land you *must join* the union *prior* to completing that job (or at least immediately following the session).

Once 30 days is over, whether you've worked more union jobs during that period or not, you become what is known as a *must-join*. You can remain a must-join for two days or two weeks or 20 years, however long it takes until you land another union booking (of the same union you secured work under).

(See Chapter 20, How Union Work Works.)

**tag**     The tail end of the commercial, such as: "Tide. No other detergent cleans better."   Or "Robitussin. Recommended by Doctor Mom." Though some tags actually open the commercial.

Tag is a "short appendage to the body of the commercial."

Much like customizations, which are a bit longer than tags and pay a bit more per spot, tags take a good deal of stamina and skill to keep them consistent and finished.

Tags can also be done by a voice-over other than the principal announcer who may have voiced a majority of the spot.

(See *customizations*.)

**take**     The performance. Also known as the read or the delivery.

(See *delivery*, *matching*, and *read*.)

**take it from the top**
Begin again at the beginning of the scene, or at the top of the script.

**talent**     *You*. The actor. The talent. The performer.  And in strictly voice over circles: The voice-over. The AVO. The narrator. The voice talent.

(See *AVO*.)

**technique**     *Technique* refers to the performance approach of the actor; any system of procedures designed to achieve the desired performance outcome.

As in any field of endeavor, from a routine comes experience. If you apply the techniques we have detailed for you in this volume you will continue to develop your skills, while making yourself accessible to the work, and thereby gain hands-on experience.

Granted, there are a number of schools of thought when it comes to technique training for the actor, from Stanislavsky's Method to *Meisner* to the *Alexander Technique*, and so on. Commit yourself to explore and study these techniques. At least you'll know what indicates to you personally, and if nothing else you'll have a better grasp on the terminology used by many of your future colleagues who might prescribe to these approaches.

**teleprompter**

This is essentially a computerized cue-card machine. This device enables a broadcaster or spokesperson to read a script during an industrial, for example, while looking into the camera lens.

**theatrical**

Feature film work that potentially is shown in movie theaters. (Thus the name).

Therefore, if you secure a talent agent for *theatrical* only, he will not be representing you for commercial work, stage, or anything other than film and television work.

(See Chapter 18, How to Get an Agent.)

**three-in-a-row** or **three-wild**

When a talent repeats a brief performance in a voice-over or on-camera performance three times in a row, leaving enough space between each delivery for the engineer to edit, while making certain each read has a *decidedly different* spin on it.

Even though each read on a three-wild has a slightly different inflection, each read will still remain within the parameters of what's needed while maintaining somewhat consistent volume, pitch, and speed.

*Three-in-a-rows* are done on every voice-over session and on every film and television shoot, or recorded medium in order to offer greater options with each take.

(See *a-b-c*.)

**throw it away**

A commonly used piece of direction, which is your cue to *ease off the delivery*, often by using less emphasis; make it sound simpler, easier, and use less effort by "throwing it away."

477

**tighten the frame**

To play closer to the other performer, object, or scenery in a scene being shot.

**track**

1. (noun) To a recording engineer, a track is a single component or channel of a mix. Dialogue, music, and sound effects may all reside on separate tracks and play back simultaneously.

2. A distinct selection on a typical music CD; each song is on its own numbered track.

3. A commercial voice-over demo is a single *track*, which consists of five to nine segments. Every demo track is different per each designated genre, such as industrial, animation, or promo, but all consist of a compilation of individual segments that segue seamlessly together to form a single, cohesive track.

4. (verb) To track can also mean to record.

(See *tracking*, *VOX*, and Chapter 3, The Purpose of a Voice-over Demo.)

**tracking**

An industry term for the recording session itself, or as a verb, it's the act of actually recording.

*Example:* "We did the tracking on Tuesday, but the spot wasn't mixed for another week," or "We're tracking the VO for the trailer."

**two-shot**

Generally a medium or close shot in which two people fill the frame.

(See *fifty-fifty*.)

**type**

The sort or style of talent you are perceived most readily as. Such as the romantic lead or the cop or the Killer. You'll see your similar type at audition after audition, over and over again.

For instance, if most of the actors at the auditions you're sent out on are all female, blonde, slender, and funny, and you are too, then it's safe to assume you are among your own type, at least looks-wise.

Type also has to do with attitude, sense of humor or seriousness, and so forth.

What *you* want to know from a talent agent, if you're shopping around for representation, is can they use your type in their talent pool?

(See *read* and Chapter 6, Identity, Branding, and Type.)

# U

**under-5**     This is union (SAG-AFTRA) on-camera work that consists of *five lines or less* for a given theatrical production. Additionally, the total number of words in these five lines must be less than 50. If the role is a recurring character for up to one year, the actor can become eligible for union status.

Under-5's increase the likelihood of becoming upgraded to a larger role, such as a guest star or featured role.

**understudy**     An actor who studies one or more roles of a professional stage production in the event he will need to step in and replace one of the actors in the production. The understudy is prepared to play the roles as close to the actor he is replacing in the event one of the production's actors can't go on.

This is easily the most difficult job in all of acting, due to the fact the understudy is expected to mimic as precisely as possible the performance of the actor they are replacing. The blocking, the business, even the rhythm of the delivery is by Actors' Equity standards, which leaves little opportunity to create an original performance.

(See *matching*.)

**union(s)**  A union is an organization of workers formed to establish and negotiate with those who hire them; you have to join the union in order to get more work.

The actor's unions set the national standards for pay, working conditions, raises, basic contracts, and establish health, dental, and pension benefits based on income, among other things.

(See *AEA*, *SAG-AFTRA*, and Chapter 20, How Union Work Works.)

**union affiliations**

The union to which you belong (or strive to belong) as a professional talent in the United States is SAG-AFTRA. Once you belong to the union this becomes your affiliation.

(See *AEA*, *SAG-AFTRA*, and Chapter 20, How Union Work Works.)

**upgrade**  This is a promotion given to an actor originally booked on a lesser pay rate commitment.  For instance, if you were booked on a commercial voice-over "demo" that is upgraded to a standard session, then you would earn both a demo fee as well as a session fee as well as the residuals based on the commercial playing in a designated market.

Additionally, if you were originally hired as an Extra on a shoot and you're upgraded to an Under-5, this would greatly improve your visibility on the production as well as your rate of pay.

**upstage**  1. The back half of a playing area on a stage.

2. To draw attention away from other actors whether deliberately or not by either physically blocking that actor or drawing attention away from other actors in the scene.

**usage**

*Usage* defines to what extent those hiring intend to the use of your performance, likeness, or voice.

In order to determine your rate for any given project, the very first element that must be determined is the projected usage of the piece. In other words, will it be used as a network television commercial, a local radio spot, Internet, trade show, theatrical release, corporate in-house, and/or new media? Each of these forms of use implies a value in terms of income for your work, no matter if the project is a buyout or subject to residuals.

The degree of difficulty for any given job is relative. The allowed usage is not.

(See Chapter 20, How Union Work Works.)

# V

**VOX**

This is an abbreviation for the term vocal tracks.

This refers to the act of recording the voice tracks or the voice tracks themselves, as a noun. VO stands for voice-over and the X for the tracks themselves.

(See *track* and *tracking*.)

**vested**

This term means that you have earned the right to a retirement benefit payable at a later date. In most plans, if you withdraw your accumulated contributions and interest, you lose your service credit and the right to a future benefit.

In most cases you must earn at least five years of eligibility service to become vested. If you leave eligible employment after you are vested and do not withdraw your accumulated contributions, you will receive a monthly retirement benefit when you reach normal retirement age.

(See Chapter 20 *How Union Work Works* for more details.)

**Voicebank.net**

This is the premier site for voice-over in North America with which talent are cast especially, but not exclusively, for union commercial voice-over work.

 The talent agency joins the site, rather than the talent (although you have that option if you wish). The primary and most beneficial way to utilize Voicebank to its fullest is to secure representation with a handful of talent agents listed on Voicebank. This site offers you access to representation in a variety of regions allowing you access to a greater body of work from multiple sources, provided you are equipped to record locally should you book a job.

Voicebank offers talent posted on their site the option to secure a premium link, which grants direct access to your voice-over-only Web page. (Which, at **Sound Advice**, we strongly recommend you do.)

**voucher**

The *voucher system* is one of three ways in which a nonunion talent can become SAG-AFTRA.

According to SAG-AFTRA, "For years, SAG had the 'three voucher rule'. After collecting three valid union vouchers for three separate days of work, a background actor can become SAG-eligible; however, employment must be confirmed with payroll data, not vouchers. SAG productions require a minimum number of SAG members be employed as background actors before a producer is permitted to hire a non-union background actor in their production. Producers are permitted (under various circumstances) to fill one or more union spots (on various on-camera productions) with non-union actors. The non-union actor chosen to fill the union spot is then issued a union background *voucher* for the day, and that non-union actor is entitled to all the same benefits and pay that the union actor would have received under that voucher. This is called *a Taft-Hartley voucher*. The SAG-Eligible background actor may continue working in non-union productions, but is required to join the Guild after obtaining 3 Taft-Hartley vouchers."

(See *SAG-AFTRA*, and *Taft-Hartley*.)

**W.N.**      The abbreviation for <u>w</u>ill <u>n</u>otify, a notation on a call sheet meaning that the actor is on call, but no call time has been decided.

(See *on call*.)

**W.P.**      The abbreviation for <u>w</u>eather <u>p</u>ermitting, a notation on the call sheet for location work.

**waivers**   Permission from SAG-AFTRA for any deviation from the terms of a union contract.

**walk-on**   A very brief on-camera role.

**walla**     A film and television industry term referring to the incidental background conversations that occur in crowds choreographed by a loop group in post-production.

A loop group or walla group may be recorded to add human ambience to a scene in postproduction.

The term *walla* implies the nonsensical vocal sounds made by actors hired to create background mumblings on early film recordings. The actors supposedly mumbled, "Walla, walla, walla" to depict groups of people in various background settings in films and television productions.

(See *ADR, looper, loop group, loop group.*)

**watermark**   In voice-over, this refers to audible tones or music that may be mixed under the voice in a recording of a voice-over audition.

Watermarks are a security measure, preventing unscrupulous talent buyers from simply "stealing" the audition/performance and using the voice-over outright in a production without paying the talent.

Watermarking is not widely used, but may prevent misuse of your performance off various pay-to-play sites across the globe.

We generally recommend auditioning only part of the script offered, rather than in it's entirety off these sites to prevent random abuse.

**work permit**   A legal document required to allow a child to work, issued by various state or local  agencies.

(See Chapter 5, Kids and Young Adults.)

**wry-wit**   A type of delivery that is currently very popular. It tends to be very dry, and at first glance may seem very monotone. It's not. There is still a great deal of vocal variety to be had in a wry-wit delivery. So don't let the direction fool you. There are a lot of levels to play within a wry-wit read. The attitude may be flat, but the actual delivery is not.

**whisper-speak**

A stage whisper. When a whisper-speak delivery is used on mic, it can read as very intimate.

**whisper room**

(See *iso booth*.)

**wrap**

Whenever completing a production or a session, it's considered a wrap.

**"yes... and"** This is an improvisational tenet that requires you *agree* with the reality that is being established in the scene and then you *add* to it. Thus the phrase "yes...and." Sounds simple. Frankly, it is very simple. The truth is, this is required of you in any and all performance.

What comes into play is employing your imagination, your ability to trust others and yourself in a scene, and your ability to risk and play.

"Yes...and" is one of the three primary concepts that are (ideally) covered repeatedly in any Improv training and practice. The other two are: reference base and Rule of 3. All three apply to creative writing, acting, and directing.

(See *improvisation, reference base*, and *Rule of 3*.)

**zoom**

A shot taken with a zoom lens, in which the focal length changes from wide to close (i.e., zoom in) or close to wide (i.e., zoom out).

# Chapter 23: If It's Meant to Be

> "There is nothing as permanent as change."
> —Anonymous

I happen to think there's a common misconception in our culture that states if a road proves too difficult then maybe "it wasn't meant to be." Instead, I happen to think the opposite might actually be true. If you _are_ on the right path, then you're likely to face far more opposition than you ever may have imagined. I don't wish this for you, it's simply an observation.

Think about it. Every great accomplishment that has ever come about has done so against terrific opposition, not the other way around. It's historic.

So it only stands to reason you're far more likely to be met with rather sizable obstacles on the road to accomplishing your heartfelt goals. You'll hear friends and loved ones pipe in, after you've gone through a setback, "Well, maybe it wasn't meant to be." And with that you'll doubt your ability to press on. You'll think, "Maybe they're right." Happens to the best of us. Perfectly supportive people saying this often gives one pause.

Of course, after the fact, after you've accomplished your goals, such as producing your demos or securing a really exceptional agent or landing an ongoing commercial campaign, for example, no one will have seen all the hard work that went into rising above great odds and the many difficulties it took to get there. All the perseverance, promotion, and patience required of you beyond what anyone might have initially considered acceptable would certainly surprise the average man on the street. But then maybe that's the whole point. To stand out, you have to stand up.

We'll never know what could have been accomplished without tenacity.

If anything is ever to come to be, such as your career, you must take a leap of faith—you must risk. This is certainly true in performance. If you consider every major, game-changing role you ever landed only came about when you ventured beyond your comfort zone and took a real chance, not because you played it safe or performed exactly within the perimeters of "what was asked of you."

Besides, if playing it safe is the best bet to accomplishing what we're passionate about and destined to do, then it stands to reason every door would swing open wide as we approached it, every opportunity would embrace us and the gods would happily smile on us, nodding their approval and there would be one simple, exact path to follow when you're setting out to establish yourself in this business. Unfortunately, history proves otherwise. Even those who dutifully conform to what they think or are told is required of them as talent are met with adversity.

In fact, every major accomplishment from the creation of the lightbulb to the iPod has come about only after meeting and overcoming terrific obstacles. But it's how we weather those obstacles ultimately that determines whether our goals will ever come to fruition.

Thomas Edison devoted more than 10,000 attempts to creating the lightbulb—and not a very good light bulb at that. But it did work. And when he was asked, given all those tries, if he felt like a failure and why didn't he give up, he replied, "Why would I feel like a failure? And why would I ever give up? I now know definitively over 9,000 ways that an electric lightbulb will not work. Success is almost in my grasp." Lucky for us, a short time later and with more than 10,000 attempts under his belt, Edison invented the lightbulb. He was intent on creating the thing!

Can you imagine if he complacently succumbed to the notion, "Well, guess it just wasn't meant to be," because he wasn't quite sure what to do next? The world is far brighter by the simple fact he was intent on the task. Literally.

So, it's safe to assume success requires dedication far beyond what anyone might first imagine.  It takes a whole lot of tenacity to make anything come about, such as your career as a working talent. Your career won't exist without you continually creating it and, yes, often against rather sizable odds.  We're here simply to help you navigate better and help getting from point A to point B faster, easier, quicker, and smarter.  That's what we do as **Sound Advice**.  Thus the name.

It's important to keep this in mind as you set out to train, produce your demos, promote yourself like never before, and generally take your career to the next level.  As talent we often harbor the hidden hope that our lives will magically hold still while we set out to implement any major advancement or change in our lives.  And like clockwork, our mettle will be tested.

It all comes down to your intention, your determination to succeed—not just to continue.  Best advice: Focus on what it is you are trying to accomplish and stay with the program. It's always been your responsibility to keep your dream alive.  Surrounding yourself with those who want to see you succeed is key to accomplishing just that. Again, this is, in part, why we're here as **Sound Advice**.

So, the next time you hear someone say, "Maybe it just wasn't meant to be," consider this: Maybe it was, it's just that the Universe demanded that much more of you to make it happen because you're made of greater stuff.  This current challenge you're facing could very well be your cue to rise to the occasion beyond what you might have ever expected from the onset.

After all, no one ever received an Academy Award, saying, "This was so easy!  Wonder why everyone doesn't have one?!"

Decide your career is meant to be and remember; they don't call it work for nothin'. Your career is meant to be if YOU say it is.  So be it!  Then get busy. There's always work to be done!  Enjoy it!

## Aim to Be a Seasoned Journeyman

We'd like to assume the aim of every talent we work with at **Sound Advice**, regardless of media specialty (television, film, stage, or voice-over) or experience level, is to become a seasoned journeyman. In other words, be a professional through and through.

One who never ceases exploring beyond the safe, the comfort zone and forever aims to expand upon his performance abilities. One who intends to go the distance, to deliver the best results, and behave at the top of his form, often in the face of unusual and often difficult obstacles and even great odds.

In short, one who seeks to master his role in this business and persist with great tenacity.

Here's how Merriam-Webster's defines these terms:

**sea·soned**, adjective
to treat so as to prepare for use; b: to make fit by experience (a seasoned veteran), to become seasoned.

**jour·ney·man**, noun
an experienced, reliable worker, athlete, or performer especially as distinguished from one who is brilliant or colorful (a good journeyman trumpeter — *New Yorker*).

We do our very best at **Sound Advice** to prepare and make you fit to deliver the goods. You simply must commit yourself to the task and make it your aim to become a seasoned journeyman.

It can be done.

Craftsmen have been committed to excellence for generations. Today is no different. It doesn't take much effort to rise above the standard and the run-of-the-mill—of which there is a terrific glut. It only takes just that much more effort and commitment to be above average.

If you dedicate yourself to raising your standard with each attempt, you will achieve it.

But it requires true intention. Apply yourself to it.

We're committed to helping you accomplish just that!

So there it all is (at least for the time being).

It's a mouthful, to coin a phrase, I know. But then, all this wouldn't be considered a profession if it weren't just a little bit involved, I suppose.

All the information you've found here will most certainly change, that much you can surely count on.

We hope to stay on top of the latest and greatest and will continue to update this material in future editions of this publication, and, of course, on our Web site (voiceoverinfo.com) as changes present themselves.

Do your best to stay true to this material by applying it fully while it's still fresh. We hope it affords you a much easier time than it has been for all of us who have tripped and plodded along without the benefit of any real resource from which to draw.

We wish you health, success, and a very long, sane, playful, and fulfilling career. Always.

Knock 'em dead. ✍

# Acknowledgments

After a great deal of trial and error, I somehow (*finally*) managed to secure a very tight, very talented, remarkable staff here at **Sound Advice**. After 20 years of operation, our crew now consists of a small but fiercely dedicated, savvy group who make coming to work everyday truly worthwhile and rewarding.

And, of course, we'd be nowhere without the contributions, technical expertise, support, and the *continued encouragement* of: Jeff Finney, Chin Yi, Travis Dunsmuir, Jen Rand, Marcie Fanning, Lori Jablons, Eve Bollin, Lynette Nisbet, Camilla Bassaly, Sean Jacobson, Ron Martin, Erik Martin, Eric Sherman, Rachel and Bob Hutcheson, Amanda Reyne, Jamie Blythe-Martin, Jessica Pantermuehl, Kourtney Vahle, Courtney Rioux, Jon Monteverde, Jon Legat, Katie Dean, Justin Mooney, Harlan Hogan, Glenn Haines, Tamra and Jim Meskimen, Pat Byrnes, Jenn Harrell, Joan Sparks, Sheila Dougherty, Kim Valkenburg, Mark Measures, Melanie Thomas, Dean Panaro, Carol Rathe, Deborah Duckett, Vickie Barraso, Carrie Kaufmann, Eva Lewandowski, Barbara Figgins, Carolyn McDermott, David Guzzone, Cynthia Barber, Patrick Tucker and the ongoing support and encouragement from my massive, remarkable family. These folks *all* deserve far more thanks and appreciation for their extended support, apt attention, and total commitment to excellence, both professionally and personally, than I can possibly convey here. Their input and encouragement have been absolutely invaluable to me personally, and **Sound Advice** as a whole.

These folks have dutifully allowed me, through **Sound Advice**, to raise the standard of delivery for each and every one of our clients, while raising the bar professionally within our industry. They are each and every one a great artist in his own right and will certainly continue to go on creating remarkable things.

As for our dedicated staff of inspired, good-natured brainiacs…well, I can't thank them enough for aligning behind me every day. I hold them in the highest regard, as friends and colleagues. I respect and value each and every one *tremendously* as professionals and know them to be of noble character of the highest caliber.

Last of all, I must acknowledge with the warmest regard our many wonderful clients over the years, who have dutifully stood by us—as we have stood by them. We wish them all continued success and many more dreams fulfilled.

*Sláinte.*

# Appendix: Other Useful References

Wernick, Erica *LA Bound:The Ultimate Guide To Moving To Los Angeles*, www.laboundguide.com , 2013.

Callan, K. *How to Sell Yourself As an Actor: From New York to Los Angeles (and Everywhere in Between)*. Studio City, CA: Sweden Press, 2002.

——. *The Los Angeles Agent Book: Get the Agent You Need for the Career You Want*. 8th edition. Studio City, CA: Sweden Press, 2003.

——. *The New York Agent Book: Get the Agent You Need for the Career You Want*. 7th edition. Studio City, CA: Sweden Press, 2003.

Callan, Kristi. *Working Actor's Guide to Los Angeles*. 18th edition. Gardena, CA: Aaron Blake Publishers, 2006.

Cartwright, Nancy. *My Life As a Ten-Year-Old Boy*. New York, Hyperion, 2000.

Gillespie, Bonnie. *Casting Qs: A Collection of Casting Director Interviews*. Hollywood, CA: Cricket Feet Publishing, 2003.

——. *Self-Management for Actors: Getting Down to (Show) Business*. 3d edition. Hollywood, CA: Cricket Feet Publishing, 2003.

Hogan, Harlan *VO: Tales and Techniques of a Voice-over Actor*. New York: Allworth Press, 2002.

Mamet, David. *True and False: Heresy and Common Sense for the Actor*. New York: Pantheon Books, 1997.

Tucker, Patrick. *Secrets of Screen Acting*. 2d edition. New York: Routledge, 2003.

# Other books from Kate McClanaghan
## from **SOUND ADVICE:**

How To Get An Agent for Acting & Voice Over

How To Break Into Voice-over and Acting for Kids & Young Adults

How To Get More Voice Acting Jobs: Marketing 101 for Actors & Voiceovers

How To Become a Valuable Voice Over:
What Every Talent Needs To Know

How To Take Advantage of Technology as an Actor & Voiceover

How To Move from Radio To Voice Overs

The SOUND ADVICE Dictionary for Acting & Voice Over:
What You Need to Know to Have a Career in Voice Acting

## Become a Better Voice Over